MANAGING YOUR BAND

Artist Management: The Ultimate Responsibility

5th Edition

Copyright, © 2010 HiMarks Publishing Co.
Copyright for previous editions held by HiMarks Publishing Co., © 1995, 1998, 2002, 2006

ISBN-10: 0-9651250-6-8

Cover Design: JonasMusicServices
             www.JonasMusicServices.com

For information:

        HiMarks Publishing Co.
        P. O. Box 2083
        Wayne, NJ 07474-2083
        Fax: 973.720.2217
        marcones@wpunj.edu

Managing Your Band

5th Edition

INCLUDES New Business Models and 360 Deals

Dr. Stephen Marcone

Branding

Building a Fanbase

Contracts

Entrepreneurship

Marketing

Merchandising

Touring

Trademarks

Web Use

For every musician who, against unbelievable odds,
was given the chance to play in the major leagues and blew it!

CONTENTS

CHAPTER FOUR

CHAPTER FIVE

CHAPTER SIX

CHAPTER SEVEN

ACKNOWLEDGMENTS

When approaching a new edition to a successful book, one must decide as to what length and depth does one revise. I decided that a quick update revision would surface. Well, I was wrong. Since the last edition (2006), the industry has changed so dramatically that a simple revision would be meaningless. Along with Professor Jim Progris at the University of Miami, I am one of the "grandfathers" in music and entertainment industry education. We have both served on the board of the Music and Entertainment Industry Educators Association (MEIEA.org) and have witnessed the growth of the discipline in higher education. I believe that the growth has come from a need, the need to educate musicians and music lovers on how to survive in this somewhat unique business. This book is a tool for that task.

For this edition, I thank friends and colleagues Adam Kornfeld, Steve Leeds, Dave Lory and Aaron Van Duyne for the updated contracts, forms, and advice, and my students for their contributions to chapters one and twelve. Also, my colleague, E. Michael Harrington for his website source list (that has been extended extensively), Richard Kearney from the Cheng Library at William Paterson University for his help with RefWorks. Clare and John Cerullo, at Hal Leonard. Lastly, *Jonasmusicservices* for their outstanding cover design.

S.M.

December 2009
Wayne, NJ

GENERAL INTRODUCTION

With barely a music graduate degree in hand, I was given the opportunity to play in the big leagues. As a band that wrote and performed its own material, we somehow generated some interest at Epic Records to give us a chance and they signed us. The group was holding down a six nights a week, six sets a night summer gig at **THE** club in Lake George New York and packing the place. We rehearsed almost everyday and were probably as tight as any band could be. We sounded great and people paid to hear (and see) us. Things were happening pretty fast and it was exciting (and foreign) to the six of us.

As we began our first tour of arenas (as an opening act) we were told on numerous occasions to concentrate on the music and let "them" worry about the business. This was the fall after the summer of Woodstock 69, and it was obvious to many that there was now big money to be made from rock 'n' roll. We had management. A friend of ours who could be trusted, a doctoral student at Syracuse University, who had been booking the band and had the intestinal fortitude to put up with us. He could swim, and although we didn't know it, but not with the barracudas!

A short time later, while we were still in demand, we realized his shortcomings and decided to try another manager. We found one, or I should say, he found us, and had his attorney draw up an agreement. He came to us with experience, and we all liked him. After all, he was hipper than our friend, lived in NYC, and had gotten high with us on several occasions. What was not to like!

We received the contract that his attorney composed, read it and were shocked that this guy, our new found friend, would demand what was written on the pages. In fact, we were so appalled (and green) that instead of asking our attorney to respond with an equally outrageous counteroffer, we decided to run (not walk) back to our original manger/friend and ask his forgiveness.

Basically this is where the story ends. In fact, we committed industry mortal sin number two and went on to manage ourselves. After all, The Beatles did it (without success), so why couldn't we. Well, this is how I learned what not to do.

Only a few years later I realized that many musicians are being short changed. For the most part, the players do not control the record business. Aren't baseball managers former players? Possibly, with the right education and information, musicians could be in control of their own destinies. However, it would take time. Today the more successful musicians understand the business, make decisions, and some control their own careers, and own their own publishing and recording companies.

This book has been written to help the cause. Today, **Personal Management** is more important than ever, but is still the weakest link in a business that operates by fragmenting its product. That is, an artist must give (license) pieces of his/her product to several people that control different fragments of the business. Holding on to all of it doesn't work. **ONE HUNDRED PERCENT OF NOTHING = NOTHING**, no matter how you slice it. An artist must understand and learn to live within this concept. The trick is to give it to the right people for the shortest amount of time possible. I hope this book helps artists and managers choose the right people to give it to, and right people learn how to do it right!

INTRODUCTION TO FIFTH EDITION

"The music business is a cruel and shallow money trench, a long plastic hallway where thieves and pimps run free, and good men die like dogs. There is also a negative side." adapted by Dr. Richard J Atkins, March 19, 2006, from the late Hunter S. Thompson (San Francisco Examiner Nov. 4, 1985)

When the third edition was completed in 2001, the industry was just beginning to feel the effects of "e" and free commerce as it emerged as a possible threat to the existing business models. Over the course of the next five years "all hell broke out" and the mantra for most young music lovers became "why pay for it when I can get it for free."

Records companies had several chances to design alternatives to the free music model, however, early attempts at solving their problem were ill advised and most everyone into downloading songs and peer to peer sharing did not buy into any of it.

Then two significant events occurred. The Recording Industry Association of America (RIAA) began suing individuals for copyright infringement, and Steve Jobs and Apple Inc. unveiled the iTunes store and the iPod. Almost overnight the virtual world of free music became legitimized and standardized with the 99 cent per song legal download. Although the subscription model was already being tested and in place, it took the per-song business to get people excited about going legit.

Presently, legal downloads are still a fraction of music downloading, however, as the CD continues to lose market share, the digital selling of music is keeping the business of selling recorded music product alive. Because of this, record companies, concert promoters, management firms, and production houses are inventing new revenue sharing business models. Whereas the record company was once the "engine" that drove the business, it is now part of the revenue sharing mix that has helped established artists gain greater control. Today, it's all about buiding a fanbase. Touring, that's where the money is. A recent *Billboard Magazine* (March 27, 2010) back cover commemorating Brad Paisley's tour (see Figure Intro. 1 below) says it all.

BRAD PAISLEY
AMERICAN SATURDAY NIGHT TOUR 2009-2010

BY THE NUMBERS:

1,196,312 FANS

1,151,880 MILES

340,000 WATTS OF POWER

230,376 GALLONS OF DIESEL FUEL

80,000 LBS TOTAL SHOW FLYING WEIGHT

41,000 TOTAL BOTTLES OF WATER

34,000 TOUR PHOTOS TAKEN (400 KEPT)

17.955 MEALS SERVED

12,840 GUITAR PICKS

4,165 LOCA TOUR PERSONNEL

3,550 AA BATTERIES

1,056 PACKS OF STRINGS

924 HOTEL ROOMS BOOKED

855 PEOPLE WHO TOOK BACKSTAGE TOUR

840 NINE VOLT BATTERIES

836 SQ FEET OF VIDEO

240 ROLLS OF GAFF TAPE

214 PAIRS OF DRUMSTICKS

95 MINUTE SHOW

74 SHOWS

74 COWBOY HATS

45 STAGE JUMPERS

12 SEMI TRUCKS

10 TOUR BUSES

9 PEOPLE ARRESTED FOR LEWD BEHAVIOR IN CHARLOTTE

8 PEOPLE ARRESTED FOR LEWD BEHAVIOR IN TAMPA

7 PEOPLE ARRESTED IN SEVERAL CITIES (YOU GET THE PICTURE)

2 BIRTHS

1 LAS VEGAS WEDDING

I LARGE BRUISE

THANK YOU COUNTRY RADIO AND COUNTRY MUSIC

Figure Intro One

In this edition, several new business models appear as well as updates to the standard existing agreements. Most labels are offering the "one revenue pot" model, however, my sources say that a model template agreement has yet to exist. Tom Silverman, CEO of *Tommy Boy Records* (along with Dave Lory, have resurrected the *New Music Seminar* to help wantabees become successful in today's business) offers this simple revenue sharing model for a label of management deal (see below) and we could end the book here.

NEXT MUSIC BUSINESS ARTIST CONTRACT
Label or Management Deal

Date:

Artist Name_____ **PKA** _____

Address:

Contacts:

Company Name:

Address:

Contacts:

Territory: (circle one)   World   North America   US

Term:

Artist Contributes:

___% of Net Master Copyright Revenues

Ownership: Yes   No

___% of Net Publishing Copyright Publisher's Share Revenues:

Ownership: Yes   No

___% of Net Merch. Revenue

___% of New Touring

___% of New Ancillary Revenues

Definition of Net:

Company Contributes:

$_____ Artist Advance (Recoupable but not returnable)

$_____ Guaranteed A&R Budget

$_____ Guaranteed Marketing Budget

      Recoupable but not returnable: Yes   No

      Taken as expense of the top: Yes   No (can't be Yes if prior is Yes)

- A&R Strategy, Direction and Management
- Long Term Artist Development and Brand Building Strategy
- Content Development and Management
- Marketing, Promotion, Press Management
- Fan Relationship Management (web, etc.)
- Music Writing Management Production Management
- Distribution
- Travel and S
- Scheduling
- Accounting
- Legal
- Financial Planning and Personal Accounting

Accounting: (circle one) Semi-annual Quarterly Monthly

Agreed and Accepted:

_____   _____

Artist   Date   Company   Date

New Music Seminar provides this template as a learning tool and not a valid contract. Please consult music attorney before executing any agreements.

Figure Intro. Two NMS Seminar

Therefore, throughout this edition, along with examples of existing new agreements there are explanations and computations of some of the agreements that have yet to materialize in standard written form.

Concerning the individual chapters, Chapter One contains a new career plan model, a list of current prominent management firms, and recent student Project Management Outlines. The second chapter includes an additional new artist-manager agreement. Chapter Three includes information dealing with domain names. The fourth chapter deals with new media marketing and branding, and includes updated statistics. Chapter Five takes our transnationals down to four (and possibly soon to be three) corporations. Six strikes the name "Record Company" for Music Entertainment Company, and includes 360 Deal computations. Chapter Seven includes several new recording contracts and additions to existing templates. The eighth chapter deals with new media again. Chapter Nine has a great deal of new information concerning the changes in the live appearance business. Ten includes much info on merch and sponsorships, and branding (again). Eleven contains information on the expanded role of the business manager, including an artist-business manager agreement. There are additional legal battles to pursue in Twelve, and Thirteen is a "rap" up chapter.

Lastly, I am not a big fan of appendices ......especially in a textbook. When teaching, I tend to ignore them. Consequently, except for the web and resource list, all information is incorporated directly into the chapters.

The Instructor's Companion has also been updated accordingly.

The subject of how to remain fair to both genders was never an issue to me.
Throughout the book I tried to use s/he and his/her when either applied.
My intention was (and is) to emphasize equality.

CHAPTER ONE
PERSONAL MANAGEMENT

"The manager is the most valuable player on an artist's behind-the-scene team of professionals….." Michael Amicone, *Billboard Magazine*, September 1, 2002

BY THE END OF THIS CHAPTER YOU SHOULD BE ABLE TO:

1. Discuss the role of a personal manager
2. List eight characteristics of a good manager
3. Discuss the three characteristics of a potentially successful artist
4. Discuss how an artist should choose a manager
5. List the artist's "team" and discuss their individual roles and how they are chosen
6. Discuss two key points found in an artist-personal manager agreement
7. Discuss models for a successful career
7. Manage a project in an organized manner
8. Define talent and success as it relates to the industry.

DO I NEED A MANAGER?

At one time or another, most artists/musicians say that they need a manager when they are either tired of booking gigs or need more gigs. They are oblivious to understanding that the role of a manager is not that of a booking agent, and in fact, managers are not licensed to find employment for a client. (Presently there is a bill in the New York legislature (A8381-S5602) that would amend the law to allow personal managers to act as agents {{91 Butler, Susan 2005;}}.) The question that follows is usually "Then do I need a manager?" The answer to this isn't always as obvious as one might expect. In fact, it may be more complicated than first imagined because there are several types of managers, and there is a big difference between the two types most often employed in the entertainment industry: a personal manager and a business manager.

The second question that is asked is……. "When do I need management?" Is the role of the manager most important when: an artist is looking for a record deal; a new artist has reached the status of John Mayer or 50 Cent; an artist has become a veteran performer (ie: Mick Jagger); or an artist has reached the residual stage of Jimi Hendrix?

The answer to all of the above is that at each stage an artist may not recognize that s/he needs a manager, but it is clear that s/he needs **management**. And unless the artist is committed to giving the 24/7 to the business side of the career, someone must take the responsibility.

WHAT IS IT?

The role of the personal manager in the music and entertainment business can be compared to the role of a football coach. Short-range strategy plays an important part of every possession in every quarter of the game. Long range strategy plays a role in determining a successful season. Each play is determined by the team's strengths versus the opponent's weaknesses. As Gary Borman, whose clients include Faith Hill, James Taylor, and the Rolling Stones states: "With each client, I play a slightly different role. But ultimately, I guess if one were to use a metaphor, I am a coach, and my job is to put together the best team with the best chemistry,{whose members} share a vision, who trust one another, who communicate well, who put the artists' needs first and who want to win" {{90 Amicone, Michael 2002/f, p. 32}}.

The personal manager coaches the artist and his or her team. Every musical set of every gig is important in winning over an audience. Each gig has an effect on the long-range game plan. How much can the team do to insure the success of the next performance?

Most managers will confess that when they landed their first client, they thought they knew a great deal more about managing then they really did. Most managers will also confess that they learned management by "doing it." Furthermore, managers that have survived in this business will confess that the most crucial aspect to surviving was ADMITTING that they neither knew the CORRECT answer to certain questions, nor did they know WHAT the correct information was that they SHOULD HAVE known. Some managers will even admit that they STILL don't know everything they should know. As Borman comments: "There's no way of learning without doing. And, when you do things, you make mistakes-and you learn form those mistakes" {{90 Amicone, Michael 2002;}}.

SO WHAT IS IT?

Personal management means being responsible for every part of the artist's career . . . twenty-four hours a day, seven days a week. It involves making decisions you and your artist can live with and developing a trusting relationship. It's a relationship that matures over time and grows out of mutual respect. This respect may be gained in two ways: by maintaining a record of not "screwing up", and by truly considering the artist's opinion about his or her career. A personal manager should never let the artist feel that his or her opinion is worthless. In fact, the artist's opinion can be and should be an integral part of the decision making process. Empowerment is a strong motivator.

AN ART OR A CRAFT?

Well it's both! The mechanics of the job can be learned, so the craft isn't very mysterious. Learning the fundamentals and routines is easy. The creative or artistic side of the job is more complex.

A successful manager has the ability to motivate people and generate excitement about a project. A successful manager senses other people's needs, not only the artist's, but the needs of the other people who are part of the "army" that works for and with the artist. This part of the creative aspect is seldom learned. A person either does it or doesn't. Personalities play a major role in the business, and at times, personal relationships are even more important than talent.

WHO SHOULD TRY IT?

The short answer is anyone who wants to. However, Figure 1.1 lists eight characteristics that contribute to success. A discussion of some of the points follows.

A GOOD PERSONAL MANAGER IS

1. patient
2. able to recognize creativity and talent
3. organized
4. able to make decisions and take responsibility
5. a self-starter
6. able to recognize uniqueness
7. able to recognize the potential value of an artist in the marketplace
8. knowledgeable about the music business

PATIENCE

A successful manager is a patient one. The creative process takes time. Composing songs or developing a concept for an album should not be rushed. Deadlines and timetables constantly need readjustment. Truly creative people cannot turn on creativity precisely at a designated time. The manager must feel comfortable with the unpredictability - - with changing schedules and unanticipated cost overruns.

A manager must also wait for information to be collected. Being "ultra" busy in this business seems to be a status symbol. It takes days, repeated phone calls and emails before decisions are finalized. Many executives (decision makers) divide their time between NYC, LA, and the rest of the world, and even some very successful and prominent managers have trouble pinning them down.

Artists' careers evolve through many levels. However, they don't always appear to be moving in the right direction (or any direction). Potential stars must "pay their dues," and a manager must wait for each level of success to be reached before another level can be attained.

In this business, success does not provide instant gratification. An audience may go wild during a concert or someone may blog a positive review of a recording, however, success is measured quantitatively. How many tickets were sold? How much airplay or downloads did the song receive? How high up the charts did the record go? It takes time for impact of these measurements to be felt. And it takes patience to allow time for success to happen. "Patience is a virtue" . . . a necessary virtue for success.

ABILITY TO RECOGNIZE CREATIVITY AND TALENT

How does one develop the ability to recognize creativity, talent, or uniqueness? Does one either have a feel for it or not? Can it be developed? Can it be taught?

Everyday, successful personal managers receive songs from new artists. (One manager said that his office receives up to 200 each week!) It's hard to explain how a manager reaches the conclusion that someone has a unique talent. Record company a&r people use their personal judgment when deciding who will be permitted to record. They say it's a feeling that one instinctively gets when they hear or see it. The late John Hammond, indisputably Columbia Records' greatest talent scout, had the ability. (Hammond brought to the label, among others; Benny Goodman, Bob Dylan, and Bruce Springsteen.) If someone has potential to recognize talent, it can probably be developed with practice, but it can't really be taught. A personal manager must possess the ability to recognize the talent in undiscovered artists. Related experience in the industry may help, but the confidence must come from within. No one is infallible. Every successful manager has probably "passed" on at least one successful artist.

RECOGNIZING THE TRUE ARTIST

Every successful performer has true artistry, or some combination of artistry and craftsmanship with market value. However, given this ingredient, what other characteristics are essential when choosing an artist with success potential? Consider the following.

1. DESIRE, DETERMINATION, AND PATIENCE

Serious determination is essential in order to survive in this business. Many stars have ALMOST quit more than once. Since success is seldom instant, an artist must have the maturity to wait for a fan base to build and the industry to react.

2. CREDIBILITY

On stage or off, an artist must have a clearly focused image in order to succeed. (Creating an Image is discussed in a later chapter.)

3. POTENTIAL TO WITHSTAND CHANGES IN THE MARKETPLACE

A manager should ask him/herself if this person has the potential to last a generation. Also, will the artist's personality mature with his or her craft? Every artist should strive to become a classic.

It's also true that many "artists" make a great deal of money for only a short of time. When managing such an artist, one correct strategy is to find a reason why the public would want to buy the act on a short term basis rather than looking to that artist for lasting potential. Although big money has been made with both kinds of artists, most managers would choose to handle the "classic" artist.

When asked why he chose to work with a particular artist, one manager summed up her qualities by saying, "her personality is clearly defined . . . she articulates a sense of self . . . with the proper guidance, she has the potential to sellout arenas."

CHOOSING A MANAGER

Most artists would like to be managed by a person with strong industry contacts and a proven track record. These elements improve the chances of success. Credibility is as important for a manager as it is for an artist. However, given these qualities, what should an artist look for when choosing a manager?

A management agreement is essentially a legal contract to enter into a relationship. **Mutual trust** is crucial to a successful working relationship. There is a very funny but also very pertinent video on YouTube (http://www.youtube.com/watch?v=5JHN5HaUg28) of Howard Kaylan and Mark Volman of The Turtles explaining how they chose the over one half dozen managers they hired (and fired), and the devastating financial consequences. In reality, they didn't really understand the role of a personal manager in their career, were swayed by various friends and enemies, and made costly decisions. Their story is not unique. The artist and manager should have **compatible personalities**. When describing their managers, most artists will list the positive qualities and conclude by saying "and I like him or her."

Prominent Management Firms and Clients

Manager/Firm	Prominent Clients
1. Azoff/**Frontline**	Jimmy Buffett, Boz Scaggs, Eagles, Christina Aguilera, Steely Dan, Seal, Aerosmith, and Jewel.
Frontline Acquisitions:	
Morris Mangt.	Kenny Chesney, Big & Rich. Gretchen Wilson
Vector Mangt.	Kid Rock, Lynyrd Skynrd, Trace Atkins
Spaulding Mangt.	Brooks & Dunn
RPM Mangt.	Shelly Fairchild, Matt Nolan
2. Coran Capshaw/**Red Light**	Dave Matthews, Phish, Tim McGraw
3. **TKO** Management	Toby Keith
4. **Fitzgerald-Hartley**	Brad Paisley
5. **Borman** Entertainment	Keith Urban
6. Burnstein/Mensch/**QPrime**	Metallica, Red Hot Chili Peppers
7. Holmes/**3D Management**	Coldplay. Interpol
8. McGuinness/**Principle**	U2, PJ Harvey
9. Guerinot/**Rebel Waltz**	Nine Inch Nails, No Doubt
10. **Wright** Entertainment	Justin Timberlake, Jonas Brothers
11. **Jon Landau** Management	Bruce Springsteen
12. McLynn/**Crush** Management	Fall Out Boy, Panic at the Disco
13. Kramer/**OK** Management	Bob Dylan, Simon & Garfunkel
14. Silva/**SAM** Management	Beck, Beastie Boys
15. Kovac/**Tenth Street** Ent.	Motley Crue, Buckcherry
16. Branch/**HipHop**	Kanye West, Lil Wayne

Figure1.1 Prominent Managers and Firms {{153 Waddell, Ray 2009;}}

CHOOSING A "TEAM"

Typically, an artist's team is composed of a manager, an attorney, an agent, a publicist, a business manager, and a webmaster (or web-service). The artist must feel secure with the team members that are directly involved with the financial aspects of the career; namely, the manager, attorney, and business manager. However, the manager must be able to work with all of the team members. A good manager will offer the artist suggestions as to who should play certain roles, and will specifically chose who will play others. The following are guidelines that maybe helpful when choosing the team.

ATTORNEY

Attorneys play a major role in the music business. There is a contract for every aspect of a career. Therefore, the manager should offer an artist at least the names of three attorneys with whom s/he would feel comfortable doing business with. Three who have exhibited sound judgment and distinguished experience . . . and leave the responsibility of choosing one with the artist. The artist should interview them and actually choose the attorney him/herself. The legal documents have the final word in business, so why should the manager take full responsibility in an area that could sour and lead to mistrust?

BOOKING AGENT

A manager must maintain a close relationship with the artist's booking agent. They will converse on the phone several times on any given day. This relationship is far more important than the booking agent's relationship with the artist. As always, the artist should be given the chance to offer input into this decision, but the manager should make the final choice.

When choosing an agent, and before signing an exclusive agreement, the manager should evaluate the degree of enthusiasm for the artist that exists **throughout the entire agency**. Large agencies usually divide the country (or world) into territories, and assign an agent to each territory. Agents will also be assigned to specific categories of the business, such as state fairs, television, or eastern colleges. Therefore, overwhelming support by one agent and no interest displayed by other agents, might present booking problems at a later date. Broad support within the agency is more beneficial in the long run.

PUBLICIST

The proper creation of publicity and handling of an image are crucial to a successful career. Most often publicists are hired to manage specific campaigns, projects, events, or tours. It is the manager's responsibility to hire the right person or agency for the job.

WEBMASTER

Virtually all artists have their own websites. The daily maintenance of the pages (which may number in the thousands) is handled by an in-house webmaster or a website service.

BUSINESS MANAGER (ACCOUNTANT)

The business manager holds the fiscal responsibilities, and controls all collections and disbursements. They offer input into all the artist's deals. When choosing a business manager, again, several names should be suggested, and the artist should make the final choice.

THE DAILY ROUTINE

In this business, each day brings a new offer or a new crisis. Some days the mail is opened in the morning and some days it sits until late afternoon. Some days the phones light up before the office is opened, and emails stack up, and on others things unravel in an orderly fashion. There are however, certain constants. Each day the manager should ask these questions: "Am I making as much money for my artist as I possibly can? Are as many recordings, concert tickets, T-shirts; etc. being sold as they're possibly can? What could I be doing to make more money for my artist?"

Asking these questions on a daily basis ensures that certain "career maintenance" routines are completed. If the artist has chosen to sign with a label, the manager talks to the record company everyday. If his/her artist is touring, he or she will converse with the agent and tour manager several times during the day; contact will be made with every individual that is involved with the amount of money being made.

Even though it seems like business can be maintained by cell phone, e-mail, the internet, Skype, etc. managers who are not located in one of the centers of the industry (NYC, LA, Nashville, or London) may be at a distinct disadvantage. Personal contacts are of great importance. In this business, absence does NOT make the heart grow fonder. In fact, "out of sight - out of mind" fits this business more closely. Daily contact is the key.

Everyone must work towards clearly defined short and long-range career goals. Musicians are conditioned to live from job to job (gig to gig). Most worry that the phone will never ring again. Most don't approach their lives in a career-oriented manner. Artists talk about what's happening today, where the manager must constantly adjust the career plan to focus on the long-range objectives.

Recently, this author asked a former student working in management, George Tortarolo, what his responsibilities are. His response follows:

My responsibilities are eclectic to say the least. As one of four managers in a firm of eight people my time is currently spent on projects that relate to Melissa Etheridge, Dave Koz, and Jeremy Toback. All three have albums that were released in the past month. The year leading up to the album releases was spent developing marketing plans, working with their labels to create artwork, staying on top of the press and PR departments to see that they arrange for TV, radio, and print spots. My law background allows me to review, consult on and negotiate the various contracts that come to the artists. Such agreements are recording, publishing, produce/engineer, management, tour riders, movie and TV licensing and songwriter. I monitor regional album sales through the use of Soundscan and airplay by BDS. In conjunction with an artist's business manager, I keep ledgers of any income and spending as well as oversee the payment of invoices. I arrange for rehearsal time and space, I assist in the hiring of session players, and I arrange for sponsorships with manufacturers such as string and amp companies. I have produced one website. I respond to email from fan websites. Recently a lot of time has been spent relating to the tours of Melissa and Jeremy. I assist in routing (calculating which markets the four should to play, and in what order so that a logistical path is followed.) With the help of a travel agency that caters to the needs of the music industry, I arrange for tour flights, hotels, and ground transportation. I also spend time looking for a job that pays a better salary!

THE CONTRACT

(A full discussion of the contract appears in Chapter Two.)

Several industry sourcebooks listed in the bibliography include artist-personal management agreements with appropriate comments (see the latest edition of Shemel & Kravilovsky, or Passman,). When it all boils down, these are two key points that are important to both parties.

1. TERM

Both parties must agree on the length of the contract, option periods, which party has the right to extend the agreement. Contingencies concerning extending the agreement must also be agreed upon, as some contracts include a minimum gross income the artist must make for the manager to continue as the manager.

2. COMPENSATION

How much should the manager be paid? Is the commission based on gross earnings, net earnings, or some formula that represents a mixture of both? Most of the remainder of the agreement contains fairly standard clauses that are negotiated in a routine manner. However, an attorney MUST represent the artist throughout the negotiations.

CAREER PLAN

STAGES OF AN AMERICAN CAREER

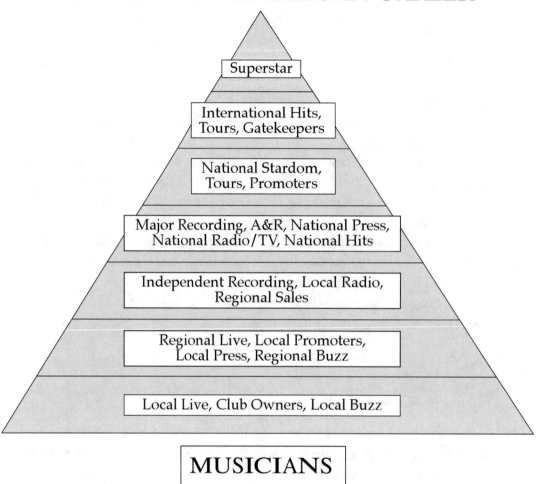

*Figure 1.2 Stages of an American Career. Frith, S.(ed.) Facing The Music. N.Y. Pantheon. 1988
{{9 Denisoff,R.Serge 1986/f, p. 37}}.*

Figure 1.2 illustrates the old model of the various stages of an American artist's career. While the lower levels of the hierarchy are fondly known as "paying your dues," it is the working up to the third level, indie recording and regional sales, that is considered the first major goal. It is the level that most driven musicians attain but unfortunately never leave. Crossing the bridge from level three to level four is what stumps even the most assertive. This model still exists and if followed one can achieve success.

Developing a Fan Base

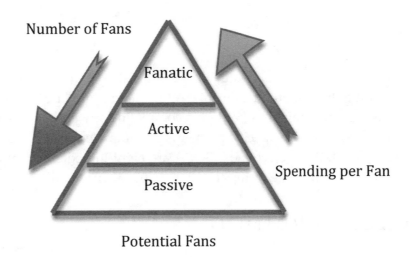

Figure 1.3 Developing a Fan Base. Adapted from New Music Seminar Presentation by Tom Silverman July 2009.

Figure 1.3 represents one of the newer models for success. This model has been adopted by successful artists that have used internet sites to their fullest potential. This route recognizes potential fans and hopeful converts them to "fanatic" fans. As fans become involved with more aspects of the artist's career, their spending on the artist's products increases. Because it is impossible to convert every potential fan to a "groupie," as fans move from passive to active to fanatic, the number of fans will decrease. Consequently, the key to monetizing this model is to constantly feed fans information and products. Since the internet has leveled the playing field, the artists that build strong communities sell products. This is a reversal of the old model. In fact, Tom Silverman, CEO of Tommy Boy Entertainment and Co-Director of the new New Music Seminar, in the New Music Seminar's *New Music Buisness Guidebook, Chicago* declares that the new model is get fans interested with your music, next comes photos and videos, and lastly, your blogs and tweets (pg. 38)

A successful career includes talent, organization, and planning. Given that the artist has a certain amount of talent (or at least appeal), it's the manager's responsibility to oversee the organization and plan. Invariably, given opportunities, an unsuccessful artist had a weak plan.

A SUCCESSFUL PLAN INCLUDES:

a) preparing,

b) securing the proper information,

c) having the proper attitude, and

d) establishing goals.

The goals should motivate both the artist and the manager. The strategy for reaching them should be flexible. A timetable should be set and tactics developed. This type of planning is helpful in completing any project successfully. Projects are developed to solve specific problems or complete specific tasks, and once they are completed, the project ends. Below are eight ingredients that are important for a successfully managed project, followed by an explanation of each point.

PROJECT MANAGEMENT

1. Problem Statement

2. Background Statement

3. Objectives

4. Procedures

5. Plan

6. Schedule

7. Budget

8. Success Indicator

1. PROBLEM STATEMENT

The problem statement is an explanation of what is the perceived need and creating the problem. For example, if the artist wants to change his/her booking agent, an investigation should be made into why this is perceived to be needed. Exactly what is the problem that the artist believes a new agent will solve? The solution may lie elsewhere. A manager must be certain that if there is a real problem, it's clearly stated, and the perceived solution (project) is the correct one.

2. BACKGROUND STATEMENT

Information about the background and significance of the problem is very useful in determining the value of a project. For example, if the artist wishes to record with a specific producer, the producer's track record may include significant information pertinent to attaining a hit record.

3. PROJECT OBJECTIVES

Are there many objectives or only one? If there are many, a prioritized list is essential. One method of writing objectives is to put each objective in a behavioral form. For example, instead of listing an objective as "learn" three new songs, in behavioral form it might read "perform" or "arrange" or "memorize" three new songs. This form makes it more obvious when an objective is completed.

4. PROJECT PROCEDURES

What steps must be completed to meet the objectives? Each step should be listed in chronological order (the project's critical path). Both **creative** and **organizational** tasks should be listed. For example, if the stated project is to complete another recording, all the creative and organizational tasks that need completion before arriving at the studio, during the recording process, and after it's finished must be listed. Obviously, some tasks occur simultaneously, but a chronological list is still useful.

5. PROJECT PLAN

Who will complete which tasks? Who will make certain each task is completed? What strategy will be used to complete each task? For example, who will write the new songs? Who will search for an outside writer? Who will hire the producer? Specific tasks must be assigned to specific people. This is what makes a plan work.

6. SCHEDULE

Realistic timetables work. Set realistic deadlines and don't require tasks to be completed long before they are needed. Schedules with a natural flow are helpful.

7. BUDGET

What is the money needed for, when is it needed, and where will it come from? These three questions need answering. Also, remember to include a 10-15% miscellaneous expense category for unforeseen expenses.

8. SUCCESS INDICATOR

How will the success of the project be determined? Realistic goals should be set. If an artist's second recording sells 2 million copies, 3 million short of the first's sales, is it not a success?

Career planning is one of the most important functions a personal manager performs. Being organized is also important. Preparing a well-organized plan greatly improves the artist's chances of success.

What follows are three examples of class projects. They have been included here with the permission of future industry leaders David Allu, Rob Benaquista, Jim Bogert, Paul Jansson, Jill Krug, John Landieri, and Rob Minnell.

Rob Benaquista
Paul Jansson
Rob Minnell

GROUP 1 PROJECT OUTLINE
AVENUE

PROBLEM STATEMENT

AVENUE, a New Jersey based pop-punk act, has the ingredients for becoming successful but needs help in getting to the next level. Their main objective is to create a local buzz. The managers of AVENUE, Rob Benaquista, Paul Jansson, and Rob Minnell, have met with the band and discussed some future goals and ideas that can be achieved over the course of the next few months. These ideas include: 1) lining up more gigs for the band outside of Bergen County, 2) improvements on their image (creating new press kit, album art, website, photo shoot), and 3) getting a sponsorship or endorsement.

AVENUE has a clearly defined goal in that it wants to create a loud and solid local buzz and then begin to expand from there. Collectively, they know that if they want to reach a higher level of success, more progress has to be made in terms of promotion, image, marketing, and networking. First, the band is planning to play more gigs because they have a demo recorded and want to promote it. Second, they want to improve their image on their album cover, press kit, and website to convey a more professional impression on the music listeners. Third, the band wants to aim for a sponsorship/endorsement to increase their funds, equipment apparel, and create more professional networking opportunities.

BACKGROUND STATEMENT

Performances, image, and sponsorship are three keys to open doors of success for any band. While many artists are reaching high levels of popularity more than before in non-conventional ways (due to the increase in digital technology), playing live performances is still the ultimate necessity for survival in the Industry. Image of a band is extremely important because it associates the artists with the music and has to be compatible with one another. When the average music listener picks up an album from a lesser known band, image pretty much can say it all and solidify the opinion of that particular band forever. Sponsorship is becoming another very important tool for bands and artists alike these days. When small and upcoming bands are endorsed by chains or retail outlets, it can do wonders in terms of advertising, professional networking, fund raising, and exposure.

These three areas were chosen because the managers felt that the intertwining goals that can be set for AVENUE are realistic, effective, and productive.

PROJECT OBJECTIVES

One of the objectives for the project is to contact local music chains and mom and pop record stores in their hometown Vernon NJ, to sponsor AVENUE for any local shows. Also, bigger corporations such as Sam Ash and Guitar Center in terms of a sponsorship to endorse AVENUE as much as possible. The next objective would be to contact local clubs, bars, and concert venues in New Jersey and NYC to line up gigs AVENUE can play.

PROJECT PROCEDURES

1. Arrange another meeting with all of the AVENUE members as a group. Restate the objectives, goals, and the plans to successfully achieve them. Listen to any additional input, opinion, or viewpoint from the leader of the band, and see if there is any changes that have to be made.

2. Contact at least 10 live concert venues in New Jersey and NYC for booking shows. Stay on top of the venues with follow up calls, in person meetings, and persistence in securing a date for the band.

3. Get in touch with as many musical retail outlets and musical instrument stores for sponsorship requests. Tackle the local places as well as the big chain outlets and see what type of offer would suit the band as well.

4. Obtain a very good camera to do a slick and professional looking photo shoot with the entire band. Make sure the photos define the set image of AVENUE and have the approval of the entire band before using them.

5. Contact a web designer or computer programmer to revamp and enhance the band's official website. Adding new elements (flash, HTML option), an official messageboard, new colors and graphics, and the new photos/image of AVENUE would project a more professional appeal.

6. Get in touch with one who does artwork, freelance or professionally, and hire that person to design an album cover for the band. Let the artist know that while he or she has enough creative input to use his or her unique style, it is AVENUE who makes the decision of what ideas are to be presented.

7. Compile a brand new press kit to be mailed and handed out to clubs. Make the press kit brief but effective. Enclose a brief bio, flyers, photos, and a CD sampler. Be aware that the kit does not have to be elaborate and overblown because it can be counterproductive.

8. Meet as a group once to twice a week to discuss progress, changes to be made, what direction to head in, and to self-evaluate the work being done. Keep each other on call for any last minute changes, sudden new opportunities, and situations which need to be resolved by more than one person.

9. Meet with the members of AVENUE once a week to let them know exactly what is being done and exactly when it will take place. If they are satisfied with how everything is going, build on the strengths and work on the weak points. If they are not happy with the process, take a different approach to the process and take more input from the leader of the band. Keep the band on call for any changes that are made.

10. Have every goal achieved by the date that it was tentatively set for. When all goals are achieved, evaluate the entire process of the project to see what worked and what did not go as planned.

PROJECT PLAN

1. Rob B., Paul, and Rob M. will assist the band in all photo shoots, organization of the press kit, and promotion of their demo and upcoming shows. Paul will arrange a time and place to take the pictures of the band members in their hometown. Rob B. and Rob M. will both create the new press kit with the photos, flyers, and CD samplers. All will help promote AVENUE's demo by attending upcoming shows of the band and handing out free samplers. This entire task will be completed by 11/12/05.

2. Paul will contact musical retail outlets and instrument stores in New Jersey and NYC. The outlets will range from corporations such as Guitar Center, Sam Ash, Tower Records to small record stores such as CD World, Vintage Vinyl, and any small record outlets in AVENUE's hometown, Vernon NJ. We will request a $1,000 sponsorship as a minimum with the possibility to extend to a higher amount if given a better deal. This entire task will be completed by 11/23/2005.

3. Rob M. and Rob B. will contact concert venues in New Jersey and NYC. They will be Connections Tavern, Dingbatz, The Loop Lounge, The Saint, Starland Ballroom, Bloomfield Ave. Cafe, Hamilton St. Cafe, The Continental, Maxwell's, and Webster Hall. We will offer the clubs money, free CDs, and any available free merchandise of AVENUE. This entire task will be completed by 11/27/05.

SCHEDULE

11/12/2005

All photo shoots and official press kit for AVENUE will be completed. Web designer will be contacted for enhancing the band's official website and artist will be contacted for designing the album cover.

11/23/2005

All musical instrument and retail stores will have been contacted for sponsorship purposes. Arrangement of the actual sponsorship will have taken place and the money/goods will have been distributed

11/27/2005

All clubs will have been contacted for booking AVENUE shows. All newspapers will have been contacted to arrange write-ups for the band. All press kits will be handed out and sent out by this time.

12/1/2005

All goals will have been achieved to an extent. Evaluation of AVENUE's goals and levels of success will take place and see what worked, what did not work, and what else can be done in the future for pushing the band to the next level.

SUCCESS INDICATORS

A. Shows

The band will have gotten at least four shows booked in four of the clubs and concert venues listed above.

B. An improved image layout

The band will have a professional image in which the members themselves are satisfied and will also generate positive feedback from outside people.

C. Sponsorship

The band will have received a substantial amount of money or product from a sponsorship with a value of no less than $1,000.

D. Conditions for the project to be successful.

1. AVENUE has to feel that they have benefitted from the managers' work.

2. The band will have gigs lined up, feel satisfied with the improvements on their image, and take advantage of a sponsorship to the fullest extent.

I.   Problem Statement

Tim Quick, of *More Then I*, believes that more exposure is needed for the band. Their new CD is going to be released on November 26th, and there will be a CD release party at the Stone Pony in Asbury Park, where they will open for Bret Michaels, lead singer of the band *Poison*. He would like us to as much press as we can on this event, and then once the CD is finished, try to get reviews on it.

II.   Background Statement

In order to most effectively promote the band's upcoming release, several markets must be reached through different mediums. *More Then I* most appeals to the 18-35 age group, often being described as *Incubus* meets *Matchbox Twenty*. Newspapers are a way to inform people about the release who may not hear of it otherwise. The niche of these papers can be crucial in helping the band gain local support. Sending press releases to papers that have printed about the band in the past, and are read by those who frequent the Stone Pony, those from the hometowns of the band members, and college students should generate the best results in terms of getting press on the event, as well as drawing a crowd.

III.   Project Objectives

Have as many papers print an article about this CD release party, and then obtain as many review of the CD as possible.

IV.   Project Procedures

1. Gather the press contact information for the major papers in the Tri-State area, and the local papers of the band's location, and the member's hometowns.
2. Mail and email news releases about the CD release party to all the press contacts gathered.
3. Follow up with the reporters 4-5 days after the releases have been sent. Since they will be sent electronically as well as by snail mail, they will have them in copy the next day.
4. Scan the papers for the press on the band and the CD release party.
5. Upon completion of the CD, send out the CD to critics for review.

V.   Project Plan

1. Jill and Jim will divide up the press contacts for the following papers, and send the releases by email and snail mail. The releases will use the following hook to grab the attention of the reporters: "New JERSEY BAND *More Then I* To Release SECOND CD Opening for *Bret Michaels of Poison*".

Jill	**Jim**
Aquarian	Asbury Park Press
Billboard/BB Events	Courier News
Daily News	Local Papers of Band Members
Local papers of band's residence	Main Line Times
NY Times	Philadelphia Daily News
Philadelphia Inquirer	Village Voice
Star Ledger	Steppin' Out
WPU Beacon	Wayne Local Paper

2. Jill and Jim will follow up with the papers that they sent the releases to by calling the reporters to whom the releases were to the attention of.

3. If the reporter has decided to print about the band, Jill and Jim will scan their assigned papers for the article.

4. Once the CD is completed, and ready to be distributed, as per Tim, Jill and Jim will contact the following papers to see if they will review the CD.

Jill	**Jim**
Star Ledger	WPU Beacon
WPU Pioneer Times	Asbury Park Press
Wayne Valley Paper	Bergen Record
	Herald News

5. If they are interested, Jill and Jim will send out the CD through regular mail.

Schedule
10/22/04   Jim and Jill send out news releases to papers.
10/28/04   Jim and Jill follow up with the papers they each sent out
11/3/04   Jim and Jill check respective interested papers for press
Approximately 11/20/04 Send out CD's for review

Budget

The band will reimburse Jim and Jill for postage to send out the news releases and CDs if necessary.

Success Indicators

5. The band feels as though they benefited from the group's work.
6. The group has participated in a positive successful learning experience.

IX.   Update – 12/6/04

After drafting a news release (attached) and sending them out to the newspapers mentioned above, we were successful with 3 of the papers. The William Paterson University Beacon printed a small section on *More Then I* with a picture of the band. Through Jim and Jill, Tim Quick and Marc Goldberg were contacted by their hometown papers for an interview. These papers are the *Hillsborough Beacon* and *The Ocean County Observer*, respectively. We were not able to obtain copies of the actual papers, but the Hillsborough Beacon published the article on their website (attached). Jay Lustig from the *Star Ledger* was not interested in covering the event, but did request a copy of the CD. As soon as it was finished, a copy was sent to him, but we haven't been able to obtain a response.

Once the CDs were completed, Tim supplied us with a list of newspapers that he would like us to send the CD to, in hopes of getting it reviewed. The CDs are packaged with a letter requesting that the CD's be reviewed. At this point we are waiting to hear from Tim on whether we should send the CDs out to the newspapers or not, because he may opt to wait on sending them out, which would be beyond the project deadline.

At the end of this project, Tim Quick seemed pleased with our work. Two papers not only covered the story, but interviewed the band members, and the new CD is ready to be sent out to obtain reviews. Both Jim and Jill were unable to attend the CD release party, but by having it published in two newspapers, more people knew about the event, and some possibly attended as a result of reading the article. In the latest *More Then I* newsletter (attached), they mention having one of their biggest turnouts ever.

This project was a positive learning experience for the group. Although it is very similar to tasks we have to perform in Mus 316 – Media Use in the Music and Entertainment Industry, this project was more in depth, and we did everything on our own, after receiving Tim's approval of the task at hand. We wrote the news releases as well as obtained some of the names and addresses of newspapers to send it to and followed up with the individual reporters. Knowing that many times your news release will not produce a story, the project can be considered successful because we did obtain press in three newspapers. Based on the total number of newspapers the releases were sent to, we had almost a 20% return. Another aspect of this learning experience was working with an actual band, with no one to answer to but the band. We got to see first hand that sometimes ideas about doing things and the way they should be done differ between the artist and the management, and a compromise must be reached.

SO WHAT'S THE SECRET?

Well there really isn't a secret. How big of a star the artist becomes will be determined by many factors; most importantly, how well the manager keeps the artist a **priority** among the industry gatekeepers (if there were a secret that would be it).

In his book *Tarnished Gold*, the late R. Serge Denisoff defines the two concepts of **talent and success**. He states, "**Talent** is the *commodity* that has economic potential." In other words, creating an original musical presentation that is marketable to an audience. And it was always the industry gatekeepers, namely, club owners, agents, radio programmers, promoters, and record company "suits" (personnel) that defined the talent. They made the decision as to which artist would receive the chance to be seen and heard.

Talent alone does not guarantee success. "**Success**," Denisoff writes, "is the artist's *ability* to persuade the industry gatekeepers to recognize the talent" {{9 Denisoff,R.Serge 1986;}}. In the past, this persuasion not only came from the music, but also from the stage presence and overall excitement and charisma as well. The artist chose the industry leader s/he believed the evaluation of his/her talent was correct.

Today that has all changed. With the new model, artists are building fan bases. The Internet has given everyone with the entrepreneurial spirit the opportunity to bypass many of the so-called gatekeepers. Success in no longer defined by major record company executives. The artist revenue streams have multiplied and a hit record is no longer the only determining factor.

So now you have two models, now go and do it. Play in the major leagues. It's a tough road to stardom. Not many who try make it. Again, according to Denisoff, "only 17 new artists per year, it is believed, ever record a Top 40 hit, while in the same year 23 persons are statistically likely to be struck dead by lightning." If you have what it takes, these odds won't stop you!

SUMMARY

1. A key to successful artist management is obtaining the proper information.

2. The artist's opinion should be part of the decision making process.

3. Management is an art and a craft.

4. The most important characteristic a manager can have is patience.

5. Artists striving for success should have talent, desire, determination, and patience.

6. An artist must have a clearly focused image.

7. The artist's and the manager's personalities must be compatible.

8. The artist's team is composed of the personal manager, attorney, booking agent, publicist, and accountant.

9. In this business, there is no such thing as a typical day.

10. Each day, the manager should ask: "Am I making as much money for the artist as I possibly can?"

11. The artist and manager must agree on the length of the contract and manager's compensation.

12. There are old and new models for success.

13. An organized career plan is essential for success.

14. Talent is the commodity that has economic potential.

15. Success is determined by many factors.

16. The manager must keep his/her artist a priority within the marketplace.

PROJECTS

1. Using the new model for success, determine a project and create a project management outline for a fictitious project and complete and a detailed plan.

2. Role-play an initial artist and manager meeting.

CHAPTER TWO
THE CONTRACT

"Fellows, forget about the contract. If it's not working like a marriage,
the contract is not going to help!" – Anonymous

BY THE END OF THIS CHAPTER YOU SHOULD BE ABLE TO:

1. Discuss why a **written** agreement between an artist and personal manager is typically used in the industry.
2. Discuss the four basic parts of any legal contract.
3. Discuss what it means to act in a fiduciary manner.
4. Discuss all the parts of a typical artist/personal manager contract, identifying fair deals for both sides.
5. List the areas where advice and counsel should be offered by the manager that are in accordance with the American Federation of Musicians' guidelines.
6. Compose a fair artist/personal manager agreement.

On several occasions, as a member of a band, the author was involved in negotiations with prospective managers and was asked to sign artist/personal management contracts. Depending upon where we were in the negotiations, some contracts were more elaborate than others. Some contracts also favored the manager more than others. Regardless of the situation, when band members inquired about the language in different sections of the contracts, the various attorneys representing the managers invariably used the marriage analogy. They assured us, in each case, that the contracts would not bind us to managers we no longer wanted to represent us.

They also assured us that we, as artists, were truly "the bosses". "The manager works for the artist, and it's never the other way around. So if the manager isn't performing to the artist's satisfaction, s/he should be fired." My response was always the same. If this is true, why do we need to sign a written agreement? If the relationship is supposed to work like a marriage and the artist is the boss, why should any problems arise? The answer is simply that problems do arise.

It's been reported that Elvis and Colonel Parker never had a written contract. Their deal was consummated with only a handshake. Unfortunately, the estate on behalf of Elvis' daughter, Lisa Marie, has sued the Colonel for a number of misappropriations (see Chapter 12). Seldom is an issue of *Billboard Magazine* published without a reported artist/manager suit.

The contract is there for protection. Both parties sign it so that each is protected from each other. It's signed with the understanding that although it is a relationship, it's first a business. And the business is more important than either party individually.

Another reason for a written contract is that a manager, as an employee of the artist, acts in a fiduciary (monetary) capacity. This means that the relationship is one involving a confidence or a trust. For this reason, the manager should never have an unfair economic advantage. Acting in a fiduciary manner implies that the artist's interest comes first, and the manager's interest second. The manager is obliged to operate in the artist's interest, and this has been the basis of many artist/manager disputes.

Most people believe that a contract must be in writing and signed by both parties to be valid. Terms of most contracts only have to be agreed upon by both parties, and if the agreement is witnessed, then it is a valid agreement. Contracts are put in writing to avoid one party denying that they agreed to something. Besides, as more time passes, people have different recollections as to what actually occurred. So even though it may be a pain to negotiate, it's easier in a long run when the contract is in writing.

There are **four basic parts** to a legal contract of this type. They are: **mutual assent, consideration, capacity, and legality.**

Mutual assent — This is the offer and acceptance by both parties. For example, John Jones wants to manage the "Dumbbells." The "Dumbbells" want a manager. This is the section of the contract that begins with "Whereas" as in "Whereas The Dubbells want advise ...."

Consideration — This is the trading process. Something of value changes hands when services are performed. For example, if Jones manages the "Dumbbells," they agree to perform and appear where they are told to, and Jones will receive compensation.

Capacity — This means that both parties are of sound mind and body, and have the legal capacity to perform the necessary functions to carry out the terms of the contract.

Legality — The contract must be for a legal purpose. A contract to buy a car that you know has been stolen is not legal.

Following are two typical artist/personal management contracts. The term "typical" is used because there is no such thing as a standard contract. Although the language may vary, the items addressed in the contracts are common. The first contract is drafted based on album cycles. The second contract's term is based on a number of named albums. For educational purposes, in the first agreement, comments that address each issue have been inserted in italics. The second agreement contains negotiated compromises; however, comments have **not** been inserted.

"THE DUMBBELLS"
EXCLUSIVE WORLDWIDE
PERSONAL MANAGEMENT AGREEMENT

In consideration of the promises and covenants set forth in this deal-memo, and for other good and valuable consideration, the sufficiency and receipt of which are hereby acknowledged, when signed by **SLICK** Management ('us" and "we"), on the one hand and **Heavyweight, Middleweight and Flyweight**, collectively p/k/a **"The Dumbbells"** (individually and collectively, "you"), on the other hand, this deal-memo shall constitute a legally binding agreement (this "Agreement") regarding your engaging our services as your exclusive personal manager throughout the worldwide entertainment industries.

The artist should make certain that the individual manager's name appears in the opening statement and not solely the name of a business or corporation so that the manager is personally responsible. The same is true for the manager. The manager should insist that each member of the performing group have personal contracts with the manager.

1.   (a) You hereby engage us as your exclusive personal manager throughout the worldwide entertainment industries for a term (the "Term") that shall commence upon the date of the Agreement and shall last until the earlier to occur of (i) end of the second album cycle (such two (2) album cycles shall hereinafter be referred to the "First Album Cycle" and the "Second Album Cycle", respectively) and (ii) five (5) years from the date of this Agreement, provided that, in the event that such five (5)-year period expires during the Second Album Cycle, then the Term shall continue until the end of the Second Album Cycle. In the event that either the applicable album released in the First Album Cycle or the applicable album released in the Second Album Cycle or the applicable album released in the Second Album cycle sells at least five hundred thousand (500,000) units in the United States prior to the end of the Term, then we shall have the option (the "Option") to extend the Term for one (1) additional consecutive album cycle, which additional cycle shall commence as of the expiration of the Second Album Cycle. The Option shall be deemed exercised by us unless we notify you in writing to the contrary prior to the expiration of the Second Album Cycle. As used herein, an "album cycle" shall mean the period of time commencing with the initial commercial release of a long-playing studio album embodying your newly-recorded featured performances and continuing until the delivery to your exclusive record company of the next long-playing studio album embodying your newly-recorded featured performances in fulfillment of your recording commitment.

Clause 1 (a) defines the term of the agreement. The term of this agreement is based on both the recording cycles and years. It also states that management will have the exclusive right to pick up the option period, and it lists the requirements. Furthermore, it states that management can exercise their option without notifying the artist, and if they choose not to exercise the option, they must notify the artist "prior to the expiration date", which could be interpreted to mean that a notification at 11:59 PM of the cycle will fulfill their legal requirement, leaving the artist no time to secure new management.
It should also be noted that five years is a long time period for an initial term.

Notwithstanding anything to the contrary herein contained, in the event that you have not entered into or substantially negotiated the terms of a recording, production or distribution agreement with a "major label" (defined below) within twelve (12) months of the date of this Agreement, then, upon our receipt of written notice to such effect, you shall be entitled to terminate the Term of this Agreement. For the purposes hereof, "major label" shall mean (i) WEA, CEMA/EMD, SONY, UNI, or BMG, or (ii) any other record, production or distribution company whose records are distributed by one of the companies set forth in the preceding clause 1(b)(i).

Clause 1 (b) describes the contract termination requirements. If a record deal is not secured, then the artist may, in writing, terminate the agreement. There is no grace period for this notification. Other contracts use a gross income amount as a barometer for how the relationship is working. If the artist does not make a certain dollar amount by a certain date, then the contract can be terminated. Also, some use both.

2.   We shall render all services customarily rendered by personal managers in the United States recording industry. Our services hereunder are non-exclusive and we shall at all times be free to perform the same or similar services for others, as well as to engage in any and all other business activities.

According to the American Federation of Musicians (the union), the artist's representative should offer to advise and counsel and render services in five specific areas. They are:

> *1. the selection of literary, artistic, and musical materials*
>
> *2. all matters relating to public relations*
>
> *3. adoption of a proper format for the best presentation of artist's talents*
>
> *4. selection of a booking agent*
>
> *5. the types of employment the artist should accept.*

Clause two also states that management is free to manage other artists. There are many advantages to employing management that manages other acts of the same genre, such as record company and booking agency contacts.

3.   (a) During the Term, you agree to account to and pay us, promptly following your (or any of your designees") receipt thereof, a commission equal to twenty percent (20%) of all the gross earnings received by you (or any of your designees) in any and all forms and from any and all sources in the entertainment industry, subject only to the exclusions set forth in **Exhibit "A"** attached hereto incorporated herein by this reference.

This is the compensation clause. Twenty percent is within the scope of personal management commissions in the entertainment industry, however, be aware that a symbol such as this in a contract (%) is begging to be negotiated….. in this case, down to fifteen percent. It is important to read Exhibit "A" to understand what is excluded from commissions.

Commencing upon the expiration of the Term and continuing for a period equal to two (2) times the length of the Term (the "Post-Term Period"), you agree to pay to us a commission (the "Post-Term Commission") equal to the following percentages of all of the gross earnings received by you (or any of your designees) in any and all forms and from any and all courses in the entertainment industry, subject only to the exclusions set forth in **Exhibit "A"**; (i) fifteen percent (15%) for the first one-third (1/3) of the Post-Term Period; (ii) ten percent (10%) for the second one-third (1/3) of the Post-Term Period; and (iii) five percent (5%) for the final one-third (1/3) of the Post-Term Period. For the avoidance of doubt, with respect to gross earnings derived from master recordings, videos and musical compositions, the Post-Term commission shall only apply to the gross earnings derived from those master recordings, videos, and musical compositions that are substantially created during the Term.

This is the "golden parachute" or "sunset" clause that protects management from losing out on commissions from income subsequent to the termination of the agreement that they believe they are entitled to receive. Usually a manager will want to continue receiving commissions on any contract that s/he negotiated, even if, for example, all of the albums under the recording contract have not yet been recorded. Note that the "Post-Term Period" is twice the length of time that the initial term represented, which could be ten years! Even though the commission rate decreases, the entire clause should be negotiable.

4.   You agree to reimburse us for any and all direct expenses incurred by us on your behalf, including, but not limited to, long-distance phone calls, FedEx or similar overnight courier charges, messenger charges and travel costs, but specifically excluding our so-called "overhead" costs. We hereby acknowledge and agree that when we travel with you or on your behalf, we shall travel in the same so-called "class" as you (including, but not limited to, with respect to air transportation, ground transportation and lodging); for the avoidance of doubt, the foregoing shall not preclude or prevent us from traveling with you or on your behalf in a superior "class", provided that any such resulting excess costs shall be our sole responsibility and obligation. We shall not, without your prior consent or request, incur any costs on your behalf in excess of (i) Five Hundred dollars ($500) for any single expenditure or (ii) One Thousand Dollars ($1000) in aggregate costs per month.

Management requires payment of expenses that go beyond normal costs. Number four also states that if the artist travels first class, then management is entitled to as well. Also, it sets a ceiling for both single and monthly expenditures.

5.   Your obligation under this agreement shall be joint and several and, for the avoidance of doubt, your obligations to pay to us commissions shall cover each of you as members of "The Dumbbells" as members or leaders of other projects and in any and all other entertainment related activities, including, but not limited to music, motion pictures and television.

The agreement requirements members of the performing group to sign and become libel individually as well as collectively.

6.   We shall have the right to assign this agreement, in whole or in part, to any entity in which SLICK Management, has a substantial ownership or control interest. You shall not have the right to assign any of your rights or obligations hereunder.

Management is stating that they have the right to assign the contract (or artist) to another subsidiary company. This entire agreement lacks a "key man" clause, which customarily states that if an individual leaves the company, the artist has the option of going with the individual or staying with the company. The artist should not sign an agreement without it. The two situations are related and should be set forth in this clause.

7.   Neither party hereto shall be deemed to be in breach of any of its respective warranties, representations, agreements or obligations hereunder unless and until the alleged breaching party shall have first received from the other party specific written notice by certified or registered mail, return receipt requested, of the nature and details of such breach and such alleged breaching party shall have failed to cure said breach within thirty (30) days after receipt of such written notice.

This is the breech and cure clause, which allows either party to respond to an alleged breech within thirty days of written notification.

8.   WE HAVE ADVISED YOU THAT WE ARE NOT PERMITTED TO SEEK OR OBTAIN EMPLOYMENT OR ENGAGEMENTS FOR YOU AND THAT WE DO NOT AGREE TO DO SO. WE HAVE MADE NO REPRESENTATIONS TO YOU, EITHER ORAL OR WRITTEN, TO THE CONTRARY. YOU ACKNOWLEDGE THAT WE DO NOT HEREBY AND HAVE NOT HERETOFORE OFFERED TO, ATTEMPTED TO OR PROMISED TO OBTAIN, SEEK OR PROCURE EMPLOYMENT OR ENGAGEMENTS FOR YOU AND THAT WE ARE NOT OBLIGATED OR EXPECTED TO DO SO.

Clause eight is in respect to the California and New York laws that are widely practiced in the entertainment industry. It states that management is not licensed to be an employment agency and cannot seek or procure employment for an artist. The only exception is the procurement of a recording contract.

9.   You warrant and represent that (a) you are free to enter into and perform the terms of this agreement, (b) no other party is presently engaged to act as your personal manager, (c) you will not during the Term engage any other person or entity to render services similar to those to be rendered by us hereunder, (d) you have not heretofore nor will you hereafter assign or otherwise encumber any of the gross earnings that may be subject to our commission or other rights hereunder and (e) you shall at all times engage and utilize proper theatrical, booking or employment agencies to obtain engagements and employments for yourselves. You and we agree to indemnify, defend and hold each other harmless from and against any and all cost, loss, damage, liability or expense arising from a breach of any of the warranties, representations or agreements, made by each of you and us hereunder and agree to execute any and all documents and take any and all actions which are reasonably necessary to secure each of your and our respective

rights under this agreement. In the event of any litigation between the parties, the prevailing party shall be entitled to recover its costs and attorneys fees.

10.   This constitutes the entire agreement between you and us regarding the subject matter hereof, and this agreement may only be modified pursuant to a written instrument signed by both you and us.

11.   Each of you and us has cooperated in the preparation of this agreement, and accordingly, in any construction to be made of this agreement, the same shall not be construed against any party on the basis that such party was the drafter.

Clause Eleven is a statement pertaining to the awareness of both parties of all clauses and their interpretations.

12.   You and we intend to enter a more formal agreement embodying the terms contained herein, as well as such other terms as are customary, in exclusive, worldwide personal management agreements of this type. Until such time, if ever, as that more formal agreement is signed, this agreement shall be legally binding contract between you and us with respect to the subject matter hereof.

13.   Promptly after the execution of this Agreement, you shall, at your sole cost and expense, use best efforts to engage throughout the Term a certified public accountant experienced in the entertainment industry (the "CPA") to act as your business manager and to collect all of the gross earnings payable to you pursuant to Paragraph 3(a) above. You acknowledge and agree that (i) you shall consult with us in good faith prior to engaging any such CPA, and (ii) such CPAshall abide by the terms and conditions of this Agreement regarding the payment of any and all monies or other consideration due to us hereunder.

Management is requiring that a CPA be engaged to collect funds. This helps to protect them from any alleged fiduciary irresponsibility. Also, they require that they take part in the engagement of the business manager.

Very truly yours,

SLICK MANAGEMENT, INC.

By: _____
        (an authorized signatory)

AGREED TO ACCEPTED:

THE DUMBBELLS

(individually and collectively)

_____   _____   _____
Heavyweight SS#   Middleweight SS#   Flyweight SS#

EXHIBIT "A"
CUSTOMARY GROSS EARNINGS EXCLUSIONS

(a)   "Recording Costs" – payments, advances, overrides and royalties payable to individual producer, engineers, musicians and vocalist, or the respective companies furnishing their services, as defined under any applicable agreement for your recording services, but specifically excluding advances, payments or other consideration retained for your personal use;

(b)   "Video Production Costs" – monies paid to you or on your behalf in connection with video or film productions featuring or incorporating your recorded performances, but specifically excluding advances, payments or other consideration retained for your personal use;

(c)   "Tour Support" – monies used to offset a deficit incurred in connection with any personal appearance of concert engagement or tour of yours (unless the relevant record company does not object to our commissioning same) and monies spent by Artist's record company on so-called "independent promotion" and "independent marketing", but specifically excluding advances, payments or other consideration retained for your personal use;

Clauses a, b, and c exempt all payments that will be used to offset recording costs, video production costs and touring expenses. However, if any money is leftover or designated for personal use, then commission will be due.

(d)   Costs incurred in connection with "sound and lights" facilities or similar or related production costs, such as the costs of video projection equipment for use during live appearances) as result of you concert or other appearances, including, without limitation, hiring such "sound and lights" facilities, the transportation thereof and travel and accommodation expenses of the personnel required to erect, dismantle, transport and operate such facilities;

(e)   Advances, fees, royalties and other costs incurred with regard to third-party engineers, producers and songwriters and/or music publishers rendering services to you, including, without limitation, artist, producer and engineer advances, fees and royalties incurred with regard to production, and/or producer agreement between you and any such third party(ies) and royalties payable to any writer(s) or others with regard to any publishing agreements(s) between you and any writer(s); and

(f)   Costs incurred in connection with "opening" acts, "support" acts and other performers employed or retained to appear before, with or after you at concert or other appearances of yours.

Conspicuously absent from exemption is the booking agency fees or any fees related to employing a public relations person for the tour. However it is understood that managers usually ask for their commissions prior to the agent's fee being paid Clauses a through f are standard commission exemptions that honest managers are willing to forego their commissions on because of the high costs involved.

ABC Entertainment Group, Inc.
46 Lexington Avenue,
New York, NY 10017

Dated as of July 1, 2010

Future Superstar ("you", or "Artist")

4 W. 69th St.

#1D

New York, NY 10008

Dear Future,

The following, when signed by you and by an authorized representative of ABC Entertainment, Inc. ("Manager"), will constitute a complete and binding agreement (the "Agreement") with respect to your engagement of Manager as your exclusive personal manager:

1.   Territory:

The world.

2.   Scope of Manager's Activities:

(a)   Manager shall be your exclusive personal manager, during the Term, and throughout the Territory, solely in connection with your activities in the entertainment industry, and shall confer with, counsel, guide, advise and assist you in all matters pertaining to such activities, including, without limitation, in connection with phonograph records, music publishing, personal appearances, modeling, acting and the use of your name and likeness for commercial purposes.

(b)   Manager's services hereunder shall include, without limitation, the following:

(i)   assisting you in the selection and procurement of literary and artistic material for your exploitation as an artist;

(ii)   assisting you in the selection and engagement of producers, engineers, mixers, writers, musical directors, choreographers, vocal coaches, video directors and producers, and other creative and technical personnel; counseling and assisting you in the development of a professional act;

(iv)   acting as your liaison to record and publishing companies, merchandisers, booking agents and other actual and potential users of your talents and services; and

    (v)   assisting you in the selection of, and preliminary negotiation with, the following: theatrical, booking and similar agencies; other third parties that seek and/or procure employment and engagement for artists; and other potential users of your talents and services; and

    (vi)   regularly reviewing with you all actual and potential venues and engagements of your services in the entertainment industry and all other matters relating to your professional career therein.

3.   Term:

The term of this Agreement (the "Term") shall consist of one contract period commencing as of the date hereof and continuing until June 30, 2011.

4.   Manager's Commission:

(a)   During the Term, and provided Manager performs its services in accordance with the terms and conditions of this agreement, you shall pay a commission ("Manager's Commission") to Manager of twenty (20%) percent of your Gross Income (as hereinafter defined) derived from any and all areas of the entertainment industry, including the music industry, to include, but not be limited to, music, TV, film, acting, writing, commercials, songwriting, publishing, Broadway and live theatre, merchandise and any new and developed areas by Manager and Future Superstar, during the term and which relate to Future Superstar's work in the entertainment business, except as specifically provided for hereunder.

(b)   Intentionally Deleted.

(c)   As used in this Agreement, "Gross Income" shall mean all income received by you in connection with your activities during the Term in the entertainment industries, as a recording artist, songwriter, producer, actor, model, writer, publisher and all other fields of endeavor and commercial uses of your name and likeness approved by you, except as specifically provided for hereunder. Income derived from agreements which were substantially negotiated prior to the expiration of the Term and entered into within three (3) months after the expiration or termination of the Term ("Post Term Agreements"), shall be deemed to have been entered into during the Term.

(d)   Notwithstanding the foregoing, Gross Income shall not include, and there shall be deducted therefrom, the following:

    (i)   all music publishing income retained by or payable to third parties including, without limitation, songwriter royalties payable to co-writers and publishing company administration fees;

(ii) bona fide third party costs and fees incurred in connection with motion picture, television and other types of synchronization or general licenses;

(iii) actual recording, production and other recoupable or non-recoupable costs of master recordings and audiovisual works (other than payments [e.g., musicians fees and producers fees] to you as a portion of those recording costs);

(iv) fees, advances, royalties and other payments paid to third parties including, without limitation, record producers, producers and directors of audiovisual works, and band members;

(v) income derived by any entity in which Manager has a proprietary or income interest;

(vi) that portion of your income from any "package" which is payable in commissions to a talent agent or is otherwise payable to third parties as part of the cost of production;

(vii) (A) reasonable tour expenses (e.g., monies paid to technical and creative personnel, monies payable for transportation and accommodations), (B) monies paid to opening or other support acts, and (C) monies paid for hiring and transporting "sound and light" facilities and other similar or related production costs (e.g., video projection and special effects equipment);

(viii) any income derived by you from any business investments, or entrepreneurial or other non entertainment related activities. Notwithstanding the foregoing, in the event that you request Manager to render any services in connection with any such activity, you and Manager agree to negotiate in good faith Manager's compensation therefor;

(ix) costs incurred to collect Gross Income, including, without limitation, reasonable attorneys' fees and other legal costs, and auditors' costs (regardless of whether any audit recovery results);

(x) any judicial or arbitrators' award which you receive in the nature of punitive or reputational damages; and

(xi) Intentionally deleted.

(xii) income derived from MTV (or related entities) in connection with voiceovers performed by Artist, as well as producing and/or writing relating thereto, unless otherwise agreed to by Artist, in writing, pursuant to an opportunity procured by Manager.

(xiii) income derived from any other voiceovers performed by Artist, pursuant opportunities not procured by Manager, or are not branded as the performances of Artist.

(xiv) the amount representing the production costs of the audiovisual work titled "The Future Superstar Band Live From NYC" (the "DVD"), but only from the gross revenues generated from the exploitation of the DVD.

(xv) the amount representing the production costs of the audio work titled "The Future Superstar Band Live From NYC" (the "Live CD"), as well as the amount representing the photo shoot and artwork therefore, but only from the gross revenues generated from the exploitation of the Live CD.

(xvi) 50% of the amount of publicist and bio fees and expenses paid by Artist during the Term, but only from the gross revenues generated from the exploitation of musical and audiovisual products.

(xvii) amounts representing the costs of any new studio recordings paid for by Artist during the Term, which such costs are mutually agreed to by Artist and Manager. Such amounts spent by Artist which would be considered reasonable, taking into consideration all reasonable facts and circumstances, shall hereby be deemed to be agreed to by Manager.

(e) Notwithstanding anything contained herein, provided Manager is not in material breach of this Agreement, Manager's entitlement to Manager's Commission after the Term ("Post Term Commission") shall be as follows:

(i) The Manager's Commission derived from agreements entered into during the Term (including agreements relating to Term Product [as defined below]) shall be as follows: (A) twenty percent (20%) of gross income in perpetuity on any and all Term Product (e.g. records, videos, films, books, movies, synch licenses, publishing, songwriting, etc.); (B) twenty percent (20%) of live dates that were booked during the Term, but were performed after the Term is over.

(ii) "Term Product" shall mean all (A) master recordings and other products embodying your performances or using your name, image, voice or likeness which are recorded, produced, manufactured during the Term, and released during the Term or within one year after the end of the Term, and (B) compositions written by you embodied in master recordings which are recorded by you during the Term, and released during the Term or within one year after the end of the Term. For clarification, the following items shall not be considered Term Product hereunder:

A.   The Future Superstar Live From NYC (DVD)

B.   The Future Superstar Band Live From NYC (CD)

C.   Happy For A Lifetime (CD)

D.   Acoustic Sessions (CD)

(f)   All Gross Income derived from your activities which are subject to this Agreement, shall be paid to and collected by your independent accountant ("Business Manager"), and such Business Manager will render monthly accountings and payment hereunder (if any) to Manager. Said Business Manager is hereby authorized and directed by you to pay the Commission (and all reimbursable expenses pursuant to paragraph 6 hereof) directly to Manager. Any and all Gross Income received directly by Manager shall be delivered by Manager, to Business Manager (or to you as set forth in this paragraph below) within five (5) days following your or Manager's receipt thereof. Notwithstanding the foregoing, until such Business Manager is engaged by you, you shall have the right to collect all Gross Income hereunder, and to pay the Commission to Manager in accordance with the terms hereof.

(g)   Notwithstanding anything contained herein to the contrary, Manager agrees to reduce Manager's Commission, in connection with gross revenues generated hereunder, from any non-music industry related services rendered by Artist if such services would customarily be subject to a commission by a third-party agent, manager, etc., in an amount equal to such third-party's reasonable and customary commission amount, but, in any event, by no more than 50% of Manager's Commission hereunder.

5.   <u>Manager's Power of Attorney:</u>

Manager's power of attorney shall be expressly limited to executing agreements with respect to live appearance "one nighters" or a series of live appearance "one nighters", not to exceed more than three (3) consecutive appearances, with your prior written approval of such activities where reasonably feasible.

6.   <u>Management Expenses:</u>

(a)   You (or Business Manager) will reimburse Manager for any and all reasonable expenses incurred by Manager with your knowledge, on your behalf, directly in connection with the activities referred to in paragraph 2 hereof, provided that: (i) you will not be responsible for any portion of Manager's overhead expenses; (ii) subject to subparagraph 6(a)(iii) hereof, if Manager incurs travel expenses on behalf of both you and other of Manager's clients, you shall be responsible only for your pro rata share of such expenses and (iii) Manager shall not incur without your prior written consent (A) any single expense in excess of One Hundred Dollars ($100) or (B) aggregate monthly expenses in excess of One Thousand Dollars ($500).

(b)   Manager shall furnish you or the Business Manager with appropriate documentation of Manager's expenses within thirty (30) days after the date such expense is incurred, and reimbursement of such expenses, as appropriate, shall be made in connection with the monthly accountings referred to in subparagraph 4(e) hereof.

7.   Accountings and Audit Rights:

Upon written notice by either party to the other, the party to whom such notice is addressed shall furnish an accounting to the other party of all transactions between the parties since the last such accounting, within thirty (30) days of such request; provided, however, that neither party shall be obligated to account to the other more than four (4) times in any one (1) calendar year period. Each party shall have the right to reasonable inspection of the other's books and records at any time within one (1) year after an accounting statement is rendered hereunder to the inspecting party in order to verify the accuracy of such accountings; provided, that such inspection may take place not more frequently than once with respect to each such statement and only once per any calendar year. Such inspection may be made only upon the inspecting party giving the other party written notice at least thirty (30) days prior to making any such inspection. Each party shall be deemed to have consented to all accountings rendered by the other hereunder and said accountings shall be binding upon each party and not subject to objection for any reason unless specific written objection, stating the basis thereof, is given to the other party within two (2) years after the date rendered.

8.   Warranties and Representations:

Each of the parties hereto respectively warrants, represents and agrees that it is not under any disability, restriction or prohibition, either contractual or otherwise, with respect to its right to execute this agreement or to perform fully the terms and conditions hereof.

9.   Indemnification:

Each of the parties hereto agrees to indemnify, and hereby do indemnify, save and hold the other harmless from all loss, damage and expenses (including legal costs and reasonable attorney's fees) arising out of or connected with any claim by any third party which shall be inconsistent with any agreement, warranty or representation made by the indemnifying party in this agreement; provided same is reduced to final adverse judgment or settled with the prior written consent of the indemnifying party. You and Manager each agree to reimburse the other, on demand, for any payment made at any time after the date hereof with respect to any liability to which the foregoing indemnity applies.

10.   Cure:

In order to make specific and definite and/or to eliminate, if possible, any controversy which may arise between the parties hereunder, you and Manager agree that if at any time you or Manager, as applicable, believe that the terms of this Agreement are not being fully and faithfully performed hereunder, you or Manager, as applicable, will so advise the other in writing by registered or certified mail, return receipt requested, of the specific nature of any such claim, non-performance or misfeasance, and the party receiving such notice shall have a period of Thirty (30) days after receipt thereof within which to cure such claimed breach.

11.   Independent Counsel:

(a)   Each of the parties hereto warrants and represents that in executing this agreement, they have relied solely upon their own judgment, belief and knowledge and the advice and recommendations of their own independently selected and retained counsel, if any, concerning the nature, extent and duration of their rights and claims hereunder, and that they have not been influenced to any extent whatsoever in executing this agreement by any representations or statements with respect to any matters made, if any, by any party or representative of any party hereto.

12.   Key Man:

During the Term, Mr. Biggie shall be actively involved in, and primarily responsible for, the activities and services to be provided by Manager hereunder. In the event that Biggie is not actively involved in, or primarily responsible for, the activities and services to be provided by Manager, your sole remedy shall be to terminate the Term, upon written notice to Manager, effective upon the date on which Lory is no longer actively involved in, or primarily responsible for, the activities and services to be furnished by Manager hereunder, and you shall be relieved of any obligation to pay Manager's Commission with regard to Gross Income received after the effective date of such termination, specifically including any income payable pursuant to paragraph 4.(e).

13.   Notices:

All notices pursuant to this agreement shall be in writing and shall be given by registered or certified mail, return receipt requested or telegraph (prepaid) at the respective addresses hereinabove set forth or such other address or addresses as may designated by either party. Such notices shall be deemed given when mailed or delivered to a telegraph office, except that a notice of change of address shall be effective only from the date of its receipt.

14.   Additional Provisions:

(a)   This agreement contains the entire understanding of the parties hereto relating to the subject matter hereof and cannot be changed or terminated, except by an instrument signed by the parties hereto. A waiver by either party of any term or condition of this agreement in any instance shall not be deemed or construed as a waiver of such term or condition for the future, or of any subsequent breach thereof. All remedies, rights, undertakings, obligations, and agreements contained in this agreement shall be cumulative and none of them shall be in limitation of any other remedy, right, undertaking, obligation or agreement of either party.

(b)   This agreement has been entered into in the State of New York, and the validity, interpretation and legal affect of this agreement shall be governed by the laws of the State of New York applicable to contracts entered into and performed entirely within the State of New York.

Very truly yours,
ABC ENTERTAINMENT, INC.

By: _____

CONSENTED AND AGREED TO:

_____

Future Superstar

SUMMARY

1. A written agreement between an artist and personal manager is employed in the industry for protection. Both parties sign it so that each is protected from the other.

2. In order to attain success, a trusting relationship is needed between an artist and the personal manager. However, the artist is always the boss.

3. The manager acts in a fiduciary capacity for the artist. This means that the relationship is one involving a confidence or a trust. The manager should never act in his or her self-interest.

4. Contracts need not be in writing to be valid. However, a dispute involving a verbal contract must rely on testimony by a witness in order to be resolved.

5. The four parts to a legal contract of this type are: mutual consent, consideration, capacity, and legality.

6. Neither the artist nor the manager should sign a binding contract between one another without counsel.

7. The American Federation of Musicians lists guidelines as to what areas advice and counsel should be offered.

8. The contents of an artist/personal manager agreement should be fully understood by both parties, and all clauses should be clearly defined.

PROJECTS

1. Role-play a negotiating session between an artist and a personal manager.

2. Compose a fair agreement for both parties.

3. Locate (from local bands or attorneys) several artist/personal manager agreements and discuss their contents.

4. Survey local bands that claim to have managers and see if they have a written agreement.

5. Research *Billboard Magazine* for articles concerning artist/personal manager lawsuits and discuss the reported reasons for the suits (more in Chapter Twelve).

CHAPTER THREE
LEGAL ASPECTS

"How to you know when an attorney is lying?"
"His/Her lips are moving! (Popular joke)

BY THE END OF THIS CHAPTER YOU SHOULD BE ABLE TO:

1. Explain the legal basis by which you can claim rights to a name.
2. Complete a name search.
3. Define trademark and servicemark.
4. Explain how to register a trademark, servicemark and domain name.
5. Discuss the rights that you are granted when you file for federal registration.
6. Explain what determines secondary meaning.
7. Define and discuss how to set up the various forms of business entities.
8. Discuss the basic tools used in bookkeeping.
9. Discuss the issues that should be negotiated in case of a performing group's breakup.

SELECTING A NAME

Naming a group or choosing a stage name is one of the most important decisions an artist will make. The name should be memorable, and should not allow your artist to be confused with any other artist. It would not be a good idea to call the group the Beetles, even though the famous group spells the name differently. This would obviously confuse the public, the Beatles would probably sue you, and besides, it is not a very original idea.

Since the 1950's, the names of rock groups have gone through many changes. There were the so called "bird" groups of the early 1950's —the "Cardinals," "Orioles," and "Ravens"— that evolved from the rhythm and blues style of the 1930's and 40's. Then, in the mid-50's there were thousands of "doo-wop" groups. Their names were associated with things that were hip and topical at the time. Some examples are: "Cadillacs," "Teen Queens," "El Dorados," "Safaris," and "Shep and the Limelites." Some argue that there was a relationship between the name of the group and the style of music performed; however, with over 15,000 groups that cut at least one single at that time, there were many exceptions {{2 Hansen, Barry 1992/f, p. 84;}}.

During the San Francisco era of the 1960's, group names took on a surrealistic tone. Names such as: "Ball Point Banana," "Blue Light District," "Dancing Food and Entertainment" and "Freudian Slips," were performing along side the more famous San Francisco bands {{1 Gleason,Ralph J. 1969/f, p. 331-333;}}. The "Disco" and the "Punk" styles of music in the 1970's spawned names that were easily associated with the sound of the styles (from "The Stylistics" to "The Clash").

Today, in this celebrity saturated business, names are used by aspiring bands to get some attention. *The New York Times* (29 September, 2005) published a list of bands as advertised in *The Village Voice*. Some of the unusual names were: "Bling Kong," "Checkbook Biography," "Deerhoof," Evil Doers," "Gonna Get Got," "The Hard Tomorrows," "No Redeeming Social Value," and "Wide Right." Whatever your reason for choosing a certain name, remember . . . originality is most important.

In terms of the legal aspects, using someone else's name without permission is an infringement. The basis of the law is what is termed **"priority of use"** {{55 Bigger, Stephen 1996/f, p. 12;}}. **It doesn't matter who owns the name or who has registered the name, but who has established first use of the name or has used the name continuously.**

TRADEMARK AND SERVICEMARK

A trademark is a brand name of a product. It can be used as the logo for a product or independently (ie: Coca-Cola). When it is used for a service, such as performing music, it is called a servicemark. In some instances, a servicemark acts like a trademark (ie: on an artist's t-shirt), and there are some legal differences between the two {{55 Bigger, Stephen 1996/f, p. 13;}}. However, for the purpose of this discussion, it is only necessary to understand that rights to either are based on **use**.

The law also permits you to use a brand name on a completely different product, such as using Remington® on something different than a shaver. However, if the use causes a high degree of confusion to the public, the courts may not permit you to continue its use.

If you are a singer and your real name is Frank Sinatra, would you be able to use it as your stage name? Unfortunately, the answer is no. The (late) Frank Sinatra has "priority of use," and the using your own name would cause confusion.

There are two classes of federal trademark and servicemark registration. They are "Principal Registration" and "Supplemental Registration." A mark must be "distinctive" (as opposed to descriptive) to qualify for the Principal Register {{4 Shemel,Sidney 1985/f, p. 337}}. For example, the group Chicago's logo is very unique and distinctive and therefore qualifies. Registration on this register gives constructive notice to the public, which means that it satisfies the legal requirements as to notification, and gives the holder exclusive rights to the name {{4 Shemel,Sidney 1985/f p. 337}}.

Registration on the Supplemental Register does not give the user exclusive rights to the name nor does it give constructive notice to the public. An example of a common name that would be included on the Supplemental Register is "The Blues Band." The name is not distinctive and does not clearly describe any uniqueness in the product.

COMPLETING A SEARCH

After a name is selected and before it is used, a search must be conducted to insure that no one is currently using it. The procedure for conducting a search is as follows:

1. Check with the local newspapers, "underground" papers, rock and music magazines, the local musicians' union, and local talent agencies for use of the name.

2. Check all of the national music and entertainment trade publications and organizations for use of the name.

3. Investigate record company and talent agency rosters for its use.

4. Check with international music and entertainment directories for its use, such as www.bandreg.com" www.bandreg.com or www.artistdirect.com" www.artistdirect.com or search myspace.com.

5. Search the web, specifically the U.S. Government agency site: www.uspto.gov" www.uspto.gov

6. Check all databases and search engines. Go to online record store sites and enter the name. Check the domain name directories, such as, www.internic.net" www.internic.net.

7. If needed, employ a professional searching bureau to ascertain if the name has been registered with the U.S. Patent and Trademark office of any state bureau.

8. Many private law firms complete trademark registration for a fee and can be reached through a google or similar searches.

Even if a thorough search has been conducted, you can never be 100% sure that the name isn't being used somewhere by someone {{55 Bigger, Stephen 1996/f p. 3}}.

If the name does appear in the course of your search, you should return to square one and come up with another name. There is an illustrious history of small-unknown acts that have successfully sued larger acts based on priority of use in a certain territory. If you believe that you'll only be successful if you use a particular name, you might try to buy the rights to that name from the current user, before you buy be certain that they do, indeed, own the rights.

REGISTERING FOR A FEDERAL TRADEMARK
OR SERVICEMARK

If you are interested in filing for a federal trademark or servicemark, and you have completed your search, you should begin by using the name across state lines. You will have to be able to prove that you've done this. Proving it may be as simple as saving newspaper advertisements announcing the appearance in another state, or keeping actual contracts. You will also have to produce a drawing of the mark and some specimens. Then you must file for federal registration with the Patent and Trademark Office in Washington D.C. (If you don't live in a particularly large state and do expect to travel over the state line, then federal registration is best.) According to Stan Soocher, in a *Musician Magazine* article, the procedure for filing is expensive for the following reasons:

1. A considerable fee is required for each class in which a name is registered (ie. a recording use fee, another for use on t-shirts, etc.).

2. Attorneys charge up to $600+ to complete the complicated federal filing procedure.

3. Companies that conduct searches for purposes of federal trademark registration charge about $300+ per search {{56 Soocher, Stan/f, p. 45.}}.

The procedure for filing a federal registration is as follows:

1. File an application with the U.S. Patent and Trademark office www.uspto.gov" www.uspto.gov). In order to file, you must be able to prove that you used the name across state lines. Keep copies of advertisements or contracts to use as proof (the process takes about a year).

2. In order to have the rights to the name, you must continue to use the name. Two years of nonuse constitutes abandonment.

3. After the fifth anniversary of the registration you must file an affidavit stating that the name has been used continuously.

4. Renewal must be completed every twenty years {{55 Bigger, Stephen 1996/f, p. 7}}.

Even though it is expensive, there are many benefits to obtaining a federal registration. Federal registration gives you the following rights:

1. You can sue someone for infringement in federal court.

2. It provides "constructive notice" so that any subsequent user cannot claim "no knowledge of your right {{55 Bigger, Stephen 1996/f, p. 6}}."

3. After the registration has been approved, you may use the symbol ® to protect your name.

Remember to check the USPTO for the latest policies and procedures.

WHO OWNS THE RIGHTS TO THE NAME

The basis of the law is **"priority of use."** If the name is registered on the Supplemental Register (as opposed to the Principal Register), the first person or group to use the name may not have the right to use it anywhere at anytime. They may need to establish **"secondary meaning."** Secondary meaning is determined by four factors:

The geographic region in which the user works.

The duration of the use of the name.

The drawing power of the user (or how big a star).

The extent of its use in advertising

Two artists may establish secondary meaning in two different geographic regions. If neither has the name federally registered then both artists may use the name in their respective geographic regions.

Continued use is the key to obtaining legal rights to a name. However, there is such a thing as **residual use** of a name. Residual use usually means that the name is still associated an artist after they have stopped performing, but their products continue to sell. Acts, such as the "Beatles," have a residual use right to the name, and it has been continuously used by EMI-Capitol Records. For further information concerning trademarks and servicemarks, contact the U.S. Office of Patents and Trademarks or consult an attorney. Worldwide use of a name is a far more complicated issue, and an attorney should again be consulted.

Domain Names

A domain name is an online address. There is a registration process, however, the process does not give you trademark rights. There are domain name registries and they are listed at www.icann.org. The fee to register is very reasonable. If the name you have chosen has already in use, and you are interested in knowing who owns the name (as you may be interested in buying the name from them), owners are listed at www.whois.net. Also, you maybe able you use the name, by changing the suffix from .com to another (.biz). You must renew your domain name (pay a fee) periodically {{93 Stim,Richard 2004;}}.

Most artists make available samples of their music on their websites. If the artist owns the music and has yet to record it for a commercial label, everything is legal as is. However, the digital world is different in that, along with the owners of the song (usually the songwriter and publisher) and the owners of the sound recording (usually the record company), the performer also receives a royalty for every download. Consequently, if you do permit downloads on your website and are not the owners of the material, you are allowing this without permission and subject to a lawsuit. If you are the owner, you should investigate www.creativecommons.org.

STARTING YOUR OWN BUSINESS

Bands usually begin performing and making money before they become an actual business. They play the gig and split up the money. Expenses are covered before anyone is paid. If each member owns his or her own equipment and there is no overhead, this method of conducting business may continue indefinitely. However, when a band decides to purchase something as a band (usually a sound reinforcement system), and wishes to pay it off in credit installations, it is forced to make some decisions about becoming a legitimate business. Either one member (or a member's parent) becomes responsible for paying off the loan, or the band becomes a legitimate business entity.

The forms of business entities practiced in the most industries are: **proprietorship, partnership,** (some form of a) **corporation,** and a **limited liability company**.

PROPRIETORSHIP

A proprietorship is the simplest and the easiest form of business to start because, by definition, it is a business conducted by one self-employed person who is the owner. The procedure for setting up a proprietorship is as follows:

1. File a "DBA" (Doing Business As) form (purchased at any stationery store) with the county clerk in the county you'll be conducting business. If you intend to use your own name (John Smith as opposed to John Smith Productions) completing a DBA form is not necessary.

2. You may have to publish a legal notice in the local newspaper stating that you're doing business under the name. Check with you local county clerk's office.

3. You should file Form SS-4 with the Internal Revenue Service to obtain an employer's tax I.D. number (even if you haven't any employees).

4. If you intend to sell (retail) goods, you must obtain a resale tax permit from the state tax authority.

5. Open a checking account in the company's name.

6. Contact your local county clerk for a free brochure explaining the specifics.

The advantage of a proprietorship is that you have complete control of any and all decisions made and make all the profit. However, you are personally libel for any accidents or suits that might occur and you also must absorb any losses. You are not protected from any creditor who may want to place a lien on you personal property.

There are many tax issues involved and an accountant should be consulted.

PARTNERSHIP

There are several types of partnerships, ie: general partnerships, joint ventures, and limited partnerships (there is also a Limited Liability Partnership which is essentially is a LLC).

1. General Partnership

    A general partnership is an "association of two or more persons conducting business on a continuing basis as co-owners for profit {{57 Hearn, Edward R. 1996/f, p. 11}}" Each partner contributes property, service, and/or money to the business. Partners may also loan property to the business.

    Each partner owns a part or interest in the whole partnership ("assets in common") and acts on behalf of the partnership. The entire general partnership (not an individual partner) is responsible for any lawsuit except where bodily harm or injury has occurred by an individual partner.

    Many bands form partnerships when they begin to purchase equipment that is used by the entire group or is too expensive for an individual to buy. It's actually a good idea for a partnership to acquire some assets because all of the partnership's assets must be liquidated before creditors have access to any individual partner's personal property. The procedure for setting up a general partnership is similar to setting up a proprietorship. However, an attorney should compose the actual terms of the agreement.

2. Joint Venture

    On many occasions a group and an entrepreneur join together to complete a project (such as writing a song, or producing a master recording, etc.). When the project is completed, there is no reason for the relationship to continue. In these situations, the two or more people are conducting business for one purpose, and are actually partners for the business transaction. This is a joint venture. One party is contributing service and one party is contributing service or money.

3. Limited Partnership

    A limited partnership is a vehicle for funding a business project. A general partner takes on the normal business responsibilities, and the limited partner contributes capital but takes no part in the management of the business and has no liability beyond his or her capital contribution {{57 Hearn, Edward R. 1996/f, p. 13}}. The limited partner acts as a backer to finance a project (usually for a limited time period). State and Federal security laws govern limited partnerships, and an attorney should be consulted before agreements are made.

CORPORATION

Most successful recording artists form one or more corporations (some literally have hundreds) to handle their business affairs. All contractual obligations are made through the corporation, who in turn, make the artist available for fulfilling the responsibilities of the specific deals.

A corporation is a separate business entity from the persons who manage it. Ownership is obtained by buying shares of stock in the corporation. Personal assets of individuals are thereby protected from business creditors. There are several types of corporations depending on the number of stockholders.

A board of directors who is elected by the shareholders governs corporations. The business affairs are managed by a group of officers, who are employees of the corporation hired by the board of directors. Or in other words:

> Shareholders
>
> **ELECT**
>
> Board of Directors
>
> **WHO APPOINT**
>
> Officers
>
> **TO MANAGE**
>
> employees

There are two types of corporations: **private and public**. The stock of public corporations is traded publicly on one of the stock exchanges and anyone can buy shares in (and own a part of) the business.

Private corporations do not trade their stock on the open market. Shareholders who have some relationship to the business hold all the stock. The procedure for forming either type of a corporation is as follows:

1. A corporation charter, or a document that describes the business and the structure of the corporation must be filed in the state in which you plan to be incorporated.

2. By-laws for the corporation must be formed.

3. Several sets of taxes and fees must be paid.

SUBCHAPTER S CORPORATION:

Many business managers are suggesting this because taxes are not levied at the normal corporation rate. This structure is somewhere between a corporation and a sole proprietorship. You receive all the benefits of a corporation's liability protection, but taxes are assessed to you at a personal level.

When forming any corporation, an attorney should be retained. Usually a corporation immediately becomes an employer because it begins paying someone a salary, even if the only employee is the artist. Therefore, there are many legal obligations, such as tax laws and labor laws, which must be followed. An accountant should also be retained.

THE LIMITED LIABILITY COMPANY (LLC)

The LLC has become very popular because it allows members to enjoy the tax benefits of a partnership and the limited personal liability of a corporation. However, it does not exempt the members of the company from being sued for negligence. States vary as to the criteria for forming an LLC. You and/or an attorney should be able to set one up for well under $1000. Each member, who will then be issued shares in the company, must sign an operating agreement.

GROUP AGREEMENTS

All the band members should sign a written agreement. Before deciding which is best for your situation, check out some excellent sources to review several models (see Stim, Rich. Music Law latest edition). Topics such as meetings, voting rights, services, ownership, revenue sharing, adding band members, etc. are all standard (boilerplate) clauses. However, the most important clauses pertain to **group breakups.**

There are several ways groups breakup. If the group totally disbands, things are not quite as messy as when one of two members want to continue with new personnel, or when the remaining group members, and the group members who are leaving both want to use the group's name. If the group is under contract with a major label, things will become more complicated, as all the major labels contractually protect themselves against not recouping any owed advance money (money they have advanced the artist for recording expenses). Sometimes they do this by requiring the continuing group (provided the record company accepts the new members) to recoup any remaining advances before they may collect any royalties. This is an important point and must be negotiated carefully (see Chapter Six). In any case, the best time to plan for a breakup is at the formation of the group. The following areas should be covered in the group's partnership agreement before anyone says "I DO!"

1. A clear procedure for changing, adding, or subtracting group members. This should include any "buy outs" or the division of any of the group's assets.

2. Who owns the rights to the group's name, domain, and/or logo. Rights to the name are usually handled in one of three ways

    a. they are the exclusive property of the group and not owned by any individual member

    b. they are the exclusive property of the group and not owned by anyone individual except that if the key "man" leaves the group, than the group will cease to use any of the group's names or

    c. they are not assets of the group but rather the property of one or more named members of the group {{93 Stim,Richard 2004;}}

3. What rights does a leaving member have to income generated after s/he leaves.

4. How to deal with the record company should any changes in the group's personnel occur. This should include the right of approval of new members, recouping advances, key man clauses (the most important group member), and any other matters

5. A procedure for the complete disbanding of the group and the dissolution of the partnership, its assets and liabilities.

BLONDIE MEMBERS SUING EACH OTHER OVER NAME USE

Now that the band is back together and recording, two former members filed a complaint against the four current members in New York Supreme Court on July 23, 1998. The two allege that the defendants have entered into "unlawful appropriation and breach of fiduciary duty" in using the Blondie name and in making business decisions for the corporation without a vote. The defendants claim that the plaintiffs "...are seeking to win a free ride on the backs of defendants' current hard work and musical enterprise."

Currently, informative text on band member agreements can be found at: www.artistshousemusic.org www.artistshousemusic.org

Additional materials concerning actual group breakups can be found at: www.spinner.com/2007/08/10/20-bitter-band-breakups-smashing-pumpkins

Band member agreements can be found at: www.musiccontracts.com www.musiccontracts.com and other sites.

BOOKKEEPING

Today, computer programs are extremely helpful in maintaining accurate financial records of all business transactions. Many programs complete several accounting procedures automatically. The basic tools used in bookkeeping are as follows:

1. **Checkbook** - It is essential to open a separate checking account under the company's name. All of the business accounts and cash disbursements should be accounted for by a check.

2. **Ledger** (monthly) - The ledger is a book containing all accounts and transactions are posted monthly.

3. **Cash disbursement record** - This is usually designed in the form of a monthly chart that shows how any cash is spent. Items usually include parking, tolls, taxi, etc..

4. **Accounts receivable** - This is a listing of all accounts from which the company receives money. It is usually posted monthly.

5. **Accounts payable** - This is a listing of all accounts the company owes money to on account, and makes payments to. It is usually posted monthly.

6. **Receipt file** - A place where receipts are kept.

7. **Balance sheet** - The balance sheet is a monthly account of the financial condition of the company. The debits and credits for the month must balance (be equal).

8. **Calculator** - "Don't leave home without it!"

9. If you cannot keep accurate records or hate to, hire someone who will!

SUMMARY

1. Choosing a group's name is one of the most important decisions a group makes.

2. Using someone else's name without permission may be an infringement. The basis of the law is "priority of use," or continued use, not who has registered the name.

3. A trademark is a brand name of a product. When it's used for a service it's a servicemark.

4. After a name is selected and before is used, a search must be conducted. If the name appears in the search, do NOT use it.

5. In order to file for a federal trademark or servicemark, you must first use the name in commerce across state lines.

6. A domain name is an online address. It does not give you trademark rights.

7. Filing is expensive.

8. There are two classes of federal registration. Principal registration automatically gives constructive notice to the public, permits you to sue someone for infringement in federal court, and gives you the right to use the symbol R. Supplemental registration does not, and "secondary meaning" must be established.

9. When two or more people on the registered on the Supplemental Register are using the name, the person who establishes "secondary meaning" has the greatest rights to a name. Secondary meaning is determined by four factors: the geographic region in which the user works, the duration of the use of the name, the drawing power of the user, and the extent of the user's advertising.

10. The forms of businesses practiced in the music industry are: proprietorship, partnership, corporation, and limited liability company.

11. A proprietorship is a business conducted by one self-employed person who is the owner. A general partnership is an association of two or more persons conducting business on a continuing basis as co-owners for profit. A corporation is a separate business entity from the persons managing it. An attorney should compose any partnership or corporation agreements.

12. The basic tools used in bookkeeping are: checkbook, ledger, cash disbursement record, accounts receivable, accounts payable, receipt file, balance sheet, and a calculator.

13. Groups' breakups can be complicated issues. The best time to plan for a breakup is at the formation of the group.

PROJECTS

1. Choose an original name and conduct a mini-search.

2. Contact an established performing group in your area, and find out if they legally have a right to their name. What evidence do they have that assures them of the right? Did they establish secondary meaning?

3. Contact an established performing group in your area and find out what business entity they are conducting business. Do they have any employees and are they receiving legal treatment under the labor laws?

4. Contact an established performing group in your area and find out if they have made any provisions for changing members or totally disbanding.

5. Read a recording contract and discuss the parts dealing with breakups and disbandment.

CHAPTER FOUR

MARKETING THE ARTIST

"Don't embarrass your fans, They've given you a good life."
Bono. *New York Times* November 28, 2005

BY THE END OF THIS CHAPTER YOU SHOULD BE ABLE TO:

1. Discuss the role of popular music in the popular culture marketplace.
2. Discuss the scope of today's market, including the prerecorded, live and digital music domestic and international scene.
3. Describe the role of the artist in the marketplace.
4. Discuss how stardom is achieved.
5. Define positive deviance.
6. Discuss the process of de-labeling a star.
7. Describe the process of creating and managing an image.
8. List the contents of a press kit and describe their roles.
9. Define media mix.
10. Write a news alert and a news release.
11. Discuss several digital music initiatives.
12. Discuss Branding and its impact on the industry.

THE MARKETPLACE

Since the 1960s, rock music has become a major player in the popular culture marketing mix. As the war babies became of age and began representing the largest segment of the population, their consumer behavior became of interest to every leisure time activity marketer in business. It was actually the first Woodstock Music and Art Festival in August 1969, that convinced retailers to take serious notice of the buying habits of these young adults. By merging the behavior of flower children with mainstream marketing techniques, the potential for making money became a reality.

The record industry saw this potential as well. In fact, the potential was so great, that until around 1980, the record industry was considered inflation proof! According to R.I.A.A statistics, in every year until 1979, sales as well as software unit shipments increased. Up until very recently, thanks to the soundtrack recordings of *Saturday Night Fever* and *Grease*, sales and units shipped figures of 1978 were considered one of the industry's crowning achievements.

As these war babies reached middle age in the early 1980s, it was originally thought that they would "grow up," leave rock 'n' roll behind, and turn to recordings by Sinatra, Steve and Edie, and various cover artists. Surprise! A new generation gap never really evolved. Their listening habits did not change. As it became hip to be square, Mick and Keith, Steven Tyler, Roger Waters, and Bruce continued to rock. Metallica's following increased (in number as well as average age of their listeners), and in her 50s, Tina Turner recorded a very sexy mainstream AC album. As the alternative scene developed, white kids had a increasingly difficult time using music as a tool for rebelling (and also discovering a music that their parents did not enjoy). This dilemma did not hurt the industry. By the mid-1980s, sales of recorded music software in the U.S. began to rise again. Helped by the new software configuration (always a sure booster of catalog sales), the CD, the industry increased sales each year (more or less) to the year 2000. For an industry that measures its achievements quantitatively, this added up to success.

What does all this mean to the artist? As a product, the artist retails his/herself through basic formats: the recorded product and the performance ticket (including the sale of merchandise). Just as the retail store sells recordings, downloads are sold online, and ringtones are made available to the consumer, the concert promoter sells tickets to the fan. All markets play significant roles in the success of the artist.

THE SCOPE OF TODAY'S MARKET

According to Nielsen Soundscan (a very difficult organization for revealing statistics), 671,000 titles sold at least one copy in 2008. Table 4.1 shows that 28% more titles were released in 2008 than in 2006, and 2006 was up almost 37% from '05 releases. Six thousand new titles sold at least 1000 copies in 2008, representing only 6% of new title releases, and 82% of new album sales came from 950 titles. The majors released 15% more titles in 2005 than the previous year, and accounted for 1/3 of the 618 million albums sold (204 million). The indies released 19% more titles (75% of the new releases) but only sold 38.8 million units. The majors sold an average of 18,454 units per title, compared to the indies 787 units per title. (Exclude indie albums selling less than 100 copies and indies sold 2880 per title.) Statistically stated: .7% of new releases in 2005 (410 titles) generated 70% of all new release sales.

2008 NEW ALBUM TITLE RELEASES

New Title Total Sales = 150,000,000

New Title Releases:

	2008 (+28%)	2006 (+25%)	2005 (+35.6%)	2004 (+16.2%)	2003
	105,575	75774	60331	44476	38269
Major Releases	?	11230	11070		9404
*Indie Releases	?	64544 (85% of new rel.)	49261 (81.6% of new rel.)		35072

2008

**Plat. titles.	16	(.015% or new releases)
**Gold	22	(.02% of new releases)
250K	110	(.10% of new releases)
100K	1515	(1.4% of new releases)

2006

33	(.04% of new releases)
54	(.07% of new releases)
93	(.12% of new releases)
184	(.24% of new releases)

Major Releases (2006):
1. 84% of NT Sales
2. Average of 16,453 units sold per title

Indie Releases (2006):
1. 16% of NT Sales
2. Average of 551 units sold per title

Other Facts:
1. 671,000 titles, including catalogue sold at least one copy in 2008
2. 6000 titles sold at least 1000 copies in 2008 (6%)
3. 82% of all new album sales came from 950 titles in 2008 (.8%)
2. 58% of all new titles sold less than 100 copies in 2004; 67% in 2005; and 73% in 2006
3. 81% of all new titles sold less than 1000 copies in 2004; 86% in 2005; and 89% in 2006

* Indie defined as all releases with indie distribution
** Approximations

Table 4.1

THE DOMESTIC SCENE
Prerecorded Music Product

According to R.I.A.A. statistics (riaa.com), in 2008, overall music sales, in terms of units, was up 4.4% from 2007, and the total dollar value slipped 18% to $8.5 billion. Physical product sales continued to fall, representing 68% of "shipments" and digital rose to 32%. Both the download of singles and albums increased 28 and 33% respectfully. Digital performance royalties (the estimated payments in dollars to artists and record companies distributed by SoundExchange) rose 74%. According to Nielsen Soundscan in 2009, total unit sales (albums, digital tracks, store singles) are up 3.5%, however, the rate of increase in digital downloads is slowing.

Based on the number of units sold, consumers aged fifteen to thirty-year olds purchased less music than in 2007, however consumers aged forty to forty–four years old purchased approximately 3% more. Thirty cents of every purchasing dollar was spent in the record store. Internet sales rose almost 3% and download sales increased 1.5%. Females bought a shade more than males, representing approximately 51.5 cents of every dollar spent on music product {{29 Recording Industry Association of America 1900s;}}.

THE INTERNATIONAL SCENE
Prerecorded Music Product

According to the International Federation of the Phonographic Industry (IFPI at ifpi.org) overall recorded music sales (including total physical and digital performance rights) fell by 8.3% in 2008. The global recorded music market is estimated to be worth $18.4 billion in U.S. currency. Although the US represents approximately 27% of world sales it is down considerably from the 1970s, when the U. S. represented almost one-half. The second biggest world market was Japan. It is important to note that Japan and the U. S. total approximately one half of the world market. However, different countries have different methods of calculating sales and many countries do not include every type of retail outlet or distribution point in the statistics they submit. Consequently, "real" sales can and do vary greatly from what is reported. For the purposes of this book, it should be noted that with approximately 70% of the records being sold outside the U. S., it is very important for artists to become international stars. Although royalty rates are lower and currency exchange rates are very volatile, there is still a great deal of money to be made from international sales.

Live Performance

In 1992, The Rolling Stones performed nine dates in Japan and grossed over $30 million (in U.S. currency) {{35 Laing, Dave 1998;}}. In 2005, the Stones grossed $162 million, however, the top tour was U2 who grossed $260 million. Total attendance was down in 2005, at 45.6 million fans, versus 47.5 million in 2004 {{96 Waddell, Ray 2006;}}.

Fans were willing to shell out almost $4 billion worldwide in 2008, up 13 percent over 2007. In North America, the average per-show box office gross was up 18 percent, with average per-show attendance up 6.3 percent. Ticket prices continued to escalate which accounts for the rise in gross with the decrease in attendance. In fact, average attendance per show was down over 35% from ten years ago, with the number of shows doubling {{144 Waddell, Ray 2008;}}.

The highest grossing tour was Bon Jovi, performing ninety-nine sellout shows to 2,157,675 people and grossing $210,650,675, with an average ticket price (excluding fees) of $97.60. Not far behind was Bruce Springsteen performing eighty-two shows to 2,094,851 fans and grossing $204,513,630,with an average ticket price of $97.60. The highest average ticket price of the top fifteen tours in 2008 was, Madonna at $136.75.

THE ROLE OF THE ARTIST

The working hours of a successful rock musician is literally a 24/7. Fans expect their fantasy to be fulfilled whether they see their favorite hero on stage or off. Today's artist is expected to hold his/her image even during off hours. Consequently, the artist's image must fit the lifestyle s/he leads.

Even before the perks associated with success are delivered, being a rock musician is a challenge. Pop musicians have been considered social deviants for many years. Not necessarily negative deviants, but deviants nonetheless. In fact, sociologist George Lewis used the term positive deviant to describe the musician. He defined one as having "behavior that deviates from the expected, but is not negatively valued {{58 Lewis, George 1980/f, p.74}}." Another sociologist, Howard Becker, used the terms legitimate occupations versus illegitimate careers.

There are characteristics of the musician's behavior that make him/her perceived as being a deviant. Firstly, there are the work habits. A musician works when others (the fans) are off. A musician works at night, and sleeps during the day. A musician plays an instrument. Secondly, the social circle of a musician is very limited. Because s/he works nights, s/he is subjected to many occupational hazards. Most of his/her fans are either musicians or night people. Drugs and other abusively used substances seem to be more available after dark. Consequently, for some, the straight life is alien and unfriendly. Lastly, conforming to the routines of day people are often difficult. Because musicians need sleep as much as anyone else, shopping, and attending to medical needs are often hassles.

Stardom

What is a star and who determines who becomes labeled as one? Lewis defines a star as "a person whose productions are so much in demand that, to some extent at least, he is able to use distributors as his adjuncts" {{58 Lewis, George 1980;}}. However, in demand by whom, and how do these productions become in demand? Lewis continues, "his success as a star depends upon his 'playing with the market' {{6 Becker, Howard Saul 1963;}}. And the star label "is bestowed upon certain people by a specific audience which intentionally wishes to bestow such a quality" {{58 Lewis, George 1980;}}. Consequently, one becomes labeled as a star by a quantitative measure.

What happens when the star no longer lives up to the audience's expectations? Is there any procedure for de-labeling the musician as a star? Few artists are able to handle both their audience generated image and their personal identity with much success. Much of the problem is due to the amount of insulation from the real world that occurs. It compounds the situation. Not only can some not distinguish between on and off stage personas, but there is "no appropriate institution for "de-labeling" the star" {{58 Lewis, George 1980;}}. The premature deterioration of Elvis is a good example of the worst-case scenario. Unfortunately, Elvis did not surround himself with people who were sensitive to his needs as a star.

Creating the Image

What determines the image? It's obvious that the artist must feel comfortable with what is fabricated for him/her, but, isn't this determined by what the fans want or need? Shouldn't a good manager and PR team identify the market that is attracted to the music and develop the image accordingly? Capitalize on what the market needs to feel hip, and then exaggerate it and make it bigger than life.

For example, it isn't coincidental that almost every time Bruce Springsteen is photographed, he is wearing a faded pair of blue jeans? Or that Pearl Jam is in baggy shorts and flannel shirts. Or any number of rappers are in gold chains etc. It would be odd if it were any other way; as strange as if Keith Richards, while guest hosting The Tonight Show, came out in a three piece suit and sang *Spinning Wheel!*

What would be wrong with this picture? For one, the image would be totally inconsistent with Keith's image of the last forty years. His fans trust him, buy his records, go to his concerts, and follow his career because he has been consistent over time. He has never "sold out" by conforming to society's middle of the road safeness. As a spokesperson for rock 'n' roll, he has gained the respect and loyalty of millions of people because of the consistency of his rebellious image.

Managing The Image

As mentioned earlier, stars are so much in demand (by fans) that insulation from them becomes, to many, a means of survival. This becomes a problem because the onstage image gets confused with the reality of life and some artists are not mature enough to keep the two separate. Also, fans are so thirsty to see the artist as a larger than life fantasy, that they do not care to see the artist as a everyday human being. Therefore, by definition, it is impossible for the artist to live up to the expectation.

The artists that have control of the situation are the artists that do not allow themselves to be so insulated from the public that they lose sight of reality. They may be surrounded by bodyguards (i.e. Madonna, Mick, Cher), however, they go about their lives in the environment of reality, compared to one constructed to fit their on stage persona (i.e. Elvis).

The second problem is the difficult process of changing the image (if needed). Some artists, such as David Bowie, Madonna, and Miles Davis have done this fairly easily. For many, the consequence outweighs the risk. The artist's audience may feel alienated if the change is too great, however, the artist may feel trapped without the freedom of artistic experimentation. One may think that his/her fans are a great group of longhaired liberals, however, the need that a consistent image fills is actually very conservative {{6 Becker, Howard Saul 1963;}}.

De-labeling the Star

How can a manager and an artist create a positive image, manage the image through a prosperous career, and then successfully transform the artist back to a life of John Doe? There is no creative procedure. Getting in touch with his/her personal identity, not the fabricated identity is the key. Avoiding burnout rather than drinking oneself into oblivion is the mature process of transformation.

Unfortunately, the music industry has never taken this task seriously. It is only recently that some members of the industry (and NARAS) have taken action to develop better health plans, detoxification centers, and old age residences for artists that either blew their "fortunes" or never really made it. For the time being, it is the responsibility of the manager and the artist to see that this transition (if needed) is completed successfully.

THE MEDIA TOOLS

The Press Kit or Media Kit

If it's hip, the physical press kit can still be one of the artist's most useful marketing tools. It establishes credibility by presenting the artist's accomplishments in an organized professional presentation. The kit must reinforce the image that was created to fit the needs of the audience, and contain a publicity angle. The publicity angle is some uniqueness about the artist. It must be newsworthy, fresh, informative and believable. For example, maybe one of the band members has played with someone famous, or the band has been politically active in their hometown. The angle must grab the attention of the press and eventually the fan. It must be consistent with the image and complement the music. Trite sayings that describe characteristics of the band, which hype the same characteristics as every other band, should be avoided. However, today many artists use only electronic kits (e-kits)

Ingredients

Every press kit should contain a **biography** (bio) of the artist (or band). It must be exciting and capture the essence of the artist's musical style as well as the most interesting characteristic of the artist (or band members). In a few short typewritten pages, it should shape the image. Important quotes may be tailored to the image desired and incorporated into the story. The bio should have a beginning, middle and an end.

The **8 X 10 black and white glossy photo** is another basic part of the kit. It may be a headshot of the artist or a full body one. A good publicity photo is the most difficult piece of the kit to get right. Like the bio, it must represent the image of the artist, look natural, and make one want to hear the music. The photo should also reproduce well for printing in a newspaper, so a picture with small details should not be considered. Most likely the photo will be cropped to fit in the available space in the newspaper. Therefore, the focal point of the photo must be kept in the center of the photo.

Legitimate **media clippings** should also be part of the mix. They are important because the media generates them. They legitimize and support the artist's efforts. A good manager and PR person will concentrate on doing everything in his/her power to get the press interested in the artist and write or talk about the him/her and the music. Clippings are especially important for a new artist. If the artist has accumulated a number of good press clippings, the best ones should be pulled and included in an easy to read one page **quote sheet**.

Depending on the objective of the artist, other materials may be included. For example, a lyric sheet may be important. If the artist does not have a record contract, an audio recording of the artist's best material should be available. If the artist is particularly visual and his/her stage presence is a strong part of the act, a video may be important. A calendar showing how busy the artist is may be impressive to a prospective purchaser of talent. Flyers or postcards with space for the date, time and place of the engagement are also recommended. This is now incorporated into a well-designed webpage.

The Webpage

In addition to being featured on record company web pages; most artists have their own web page. The website is the first place fans look for information and a good spot for the virtual media kit. The obvious should be displayed on the page: calendar, tour itinerary, bio facts, fan club information, merchandise for sale; however, it will also be useful to link the page to other pages so that search engines can display the page when someone isn't necessarily looking for the artist by name. An example of this is the following: Suppose everyone in the band is a left-handed. Link the band's web page with a page on left-handed products (i.e. www.google.com/Top/Shopping/Niche/Left-Handed_Products/). This is a useful tool to introduce the artist to a new audience without any major expense.

Using the web to build a fan base is essential. The artist's webmaster and the manager must devise a plan with the objective to convert the casual/passive fan to the fanatic fan. Community sites, including Facebook and Twitter, that generate activity must be a part of the artist's arsenal. Artists should also blog about their life. Every form of communication with fans must be employed.

THE MEDIA MIX

Print, radio, television and the internet make up the media mix. Compiling a media list is the job of the PR person working for the artist. A new artist must do the legwork his/herself. Today, media lists may be bought (either in hardcopy or as a file), or are found in any number of industry sourcebooks and by surfing the net. However, names and addresses change often, and it is difficult to stay current. It's a jungle out there and compiling mailing labels and lists is very time consuming, so target the outlets carefully.

A great example of a comprehensive media blitz was executed for the CBS' "Elvis Week" which occurred during the second week of May in 2005. The campaign centered around two television shows, one fictional and the other factual. The miniseries, "Elvis" and the stand alone factual show, "Elvis by the Presleys" was partnered with Bertelsmann's (parent company to BMG and Elvis' label RCA Records) Random House division release of a book, "Elvis by the Presleys", and the quiz show, "Jeopardy" (owned by Sony, other half of SonyBMG at the time). Viacom billboards, radio stations, MTV and VH1 were all part of the mix (along with CBS, all part of the Viacom family at the time). A musical inspired by Presley opened on Broadway and the cast album was recorded by SonyBMG. Presley was a major part of the 100th anniversary celebration of Las Vegas, which included a new Presley album live from Las Vegas. The first commercials encouraging tourists to visit Graceland appeared on television in April. As was noted, "It's the re-emergence of Elvis Presley as a brand" {{98 Elliott, Stuart 2005;}}.

THE CAMPAIGN

Planning and managing a media campaign is a fulltime job. Staying focused on the objective of the campaign, and understanding what the media needs to do their job is essential. The key to getting any type of publicity is offering something unique and meeting deadlines…. real deadlines.

It is very important to create and follow a campaign **timetable**. Just as media centers adhere to deadlines, the campaign must follow a organized routine. If your campaign is concentrating on a performance, the work begins three to four weeks prior to the gig. Release a news alert so that it will have plenty of time to be published in a calendar listings. About two weeks before the performance send out a news release and have a street-team begin hanging flyers and cards where they will do the most good.

On the day of the show, make certain that those invited are on the guest list. Remember, one of the objectives is to generate press reviews, so reminder phone calls and emails to the local reviewers is recommended. Immediately after the performance check all the local rags and sites and save all the reviews, good or bad. And don't ignore e-mail or the web, a following can easily be developed by publishing a hip web page linked to e-mail address. This legwork is extremely tedious, but a required activity . . .persevere {{31 Rapaport, Diane Sward 2003;}}!

NEW MEDIA

Chapter Six contains parts of several marketing campaigns. Study them and use them as a guide for creating your own campaign. Presently, the web is the best tool. All of the community sites, listing sites, calendar sites, unsigned band sites, etc. are great opportunities. A *Google* search is a place to start.

Initiatives

In 2008, Billboard Magazine offered it's first "Maximum Exposure List" by consulting twenty of biggest media experts to create the ultimate media-matrix. Below are the first ten:

1. Synch-placement in a TV ad for Apple

2. Performance on the Oprah Winfrey Show

3. Song in a TV commercial that runs in a special event (Super Bowl, Olympics)

4. Song featured as itunes' free single of the week

5. Song covered on American Idol

6. Synch-placement in Activision's Guitar Hero video game

7. Song played during a hit movie's opening credits

8. Synch-placement in a highly rotated TV ad for Nike

9. Performance on Lollapalooza Mainstage

10. Synch-placement in MTV's Rock Band video game
     {{155 Harding, Courtney 2008;}}

DIGITAL

Several beverage giants began separate marketing campaigns that used digital music to connect with consumers. Coca-Cola created the entertainment Web site *Stageside.tv* (no longer in operation) from which fans downloaded exclusive videos from select acts using peer-to-peer file-sharing networks. Coke payed artist Ne-Yo and his label and publishers for the right to exclusively film a short "coke side of life" mini-documentary with two minutes of music.

Bacardi spent $40 million to start an online and mobile radio station. The station called, *Bacardi B Live Radio* streams dance music with exclusive mixes. Other beverage initiatives include *Pepsi Smash*, a live music feature of Yahoo Music Service; *The Scenario*, MSN and a Sprite-branded online music service; and in 2006, Pepsi/iTunes offered 100 million free iTunes music downloads through codes under bottle caps. However the campaign was plagued with cheaters tilting unopened bottles to see winners {{105 Bruno, Anthony 2006;}}.

Below is an example of the process of building a fanbase to create sales.

CHATTING' A SINGER UP THE POP CHARTS
SELLING CHRISTINA

STAGE ONE: LISTENING TO TEENS

To see what, if anything, kids were already saying about Ms. Aguilera, Marc Schiller and Electric Artists monitored popular teen sites like www.alloy.com, www.bolt.com and www.gurl.com, as well as fan sites for teen acts like Britney Spears and Backstreet Boys. They picked up some early talk on "Genie in a Bottle" as well as a budding rivalry between Ms. Aguilera's fans and Ms. Spears.

STAGE TWO: FUELING BUZZ ON "GENIE"

Electric's team started to email information to the sites, newsgroups and individual fans they found during Stage One: "Does anyone remember Christina Aguilera – she sang the song from "Mulan," "Reflection"? I heard she has a new song out called "Genie in a Bottle." The team also lobbied big web sites like America Online to run features on Ms. Aguilera.

STAGE THREE: GEAR UP FOR THE ALBUM

Electric's postings shifted emphasis to the album rather than the single "You've got to convince them to go from a $1.98 purchase to a $16 purchase." Also, key now was making sure the album cover was on the big retailers' web sites. That helps parents shopping for their kids remember the album's name.

STAGE FOUR: BROADEN THE FAN BASE

To promote her second single, Electric may target Mariah Carey and Whitney Houston fan sites. It's important to show that this was not Britney Spears, this was not a one shot thing {{5 White, Erin /f, p. B1}}.

BRANDING

A *branding iron* has been used for years to identify the ownership of livestock out on the range. Ranchers mark their cattle, etc. with a "logo" that secures their stake in the animal. The same mark appears on all the different animals owned by the rancher. The bigger the ranch the more important is the brand marking. In fact, if the ranch is very prosperous, the marking adds value to the animal.

The fifth definition of "brand" by *Webster's New World Dictionary* states: a. "an identifying mark or label on the products of a particular company" b. "the kind of make of a commodity." In concert with this definition, the entertainment business has embraced "branding" as both a way for the artist to reach a broader audience and add value to the artist as a product (not much different than the rancher). This is usually accomplished by an active association with a successful product line, however, artists can and do develop into a brand within themselves (think Beatles, or Beyonce). What was once considered taboo for many artists has become an integral part of many marketing plans.

A SURVEY

A partnership with national brands has become a significant means of generating buzz and sales. In a survey of 2500 music fans conducted by PromoSquard/Hit Predictor and completed in August, 2005, "63.5% of respondents said an artist's participation in a TV commercial for a product did not affect their attitude toward the artist." And, almost twice as many respondents said such TV spots actually built their interest in the artist, than those that were turned off. Throughout the survey, blacks were more receptive to product placement in songs. The goal of the survey was to "measure fans' attitudes toward artists who participate in ad campaigns and to gain insight into the effectiveness of those campaigns {{99 Paoletta, Michael 2005;}}. Other findings included: 39% said it was "OK" for an artist to take part in a campaign; however, another 32% said that it depended on the product. This reinforces the notion that bands and brands must be carefully matched.

One of the most important findings concerned the effectiveness of brand and band hookups. Almost 30% of respondents said it builds their interest in the product when they see an artist they know and like in a spot, and nearly 24% said the ads build their interest in the artist as well (the younger the respondent the more easily influenced). Lastly, 66.3% of respondents said acts should only do spots for "products they actually use and believe in"; however, somewhat contradictory, "only 21% said they assume an artist endorsing a product actually uses it" {{99 Paoletta, Michael 2005;}}.

SUCCESSFUL PARTNERSHIPS

Today, many vehicles are needed as part of the marketing mix. Product advertisement offers exposure that record labels can't supply. For example, Josh Stone's *Gap* ads feature her singing or talking about her favorite artist dressed in the retailer's threads. Her manager, Marty Maidenberg believes that the spot helped to sell jeans and Stone's CD. *Kings of Leon* and Volkswagen teamed up in the summer of 2005, featuring KOL's tune *Molly's Chambers*. During the campaign, the album sales increased and the iTunes store was selling 10-15K downloads of the song per week.

Sometimes deals that seem strange actually work well, as was the case with *50Cent* and *Glaceau Vitamin Water*. The artist wanted a healthy partnership to counteract his gangsta image {{99 Paoletta, Michael 2005;}}. No one can deny the benefits of connecting with a brand, but it must be one that makes smart business sense for the band and the brand.

CHANGING ATTITUDES

"We're living in an age where there is no such thing as over exposure...if an ad agency wants to use my song I'm fine with it as long as the brand makes sense. I love selling records [and] I'm proud of my music. But just making a good album and going on tour doesn't seem to be enough," says Goo Goo Dolls' John Rzeznik {{100 Paoletta, Michael 2006;}}. "We like having our songs in commercials. We never wanted to be underground. We want to reach as many people as possible," exclaimed Allison Robertson of the Donnas {{100 Paoletta, Michael 2006;}}.

BRAND-DROPPING ARTISTS

Many hip-hop artists are fond of the finer things in life and have no problem dropping well-know consumer brand names into their lyrics (remember My Adidas in 1986 by Run-D.M.C. or better yet, Janis Joplin's Mercedes Benz sung a capella). While most of these mentions appear to be unpaid, many companies actively pursue acts to name-check their products. Sometimes, formal brand-marketing partnerships can result from the initial name-dropping. The following is a list of the top brand mentions for 2005.

Brand	Number of Mentions
Mercedes-Benz	100
Nike	63
Cadillac	62
Bentley	51
Rolls Royce	46
Hennessy	44
Chevrolet	40
Louis Vuitton	35
Cristal	35

Both Cadillac and Mercedes experienced sales increases in 2005, as well as Nike and Hennessy.

Some top artists have their own brands and are not shy about mentioning them in their lyrics. For example:

Jay-Z	Rocawear and Armadale Vodka
Gwen Stefani	L.A.M.B.
Sean "Diddy" Combs	Sean Jean
Beyonce	House of Dereon

With the proliferation of brand mentions in lyrics, music publishers cannot help but guess what effect it will have on the song's future publishing potential {{104 Paoletta, Michael 2006;}}

THE IMAGE MAKERS

The publicist must create a trust between s/he and his/her client. The artist puts his/her pubic image in the hands of the publicist and relies on the credibility of the publicist to do his/her work justice. What follows are a series of quotes by industry image-makers. They were found in an out of print book, The Making of Superstars, by Robert Stephen Spitz.

Next to music, image is perhaps the most important aspect of recording artist's career. The way a particular artist looks and feels, thinks and reacts to situations plays heavily upon the way the public views that person and, many times, creates an appeal equally as important as the music. But unless the artist is so unique a talent or a personality before embarking on a recording career, it is up the publicist to create an image that will catch the public eye and lure them into giving this artist a chance to be heard.

Publicity is an art in itself, distinguished by those in the profession who have achieved credibility by creatively formulating an image within the bounds of reality from those who merely "hype" false praise.   Robert Stephen Spitz.

My responsibility to my clients is to represent them accurately and to better translate their interesting points to the public. An artist does not know what makes him interesting to a magazine or to the public and that's what I'm there to tell him.

I think even the big acts need press all the time. A career should build. It's very hard for an artist to get a record company behind them when their record in five months old and they won't have another one coming out for three or four months.

Credibility is perhaps the most useful quality which a publicist can develop. I maintain my credibility by trying never to lie about the proportions of the act I'm publicizing.   C. J. Strauss

Breaking a new artist by press is extraordinarily difficult. There is a certain amount of luck involved. First of all, the music has to be there. You cannot hype anything for very long that is either not musically valid or entertaining. But we'll try, though.

When conferring with a new artist, we spend a lot of time discussing the strong character points of an artist and how to bring them out.

I always strive to have our publicity department "bunch" things. We try to get as many things going on a particular artist in the hope that they will all break around the same time. Concentration of that nature, I always find, inundates the public's awareness. If it's spread out over a year, publicity loses its effectiveness.   Bob Regehr

Basically, my job is to get my clients the best possible space in the best possible public showcases. I try to take the real part of my clients and build those aspects into publicity so that when they are in the public eye they don't fall short of the press which they received. I am careful not to overbuild an artist- especially a new artist- because people will become disappointed and turn off to them.   Pat Costello

DIRECT TO CONSUMER MARKETING

One of the strongest attributes of the web is its employment of direct to consumer marketing. Most artists have well designed web pages that help to gather information about their fan base and buyers of their music and merchandise, and create databases to use in direct to consumer marketing. Independent music marketing firms create web campaigns (see above) and databases, and contact the buyers of products, making use of the demographic information to alert these buyers of other products s/he may be interested in, or to the artist activities.

Some record companies are completing this task in-house, because it is a very effective tool for artists that are not very "radio friendly" but have a loyal fan base. And besides, radio is becoming less and less important as an outlet for new music. As long as there is product in the marketplace, a marketing company can expand on the marketing tools.

SUMMARY

1. Since the 1960s, rock music has played a major role in the pop culture marketing mix.

2. Domestic shipments of physical prerecorded product decreased by 8% last year.

3. Last year, 6% of recorded music revenue was from digital sales.

4. In 2005, the U.S. continued to account for more than 1/3 of the world sales of prerecorded music.

5. The artist's image must fit the lifestyle s/he leads.

6. Being a rock musician is a risky existence.

7. Musicians can be considered positive deviants because they exhibit behavior that deviates for the expected, but not in a negative way.

8. A star is a person whose productions are so much in demand that s/he is able to use distributors as his/her adjuncts.

9. His/her audience bestows the star label upon an artist.

10. There is no appropriate institution for de-labeling a star.

11. The fans' wants and needs determine the image that is created.

12. Many artists insulate themselves so much from their audience that they have trouble separate their stage image from real life.

13. It is a difficult process to change an image.

14. A media kit should include a bio, glossy photo, newspaper clippings, and a quote sheet.

15. Two types of press releases are the news alert and the news release.

16. It is important to follow a media campaign a timetable to respect deadlines.

17. Branding is very lucrative for today's artist and fans support the efforts.

18. Direct to consumer marketing via the web is very useful to some artists.

PROJECTS

1. Compile a press kit.

2. Locate an artist that is performing live, and write a news alert and a news release announcing the event.

3. Choose an artist on tour and track the gross receipts for a leg of the tour.

4. Discuss the images of three current stars and determine if they are fabricated.

5. Formulate a marketing campaign for a local artist, including a timetable and the media mix.

6. Examine five different artist's web pages for ideas.

7. Set up a webpage (or a community spot on myspace.com).

CHAPTER FIVE
THE TRANSNATIONALS

"A Leader in Media & Telecommunications." Vivendi; "Music is Central to all Cultures and Communities." EMIGroup; "We enrich the lives of individuals across many cultures through our innovative technology and creative entertainment content." Howard Stringer, Sony. (from their respective webpages)

BY THE END OF THIS CHAPTER YOU SHOULD BE ABLE TO:

1. Describe a multi or transnational company.

2. Discuss, with examples, how they have become so powerful.

3. Discuss the "big four" transnationals that control the music industry and give examples of their music related and non-music related businesses.

The term multinational or transnational company is used to describe a company that conducts business on an international scale and who has a global presence. This mega-company may be headquartered on the other side of the globe, but is able to complete business transactions as if it lived right next store. It is truly international in its ability to look and behave as if its interest lies on the local level as well as all across the globe (think globally, act locally).

In fact, many transnational and international companies behave as if they were from only one country, but that perception is a product of their marketing and not necessarily their location. For example, Grey Poupon, Yoplait, and Vidal Sassoon seem French but are actually American companies. *Car & Driver* magazine, Donna Karan, and Wild Turkey seem American but are really French {{102 Freedman, Johnah 2003;}}.

Globalization is an important part of the mission statements as exemplified in the slogans of several transnationals (see italics below this chapter's title). Reading between the lines, the feeling that is generated is that the transnationals envision a world business community that is expanding, as it's becoming smaller. That is, more countries are participating in the trading of merchandise (enlarging the community), but new delivery systems and distributions channels are shortening the time it takes for products to arrive at their destinations.

The ownership of the transnationals that control the prerecorded music industry is also truly international. One is located in Japan (Sony), one is in England (EMI), one is in France (Vivendi), and ownership of one is still in the good old USA, with ties to Canada (Warner). This is a far cry from the pre-1980s, when Americans owned all but one.

INTEGRATION AND CONCENTRATION

The four transnationals account for almost 90% of the world's prerecorded music distribution and sales. They have become so powerful because they have created conglomerates that have expanded both horizontally and (or) vertically, and (or) because they have gained control of a specific segment of a business.

An example of **horizontal expansion** is when a record company buys another record company or merges with another company. Companies that once competed join forces to create an even larger company. An example of this is Universal Music Group's purchase of DreamWorks Records in 2003. Through The Seagram Company Ltd., UMG had already acquired PolyGram in 1998, after PolyGram went on a huge buying spree, acquiring Motown Records, A&M Records and Island Records (just to name a few). On the positive side, the acquisition allows the parent company to increase in size and revenue, but the company's affiliated labels continue to fight for home run hitting artists within the company.

An example of a **vertical merger** is when a record company buys a distribution or Retail Company. It increases in size and decreases its expenses by owning another piece of the product merchandising chain (ie; producing and manufacturing, or distributing and retailing). EMI owns Virgin Records, which brought with it the Virgin Megastores.

Concentrating on a specific segment of the entertainment industry and controlling every phase of that segment has also proven to be a profitable way of gaining market share. For example, if a company envisions itself as a media company, then its ownership will include: film, video, print, and record companies. It will share in all profits to the rights of the **artist** performing in the **video** of the **single** from the **soundtrack** album of the **movie (and DVD)** of the **book (print and audio version)**, as they are all part of its business. On its corporate webpage, Bertelsmann calls itself "the world's most international media company." Sony and Vivendi are also examples of this (also see Chapter Four, The Media Mix).

*THE BIG FOUR

* All the information concerning the corporations was found on the individual corporation web sites.

EMI GROUP

For over 100 years, EMI has been one of the world's leading music companies. Its record labels and music publishing businesses have worked with and represented some of the top recording artists and songwriters of all time. In 1992, EMI bought the Virgin Music Group, which at that time was the largest independent music company in the world. Today, the EMI Group operates directly in 50 countries, with licensees and distribution agreements in a further 26. In 2007 EMI was acquired by leading private equity partnership Terra Firma, making EMI the only privately owned major music company. The company comprises two divisions; EMI Music, and EMI Music Publishing, the world's largest and most successful publisher controlling over a million copyrights. EMI Music is divided into three business units: New Music, Catalogue and Music Services. Its record labels include Angel, Astralwerks, Blue Note, Capitol, Capitol Nashville, EMI Classics, EMI CMG, EMI Records, EMI Televisa Music, Manhattan, Mute, Parlophone and Virgin. (Japan). The company employs about 6000 employees worldwide. EMI global market share is approximately 13.5%.

SONY MUSIC

Sony Corporation is headquartered in Tokyo. Sony is one of the world's premier entertainment and electronics companies, providing top quality entertainment and electronic products and services to consumers around the world. Sony is poised to be the leading provider of digital content, service, and devises in the 21st century. Sony's principal U.S. businesses include Sony Electronics Inc., Sony Pictures Entertainment Inc., Sony Computer Entertainment America Inc., and Sony Music Entertainment. Its workforce numbers 171,300 employees worldwide.

In January 1988, Sony Corporation acquired CBS Records Group, known today as Sony Music Entertainment Inc. CBS/Sony is known as Sony Music Entertainment (Japan) Inc. Prior to October 1 2008, Sony's non-Japanese music entertainment business was conducted by Sony BMG Music Entertainment (SONY BMG), a 50% joint venture with Bertelsmann AG. On that date, Sony acquired Bertelsmann AG's 50% stake in the company, and SONY BMG became a wholly owned subsidiary. From January 1, 2009, the company changed its name to Sony Music Entertainment.Their labels include: American, Arista Nashville, Arista Records, Aware, Battery Records, Beach Street Records, BNA Records, Burgundy Records, Canvasback, Cinematic, Columbia Nashville, Columbia Records, Epic Records, Essential Records, Flicker Records, Fo Yo Soul, Gospocentric, J Records, Jive Records, LaFace Records, Legacy Recordings, Modern Art, Music With A Twist, Music World Music, RCA Records, RCA Nashville, RCA Victor, Reunion Records, RTEL, Slightly Dangerous, Sony Music Masterworks, Sony Music U.S. Latin, Star Time

International, Verity Records, Volcano Records. In the latest annual report, the music division of Sony is now listed under "other revenue" which represents 9.3% of total revenue.

VIVENDI (UNIVERSAL MUSIC GROUP)

Vivendi is the world leader in media and telecommunications. The company employs 39,900. Its divisions include; Universal Music Group; The Canal+ Group; Activision Blizzard; and SFR. UMG represents 18% of its operation revenue. In 1998 Universal Music Group acquired Polygram. Its labels include: Universal Music Group, Vivendi France, Interscope, Geffen, A&M, Island Def Jam MusicGroup, Universal Music Classics Group (Decca

Grammophon, Philips, ECM), Universal Records Group Nashville (MCA Nashville, Mercury Nashville), Verve Music Group

WARNER MUSIC GROUP

The Warner Music Group (WMG) is the only stand-alone music company to be publicly traded in the U.S. Once a division of Time and AOL, in 2004, Edgar Bronfman of the Seagram distilleries family and a group of investors acquired WMG from Time Warner for $2.6 billion {{103 Christman, Ed 2005;}}. In May 2005 they took the company public. Bronfman was originally associated with PolyGram.

The Warner Music Group's controls national and international repertoire through numerous international affiliates and licenses in more than 50 countries, and is home to over 1000 established stars and new artists worldwide. Its labels include: Asylum, Atlantic, Cordless, East West, Elektra, Nonesuch, Reprise, Rhino, Roadrunner, Rykodisc, Sire, Warner Bros. and Word. Warner/Chappell is one of the world's leading music publishers and controls over one million copyrights worldwide. WEA Inc. is one of the largest distributors of recorded music in the world. WMG represents approximately 12% of the world's prerecorded music sales and employs 3800 worldwide.

As of November 29, 2009 U.S. distribution Total Album market share (%) of each company (Nielsen Soundscan) was:

UMG	30.5
Sony Music	27.5
WMG	20.7
Indies	12.6
EMI	8.8

The entertainment business is clearly an internationally owned industry.

SUMMARY

1. The term transnational company is used to describe a company that conducts business on an international scale and who has global presence.

2. The ownership of the transnationals that control the recording industry are truly international.

3. The four multinationals account for almost 90% of the world's record sales.

4. They became so powerful because they expanded horizontally and vertically and also took control of a specific segment of the industry.

PROJECTS

1. Visit the web pages of the big four and see who are the leaders of each division.

2. Research the big four and find out what percentage of their sales, revenue, and expenses the music division is of each.

CHAPTER SIX

~~THE RECORD COMPANY~~ THE MUSIC ENTERTAINMENT COMPANY

THEN:

Vice President/NYC

Manage & direct heavy metal, country, alternative & dance music sectors of international music recording & distributing company. Exercise final approval discretion on selection of talent. Identify promising artistic talent. Negotiate contract terms w. agents of artists, exercising final approval agreements. Coordinate with Company attorneys in foregoing task. Create broad plans & policies for achieving corporate financial & development goals established by management, including budget & sales forecasting. Conceive, supervise, coordinate & implement activities that create public awareness & demand for corporate products & artist, by way of advertising, sales campaigns, market analysis, & media exposure. Develop image strategies for recording artist, including supervision of artwork, photography, image consultants posters & packaging, editorial & label copy. Develop & exercise final discretion on methods to enhance career growth of Company artist, including finding & selecting material to be recorded & recordings to be released. Spvse & direct artists tour support, incl. market & venue selection, budgetary control & timing. Use all available mkt info to guide decision making. Hire & fire staff. Direct Company's outside recording studio activities, incl. studio selection, product & staff quality evalu. & cost oversight. Associate's degree, or foreign equiv. in Business Administration; 5 yrs. exp. in job. Exp. Must be with internally distributed recorded media. At least 2 yrs. extensive exp. Providing interntl. & domestic tour booking & supervision to groups playing 200 seat club to 15,000+ seat arena venues. Reqs. at 2 yrs. recording exp. as producer or exec. producer. 2 yrs. exp. in music publishing (finding & selecting material to be recorded). $200,000/yr.; 40 hr./wk. Resume in dupl. To CJ-112, Rm 501, One Main St., Brooklyn, NY 11201."

Classified ad. Billboard Oct. 19, 1991

AND NOW:

"We decided that you wouldn't want to build a record label today…you would start from scratch and build an all-encompassing entertainment company."
Bob Chiappardi, president of Concrete Marketing, *Billboard*, March 12, 2005.

BY THE END OF THIS CHAPTER YOU SHOULD BE ABLE TO:

1. Discuss the role of the record company in the life of the artist.
2. Discuss the three types of financial advances offered to an artist.
3. Discuss, with examples, the three types of record companies in the industry, and the advantages and disadvantages of each.
4. Discuss several new models for generating revenue
5. Discuss the structure of a record company and the functions of the various departments.
6. Describe the internal path of a product thorough the various departments.
7. Discuss, in detail, the various ingredients in marketing campaign.
8. Describe, with examples, the costs of releasing a product and how to calculate royalties.
9. Calculate the artist's and the record company's share of royalty revenue.

This is it!

I've made it!

I'm one of the best!

These are the thoughts that run though the mind of an artist during his/her first visit to his/her record company as a royalty artist. After all, this is the stuff dreams are made of! It is truly one of the most exciting off stage appearances an artist makes. You feel like you're a part of one big happy family, and not only does everyone get along with each other, but everyone can't wait to help you deliver a hit. You envision a long association with the label as your career develops. Feeling a bit guilty, you repeat to yourself, "Boy, what did I do to deserve this life."

Record companies are tuned into this feeling and create slogans that help convince people that music and careers are as important as the bottom line of product sales. Arista Records has used the slogan "Where Careers are Launched." With this slogan, rather than just being interested in releasing a bunch of records with the hopes that a few will make money and pay the bills, Arista announces that their interest and intention is in discovering new talent and developing solid foundations for long and prosperous careers. Another example is CBS Records, now Sony. For years, CBS had the indignation to call itself "**THE** Music Company". The slogan positioned CBS as the knowledgeable company that recorded material that deserved to be recorded and classified as music, and the other labels didn't. Certainly CBS would have a hard time convincing most of us that everything they've released over the years should be considered great music. However, as a former artist with the company, this author recalls the feeling of being something special signed to CBS.

These assurances are very healthy for the artist and the manager. However, if all or even most of the above is true, why do the overwhelming majority of recordings released never recuperate their recording costs? (The data in Table 4.1 of Chapter Four, shows that 105,575 albums were released in 2008 and only *16 "went" platinum representing 0.015% the new releases. Only *22 titles went gold and 110 sold at least 250K copies. Using the 250K as a benchmark for recording costs, only 0.10% of the artists recouped their costs. The table further shows that 82% of all new album sales came from 950 titles in 2008 (.8%).   However, artists who are signed to a major label are presented with a much greater chance of success, as the majors release approximately 20% of the new titles each year and account for over 80% of the sales. So why are there so few hits? Why do so many managers say that they do not feel secure in leaving the record company alone to run the show? Why do so many artists fail to sell records and are eventually dropped from the label's roster? Why do so many good records get lost in the shuffle? How can companies continue to operate with what might be considered such a dismal track record? These questions will be addressed later in this chapter when we look at the typical route of a new recording as it travels through the many departments of the company.

That was then.

THE ROLE OF THE ~~RECORD~~ MUSIC ENTERTAINMENT COMPANY

Choosing a label was by far the most significant business decision the artist and his/her manager made together. Today, record companies play many roles in the life of the artist and are currently becoming "music entertainment" companies, rather then recording companies. Because of the continuing declining sales of prerecorded physical products (CDs), record companies are demanding a share from most of the artist's revenue streams (see "the revenue-sharing deal" below). "… in the world of the "new" music business the name of the game is capturing revenue anywhere and everywhere" {{106 Garrity, Brian 2006;}}. Consequently, their importance has diminished to a lesser significance in the overall career of today's artist.

Traditionally, record companies played two distinctive roles in the artist's life. One is obvious and the other not. The obvious role a company played was to produce, manufacture, release, promote, manage and distribute the artist's recorded product, and through sales, generate income for the artist. Although not an easy task, it had been the company's main function in the industry since the beginning, and an artist expected these tasks to be completed effectively and efficiently.

A subtler role was one of a financial backer. Through various types of financial "advances" which were charged against the artist's royalty account, the record company acted as a reservoir or bank for the artist to obtain funds.

For many artists these roles still exist, however labels are not satisfied with loaning or "advancing" artists money and collecting from the recording's revenue stream.

ADVANCES

The term advance is used to describe the loaning of money to a royalty artist (sometimes with interest charged), with the understanding that the money will be paid back to the company before any royalty checks are delivered to the artist. As we will learn in Chapter Seven, The Record Contract, record companies will seek every conceivable way to generate the revenue to recoup any of the expenses (including advances) that they have incurred. If permitted, they will "cross-collateralize" revenue generated into royalty accounts from past and future recordings, merchandising, endorsements, sponsorships, etc., to guarantee as many sources of revenue as possible. Therefore, the artist and manager should be careful not to over extend the debt to the company. Remember, because it is charged to the royalty account, it's the artist's money that is being spent. Three types of advances commonly given by the company are **personal, production, and inducement** advances.

Personal Advance

A personal advance is the lending of money to the artist for such needs as normal living and household expenses when there is insufficient revenue being generated by personal appearances and/or recording sales. The artist is loaned money to pay the bills and even though s/he is not obligated to pay back any of it (should the sales of the recording never reach their expected level), every precaution should be taken to see that the artist does not accumulate unnecessary personal expenses prematurely. Sometimes, personal advances are used to pay the salaries of employees. Again, the number of employees should be kept at a minimum until desperately needed.

Production Advance

A production advance is the lending of money by a company for the production of a recording. These expenses might include new instruments, or technical support items such as lighting, staging, or a rehearsal hall. Production advances are usually part of the all inclusive "recording fund" as are personal advances needed specifically during the recording process. This is discussed later in this chapter and in Chapter Seven.

Inducement or Bonus Advances

This type of advance is usually reserved for the established artist with a proven track record of successful sales. In some rare instances, in order to sign the artist, the record company becomes involved in a bidding war for the artist against another label, and the artist's manager seizes the opportunity to ask for a sum of money to be delivered upon signing. Although the adage "one in the hand is worth more than two in the bush" may be true, rather than taking the fast buck, the artist and manager should be concerned with the longevity of the relationship with the company and what the company can accomplish to insure a successful career.

TYPES OF RECORD COMPANIES

The simplest way to distinguish between record companies is by size. However, other terms are used in the industry, ie: major, independent, specialty, or boutique. Efficient companies come in all sizes, and hit artists have become enormously successful regardless of the size of the label. For example, the group Creed recorded multi-platinum records for Wind-Up Records, as the only artist on the label. U2 did the same for Island Records, a label mostly associated with reggae music (U2 now records for Interscope, part of UNI).

MAJOR LABELS

Major labels with their subsidiaries and associated labels, dominate the business and account for over 80% of the recordings sold worldwide. As stated earlier, distinguishing a label as major does not relate only to size. A monster hit can launch an act into superstardom and increase the size and distinction or the label almost overnight (Wind-Up Records as an example). Most of the time, a record label is considered a major label if it owns or controls the distribution of its releases and employs its own radio promotion force. Majors also distribute their subsidiary and associated labels, as well as other label's product. Using this definition of a major, there are currently four in the U.S. They are:

Record Company	Distribution Company
EMI Records	EMI Distribution
Sony Music Entertainment	Sony Distribution
Universal Music Group	Universal Music Distribution
Warner Music Group	WMG Distribution

Major labels offer the following **advantages** to their artists:

1. an in-house distribution network

2. an in-house promotion department

3. prestige

4. large financial resources

5. stability

However, there are disadvantages and they are:

1. the risk of getting lost among a large roster of talent

2. the possible lack of individual attention

3. the administration of the company may not be in total control of the company and may have to answer to the parent company which may have little involvement with the music and entertainment business

INDEPENDENT LABEL

Although total independence in record companies is almost a thing of the past, Nielsen Soundscan classifies any label that is not distributed by one of the major distributors as an independent (Indies are hoping to reclassify themselves as labels that are not owned by any of the big four.). However, a label owned by an artist or a producer may also be considered an independent even though it may rely on another label for one or more of the following services.

Distribution – An independent label may be distributed by an independent distributor that has a deal with a major distributor (ie. RED Distribution and Sony Music Entertainment).

Promotion – Depending on the size of the record label, the services in the distribution deal may also include a promotion staff.

Merchandising/Sales – same as above

Financial Resources – It is common for someone (or company) to give start-up money to an artist's or producer's new independent label and financially back it for a period of time.

The **advantages** of an independent label to an artist are:

1. receiving individual attention in all of the record company's departments

2. becoming a big fish in a smaller pond and generating more publicity than they would on a major.

However, the **disadvantages** to an artist are:

1. limited available resources

2. inadequate distribution network (In 2005, indies sold an average of 787 units per title vs. 18,454 units by the majors {{101 Marcone, Stephen 2006;}}.

3. less prestige

SPECIALTY LABEL

Specialty labels usually release only one style of music. There are jazz, classical, folk, children, etc. specialty labels. The style of music need not be without financial success, as there are labels that move a great deal of urban, metal, dance, and new age music. Many artist owned labels fall into this category as do many subsidiary labels of majors.

The **advantages** to an artist are:

1. the expertise of a company's staff in the genre

2. the ability to communicate easily with other artists in the same genre on the label.

The **disadvantages** might be:

1. a lack of financial resources

2. the inability to distribute to large chain record retailers

BOUTIQUE LABEL

Although it is not an "official" term, it is used to describe a midsize company that behaves like a major, but is more selective in its choice of artists. These companies usually have a higher percentage of hit makers within a smaller roster of artists. Nonesuch Records is an example of these so-called labels. The advantages to an artist are obvious and many. The downside is very minimal.

THE REVENUE-SHARING DEAL (360)

A LABEL-ARTIST EXAMPLE

At the turn of this century, record companies made money from two sources: CD sales, and the licensing of master recordings. Since then, the only prerecorded software configuration available (the CD) has grown out of favor with the consumer and diversification has become a necessity for survival. Music publishers have had multiple revenue streams for years. Thomas Hesse, the president of the global digital area for Sony (BMG) says: "To them [publishers], nothing is ancillary. Everything is revenue. That's how record companies are increasingly thinking about their projects. Marketing and licensing and sales are completely intertwined {{106 Garrity, Brian 2006;}}. The following are some new revenue streams that major labels are pursuing.

1. <u>Downloads:</u> According to Soundscan, digital track sales are up 89% from last year.

2. <u>Mobile:</u> It is estimated that the global 3G phone penetration will grow from the current 71 million units to 576 million units in 2009.

3. <u>Subscriptions:</u> More and more big brands are planning to offer new services.

4. <u>Video Downloads:</u> The number of companies offering video downloads is expected to rise; however, currently, only iTune files are compatible with the iPod.

5. <u>Kiosk:</u> Starbucks is currently testing the concept of kiosks that can manufacture albums and customize compilations in store.

6. <u>Radio:</u> Emerging forms of radio are growing and the digital performing rights are established. However, labels are at odds with webcasters and satellite radio over rates.

7. <u>Ad-Supported On-Demand:</u> "Licensing, usage rights and royalty rates associated with ad-backed-audio-on-demand models still have to be worked out." However, according to BigChampagne's research, P2P network usage is up 26% this year.

8. <u>Strategic Investments:</u> The majors are transforming their record companies into music entertainment companies and are looking to participate in their acts' merchandising, touring, and sponsorship dollars (ie: EMI's deals with Korn and Robbie Williams) {{106 Garrity, Brian 2006;}}.

A standard 360 deal doesn't exist. Similar to recording contracts, there are many variations. Below is one example. In this example the artist signed a typical label-artist contract with a royalty of 10% of retail and then was given a 360 deal. This is only one example.

Eight Year Term

Part One—-

$5 mil. advance: artist royalty will be a 60/40% split (60% to artist) with label after recoup.
Total annual royalty will average $750K

Part Two—-

$3 mil. advance to be recouped from the following income streams: 30% of artist share of touring revenue before agency fee, with artist averaging $5 mil. per tour. (Artist will guarantee a tour every 2 years)

   B. 30% of artist share of merchandise @ $125k per year

   C. 20% of artist publishing income, including writer/publisher share (which includes performance royalties) that average $750K per year

The computation is as follows:

DEAL		LABEL		ARTIST	
Deal Point		Deal Balance	Add. Balance	Deal Balance	Add. Balance
Part I:					
$5 mil. advance: artist royalty @10% will be split 60/40% (60% to artist) with label after recoup.		(5,000,000)		5,000,000	
Total annual royalty will average $750K					
750K X 8 yrs = 6 mil		5,000,000			
6 mil – 5 mil = 1 mil artist 60% = 600,000		400,000		600,000	
label 40% =400,000					
TOTAL		**400,000**		**5,600,000**	
750K X 8 = 24,000,000 X .90 = 21.6 mil (minus manufacturing etc.)				5,400,000	

		LABEL		ARTIST	
Part II:		Deal Balance	Add. Balance	Deal Balance	Add. Balance
$5 mil. advance to be recouped from the following income streams:		(5,000,000)		5,000,000	
A. 30% of artist share of touring revenue before agency fee, with artist averaging $5 mil. per tour. (artist will guarantee a tour every 2 years)					
5 mil X 4 = 20 mil X .30= 6 mil		6,000,000		(6,000,000)	
20 mil X .70 = 14 mil					14,000,000
B. 30% of artist share of merchandise @ $125k per year					
125K X 8 = 1,000,000 X .30 = 300,000		300,000		(300,000)	
1 mil X .70 = 700,000					700,000
C. 20% of artist publishing income, including writer/publisher share (which includes performance royalties) which average $750k per year					
750,000 X 8 =6 mil X .20 = 1,200,000		1,200,000		(1,200,000)	
6 mil X .80 = 4,800,000					4,800,000

Figure 6.1

The computation is self-explanatory, except for the columns that read "additional balance." This is revenue that is not part of the deal, but is revenue that will be received. For example, in Part I, the label is sharing in the 10% artist royalty (60/40 split) and is also receiving the other 90% (expenses have been intentionally omitted for easier computation). In Part II, the artist is receiving additional revenue from touring, merchandising, and publishing.

ONE INVESTOR-ARTIST EXAMPLE:

The following is an example of a 360 deal between a group of investors (a company) and an artist. Since this company is not a label, they will not receive additional revenue from the recordings. However, the artist does receive additional revenue from touring, merchandising, and publishing.

Artist/Company 360 Deal: Ten-Year Term

Part One—-

$5 mil. advance recoupable from the following:

A. 30% of net touring, expecting to tour every two years @ $2mil per tour

B. 30% of net merchandise and licensing @$300K/year

C. 30% of all net publishing revenue @@$600K/year

Part Two –

$5 mil. non-refundable/recoupable advance for 5 albums to be recouped from the artist's 20% royalty earnings on the five albums and 60 company/ 40 artist split after recoup. Artist recording royalties averages $1.3mil/album at the 20% rate.

DEAL	COMPANY		ARTIST	
	Deal Bal	Add. Bal	Deal Bal	Add. Bal
Part I: $5mil. Advance recoupable from the following:	(5,000,000)		5,000,000	
A. 30% of net touring, expecting to tour every two years @ $2mil gross per tour 2 mil X 5 = 10 mil X .30 = 3,000,000 10 mil X .70 = 7,000,000	3,000,000		(3,000,000)	7,000,000
B. 30% of net merchandise and licensing @$300K gross/year 300K X 10 = 3,000,000 X .30 = 900,000 3 mil X .70 = 2,100,000	900,000		(900,000)	2,100,000
C. 30% of all net publishing revenue @$600K gross/year 600K X 10 = 6,00,000 X .30 = 1,800,000 6,000,000 X .70 = 4,200,000	1,800,000		(1,800,000)	4,200,000
Part II:				
$5 mil. non-refundable/recoupable advance for 5 albums to be recouped from the artist's 20% royalty earnings on the five albums and 60 company/40 artist split after recoup. Artist recording royalties averages $1.3mil/album at the 20% rate. 1.3 mil X 5 = 6,500,000 (6.500,000 – 5,000,000 = 1,500,000) 1.5 mil X .60 = 900,000 1.5 mil X .40 = 600,000	(5,000,000) 5,000,000 900,000		5,000,000 (900,000) 600,000	

Figure 6.2

ONE INDEPENDENT LABEL EXAMPLE

Canadian based management entertainment company, Nettwerk Music Group, founded in 1984, is the umbrella company for Nettwerk Management, Nettwerk Productions, Nettwerk One, Afrtwerk, and Nutone. Nettwerk allows its artists to setup their own record labels (and publishing companies). Their roster includes Sarah McLachlan, Avril Lavigne and Dido, and CEO Terry McBride estimates that "probably 80% of releases from his management clients will be through their own labels." Nettwerk has developed an infrastructure, including four marketing teams spread across their offices in Vancouver, Los Angeles, Nashville, Boston, New York, and Europe. "I'm advocating for artists we manage not to sign-or re-sign-with a label unless it's a pressing – and – distribution deal to work back catalog with new projects" {{107 LeBlanc, Larry 2006;}}.

OTHER MODELS

SellaBand, a Netherlands-based site that helps artists create fan-financed recordings, announced that legendary hip-hop group Public Enemy will use the service to raise funds to record its thirteenth studio album. Frontman Chuck D said that band aims to raise $250,000 through the service, which will let fans pledge $25 and receive a limited edition version of the CD, as well as a pro ratio share of 33.3% of all net revenues generated by sales of the resulting album {{146 Hefflinger,Mark 2009;}}. Through its partnership with SellaBand, PE is offering a total 10,000 parts for believers at a value of $25.00 each to raise a total of $250,000. The $250,000 will be used to: a) fund the complete recording costs and expenses for its next album and b) fund a strategic marketing plan for the worldwide release of the SellaBand album in 2010. According to www.sellaband.com as of November 13, 2009, eighty-six believers have partnered for $65,525 {{147 Anonymous}}.

Radiohead's name-your-own-price experiment for their *In Rainbows* album has been reported very successful (there is still controversy concerning the success of the experiment). Rather than release their seventh album through the normal retail channels, they released it online only and the average price paid for the album was six dollars. As reported, the album sold three million copies worldwide and the eighty-dollar boxed set sold one hundred thousand copies. In fact, the group made more money before the release of the physical copies than its previous album {{150 Anderson, Chris 2009;}}.

In July 2007, Prince debuted his album *Planet Earth* by stuffing the nineteen-dollar recording into 2.8 million Sunday editions of the London's *Daily Mail*. The paper paid one million dollars for the copies and Prince used this to promote his live shows. He sold out twenty-one shows that brought him record concert revenue for the region {{151 Anderson, Chris 2009;}}.

THE STRUCTURE

Record companies are obviously in business to make money. Structurally there are two major divisions in any company. They are the creative division and the business/administrative division. Although the creative areas are concerned with making a profit, the tug or war between areas concerned primarily with the bottom line and areas concerned with the artistic merits of a release are common. In fact, in some a&r departments there is the distinction made between "pop product" that is released to rocket up the charts and disappear after one or two monster releases, and product with artistic quality that has the promise of longevity.

Today, much criticism is given of the labels for the lack of artist development. It seems that artists are not given the opportunities they once had to nurture and develop into superstars. Much of that blame has been attributed to the ownership of labels by large conglomerates whose officers must answer to stockholders with quarterly accounting, therefore not allowing the time for artist development (read *Howlin' at the Moon* by former CBS Records Group President, Walter Yetnikoff).

Figure 6.3 is a representation of the structure of a major record company. The departments or areas in italics represent the creative areas and the departments in plain text represent the business areas. At the top of the chart are the stockholders of the "parent company." They are the owners of the company and are the true "bosses." The company as a corporation may be a public company, with stockholders that invest capital through the purchase of shares on the open stock markets; or they may be private investors who purchase shares in return for financial support. As with any corporation, the board of directors is directly responsible to the stockholders and is represented by their chairperson. The board of directors receives its information concerning operations of the (parent) company from the president of the company. The operation of the record label is represented to all of the above by the label president. S/he is in the hot seat! If the entertainment business is newly acquired or only a small part of the central operations of the parent company (ie: Sony Music), then the label president's ability to communicate the successes and failures of the label becomes crucial to its future.

STRUCTURE OF A RECORD COMPANY

Stockholders of Parent Company

Chairman & Board of Directors

President of Parent Company

Label President

Vice Presidents of:

Artist Dev.	Manuf.	Bus. & Legal Aff.	*A & R*	Dist. & Merch.	Finance	Int. Op.	*Promo.*
1. Per. Appear 2. Tour Supp. 3. Career Dv. 4. Publicity 5. Media Ser.	1. Press. Plants 2. Printing 3. Duplication	1. Artist Cont. 2. Licenses 3. Labor Agr. 4. Prod. Cont. 5. Comp. Ads. 6. Copyright Mgt. 7. Ent. Law	1. Artist Sign. 2. Master Pur. 3. Prod. Coor. 4. Admin.	1. Trans 2. Acct. Ser. 3. Sales 4. Warehouse 5. POP Ads. 6. Co-op Ads 7. Invtry	1. Acct. 2. Inventory Control 3. Royalty Payments 4. Taxes	1. Commun. 2. Personnel 3. Phy. Pl.	1. Radio 2. Video 3. Internet 4. Field 5. Indie

New Media

1. Downloads
2. Mobile
3. Kiosks
4. Satellite
5. Streaming

Marketing

1. Prod. Dev.
2. Artwork
3. Mktg. Plans
4. Publicity

LEGEND
Creative Areas = Italics
Business Areas = Plain

Figure 6.3

Reporting to the label president are the senior vice presidents and/or vice presidents of each department. Their job is to make the president look credible, responsible, and in control. The chart describes, in outline form, the functions of each department. What follows is a short synopsis of each of the department's responsibilities.

ARTIST DEVELOPMENT

The activities of this department involve increasing the artist's (not necessarily his/her product) recognition in the marketplace, including short and long-term career development, tour support, and publicity.

ARTISTS AND REPERTOIRE

Until the mid 1960's, when the industry superstars began employing independent producers, the A&R department would discover the talent, pick the songs to be recorded, and produce the records. Everything was completed "in house" and the "head" of A&R was considered the most important person in the company. Mitch Miller, who was responsible for the careers of Doris Day, Tony Bennett, and others, was head of A&R at Columbia Records in the 1950's and considered the most influential person in the industry.

Presently, A&R still plays the largest role in the musical direction of the company. The staff discovers artists, locates material to be recorded, matches artists with producers, and deems the recorded product acceptable for release. Although still considered to be the most creative department in the company, an independent producer completes the actual production of the record. Consequently they are not usually active in the actual recording or mixing of the recording. When asked what the letters stand for, one A&R rep. said "airports and restaurants". The administration of the department keeps track of the budget for each recording session.

Because the large umbrella category known as popular music is subdivided into narrow-casted "micro" formats (such as metal, urban, rap, dance, house, hip-hop, etc.), each department usually employs a specialist to discover artists, and direct activities in his/her area of expertise. Although being a musician is not a qualification for the position, these are the few **MUSIC** people left in a company.

BUSINESS AND LEGAL AFFAIRS

Although they are separate departments by name, these two departments work closely in composing various agreements that concern the revenue flow of the company. These include artist agreements, licensing agreements, labor agreements, and any regulatory agreements that involve income and expenditures. These departments employ the people that wear the suits (and/or high heels) to work and make the important but not glamorous bottom line decisions. Artists and managers tend to question the rationale of many of their decisions.

DISTRIBUTION AND SALES

These two departments also work closely in servicing the branch distributors, tracking inventory, and servicing point of purchase promotional vehicles for in-store display. Because *Billboard Magazine* and Nielsen have developed "Soundscan," the computerized sales tracking device for servicing their charts, retail sales have taken on greater industry significance.

FINANCE

Again, this important but non-glamorous department accounts for every penny that the company spends and receives. These people tend not to have sole decision-making power, but consult with the administration and business affairs to offer the most cost effective options for the company.

INTERNAL OPERATIONS

This department has the greatest variety of responsibilities, from paper clips to personnel to telephone and data processing systems to tropical plants to kosher meats for the kitchens. Their goal is the most cost effective efficient operation of the company.

MARKETING AND PROMOTION

Once the producer delivers the recording to the company and the A&R department has pronounced it acceptable for release, the marketing department is an umbrella department that is responsible for the integrity of the recorded product. They design a marketing campaign for the record that includes the visual concept for the artwork, media mix, point of purchase displays, and any merchandise that will be sold in conjunction with the release.

A great number of companies separate the marketing and promotion departments with individual vice presidents for each. Promotion departments are also separated by radio formats, with National Directors leading the staff in each. Promotion departments live and die by airplay, and are responsible for completing the radio and video and now internet portions of the campaign. The decision to employ free-lance or independent experts for any of the marketing plan's responsibilities is made by this department's vice president.

MANUFACTURING

The goal of this department is attaining the most cost-effective efficient method of product duplication possible.

NEW MEDIA

This newly formed department is responsible for the digital delivery of the product and any new and different avenues yet to be employed.

PRODUCT FLOW

The following describes the internal path a physical product takes from the time the master is delivered, and the A&R department decides to "sign off" on the recording as being "commercially acceptable," and all necessary forms and releases have been completed. In Figure 6.4, the diamonds represent decisions that must be addressed, and the rectangles represent actions. The diagram represents the linear flow of the product but does not represent simultaneous actions completed by separate departments.

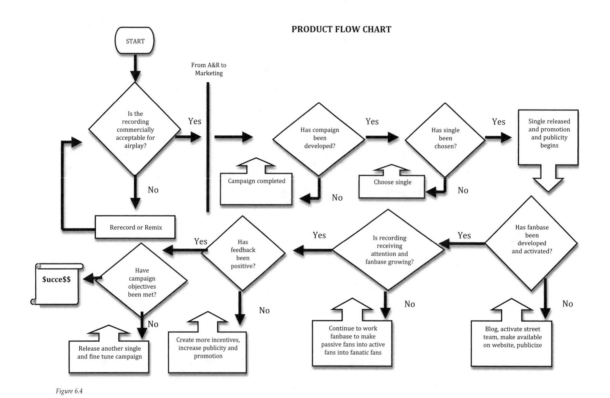

PRODUCT FLOW CHART

Figure 6.4

Is the Product Commercially Acceptable for airplay and sale, and the first single chosen?

If the artist is going the traditional route, this is a important decision, and it's A&R's responsibility. The term **"commercially acceptable"** is the term used in the recording contract that allows the record company to make a release decision based on more than just the technical integrity of the recording. It allows the company to censor the recording. They may feel the lyrics may offend a certain segment of society and if aired, have a negative effect on sales, or they may deem the lyrics as obscene. The company may feel that the recording sounds too much like a previously copyrighted work and may be bordering on infringement. Whatever the "problem" with the recording, the term commercially acceptable allows the company the legal freedom to hold back a release for reasons beyond a recording's technical inefficiencies. Recently, several record companies have required the legal department to review (and sign off on) the lyrics on all material scheduled for release. As also stated in the recording contract chapter, artists are very skeptical about this term and should be. However, very few artists (if any) have the term struck from the contract.

Choosing the first single to be released is also an A&R decision. It is the manager's responsibility to make certain that the right song is selected. Major battles are fought everyday over this decision, and a good manager persuades A&R to make the right choice. Sometimes the company's administration is involved with the choice, and managers find themselves trying to persuade a president that the record s/he really wants as the single is the same record the manager and artist want.

There is quite a bit of paperwork involved in delivering the master recording to A&R for release. The names and social security numbers of each performer on the record must be submitted and a host of other forms completed. For example, immigration forms must be completed when necessary because the federal government is very concerned that foreigners do not replace working citizens of the USA. Various labor forms must also be completed. All expenses pertaining to the actual recording and other debits to the recording fund must be accounted for. The manager and artist's accountant and attorney should review all expense statements as well as other "official" documents.

Has Product Marketing Campaign Been Developed?

The actual marketing campaign has many facets that must be coordinated by the product manager responsible for the project. Although names of the categories may differ among record companies, the objectives are the same. Following are parts of two marketing plans employed in recent years. Marketing campaign models are readily available on the internet.

First Marketing Plan

POSITIONING STATEMENT:

One of the most gifted and versatile song stylists in the world, Jane Doe's distinctively beautiful, powerful voice and her extraordinary ability to command diverse musical idioms — including country, rock, punk, pop, Broadway, jazz, opera, Mexican, and Afro-Cuban — have led to one of the most spectacular and enduring careers in popular music. The 10-time Grammy-winner has a stunning string of platinum and multi-platinum recordings to her name and dozens of top-40s hits in a career that spans nearly three decades.

Her groundbreaking trio of recordings made her the **first pop/rock megastar to have runaway, multi-platinum success with recordings of American song standards**. Those records are perennial favorites, scanning around 10,000 discs a year nearly 20 years later. This album celebrates her return to standards repertoire for the first time since then. These are grown-up songs for grown-up hearts that have loved and lost and lived to sing about it and she has never sounded better.

TRACK LIST:

1 through 10

PERSONNEL:

Jane Doe – vocals

TIME LINE HIGHLIGHTS:

OCTOBER

7 – Limited quantity advance CDs for press arrive in-house, press release draft

11 – Solicitation begins

11 – 1x1s available to ship

13 – ABC Group sends gay press servicing to 125 weekly, bi-weekly, and monthly gay press outlets as well as gay and theater online editorial outlets

13 – Full-length album ships to Jazz, Adult Standards, and AC Radio with postcards

13 – Commercial CD servicing to field reps, Regional Directors, Sales VIP list, and Strategic Marketing outlets.

15 – Postcards available to ship

15 – Press servicing to over 600 outlets

late-Oct – 2x2s and 3x3s ship to retail

NOVEMBER

4-26 – ABC Group launches campaign to gay/theater/cabaret audiences.

- listening/release events at clubs in 25 markets, with advertising in gay publications, enter-to-win contest and sampler giveaways at each event
- Postcards will also be included in gift bags at gay/theater/fashion/ lifestyle events
- Gay press campaign continues
- Event marketing to NY theater/cabaret audiences with postcards and stickered Verve samplers

4 – Add date at Jazz and Adult Standards radio

7 – Ads run in New York Times, Los Angeles Times, and San Francisco Chronicle Sunday Arts sections

8-12 TBD 2-3 promotion days in New York or LA for press, radio, satellite radio interviews, etc.

9 – STREET DATE

9 – Web feature launches

9 – Animated e-card is sent to news list

DECEMBER

12 – ad cut runs in New York Times Magazine

JANUARY

Second week in January *Tracks* magazine ad in Feb/March issue streets

SALES

KEY SELLING POINTS:

- **She was the first major pop/rock star to have multi-platinum success recording American pop standards with her groundbreaking trio of platinum- selling records** in the mid-80s.

- **Her previous three standards albums were all platinum-selling hits that have sold over 6 million in the US alone.**

- An ever-popular artist, **her catalog scans over 200,000 units a year** in the absence of a new release.

- **Her records have scanned over 5.6 million in the Soundscan era alone**

TELEVISION
McEnroe
Entertainers with Byron Allen
CNN Headline News
CNN "The Biz"
Fox News Live
20/20
60 Minutes II
A&E Breakfast With The Arts
A&E Live By Request
Access Hollywood
Bravo Profiles
CBS Early Show
CBS Sunday Morning
Charlie Rose
CNN – Various shows
Dateline
E!
Ellen Degeneres Show
Emeril Live!
Entertainment Tonight
Extra
Fox & Friends
Fox News Channel
Good Morning America
Larry King Live
Oprah
Primetime Live
Today Show
Wall Street Journal TV

MAGAZINES
We will be pursuing features
where appropriate; otherwise, we
will be seeking to place CD
reviews or column mentions.

General Interest Publications
Atlantic Monthly
Entertainment Weekly
Harper's
In Style
Interview
Los Angeles Magazine
AARP
New York Magazine
New Yorker
New York Times Magazine
Newsweek
Paper
Parade
People
Readers Digest
Time
Town & Country
US
USA Today
USA Weekend

Vanity Fair
Venice Magazine
US News & World Report

Women's Magazines
Cosmopolitan
Elle
Harper's Bazaar
Ladies Home Journal
More Magazine
New Woman
O. Oprah Magazine
Good Housekeeping

Music Magazines & Trades
Billboard
Down Beat
Goldmine
Ice
Jazz Times
Jazziz
Music Connection
Spin
Tracks
Vibe

REGIONAL PUBLICATIONS
NEWSPAPERS
**Major Market Dailies and
National Newspapers**
Atlanta Journal Constitution
Baltimore Sun
Boston Globe
Chicago Tribune
Dallas Morning News
Detroit News
Los Angeles Times
New Orleans Times-Picayune
Nashville Banner
Miami Herald
New York Times
Philadelphia Inquirer
San Diego Union-Tribune
San Francisco Examiner
Seattle Times
Tampa Tribune
USA Today
Washington Post

RADIO
ABC Radio Networks
NPR: Fresh Air, Morning Edition,
Weekend Edition, All Things
Considered, Jazz Riffs,
Associated Press Radio
Voice of America
Local & National talk radio
shows

Launch Radio
Sirius XM Satellite Radio

NATIONAL WIRE SERVICES
Columns and Wire Services
Associated Press
Bloomberg News
Copley Wire
Cindy Adams
Gannett Wire
Hearst News Service
Jeanne Williams
King Features Syndicate
Knight-Ridder
Liz Smith
Los Angeles Times Syndicate
Marilyn Beck
New York Times Syndicate
Newhouse News Service
Reuters Wire
Scripps Howard News Service
Tribune Media Services
Universal Press Syndicate
UPI Wire

WEBSITES
All Music Guide
Amazon.com
Billboard Online
BN.com
Citysearch
Contemporaryjazz.com
E! Online
Jazz Online
Jazz Review.com
Jazz USA
Launch
Musictoday.com
PopMatters.com
Rollingstone.com

Airline Publications/Inflight
Music Programs
Air Tran Arrivals
Alaska Airlines Magazine
America West Airlines Magazine
American Way (American)
Attache (US Air)
Continental
Frontier
Hemispheres (United)
Meridian (Midway)
Northwest Airlines
WorldTraveler
Sky (Delta)
Skywest Magazine (Delta
Connection/United Express)

KEY RETAIL:

- in-store play, and co-op priority

- Aggressive price and positioning programs at retail will create a high-profile

- Key Accounts for 4th quarter listening stations and/or P&P programs: Borders, Barnes and Noble, Target, Anderson, Costco, Best Buy, FYE

- Key 4th quarter programs will be set up with appropriate independent retailers and coalitions.

- In-store merchandising fund for blow-ups, light boxes, etc. at key accounts.

- This will be a featured title on Amazon.com, B&N.com, Borders.com, itunes and all digital partners.

- staff and Market Directors will create marketing plans to support the release focusing on adult, pop, and jazz retail outlets with a focus on lifestyle marketing.

TOOLS:

- In-store play CD servicing

- 1x1 (4-c cover art only) – available October 11

- Postcard (mid October)

- Animated e-card by street date

- CD sampler

- Publicity photos, cover art, copy points available on Extranet

DISCOGRAPHY/SALES HISTORY:

- **Soundscan only includes sales after 1992**

- **Nearly 6 million records scanned in the US in the Soundscan era**

TOTAL	**4,705,445**
Plus Misc albums and compilations	899,650
TOTAL ALBUMS SCANNED	**5,605,095**

TOP SOUNDSCAN DMAS:

New York, Los Angeles, San Francisco, Chicago, Washington DC, Philadelphia, Boston, Atlanta, Seattle, Dallas-Ft. Worth, Houston, Denver, Minneapolis, Portland

HOMETOWN:

Tucson, Arizona

PROMOTION:

JAZZ RADIO –

- Full CD ships October 15. Impact date: November 4
- Win-it-before-you-can-buy-it campaigns and on-air ticket giveaways in key markets

ADULT STANDARDS RADIO –

- Full CD ships October 15. Impact date: November 4
- Pre-promote second half of October
- Independent promoter Don Graham will work the project to the format
- Win-it-before-you-can-buy-it campaigns and on-air ticket giveaways in key markets

ADULT CONTEMPORARY RADIO –

- Full CD will ship to select AC stations October 15.
- Interviews will be scheduled at Jazz, Adult Standards, and AC radio, as well as syndicated shows and satellite radio.

PUBLICITY/MEDIA RELATIONS:

Press plan will pitch

- **key TV appearances**, (pending her availability to perform) including Oprah, CBS Sunday Morning, The Today Show, The Tonight Show, Ellen, Good Morning America, Charlie Rose, PBS Soundstage, and A&E Live by Request
- **NPR**, including Morning Edition, Fresh Air, Weekend Edition, and All Things Considered
- **entertainment and mainstream press,** including *Newsweek, Time, Atlantic Monthly, The New York Times, Entertainment Weekly, USA Today, The New Yorker, The Los Angeles Times, Parade*
- **women's magazines**
- **major market dailies/weeklies, columns and wire services** for reviews
- **national and local talk radio**
- **music and lifestyle websites** for editorial coverage.

INDEPENDENT PUBLICITY

The ABC Group is hired to work gay publicity for the project

- **Syndicated feature:** a feature article will be serviced to regional gay press in every market and also major gay websites. This would be timed to run immediately preceding street date, and can gather well over 500,000 impressions.

- **Reviews:** As an adjunct to the mainstream press campaign, ABC will target gay and lesbian newspapers, magazines, and websites in major markets nationwide, servicing them with press kits and CDs for album reviews. Publications would include such outlets as *The Philadelphia Gay news*, *HX* and *Next* (New York), *In Newsweekly* (Boston), *The Gay and Lesbian Times* (San Diego), *The Dallas Voice*, among dozens of others and website would include gay.com, planetout.com, and queery.com. National, long-lead publications would include *Out*, *The Advocate*, *Instinct*, *Genre*, *XY*, *Curve*, *Girlfriends*, and *Metrosource*.

CONSUMER MARKETING:

- Ads will appear in the Sunday arts sections of *The New York Times*, *The Los Angeles Times*, and *The San Francisco Chronicle* on November 7, the Sunday before street date.

- A cut will appear in a New York Times Magazine music ad on November 12, featuring six to eight total titles, with a short paragraph of copy and an 1-800 number to call in for orders.

- Half page, 4-color ad in February/March issue of *Tracks* magazine.

ADVERTISING:

Publication (circ.)	Issue	On Sale	Size	Color	Account Tags
The New York Times Sunday A&E	Nov. 7, 2004	11/7/04	1/3 pg.	B&W	TBD
The Los Angeles Times Sunday Arts	Nov. 7, 2004	11/7/04	1/3 pg.	B&W	TBD
The San Francisco Chronicle Sunday Arts	Nov. 7, 2004	11/7/04	1/3 pg.	B&W	TBD
Tracks magazine	Feb/Mar 2005		? pg.	4C	TBD
New York Times Magazine	Dec. 12, 2004	11/1/04	1/6 cut	4C	800 # to call

STICKER COPY

THE VOICE THAT SET A STANDARD
Her return to American pop standards

DIRECT MARKETING:

The ABC Group: Gay/Theater/Lifestyle Marketing

With a number of songs originating on Broadway or in movie musicals, the album will also be well-received by lovers of Broadway and show-tunes. The ABC Group is hired to work album to both the gay market and the theater-lover audiences across the country.

- Priority markets: New York, Los Angeles, San Francisco, Chicago, Seattle, Detroit, Boston, Miami/Ft. Lauderdale, Houston, Dallas, Denver, Minneapolis, San Diego, Washington DC, Baltimore, Atlanta, Austin.

(Additional markets will be added to this list, based on influential bars or clubs in surrounding suburban and second tier markets.)

CD RELEASE EVENTS in 20 top markets

- A special release party for the album (in conjunction with album release date) will be arranged in bars and lounges in 20 + major markets across the country to elevate word-of-mouth and drive this audience to record stores. The venue will give out posters, postcards, and CD samplers which include a track, as well as run enter-to-win contests for the CD.

- In major markets multiple venue spaces will be targeted for release events.

- Print ads give excellent free visibility in gay papers throughout the country. These ads provide an excellent means of audience impressions, with readership of these publications ranging from 5,000 to 75,000+ each; the cumulative amount of people that see these ads across the country is well into the many hundreds of thousands. Key art, album street date and logo placement are focal points of the ads.

- Additional promotions around these events will include flyering, DJ announcements, website announcements and/or email blasts will be designed by venues emphasizing album artwork and key artwork.

STREET TEAM OUTREACH

- In the top 12 major markets, postcards will be distributed in gay neighborhoods via heavy grassroots street team penetration. Hired "experts" in each key neighborhood/territory would hand these out. This would take place outside of the most popular bars/clubs in each market, on key corners in the appropriate gay-borhood and in key lifestyle outlets where postcards are left to be taken.

THEATRE COMMUNITY VISIBILITY

- Karpel Group will create visibility for the CD by distributing samplers and postcards at New York theater community hangouts in mid-town Manhattan.

- In-store play copies of the CD will be distributed to stores, bars, and restaurants where the Broadway audiences spend time

- Other theater targets in New York include cabaret bars in Chelsea and the West Village and theater-related shops

Piano Bars/Cabarets

- Several key markets have cabarets or piano bars that highlight vocalists, Broadway show tunes and other similar genres. This will be a natural audience for this album, and reaching out to them will maximize awareness to this segment of the community.

TOUR:

No tour dates are scheduled.

NEW MEDIA:

- A major pre- and post-street online campaign focuses on features, interviews, downloads and contests on major music and portal websites.

- **Animated e-card**, including audio samples, track list, bio, tour dates

- she will be featured on the label's website

- **Send-to-a-friend campaign** (where the fan who sends out the most e-cards to friends to tell them about the CD wins)

- **Flyaway contest** — online contest placed on major websites for entrants to fly to see a concert

- **Grassroots marketing** — targeting chatboards and affinity artist sites. Features will be pitched to a variety of online outlets, including major portals like **MSN.com**, **AOL.com**, **Yahoo/Launch**, **MusicMatch.com**, all jazz and music websites.

- **iTunes** will offer a track for sale pre-release

- **Amazon.com** pre-release ordering campaign.

- Tracks will be available for sale on street date at all the online music outlets.

- Many more online editorial and promotional opportunities pending.

PRESS RELEASE:

JANE DOE SIGNS WITH LABEL, RELEASES NEW CD NOVEMBER 9

This album celebrates the singer's return to American pop standards repertoire

On Tuesday, November 9 ……

Second Marketing Plan

A unique series bringing together two great brands and one new vision.

Introducing an unprecedented initiative that keys in on the lifestyle and proactive home entertaining consumer - Classics, the leader in adult music, joins forces with HGTV, America's leading destination for home & garden information and the leader in defining today's proactive lifestyle. HGTV's network and website, HGTV.com, provide the most current and practical information to help you enhance your home and lifestyle. Home Design & Home Improvement is one of the hottest trends today with HGTV leading the way!

ABOUT HGTV

∞ Take a fresh approach to the way you live with Home & Garden Television. You'll find ideas and inspiration to transform your space and home, and the expert help you need to accomplish it.

∞ HGTV is one of the world's most recognizable brands and a symbol of integrity, excellence and quality.

∞ HGTV is distributed in over 89 million U.S. households and is one of the fastest-growing networks in cable television history.

∞ HGTV is a TOP 15 television network overall based on ratings.

∞ HGTV is TOP 5 network in terms of appeal to its specific audience demos (25 – 55) [Beta Ad Exec Evaluation Group]

∞ HGTV.com is the nation's leading online home and lifestyle destination, drawing an average of 104 million page views and 5.1 million visitors per month.

∞ HGTV produces three e-newsletters: HGTV Ideas, HGTV Decorating and HGTV Gardening, with approximately 3 million subscribers each.

HGTV MARKETING

HGTV.COM

The following placement will be used to promote the HGTV CD's beginning with the product launch and running on an ongoing basis:

∞ Banner rotation on main page of HGTV.com

∞ Sidelight banners rotated throughout the web site

∞ CD's can be sold via "Shop" online retail section HGTV.com

∞ A consumer contest featuring Panasonic equipment or another HGTV.com contest is tentatively planned, contingent on sponsor availability.

∞ Develop a promotional package accessible by the following URL HGTV.com/music. The site will include:

   o CD covers for the first four releases: Dinner Party, Creative Moods, Morning Coffee, Outdoor Entertaining

   o Names of all songs on each CD

   o Samples of 5 tracks from each CD, 30 seconds each (*Exact number of samples and length TBD)

   o Related links for each CD. This will include content on HGTV that complements the theme of the CD, for example "craft ideas" may appear on the Creative Moods cd. All links will stay within HGTV.com.

   o Links to buy the CDs at the HGTV Store (part of Shop At Home.com)

E-MAIL

The HGTV CD's will be promoted periodically in the following HGTV e-mail newsletters:

∞ The music series will be promoted in the HGTV Ideas newsletter twice during the first month of the launch. The newsletter has 3.1 million self-subscribed recipients.

∞ "Creative Moods" will be promoted in the HGTV Decorating newsletter, which has 2.9 million self-subscribed recipients.

∞ "Outdoor Entertaining" will be promoted in the HGTV Gardening newsletter which has 2.7 million self-subscribed recipients.

* Note: E-mail membership is not mutually exclusive.

ON AIR PROMOTION

∞ July 1 – Aug 31: Spots scattered throughout daytime pushing to HGTV.com and "where CD's are sold." We will run approximately 4-5 spots per day or about 300 spots over the 9 week period.

∞ June 13 – Aug 31: Dekos scattered throughout daytime pushing to HGTV.com to purchase the HGTV CD's. HGTV will run approximately 3 deckos per day during this time.

EVENTS

∞ The HGTV music series will be promoted at 2 HGTV Block Party events in Baltimore and San Francisco. Samples can be played, and promotional materials can be handed out.

∞ The HGTV.com music site can be highlighted via on site computers at the events.

OTHER MARKETING

∞ Consumer contest featuring equipment - online sweepstakes with retail (on-line, brick-n-mortar) promoting series, other contest in the works

∞ Home show/Gardening show outreach – explore mailers, promotions, mentions, ads in programs, fliers, etc. Create & use postcard.

PACKAGING

∞ Titles that will launch series in June

o Creative Moods

o Dinner Party

o Morning Coffee

o Outdoor Entertaining

∞ First four in June, four additional titles in September, then one Christmas title and boxed set (size tbd) scheduled for October.

∞ Track list designed especially to reflect concept, mood and title.

∞ Cover art and title are key elements as each CD conveys a different aspect of home life and décor.

∞ Brilliant photography presented in jewel boxes at a great price.

∞ Each package includes a detailed booklet as well as an insert with HGTV information.

∞ Enhanced CD (ECD) – which will feature

o Picture Gallery showing cover art, track lists, music excerpts and other cool information

o HGTV TV spots (Design to Sell, HGTV-HD)

o Hyperlinks to HGTV.com, etc.

RETAIL

∞ Traditional retail - will actively seek retail positioning and promotion throughout account base.

∞ Nontraditional retail – seeking positioning at alternative retail (Pottery Barn, Bed Bath & Beyond, William Sonoma, etc)

∞ Selling assignment: 10,000 units each title (40,000 total)

∞ Production: recommended we back up with 15,000 in paper per title initially.

PUBLICITY

∞ Will target lifestyle & music media (Print, TV, Radio)

∞ National dailies - The home/garden, food and lifestyle sections will be pitched for placement/mentions in all top 200 daily papers (NY Times, LA Times, USA Today, etc).

∞ Pitch series to select business/music writers (Billboard) for story on the unique branding partnership between label and HGTV.

∞ Long-lead lifestyle, home and women's magazines (that aren't in conflict with HGTV's publications) for placement (Real Simple, Ladies Home Journal, House & Garden etc).

∞ Coordinate efforts with HGTV's publicist - use their list.

∞ Service to select music writers who cover lifestyle/compilation CDs & series.

∞ Service to gift guide columns in dailies and magazines (seasonally).

∞ The series will be recommended as radio premiums for classical stations nation-wide (a number of stations with "lighter" formats often use lifestyle lines).

NEW MEDIA

∞ Lifestyle Campaign - Aggressive lifestyle campaign with XYZ Media – specializing in lifestyle targets (do-it-yourself, home decorating, women's websites, home entertaining, cooking/recipe sites, book clubs, etc) and tastemaker outreach. To run three months (June – August)

∞ Robust internet campaign on HGTV.com includes features on home page positioning & e-newsletters to a subscriber base of 3 million loyal consumers.

∞ The series will feature prominently on the front page and throughout the HGTV site.

∞ HGTV's e-newsletter list goes out to three distinct categories Ideas newsletter (3 million subscribes every Wednesday), Gardening (2.7 million weekly) and Decorating (2.9 million weekly).

∞ Microsite at HGTVmusic.com will contain album information, audio streaming of songs from the each release as well as tips on HGTV lifestyle activities (eg. Gardening, cooking, decorating, entertaining, etc.)

∞ Targeted promotions and sweepstakes opportunities will be schedule with the HGTV consumer in mind on the HGTV site.

∞ Dedicated section on iclassics.com.

∞ Albums will be available on itunes.

RADIO PROMOTION

∞ Radio – seeking promotions, mentions, contests, etc with selected formats.

TOOLS

∞ Press kits – joint press release with HGTV (tbd)

∞ Bin header cards

∞ Dedicated CD counter/floor bin

∞ H-clips (tbd)

∞ Window cling (tbd)

∞ Postcard

CD TRACK LISTS

∞ Each album is 62-65 minutes in length – over 1 hour.

Creative Moods

1 through 10

Dinner Party

1 through 10

Morning Coffee

1 through 10

Outdoor Entertaining

1 through 10

The media mix is vital to a campaign. Notice that new media is being vigorously employed in both campaigns. The timetable for each phase of the plan must create and maintain a momentum for airplay and product sales. Carefully, study all the categories in both marketing campaigns.

What follows in an example of how a release became a hit for rapper T.I. It is the result of a thorough campaign by Atlantic Records. Note the timeline and the series of events to combat the illegal consumption of the music.

2003: T.I. releases *Trap Muzik* and sells one million copies. He releases Down with the King mix tape.
2004: T.I. goes to Fulton County Jail in Georgia for a 1998 drug charge and parole violation. He is released in summer and releases *Urban legend* which goes platinum.
2005:
August: Establishes publishing deal with Warner/Chappell for Grand Hustle Music to sign artist to publishing deals.
September: Performs VH1's Hip-Hop Honors. Wins *Vibe* magazine's Street Anthem award for single *U Don't Know Me*. Releases T.I. Presents the P$C debut CD *25 to Life* in stores. Headlines Boost Mobile's RockCorps concert at Radio City.
October: Performs his own set at Jay-Z's sold-out "I Declare War" concert, where Jay reunites with longtime for Nas.
November: Goes on six-week Georgia Power Tour circuit. Nominated for two Grammys: best rap/song collaboration for Destiny's Child *Soldier* and best rap solo performance for *U Don't Know Me*. Also, nominated for rap artist of the year at 2005 Billboard Music Awards.
December: Early recording for *King* are leaked onto Internet, developing an instant buzz among fans. T.I. refuses to include any leaked songs on album and records all new material.
2006:
January: Releases DJ Drama's *Gangsta Grillz Mixtape: The Leak* to whet the appetite of fans and to combat piracy.
March: Releases fourth album *King* and first feature film *ATL* the same week. Album hits #1 on Billboard Top R&B/Hip-Hop Albums chart and *ATL* charts #3 at the box office.
April: *King* reaches #1 on The Billboard 200 chart {{108 Crosley, Hillary 2006;}}.

Figure 6.5

The band, Tool's album, *10,000 Days*, also takes measures to combat piracy with a value-added approach. Tool doesn't sell their material through iTunes, and the latest release is "purely a CD," although it's an elaborate one. Tool is known for their songs being quite long. (The single, Vicarious, is six minutes long, and they don't rely on pop airplay.) So the CD is 77 minutes of music with a wraparound hardcover case; the booklet is printed stereoscopically, with lenses built into the cover {{109 Sanneh, Kelefa 2006;}}

Videos were once considered an essential part of the marketing campaign. In fact, according Denisoff in his book "Tarnished Gold," in 1984, 68% of survey respondents indicated that they purchased the record after viewing it on MTV, and only 63% of respondents indicated that they purchased the record after listening to it on the radio. MTV claimed that it was the number one vehicle for record recognition among buyer (over radio). However, this is no longer true. Later studies showed that overwhelmingly, radio was the first contact that buyers had to new product. In fact, it was reported in *Billboard Magazine* in August, 1997 that according to Strategic Record Research, 80% of record buyers said that radio influenced them to buy the record. Seeing the video only influenced 43% of the record buyers. This is also no longer true. Today the elements of both the New Media campaign and Direct Marketing aspects have become the essential keys to success and for most artists, video plays a lesser of a role.

HAS A SINGLE BEEN CHOSEN?

Choosing the first single to be released off of a record is not a scientific process. Companies usually have a weekly meeting to decide what is to be released and when. Obviously, the A&R department plays the biggest role in the decision, but company administrators also like to get their egos in on the decision. In fact, Clive Davis, former president of Arista Records has been involved in choosing singles and editing down album cuts for single release since his reign as President of Columbia Records forty years ago. Release meetings may also include personnel from the marketing and merchandising departments.

A fierce battle can occur if the artist's manager and the A&R department do not agree on the release schedule of the singles. It is the manager's responsibility to convince the A&R department that the single s/he and the artist want to be released, is the same single that they have chosen. If the manager muscles the company and wins the battle but the project loses priority status, the artist may lose the war as the company's interest in the project may be jeopardized. Consequently, the strength of the manager's persuasive skills may be of extreme importance.

HAS FANBASE BEEN DEVELOPED AND ACTIVATED?

Success is converting the passive fan into the fanatic fan. Fans must be made to feel special. The artist must connect with the fans in creative ways. Daily blogs are important. Free giveaways are essential. Developing a presence on the community websites increases a fan's interest.

IS THE RECORD MOVING UP THE CHARTS?

The recording industry measures success quantitatively. How high up the charts did it go? How much airplay did it receive? And ultimately, how many recordings and downloads did it receive. Therefore the goal of the marketing campaign is to monitize the fanbase. The key to the bottom line of project is for a the objectives of the campaign to be met.

Record companies believe that airplay is one of the keys to exposure. Many industry studies have shown a strong correlation between heavy radio listeners and buyers and down-loaders. Airplay is the job of the promotion department.

Record promotion is handled either in-house by the company's staff field promotion people, or by an independent record promotion person hired by the company or the artist's manager. On line promotion is accomplished by having an active fanbase that blogs, talks, and listens to the recording.

E-commerce is playing a greater role as a revenue producer for the labels (see chapter four and five and previous paragraphs in this chapter) and is handled by the New Media department at the label. Legal downloads through the iTunes store and other services are only a part of the revenue pot. Many labels have also added Strategic Marketing departments to create e-commerce campaigns (more in other parts of book).

So what happens if the record isn't "growing legs?" Does the manager scream at the record company to get "on" the record? Does the promotion department hire a few "indies" to work the record? If the promotion department doesn't do enough to increase the record's airplay, does the manager hire an indie? Does the artist increase his/her web publicity activities? Can the fanbase be better activated? Does the manager start calling radio stations to try to increase airplay? Does someone hound the video channels for more exposure? Is a deal made with itunes? Does the company's field merchandising staff push for in-store (BestBuy, Target, Walmart) airplay? The answer is one or all of the above…. plus anything else that can be thought of. Few singles have ever received a second chance to become a hit. Few artists have ever been given priority status in a company after recording a "dog."

HAS FEEDBACK BEEN POSITIVE?

The old adage, "any publicity is better than no publicity" is still true. However, lukewarm feedback does a record little good. Although it has been reported that less than eight percent of record buyers are influenced by record reviews, the industry still enjoys positive responses. Because the company has relatively little control of the media, the marketing campaign spends a great deal of the artist's money giving free publicity paraphernalia to whom it considers influential people. Their stamp of approval gives the record and the artist credibility, and once they publicly announce their approval of artist's work, additional positive responses are expected. Today, the stamp of approval by the artist's fanbase is most important factor. If feedback has not been positive, the record company should alter the promotional and publicity activities to induce the kind of feedback that is needed. This usually requires additional financial commitments by the company, which, of course, is ultimately the artist's money.

In 2005, *myspace.com* became extremely influential in exposing music to its community of users. On a daily basis, record labels are all over the site checking out the responses to music being talked about by millions. One major label A&R guy told this writer that it is the first site that industry A&R people look for a buzz about unsigned artists. Today all the community sites are constantly monitored. This ground swell approach by the consumers/listeners validates the credibility of the artist. The importance of converting fans cannot be over emphasized.

HAS FEEDBACK BEEN POSITIVE?

This s really the third time the same question has been voiced in the chart, and doing all that can be done to make the campaign a success can not be emphasized too strongly. If the recording has not grown its own legs, it is probably time to release another single and fine-tune the campaign. If the artist's manager was very insistent on the choice of the first single and it was a dog, no matter what the reason was (ie; lack of promotion), his/her power is now diminished and A&R will have the upper hand in choosing this one. Hopefully this new activity will generate action on the chart.

WHERE THE MONEY GOES

Keeping track of the recording budget during the recording is the responsibility of the A&R administration department. Record companies use a *Recording Authorization Form* to keep track of the expense. Each line item is estimated at the time the recording proposal is submitted. When the budget is approved by the Vice President of A& R, the artist and manager or producer must seek to have budget re-approved if additional funds are needed. Therefore, estimates should be made as accurately as possible. Some of the typical expense categories found in most *Recording Authorization Forms* are listed below. They are:

- producer fee

- artist advance

- AFM payment

- AFTRA payment

- travel/hotel

- per diem

- Studio time

- mixdown time

- engineer fee

- tape

- rental instruments

- misc.

- unforeseen expenses

For example, let's assume the studio time for an initial recording of a rock group is estimated as requiring 200 hours of studio time (24 track) @@$250 per hour including the mixdown and engineer. Tape costs are minimal because most studios use ProTools instead. AFM and AFTRA payments to a four member group might be $5000 plus additional studio musicians and instrument rental is another $4000. The producer might have a fee of $50,000 plus accommodations for everyone is another $10,000, and miscellaneous expenses could equal $5000. The bottom line of the Recording Authorization form could read $100,000 without any waste. Additional money might also have been spent on recording one or several videos totally $200,000, plus additional advance incentive money of $75,000.

Therefore it would not be outrageous for a new artist to be in debt to the record company for approximately $300,000+ on the day the record is released.

Remember these expenses are all charge-backs that are recoupable out of the artist's royalty account and paid back or credited to the record company out of record sales before the artist realizes any royalty checks. Consequently, the artist and his/her manager should be very interested in the number of records (units) that must be sold in order to bring the artist's royalty account out of the red and back to zero. Or, in other words, what is the break-even sales point.

To understand this, let's use the example that the artist's royalty rate is 12% of the retail list price (superstars may demand a 15% + rate). Let's use a retail list price of $13.98 and multiply this figure by 12%. The answer is $1.68. $1.68 will be credited to the artist's royalty account for every record sold. To find the break-even point for the artist we need to calculate how many $1.68s (or albums sold) will equal $300,000. So by dividing $300,000 by $1.68 we arrive at 178,571 albums (units) must be sold in order for the artist's royalty account to break-even.

$13.98 (retail list price)
x .12 (royalty rate)
$ 1.68

$300,000 divided by 1.68 = 178,671 units

Although this is an incredible number of records to sell before the artist sees any royalties, the calculations are a bit more complex than this, and the number of records that need to be sold is even greater. We need to calculate various account allowances and adjustments. For example,

Packaging Allowances are deducted from the royalty base as a percentage. The record company may seek a package or container allowance as high as 25%. Along standing pet argument of this author's has been the packaging allowance. Isn't normal packaging just part of the cost of manufacturing records? If an artist doesn't ask for anything out of the ordinary, why is a packaging allowance debited to the royalty account? Wouldn't a similar example be if you were charged extra for the standard tires on a new car? If the artist is going to be charged, shouldn't the record company give the artist the right to shop for packaging by an independent company? However, attorneys say that packaging allowances are nonnegotiable.

For many years, record companies charged a **CD Reduction** rate of 20% through a New Media Reduction Clause in the contract. However, for this example, let's assume a 25% packaging allowance, and not calculate a reduction rate.

The **Free Goods Allowance** is usually 10-15%. Stated another way: "of every 100 albums shipped, 15 will be royalty fee." Some companies add a clause that states that they will pay on 85% of the records shipped and some companies use 90%. When attorneys approach this clause with the argument that it replaces the free goods allowance clause, some companies deny it. Executing both clauses would allow the record company to pay 85% of 85% (which has occurred) before the packaging allowance! For this example let's assume 15%.

The industry is not standardized on its use of several contractual terms. For example, some companies do not use the term wholesale price, but choose to use the term "normal retail channels." **Royalty base** is another confusing term. For our purposes, we'll define it as **the percentage of the retail list price on which the royalty rate is based, after all allowances and deductions.**

Now we can calculate the artist's royalty amount more accurately by using the royalty base and the royalty rate figures. If we subtract 25% for packaging and 15% for free goods from a royalty base retail list price of $13.98, the answer is $8.39. The artist's royalty rate is 12% of the retail list price, however, to calculate, we must multiply 12% by the adjusted list price of $8.39. The artist's royalty rate is really $1.01 on every record sold. Now if we divide $300,000 by $1.01 we arrive at 297,030 albums (units) must be sold in order for the artist's royalty account to break-even.

The calculation is as follows:

1. **retail list price x (royalty base or 100% - allowances) = adjusted retail list price**

2. **adjusted retail list price x artist royalty rate = royalty per unit**

3. **royalty account debit / royalty per unit = break even number**

Although we will not go into other scenarios here, there could be further allowances deducted from the original royalty base. For instance, a breakage allowance, the New Media reduction rate, and/or a "Special Marketing Discount" is common, or the addition of a producer's cut in an "all in deal." (The royalty rate on digital product may be different, see Chapter Seven).

THE RECORD COMPANY'S SHARE

Using a wholesale price of $8.39 and subtracting the $1.01 royalty to the artist per unit, there remains $7.38 that the record company receives. Out the remaining $7.38 manufacturing costs, distribution costs, mechanical royalties, and union benefits must be paid.

Let's use as an example a ten-song recording, and the record company will pay a 25% percent reduction from the statutory rate, currently at $.091 per song, on negotiated mechanical licenses, which equals $0.68 (without a mechanical royalty ceiling). Add to this a manufacturing cost of $.75 (or less). Subtract the $1.43 from $7.38 and the company is left with $5.95.

By law, record companies must contribute to two American Federation of Musicians (AFM) funds. They must contribute about $.05 to the Special Payments Fund, and about $.03 to the Music Performance Trust Fund (if it still exists). The record company may also have to contribute a lump sum to the vocalists' union, the American Federation of Television and Radio Artists (AFTRA). For our example let's assume that it contributes $2000, which we will compute in a moment. If we subtract $.08 from the remaining $5.95 we are left with $5.88.

If we multiply $5.88 x 297.030 (the number of units that must be sold for the artist to break-even) we arrive at $1,746,536. Now subtract a $2000 AFTRA payment and we have $1,744,536 as the amount the record company receives. (Incidentally, to calculate the number of units the record company needs to sell to breakeven, we would divide the $300,000 advanced the artist by the net wholesale price of $5.88. The answer is 51,020 units.) However, this is not all profit for the company. Promotion and advertising expenses must be subtracted from this, as well as a portion of the general overhead and operating costs. Another way of looking at was summed up in the 8th edition of the Music Business Handbook:

> A typical major-label record contract grants the artist between 12% and 15% [the author believes that this is a misprint and the calculation should be on 24% and 30% in this example] of the wholesale price of the record, which has ranged between $10 and $17 for much of the last 25 years. But contracts had numerous provisions that reduced the artist's share of the revenue, including often vague "reserves" held to cover the cost of unsold albums returned to the label by retailers, as much as 20%. Furthermore, of the artist's royalty points, both record producer and artist management typically participate, often with as much as 3% each. An RIAA-certified Gold record (500,000 units) theoretically generates $5.5 million, with each point worth $55,000. But paying back the recoupable cost of recording and other expenses are largely the artist's responsibility. Even assuming that half the theoretical revenue was netted after costs, each of those points in now worth $27,500. A five-member band splitting the net proceeds would earn less than $50,000each, before taxes {{111 Baskerville, David 2006;}}.

Figures 6.6, 6.7, & 6.8 illustrate where the money goes from the sale of a traditional recording, digital download, and master ringtones. With well over 90% of the records released never regaining their recording costs, superstars and catalog product have big jobs in the record business. They must deliver the multi-platinum sellers that pay the bills for all the "stiffs." This also illustrates the reasons why music entertainment companies are seeking revenue from a multitude of sources. As CD sales continue to decline, new and different revenue streams must continue to be explored and nurtured. Always remain aware that record companies are in the business for one reason, to sell product! For the traditional recording, if mechanical license fees and union fees are added to the manufacturing cost, the revenue percentages are still applicable (from the 3rd edition of this text).

Revenue Cuts on a Recording

artist royalty	14%
record com.	35%
manufacturing	6%
distribution	10%
retail	35%

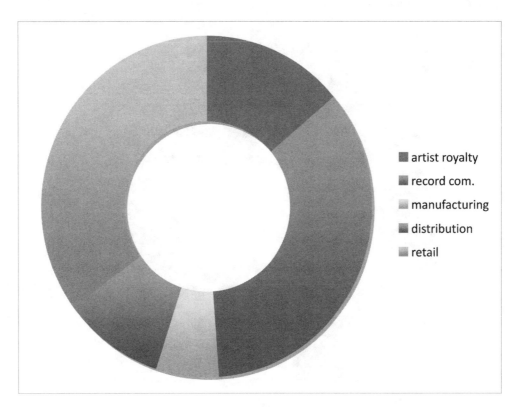

Figure 6.6.

Digital Downloads (%)

label	50
artist	11
publisher	8
service provide	14
distributor	10
bandwidth	2
creditcard	5

Figure 6.7. {{110Bruno,Anthony 2005:}}

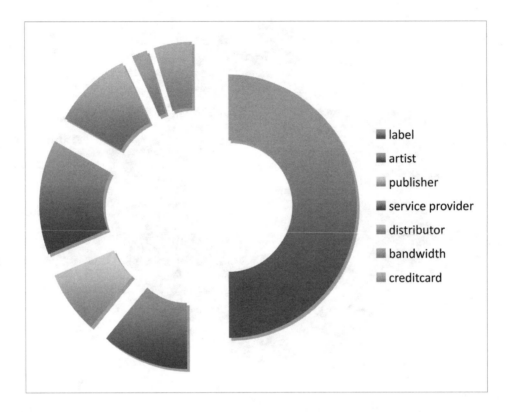

Figure 6.7.

BREAKDOWN OF MASTERTONE FEES

There is sobriety in math. This is a very likely scenario of how the finances will play out. Although prices for ringtones may go down--making a fixed fee more desirable--there is no guarantee that they will not go up. (All amounts below are rounded)

Prior To New Ruling:

$3.00 – typical (high-side) cost to consumer. ($1.99 to $3.99 per mastertone) X 45% (total typical bundled license paid to labels by phone companies. Percentage may vary +/- 5%) - $1.35 (Gross to labels) - 36 cents (12% Publisher's share) - 12 cents (4% PROs) - 45 cents (Artist's share @ 15% of SRLP) - 10 cents (aggregator and other delivery charges) ------------------

Net to labels: 32 cents.

Net to top-line artists under most recording contracts: 45 cents.

Net to publishers: 20 cents.

Net to writers under most publishing contracts: **16 cents.*** Plus any additional income filtered through PRO collections to writers & publishers—maybe another 1 penny each.

Under New Ruling: (If The Current Statuary Rates Apply and PROs are Excluded)

Net to labels: 71 cents. ($1.35 minus payments only to artist and aggregators and 9 cents to publishers)

Net to top-line artists under most recording contracts: 45 cents.

Net to publishers: 5.5 cents.

Net to writers under most publishing contracts: **3.5 cents.***

Publishers typically deduct 10% for administrative fees and then split revenue 50/50 with writers.

Figure 6.8 {{168 Avalon, Moses 2006;}}

SUMMARY

1. Record Companies are becoming Music Entertainment Companies.

2. The relationship of the artist and his/her record company is a business relationship and an emotional one.

3. The record company manufactures, releases, promotes, and distributes the artist's works, but also acts as a financial backer.

4. The three types of advances given to an artist under contract are: personal advance, production advance, and bonus advance.

5. The types of record companies include: major, independent, specialty, and boutique.

6. The major record companies own their own distribution networks.

7. A record company has creative divisions and business/administrative divisions.

8. Record companies demand masters that are "commercially acceptable".

9. A product flows through the record departments in an organized manner.

10. New business models are creating new and additional revenue streams for the company and their artists, these are called 360 Deals.

11. The artist's royalty account is credited after all record company expenses are met.

PROJECTS

1. Set up a record company in class and ask individual students to list the responsibilities of each department.

2. Create a listening party in class. Have students listen to a new release and as they represent various departments of the company, formulate a marketing plan.

3. Design several 360 Deals and complete the computation.

CHAPTER SEVEN
THE RECORDING CONTRACT

"Astute artist attorneys recognize that having key record company executives excited by an artist's music and committed to breaking the artist in the marketplace is far more important than specific contractual guarantees, particularly if the guarantees being requested are of dubious practical value."

Michael J. Pollack, V.P. and General Counsel, Arista Records.

Billboard Magazine. July 23, 1988.

BY THE END OF THIS CHAPTER YOU SHOULD BE ABLE TO:

1. Intelligently discuss every clause of the example agreements in this chapter.
2. When given different examples contract, transfer what you have studied in this chapter to the corresponding clauses of the new contract and discuss its content.
3. Discuss the current royalty rates and revenue streams negotiated in new artist recording contracts.
4. Discuss the "new" business models currently being employed.

The brass ring

The major leagues

The big time

The beginning

(What follows is the model that existed in the industry since the beginning of the business. Although there are new business models in play today, some artists, particularly new artists, fit the description that existing labels look for. A form of the 360 Deal is what the majority of labels request, however in some cases, the actually "standard" recording contract is still employed.)

All these phrases describe what securing a long-term royalty artist recording contract from a nationally distributed label means to an artist. It also means that the artist is no longer just a local or regional phenomenon. In fact, it is the most important goal of any new artist, and the payoff to years of practicing, rehearsing, and also performing in the endless number of beer joints and at nondescript fraternity parties. It is a payoff…. a payoff that very few musicians ever receive.

However, it is also the beginning. It's the beginning of a career. It is the chance to be idolized by the hometown musicians. This is the chance for the artist to be respected by his or her parents and relatives. But most importantly, it is the chance for the artist to perform original material in his or her own unique style, and not be required to work another job to pay the bills!

Then why do so many artists blow their chance? Many artists are dropped by labels after only one release, and play out their "careers" performing their "hit" in hotel cocktail lounges. Actually a "stiff" is not always the artist's fault. However, the consequence is the same.

When selecting an artist for a long-term royalty agreement, what does a company look for? What is the selection criteria used by a company's A&R staff? How does an A&R rep. judge the value of the artist in the marketplace six to nine months (the minimum amount of time needed to negotiate a contract with a major label and complete the recording of an album) after he or she is convinced that the artist is worthy of a deal?

These are some of the usual answers. "Intuition!" "It's just a feeling I have about the artist and the songs." "You can feel the electricity in the air when he or she performs." "He or she is a unique talent." None of this offers any insight for the unsigned musician. However, some helpful criteria might be:

1. charisma — The magnetic quality of a personality.

2. stage-presence — The artist's command of an audience.

3. uniqueness — Is the artist new or different?

4. worth in the marketplace — Is the artist and his or her music a saleable commodity? And for how long?

There are many ways a new artist may attempt to secure a recording contract. Here are some:

1. The artist makes a demo recording and the manager or an attorney tries to secure a deal (shops the demo).

2. The artist locates a producer and makes a demo recording and the producer (or the production company) shops the demo (an all-in deal).

3. The artist, with or without a producer, makes a demo or master recording and shops the master.

4. The artist is signed with and indie and makes a deal with a major for distribution.

5. The artist records and makes a distribution deal with a label.

6. The artist decides to release digital only product through internet portals and becomes essentially a label

7. The artist put up his/her music on a website and a community of consumers validates the music and a label becomes interested in signing the artist.

8. The artist signs with an entertainment entity that offers the artist one of many types of partnerships with an independent record label

When securing a recording contract, it is generally not a good idea for an artist to be tied to a not so well-known producer (as a third party). This may hinder any attempt to record or re-record with an established producer until someone offers to buy the original producer out of the deal. Upon signing, major labels like the artist to be as free and clear of any side deals.

THE CHANGING DEALS

THE MAJORS

By now most people have heard of the Robbie Williams/EMI record deal and the Korn/EMI deal where for a large guaranteed advance, these artists have agreed to allow the record label recoup money advanced from a variety of revenue streams (360 Deals). Other deals on the table these days are presented by independent labels that offer artists a bigger piece of the royalty pie, provided that the artist is willing pay for some of the cost of the recording (see Chapters Five and Six). And new deals are being offered, "as we speak."

Ironically, these "one revenue pot" deals were being offered to artists as late as the 1970s. Robert Stigwood had an even broader "across the board" deal with The Bee Gees which included management, publishing, record company, agent, and promoter (see Chapter Twelve). It's been said that Brian Epstein had a similar arrangement with The Beatles. Although to this author's knowledge the Williams and Korn contracts are not in circulation (it's been reported that EMI receives 30% of Korn's revenue streams), two aspects are very important:

1. The label's share of the money. The label is getting paid directly from the concert promoter and/or agent. The labels are aware that with the check in the bank they have the control and leverage. The same holds true for publishing, merchandising, and new media collections

2. Term of the agreement. The term may be shorter and is in direct proportion to the label's calculations of the length of time needed to recoup the substantial advances.

Here are some of the ways in which the major labels are directly asking for pieces of the artist's revenue streams:

1. Labels are asking for permission to advertise, license and sell label-created merchandise on official artist websites.

2. Labels are asking for control of licensing of album artwork that incorporates the artist's name and likeness. The split is not 50-50 as in the past, and some new artists may receive as little as 12%.

3. Labels are asking for a portion of tour and/or merchandise revenue.

4. Labels are requiring some artists to create royalty free new products for the mobile communications market, such as voice tones, ring backs, and electronic wallpaper for computer screens.

5. Labels are increasing the percentage of expenditures that are recoupable

{{112 Milom Esq., Michael 2006;}}

TWO INDIES

Founded by Kevin Lyman and Bob Chiappardi, Warcon Enterprises deal, includes recording, publishing, touring and merchandising operations. Here are the essentials of their deal:

1. Warcon and its acts will split profits from recordings 50/50 after marketing costs.

2. Warcon will receive 25% of publishing revenue.

3. Acts will keep revenue from merchandising and touring until it goes into the black, then Warcon will get a small share tht will increase as the profit grows.

4. Warcon will own master recordings, however, it will also accept a distribution-only deal.

5. Warcon will give 5% of its annual profit to its roster, with allotments based on sales {{113 Christman, Ed 2005;}}

According to Mike Kraski, President of Equity Music Group, the contract is "partnership based." The outline of his deal is as follows:

1. 50/50 share of revenue that includes recordings, merchandise, and touring

2. artist keeps 100% of publishing revenue

3. only charge back is recording costs

4. artist owns master {{114 Kraski, Mike 2005;}}.

A MANAGEMENT/ENTERTAINMENT COMPANY

Rob Kos of DoyleKos Entertainment says that they offer their artists a "pass through" deal, where they pass through to the artist what is received from RED Distribution from the sale of recordings after taking a 10% commission. DK Records offers no advance and the artist funds the recording costs. This setup works great for artists that do not rely on airplay and have a fan base that locate the new releases as physical product and on websites. The splits are roughly as follows (Interview with Rob Kos, November 3, 2005, New York, NY):

18.98	List Price
12.04	Wholesale Price
- .60	Discount 5%
11.44	
-4.32	RED Dist Fee 20% + DK Records 10%
7.12	
-1.00	Manufacturing Cost
6.12	
-2.00	Co-op Advertising
4.12	**Artist Revenue**

(Other models appear elsewhere in text.)

THE CONTRACTS

What follows are actual recording contracts. The first is an actual first draft recording contract submitted to a new artist by a major recording company in 2001 that was published in the 3rd edition of this book. Upon examination of a contract issued by a different major in 2005, the author decided that the similarities were so significant that only a few new and different clauses needed to be included. These clauses are clearly identified. Also included are my editorial comments.

MAJOR LABEL:

RECORDING CONTRACT FORM

AGREEMENT made as of this _____ day of _____, 200__, by and between
_____, {address} (hereinafter "Company"), and
_____ {address} (hereinafter "you").

*Many attorneys suggest that the **definitions** section of the contract, in this case **Section 19**, be read and understood before trying to understand the rest of the agreement.*

1. SERVICES.

1.01   During the term of this Agreement (the "Term") you will render your exclusive services as a performing artist for the purpose of making Master Recordings for Company, you will cause those Master Recordings to be produced, and you will Deliver those Master Recordings to Company, as provided in this Agreement. (You are sometimes called "the Artist" below; all references in this agreement to "you and the Artist," and the like, will be understood to refer to you alone.)

Your obligations will include furnishing the services of the producers of those Master Recordings and all other third parties rendering services in connection with those Master Recordings, subject to the terms of this Agreement, and you will be solely responsible for engaging and paying them.

This agreement is known as an "all in royalty" deal, meaning that the artist will supply the producer for the recordings and is responsible for paying him or her. Therefore the royalty rate reflects this.

2. TERM.

2.01   The Term shall consist of an Initial Period and of the Option Periods (defined below) for which Company shall have exercised the options hereafter provided. The Initial Period and each Option Period are each hereafter sometimes referred to as a "Contract Period". The Initial Period shall commence on the date hereof and shall continue until the earlier of the dates referred to in paragraphs (a) and (b) immediately below:

> (a) the date twelve (12) months after the Delivery to Company, as defined in paragraph 19.09 below, of the fully equalized, digital tape Masters to be used in manufacturing the Phonograph Record units to be made for distribution in the United States from the last Master Recordings made in fulfillment of your Recording Commitment for the Contract Period concerned under Article 3 below; or

> (b) the date nine (9) months after the initial commercial release in the United States of the Album required to be delivered in fulfillment of your Recording Commitment for the Contract Period concerned; but will not end earlier than one (1) year after the date of its commencement.

Clause 2.01 describes the contract period of the term of the agreement, which in this case reads twelve months. However, the beginning of the term occurs on the earlier of the two dates describe in (a) or (b).

2.02

(a) You grant Company _____ (___) separate options to extend that Term for additional Contract Periods ("Option Periods") on the same terms and conditions, except as otherwise provided herein. Company may exercise each of those options by sending you a written notice not later than the expiration date of the Contract Period which is then in effect (the "Current Contract Period"). If Company exercises such an option, the Option Period concerned will begin immediately after the end of the Current Contract Period and shall continue until the earlier of the dates referred to in paragraphs 2.01 (a) and (b) above.

(b) Notwithstanding anything to the contrary contained in this Article 2, if Company has not exercised its option to extend the Term for a further Contract Period as of the date on which the Current Contract Period would otherwise expire, the following shall apply:

(i) You shall send Company written notice (an "Option Warning") that its option has not yet been exercised.

(ii) Company shall have the right to exercise such option at any time until the date ten (10) business days after its receipt of the Option Warning (the "Extension Period").

(iii) The Current Contract Period shall continue until either the end of the Extension Period, or Company's notice (the "Termination Notice") to you that Company does not wish to exercise such option, whichever is sooner.

(iv) For avoidance of doubt, nothing herein shall limit Company's right to send a Termination Notice to you at any time, nor limit Company's right to exercise an option at any time if you fail to send Company an Option Warning in accordance with (i) above.

Record companies negotiate from the position that, the more option periods to extend the contract, the better. It gives them an easy way to move to the option periods. However, if the artist is unsuccessful, a longer contract will not force the record company to allow the artist to record, or release any product.

In the third line of 2.02a after "sending you a notice," the phrase 90 days, or 60 days, or at least 30 days prior to the expiration date may be inserted. The artist should have the right to know whether the record company is going to exercise the option period before it expires, in order to have time to shop for another deal. Usually, record companies are not willing to change this clause.

In (b) (i) the responsibility is on the artist to notify the company that they have not exercised the option, and then they have ten days to rectify the situation. However, if you fail to send the notice, the company can still drop you!

3. RECORDING COMMITMENT.

3.01   Your Recording Commitment hereunder is as follows. During the Initial Period you shall record and you shall deliver to Company one (1) Album. During each Option Period you shall record and you shall deliver to Company one (1) Album. The Albums delivered hereunder in fulfillment of your Recording Commitment are sometimes referred to collectively herein as the "Committed Albums" and individually as a "Committed Album". The Committed Albums are sometimes herein called the "First Album", the "Second Album", the "Third Album", the "Fourth Album", the "Fifth Album" and the "Sixth Album", respectively, in order of their Delivery to Company.

This contract is really a one-album deal.

3.02   You shall deliver to Company the Album constituting your Recording Commitment for a Contract Period no later than ninety (90) days after the commencement of that Contract Period.

It would better serve the artist if the three-month period was longer, and extended to, for example, at least five months.

4. RECORDING PROCEDURES.

4.01   You shall designate and submit to Company for Company's approval the producer of each of the Masters, all other individuals rendering services in connection with the recording of those Masters, the Musical Compositions or other Selections or materials which shall be embodied in those Masters, the studios at which those Masters shall be recorded, and the dates of recording of those Masters (the "Recording Elements"). You shall also prepare and submit to Company in writing for Company's approval a recording budget for those Masters in such detail as Company shall require (the "Recording Budget") at least fourteen (14) days before the planned commencement of recording. You shall advise Company of the content of each medley before it is recorded. Company shall not be deemed to be unreasonable in rejecting any request to begin recording any Album which is a part of the Recording Commitment within six (6) months after the Delivery of a prior Album under this agreement. The scheduling and booking of all studio time will be done by Company. No recording sessions shall be commenced nor shall any commitments be made or costs incurred hereunder with respect to any Masters until and unless Company shall have approved in writing each Recording Element and the Recording Budget for those Masters. If Company shall disapprove the Recording Budget submitted by you, then Company's decision shall be final.

This agreement is known as an "all in royalty" deal, meaning that the artist will supply the producer for the recordings and is responsible for paying him or her. Other costs are also your responsibility.

4.02

(a) You shall notify the appropriate Local of the American Federation of Musicians in advance of each recording session.

(b) You will comply with the following procedures in connection with the requirements of the U.S. Immigration Law:

(1) Before each recording session:

(i) You will require each background instrumentalist, background vocalist, and other person to be employed in connection with the session to complete and sign the EMPLOYEE INFORMATION AND VERIFICATION ("employee") section of a U.S. Immigration and Naturalization Service Employment Eligibility Certificate (Form I-9), unless you have already obtained such a Certificate from the person concerned within the past three (3) years;

(ii) You will complete and sign the EMPLOYER REVIEW AND VERIFICATION ("employer") section of each such Certificate; and

(iii) You will attach copies of the documents establishing identity and employment eligibility which you examine in accordance with the instructions in the employer section.

If any such person is engaged during a session you will comply with subsections (i) through (iii) above, with respect to that person, before (s)he renders any services.

(2) You will not permit any such person who fails to complete the employee section, or to furnish you with the required documentation, to render any services in connection with Recordings to be made under this agreement.

These clauses that use the terms employer and employee allow the record company to maintain its copyright claim as the artist is employed on a "work for hire" basis.

(3) You will deliver those Certificates and documents to Company promptly, and in no event later than the Delivery of the Recordings concerned.

(4) You will comply with any revised or additional verification and documentation requirements of which Company advises you in the future.

(c) As and when required by Company, you shall allow Company's representatives to attend any or all recording sessions hereunder.

(d) You shall timely supply Company with all of the information Company needs in order: (i) to make payments due in connection with such Recordings; (ii) to comply with any other obligations Company may have in connection with the making of such Master Recordings; and (iii) to prepare to release Phonograph Records derived from such Master Recordings. Without limiting the generality of clause (ii) of the preceding sentence:

(A) You shall furnish Company with all information Company requires to comply with its obligations under Company's union agreements, including, without limitation, the following:

(1) If a session is held to record new tracks intended to be mixed with existing tracks (and if such information is requested by the American Federation of Musicians), the dates and places of the prior sessions at which such existing tracks were made, and the AFM Phonograph Recording Contract (Form "B") number(s) covering such sessions;

(2) Each change of title of any composition listed in an AFM Phonograph Recording Contract (Form "B"); and

(3) A listing of all the musical selections contained in Recordings Delivered to Company hereunder; and

(B) You will furnish Company with all of the immigration control documentation required by subparagraph 4.01(b) above, at the same time as the AFM or AFTRA session reports, tax withholding forms, and other documentation required by us in order to make the payments to the session musicians and other employees concerned, if any.

(e)

(i) All Master Recordings shall be recorded under Company's current Phonograph Record Labor Contract with the AFM; all musicians who render services in connection with the recording of such Master Recordings (including instrumentalists, if any) will be paid by Company, on your behalf, the scale set forth in the said Labor Contract; and Company, on your behalf, shall pay the required contributions to the Pension Welfare Fund.

(ii) All AFTRA members whose performances are embodied in the Master Recordings will be paid by Company, on your behalf, the rates applicable under the current AFTRA Code of Fair Practices for Phonograph Recordings. Company shall, on your behalf, if necessary, also pay to the AFTRA Pension and Welfare Fund any contribution required to be made under the AFTRA Code based on compensation to other performers whose performances are embodied on the applicable Master Recordings recorded hereunder.

(iii) The foregoing representations and warranties are included for the benefit, respectively, of the AFM, AFTRA, and the AFM and AFTRA members whose performances are embodied in the applicable Master Recordings, and for the benefit of Company, and may be enforced by AFM and/or AFTRA or their respective designees, as the case may be, and by Company.

(iv) You shall furnish or shall cause the applicable Producer to furnish Company with copies of all union contracts and/or union session reports so that all payments may be made by Company, on your behalf, in a timely fashion to the proper parties thereunder; and if you fail to do so with the result that Company is required to pay any penalty sum for making a late payment under the applicable union agreements, such payments shall be a direct debt from you to Company which, in addition to any other remedy Company may have, Company may recover from any monies otherwise payable to you.

4.03

(a) You shall deliver to Company the Masters promptly after their completion. All original session tapes and any derivatives or reproductions thereof shall be delivered to Company concurrently, or, at Company's election, maintained at a recording studio or other location designated by Company, in Company's name and subject to Company's control. Each Master shall be subject to Company's approval as commercially and technically satisfactory for the manufacture and sale of Phonograph Records, and, upon Company's request, you shall re-record any Musical Composition or other Selection until a Master commercially and technically satisfactory to Company has been obtained.

Every artist would love to change the phrase to only technically satisfactory. The issue is creative control and the record company will not give it up. However, superstars may be able to negotiate this, thereby giving the record company only the right to make certain that it is acceptable for airing on radio, but a new artist would not stand a chance.

(b) You shall Deliver to Company fully mixed, edited, and unequalized and equalized Master Recordings (including but not limited to a final two-track equalized tape copy), commercially satisfactory to Company for its manufacture and sale of Phonograph Records, and all original and duplicate Master Recordings of the material recorded, together with (i) the multi-track tape and three (3) safety copies thereof; (ii) all necessary licenses and permissions; (iii) all materials required to be furnished by you to Company for use in the packaging and marketing of the Records, including without limitation, complete "label copy" information with respect to such Master Recordings; such "label copy" shall include, without limitation (A) the title, recording dates, timing, publisher(s) songwriter(s), performer(s) and composer(s) of each musical composition embodied on the Master Recordings; (B) the producer(s) thereof; and (C) any other credit and information that is to appear on the labels, liners and packaging of Records embodying such Master Recordings; (iv) all "sideman" and any third party clearances and consents, including, without limitation, all written consents in connection with Embodied Copyrighted Materials (as defined in paragraph 13.04(a) below), together with your written warranty and representation, in a form satisfactory to Company, that you have obtained for Company the unrestricted right to exploit the Master Recording(s) concerned; (v) a document, in a form satisfactory to Company, signed by the producer of the Master Recording(s) concerned which confirms Company's ownership of such Master Recording(s) in accordance with the provisions of Article 6 hereof; (vi) all mechanical and first-use licenses for each musical composition embodied in the Master Recording at the rate specified herein; and (vii) all liner notes, approved artwork, and credits for all configurations of records

(c) You further agree to irrevocably direct in writing the person who has possession of any and all tapes of masters or digital masters recorded hereunder that all such tapes and masters are Company's property and that such person shall be obligated to deliver such tapes and masters to Company upon its written request.

4.04   Each Master shall embody the Artist's performance as the sole featured artist of a single Musical Composition previously unrecorded by the Artist and shall be recorded in its entirety in a recording studio. No Masters shall be recorded in whole or in part at live concerts or other live performances unless an authorized officer of Company agrees to the contrary in writing. Each Committed Album shall embody no fewer than forty (40) minutes in playing time and containing no fewer than eight (8) and no more than ten (10) Musical Compositions unless Company otherwise agrees to the contrary in writing. You shall not record or deliver hereunder, nor shall Company be obligated to accept, Masters constituting a Multiple Album. However, if you shall do so and Company shall accept those Masters hereunder, then, at Company's election, for the purpose of calculating the number of Masters recorded and delivered hereunder, those Masters shall be deemed to be only one (1) Album. Masters delivered hereunder shall not contain selections designed to appeal to specialized or limited markets including, but not limited to gospel, Christmas and/or children's music.

The record company will not accept a recording of a live performance, or any old recording as fulfilling the recording commitment. Only compositions recorded specifically for the commitment will be considered.

4.05   Any Masters which are not recorded or delivered in all respects in accordance with the terms hereof shall not, unless Company otherwise consents in writing, apply towards the fulfillment of your Recording Commitment. Furthermore, if Company shall make any payments with respect to any Master which shall not have been recorded or delivered in all respects in accordance with the terms hereof, you shall, upon Company's demand, pay to Company the amount thereof and Company may, without limiting Company's other rights and remedies, deduct that amount from any monies payable by Company hereunder or any other agreement between you and Company or Company's affiliates.

4.06   If you or the Artist shall for any reason whatsoever delay the commencement of or be unavailable for any recording sessions for the Masters, you shall, upon Company's demand, pay Company an amount equal to the expenses or charges paid or incurred by Company by reason thereof. Company may, without limiting Company's other rights and remedies, deduct that amount from any monies payable by Company hereunder or under any other agreement between you and Company or Company's affiliates.

Company may, at its election, discontinue any recording sessions for the Masters if in Company's judgment the Recording Costs incurred or to be incurred will exceed the approved Recording Budget or if the Masters being produced will not be satisfactory.

This clause allows the record company to pull the plug if the recording budget is exceeded or the company anticipates that the budget will be exceeded. However, the question is, exceeded by how much? One dollar? One thousand dollars? Obviously the record company wants the project finished and will allow the master to be delivered over budget.

5. RECORDING COSTS.

5.01   Company shall pay the Recording Costs of the Masters recorded at recording sessions conducted in accordance with the terms hereof in an amount not in excess of the Recording Budget approved by Company in writing. If the Recording Costs of any Masters shall exceed the Recording Budget approved by Company, you shall be solely responsible for and shall promptly pay the excess. If, however, Company shall pay the excess, you shall, upon Company's demand, pay to Company the amount thereof and Company may, without limiting Company's other rights and remedies, deduct that amount from any monies payable by Company hereunder or under any other agreement between you and Company or Company's affiliates. You shall be solely responsible for and shall pay any payments to any individuals rendering services in connection with the recording of the Masters which exceed union scale unless the excess and the recipient thereof shall have been specified in the Recording Budget approved by Company. You shall also be solely responsible for and shall pay any penalties incurred for late payments caused by your delay in submitting union contracts forms, report forms, or invoices or other documents. If, however, Company shall pay any excess not approved by Company or any penalties, you shall, upon Company's demand, pay Company the amount thereof, and Company may, without limiting Company's other rights and remedies, deduct that amount from any monies payable by Company hereunder or under any other agreement between you and Company or Company's affiliates.

5.02   Recording Costs shall mean and include all union scale payments (including "excess" scale payments) made to the Artist, all payments made by Company to any other individuals rendering services in connection with the recording of the Masters, all other payments which are made by Company pursuant to any applicable law or regulation or the provisions of any collective bargaining agreement between Company and any union or guild, all amounts paid or incurred for studio or hall rentals, tape, engineering, editing, instrument rentals and cartage, mastering, mixing, re-mixing, "sweetening", transportation and accommodations, immigration clearances, trademark and service mark searches and clearances, "sample" clearances any so-called "per diems" for any individuals (including the Artist) rendering services in connection with recording of the Masters and for Company's A&R employees attending recording sessions hereunder, together with all other amounts paid or incurred by Company in connection with the recording of the Masters. Recording Costs shall be recoupable from royalties payable by Company hereunder or under any other agreement between you and Company or Company's affiliates. The costs of metal parts other than lacquer, copper or equivalent masters, and payments to the AFM Special Payments Fund and the Music Performance Trust Fund based upon record sales (so-called "per-record royalties"), will not be recoupable from your royalties or reimbursable by you.

5.02 conveys that the artist will receive AFM union scale for recording his or her own record. At the rate or approximately $250+ per three hour session per musician, substantial money can accumulate fairly quickly. All costs are considered advances and recoupable.

5.03   If packaging for Phonograph Records hereunder contains special elements or requires additional fabrication costs (e.g., for embossing, die-cutting, special ink or paper, additional color separations requested by you, etc.) such that Company would incur manufacturing or fabrication costs in excess of Company's standard per-unit costs without such special elements or costs, or if the origination costs of the artwork embodied in such packaging exceeds Company's standard artwork origination costs (such standard manufacturing, fabrication and origination costs are collectively referred to herein as "Standard Packaging Costs"), and provided you have requested or consented to such special elements or additional fabrication costs, the excess above Company's Standard Packaging Costs ("Special Packaging Costs") may be deducted from any monies (other than mechanical royalties) required to be paid by Company pursuant to this Agreement. (Nothing contained herein shall be deemed to require Company to utilize any artwork elements which would cause Company to incur any Special Packaging Costs.)

Special packaging costs are the artist's responsibility.

6. RIGHTS.

6.01   All Master Recordings recorded during the Term which embody the performances of the Artist, from the inception of the recording thereof, shall, for purposes of copyright law, be deemed "works-made-for-hire" for Company by you, the Artist, and all other persons rendering services in connection with those Master Recordings. Those Master Recordings, from the inception of the recording thereof, and all Phonograph Records and other reproductions made therefrom, together with the performances embodied therein and all copyrights therein and thereto throughout the Territory, and all renewals and extensions thereof, shall be entirely Company's property, free of any claims whatsoever by you, the Artist, or any other person, firm, or corporation. Company shall, accordingly, have the exclusive right to obtain registration of copyright (and all renewals and extensions) in those Master Recordings, in Company's name, as the owner and author thereof. If Company shall be deemed not to be the author of those Master Recordings or those Master Recordings are deemed not to be "works-made-for-hire", this agreement shall constitute an irrevocable transfer to Company of ownership of copyright (and all renewals and extensions) in those Master Recordings. You and the Artist shall, upon Company's request, cause to be executed and delivered to Company transfers of ownership of copyright (and all renewals and extensions) in those Master Recordings and any other documents as Company may deem necessary or appropriate to vest in Company the rights granted to Company in this Agreement, and you and the Artist hereby irrevocably appoint Company your attorney-in-fact for the purpose of executing those transfers of ownership and other documents in your names. Without limiting the generality of the foregoing, Company and any person, firm, or corporation designated by Company shall have the exclusive, perpetual and worldwide right to manufacture, sell, distribute and advertise Phonograph Records embodying those Master Recordings under any trademarks, trade names or labels, and to lease, license, convey or otherwise use or dispose of those Master Recordings by any method now or hereafter known in any field of use and to perform publicly Phonograph Records and other reproductions embodying those Master Recordings, all upon such terms as Company may approve, or Company may refrain from doing any or all of the foregoing.

This clause allows the company to file the SR Copyright Registration form as owner.

7. MARKETING.

7.01

(a)

(i) Company and any person, firm or corporation designated by Company shall have the perpetual right throughout the Territory to use and to permit others to use the Artist's name (both legal and professional, and whether presently or hereafter used by the Artist), likeness, other identification and biographical material concerning the Artist, and the name and likeness of any producer or other person rendering services in connection with Master Recordings recorded by the Artist during the Term for purposes of trade and advertising. Company shall have the further right to refer to the Artist during the Term as Company's exclusive recording artist and you and the Artist shall in all your and the Artist's activities in the entertainment field use reasonable efforts to cause the Artist to be billed and advertised during the Term as Company's exclusive recording artist. The rights granted to Company pursuant to this paragraph with respect to the Artist's name, likeness, other identification and biographical material concerning the Artist shall be exclusive during the Term and nonexclusive thereafter. Accordingly, but without limiting the generality of the foregoing, neither you nor the Artist shall authorize or permit any person, firm, or corporation other than Company to use during the Term the Artist's legal or professional name or the Artist's likeness in connection with the advertising or sale of Phonograph Records.

The artist may not want to guarantee that he or she will be able to secure this information for everyone on the recording. The phrase "with artist's approval" should be added to the entire 7.01(a)(i).

(ii) Company will make available to you for your approval any pictures of the Artist or biographical material about the Artist which Company proposes to use for advertising or publicity in the United States during the Term of this Agreement. Company will not use any such material which you disapprove in writing within five (5) days from the time such materials are made available to you, provided you furnish substitute material, satisfactory to Company in its sole and reasonable discretion. This subparagraph will not apply to any material previously approved by you or used by Company. No inadvertent failure to comply with this subparagraph will constitute a breach of this Agreement, and you will not be entitled to injunctive relief to restrain the continuing use of any material used in contravention of this subparagraph. You shall have the right to submit photographs, likenesses and biographical material of Artist and your submission of same shall constitute your approval thereof.

(b) Neither you or the Artist shall render any services or authorize or permit your or the Artist's name or likeness or any biographical material concerning you or the Artist to be used in any manner by any person, firm or corporation in the advertising, promoting or marketing of blank magnetic recording tape or any other product or device primarily intended for home use, whether now known or hereafter developed, which may be used for the fixation of sound alone or sound together with visual images.

7.02   During the Term of this Agreement, with respect to audio Records manufactured for sale in the United States, Company shall not without your consent:

(a) License Master Recordings made under this Agreement for commercials other than commercials for Phonograph Records hereunder. This restriction will apply after the Term for the following: (i) political, religious or hygiene related advertisements; and (ii) all other commercials if Artist's account is in a fully recouped position;

(b) License Master Recordings made under this Agreement for featured use in a motion picture, television program or video game, provided that Artist's account is in a fully recouped position. This restriction will apply during and after the Term (regardless of recoupment) for NC-17 and X rated productions;

(c) Use Master Recordings made under this Agreement on premium Records or other commercial tie-ins to promote the sale of any product or service other than Records or other derivatives of the Master Recordings, which bears the name of the sponsor for whom the Record is produced. This restriction shall also apply after the Term of this Agreement;

(d) Commercially release "out-takes" on Phonograph Records or otherwise exploit such recordings ("out-takes" are preliminary unfinished versions of Master Recordings made under this Agreement). This restriction shall also apply after the Term of this Agreement;

(e) Couple during any one (1) year period more than three (3) Master Recordings made hereunder with recordings not embodying your performances, except promotional samplers (including those sold to the general public for less than full price), institutional samplers and programs for use on public transportation carriers and facilities;

Company shall undertake to inform its affiliates outside of the United States of the restrictions contained in this paragraph 7.02. Company shall use commercially reasonable efforts to correct its failure to comply with the immediately preceding sentence following its receipt of your notice of such failure. No inadvertent failure to comply with this paragraph shall constitute a breach of this Agreement, and you shall not be entitled to injunctive relief to restrain the sale of any Record released in contravention of this paragraph. The provisions of this paragraph 7.02 shall not apply to any Master Recordings which are not Delivered within ninety (90) days after the time prescribed in Article 3 or if you have breached any of your other material obligations hereunder.

In sentence two, the word "reasonable" could be changed to "best".

7.03   If Company determines during the Term hereof to edit or remix any Master Recordings made under this agreement for use on an Album, it will accord you a period of seven (7) days in which to do that work in accordance with Company's requirements unless that delay would interfere with a scheduled release. After Company has afforded you such first opportunity to edit or remix, Company may edit or remix the Master Recording concerned, provided that you may reasonably approve such remixed or edited version. Unless you notify Company that you disapprove such remixed or edited Master Recordings within five (5) business days after Company offers you the opportunity to approve such version it will be deemed approved. This paragraph will not apply to editing necessary for the release of Singles (including radio edits), Long Play Singles or non-disc configurations, or to eliminate material which in the reasonable good faith opinion of Company's legal counsel is likely to constitute a defamation, libel or violate or infringe upon any right, including, without limitation, the right of privacy of any person. An inadvertent failure by Company to comply with the requirements of this paragraph shall not be deemed a breach of this agreement. Any costs incurred in connection with the re-editing or remixing shall be deemed Recording Costs in connection with the project concerned, provided that such costs shall not reduce the applicable Recording Fund if the costs are incurred after satisfactory Delivery of the Album concerned.

7.04

    (a)

        (i) Company will commercially release each Album recorded and delivered in fulfillment of your Recording Commitment hereunder in the United States within six (6) months after Delivery of the Album concerned if the Album is delivered between January 1, and September 30, of a given year or within eight (8) months after Delivery of the Album concerned if the Album is Delivered after September 30, of a given year. If Company fails to do so you may notify Company within forty five (45) days after the end of the applicable period concerned, that you intend to terminate this Agreement unless Company releases the Album within ninety (90) days after Company's receipt of your notice (the "cure period"). If Company fails to commercially release the Album in the United States before the end of the cure period, you may terminate the Term of this Agreement by giving Company notice within thirty (30) days after the end of the cure period. On receipt by Company of your termination notice, the Term of this Agreement will end and all parties will be deemed to have fulfilled all of their obligations hereunder except those obligations which survive the end of the Term (e.g., warranties, re-recording restrictions and obligations to pay royalties). Your only remedy for failure by Company to release an Album will be termination in accordance with this paragraph. If you fail to give Company either of those notices within the period specified, your right to terminate will lapse.

This is the release commitment which "allows" you to terminate the agreement if the recorded material is not released. The company, of course, will own the recordings and not revert their ownership back to the artist.

        (ii) The running of the six (6) month and the ninety (90) day periods referred to in paragraph 7.04(a)(i) will be suspended (and the expiration date of each of those periods will be postponed) for the period of any suspension during such periods of the running of the Term of this Agreement under paragraph 17.01.

7.05   Company will commercially release each Committed Album hereunder in the United Kingdom , Canada, France, Germany, and Italy, (the "Foreign Release Territories") within one (1) year after the date such Album was released in the United States . If Company does not release the applicable Committed Album in a particular Foreign Release Territory(ies) within the applicable time period, then you may give Company notice within forty five (45) days following the expiration of one (1) year period of such failure to release such record in the particular Foreign Release Territory, and Company shall have a period of sixty (60) days following the date of such notice to cure such failure. If Company does not cure such failure within said sixty (60) day period, you shall have the option, which may be exercised by giving Company written notice within forty five (45) days following the end of such sixty (60) day period, to require Company to enter into an agreement with a licensee designated by you, which licensee is actually engaged in the business of manufacturing and distributing Records in the particular Foreign Release Territory concerned, authorizing such licensee to manufacture and distribute Records derived from the Master Recordings not released in accordance with this paragraph 7.05 in the applicable Foreign Release Territory. Fifty (50%) percent of all revenues actually received by Company under the licenses referred to in this paragraph 7.05 will be credited to your royalty account under this Agreement. Each such license agreement will provide for such compensation for the license as you negotiate with the licensee, and will contain such other provisions as Company shall require, including but not limited to the following:

These are the term of any straight licensing deals with a foreign company should the company exercise their right to do so. The revenue will be split evenly between the company and the artist.

(a) The licensee will be required to deliver to Company all consents required by Company, and all agreements which Company may require for any third party to look to the licensee, and not to Company, for the fulfillment of any obligations arising in connection with the manufacture or distribution of Records under the license. The licensee will also become a first party to any agreements or funds required pursuant to any union agreements to which Company is a party. The license agreement will not become effective until the licensee has complied with all that provisions of this subsection 7.05(a).

(b) The licensee will make all payments required in connection with the manufacture, sale or distribution, by parties other than Company, in the applicable Foreign Release Territory of Records made from those Master Recordings after the effective date of the license, including, without limitation, all royalties and other payments to performing artists, producers, owners of copyrights in musical compositions, and any applicable unions and union funds. The licensee will comply with all applicable rules and regulations covering any use of the Master Recordings by the licensee.

(c) No warranty or representation will be made by Company in connection with the applicable Master Recordings, the license or otherwise. You and the licensee will indemnify and hold harmless Company and its licensees against all claims, damages, liabilities, costs and expenses, including reasonable counsel fees, arising out of any use of the Master Recordings or exercise of such rights by the licensee.

(d) Company will instruct its licensee in the applicable Foreign Release Territory not to manufacture Records derived from the Master Recordings licensed to the licensee. If the licensee notifies Company of such manufacture, Company will instruct its licensees to discontinue it, but neither Company nor its licensees shall have any liability by reason of such manufacture occurring before Company's receipt of such notice and Company shall have no liability by reason of such manufacture at any time.

(e) Each Record made under the license will bear a sound recording copyright notice identical to the notice used by Company for initial United States release of the Master Recording concerned, or such other notices as Company shall require, but those Records will not otherwise be identified directly or indirectly with Company.

(f) Company shall have the right to examine the books and records of the licensee and all others authorized by the licensee to manufacture and distribute Records under the license, for the purpose of verifying the accuracy of the accountings rendered to Company by the license.

(g) The licensee will not have the right to authorize any other party to exercise any rights without Company's prior written consent.

(h) Company and its licensees will have the continuing right at all times to manufacture and sell recompilation Albums in the Foreign Release Territory concerned which may contain the Master Recordings. A recompilation album is an Album, such as a "Greatest Hits" or "Best Of" type Album, containing Master Recordings previously released in different Album combinations.

For purposes of computing each of the one (1) year and sixty (60) day periods described in this paragraph 7.05 the period between October 15 and January 15 shall not be counted.

7.06

(a) A "qualifying recompilation Album", in this paragraph 7.06, means an Album, such as a "Greatest Hits" or "Best of" Album, consisting of: (i) Master Recordings made and/or released under this Agreement or otherwise recorded by you and previously released in different Album combinations; and (ii) two (2) new Master Recordings (the "New Recordings" below) of at least two (2) Compositions, made expressly for initial release in that Album and not applicable in reduction of your Recording Commitment.

(b) Within thirty (30) days after Company's release of a qualifying recompilation Album on top line Records sold Through Normal Retail Channels in the United States, Company shall pay you an Advance of one hundred thousand dollars ($100,000) less the Recording Costs for the New Recordings. No other Advance shall be payable in connection with the New Recordings. The Advance, if any, shall be payable to you promptly following the Delivery of such New Recordings. If your royalty account is in an unrecouped position (i.e., if the aggregate of the Advances and other recoupable items charged to that account at the time of payment of that Advance exceeds the aggregate of the royalties credited to that account at the end of the last semi-annual royalty accounting period), the Advance payable under the first sentence of this paragraph shall be reduced by the amount of the unrecouped balance.

(c) If Company releases in the United States a qualifying recompilation Album consisting of Master Recordings hereunder, the selection of Master Recordings to be embodied on such Album(s) shall, during the term, be subject to your written consent (not to be unreasonably withheld), provided that all Master Recordings which have been previously released as a Single in the United States shall be deemed approved by you. If you and Company cannot agree as to all Master Recordings to be included, then such Album shall include all agreed-upon Master Recordings, and Company and you shall then alternate selection to fill the Album, with Company selecting first and determining in its sole discretion when such Album will be deemed filled. During the Term, Company will have the right to release one (1) recompilation Album after the third Album released in the United States during the Term. After the Term Company will have the right to release one (1) recompilation Album.

These clauses discuss a "best of " release and what material will constitute its contents. The advance or royalty account credit of $100,000 is negotiable.

7.07

(a) In preparation of the initial release in the United States of each Album of the Recording Commitment, the following procedure shall be followed:

(i) Company shall obtain your approval regarding the proposed Album cover layout and the picture or art to be used on the Album cover, in accordance with this paragraph 7.07. The proposed Album cover shall be made available to you at Company's offices for review and comment. Unless otherwise provided in this paragraph 7.07, Company shall make such changes in the artwork as you reasonably request.

(ii) Company shall not be required to make any changes which would delay the release of the Album beyond the scheduled date or which would require Company to incur Special Packaging Costs. Any premium charges incurred to meet the release schedule because of delays in approval by you shall constitute Special Packaging Costs.

(b) In preparation for the initial release in the United States of each Album of the Recording Commitment, if you request to prepare the Album packaging layout and/or the pictures or art to be used in connection with the Album, and if Company agrees in writing to such request, then you shall have the right to produce and deliver to Company, as applicable, such Album packaging layout and pictures or art, but only on the following conditions:

(i) Your plans for the proposed artwork shall be discussed with Company's Executive Vice President, Marketing, or his or her designee, before it is produced and a budget shall be assigned for artwork costs.

(ii) You shall produce the artwork in accordance with plans approved by Company and shall deliver "camera-ready" artwork to Company, in the form of mechanicals and art (including, without limitation, pre-separated film and chromes of the original artwork) conforming to Company's specifications, together with all licenses and consents required in connection with it, not later than sixty (60) days before the scheduled release date of the Album. If any of the aforesaid materials have not been delivered to Company within that time, Company shall have the right to prepare and use its own artwork without further consultation with you, and Company shall not be obligated to make any payments to you or any other Person to whom you have incurred any obligation in connection with any artwork produced for the Album concerned.

(iii) You shall deliver to Company, together with the artwork, an itemized statement of the actual costs paid by you in connection therewith. Company shall reimburse you promptly after Company's acceptance of the artwork and the aforesaid statement of costs in the amount of those costs, provided such costs do not exceed the approved budget therefore. If Company in Company's sole discretion shall elect to reimburse you for costs in excess of the approved budget, such excess shall constitute Special Packaging Costs.

(c) All matters relating to Company's trademarks or to notices or disclosures deemed advisable by Company's attorneys, and any matter other than the Artwork (i.e., the artwork to be used for the front cover of the initial United States release of each Committed Album) shall be determined in Company's sole discretion. Company shall not be deemed unreasonable in rejecting any requested change upon the advice of Company's attorneys.

(d) Company shall have the right to reject any artwork which is not commercially satisfactory in Company's reasonable judgement. Company shall not be deemed unreasonable in rejecting any artwork or Record packaging which includes so-called "commercial tie-ins", endorsements, advertising or marketing materials in respect of anything other than Records of the Artist's performances hereunder, or which Company anticipates would require Company to incur Special Packaging Costs. Company shall not be deemed unreasonable in rejecting any artwork which Company deems patently offensive or which, in the judgment of its attorneys, might subject Company or Company's licensees to liability for any reason. If Company accepts the artwork, all engraving and manufacturing costs in excess of the amount specified above shall be reimbursed by you on Company's request; all such excess amounts not reimbursed by you shall constitute Advances and may be recouped by Company from any monies becoming due to you.

You may "prepare" special packaging, however, veto power is with the company.

(e) You shall act as an independent contractor in all arrangements you make with other Persons in connection with the production of the artwork; you shall not purport to make any such arrangements as Company's agent or otherwise on behalf of Company.

(f) This paragraph 7.07 shall apply only to Albums Delivered within the time prescribed in Article 3 and initially released in the United States during the Term, and only if you are not otherwise in default under this Agreement.

7.08   It is hereby expressly agreed that, as between you, Artist and Company, Company shall exclusively own and control all materials comprising the artwork (including, without limitation, art, photographs, graphic designs, etc.) and other items created or used in connection with the exploitation of Phonograph Records hereunder (the "Art Materials"), including, without limitation, all copyrights and the right to secure copyright throughout the world and in perpetuity.

7.09   Company hereby agrees to spend not less than _____-Thousand ($_____) Dollars in connection with its promotion and sales and marketing activities for each Album Delivered hereunder in fulfillment of your Minimum Recording Commitment. The costs for videos, tour support and independent promotion will be among the items drawn from such marketing budget. Except as set forth in the following sentence, all sums paid or incurred by Company in connection with independent marketing and publicity of Phonograph Records hereunder, including the sums set forth in the preceding sentence, shall be deemed to constitute Advances hereunder. Only fifty (50%) percent of all sums paid or incurred by Company in connection with the independent promotion of Phonograph Records hereunder shall constitute Advances. Company shall endeavor to consult with you with respect to its marketing expenditures, including its independent promotion expenditures, provided, Company's inadvertent failure to do so shall not constitute a breach hereof.

Clause 7.09 discusses the promotional campaign finances and is negotiable. If it is necessary to use indie promo guys, the artist, will have "no" say in who, when, or where, but will be responsible for half of the expenses incurred! The entire clause needs to be clearly negotiated.

8. ADVANCES.

8.01   All monies paid to you or the Artist or on your or the Artist's behalf or to or on behalf of any person, firm or corporation representing you or the Artist, other than royalties payable pursuant to this Agreement, shall constitute Advances hereunder. You agree that the Advances hereunder include the prepayment of session union scale as provided in the applicable union codes, and you and Artist agree to complete any documentation required by the applicable union to implement this sentence.

8.02

(a) Conditioned upon your full performance of all your obligations hereunder, Company shall pay you the following amounts, which shall constitute Advances hereunder. With respect to each Album recorded and delivered hereunder in fulfillment of your Recording Commitment, the amount, if any, by which the sum designated below as the "Recording Fund" exceeds the Recording Costs for that Album:

(i) For the First Album, the Recording Fund shall be _____ thousand Dollars ($_____).

(ii) For the Album recorded during the first Option Period, the Recording Fund shall be the Formula Amount, but no less than _____ hundred and _____ thousand Dollars ($_____) and no more than _____ hundred and _____ thousand Dollars ($_____).

(iii) For the Album recorded during the second Option Period, the Recording Fund shall be the Formula Amount, but no less than _____ hundred and _____ thousand Dollars (\$_____) and no more than _____ hundred and _____ thousand Dollars (\$_____).

For the Album recorded during the third Option Period, the Recording Fund shall be the Formula Amount, but no less than _____ hundred _____ thousand (\$_____) Dollars and no more than _____ hundred and _____ thousand Dollars (\$_____).

For the Album recorded during the fourth Option Period, the Recording Fund shall be the Formula Amount, but no less than _____ hundred and _____ thousand Dollars (\$_____) and no more than _____ hundred and _____ thousand Dollars (\$_____).

For the Album recorded during the fifth Option Period, the Recording Fund shall be the Formula Amount, but no less than _____ hundred thousand Dollars (\$_____) and no more than _____ hundred thousand Dollars (\$_____).

Possibly a graduated scale which would look something like below would be appropriate. Remember that all figures are negotiable.

	Minimum	Maximum
Albums Delivered during the first Option Period:	\$200,000	\$400,000
Albums Delivered during the second Option Period:	\$225,000	\$450,000
Albums Delivered during the third Option Period:	\$250,000	\$500,000
		etc.

The "Formula Amount" for a particular Album recorded and Delivered hereunder in fulfillment of your Recording Commitment shall mean an amount equal to sixty-six and two-thirds (66 2/3%) percent of whichever of the following amounts is less: (A) the amount of the royalties, after the retention of reserves (which, solely for purposes of this calculation, shall not exceed twenty [20%] percent), earned by you hereunder from Net Sales through Normal Retail Channels in the United States on which royalties are payable hereunder ("USNRC Net Sales") of the immediately preceding Album delivered hereunder in fulfillment of your Recording Commitment; or (B) the average of the amounts of such royalties so earned by you hereunder on the two (2) immediately preceding Albums delivered hereunder in fulfillment of your Recording Commitment. In either case, the amount of royalties with respect to any preceding Album shall be computed as of the end of the month in which occurs the date which is twelve (12) months following the initial commercial release in the United States of the preceding Album concerned. Notwithstanding the foregoing, with respect to any applicable Album which is not delivered to Company within the applicable period provided for in paragraph 3.02 above, the Recording Fund for that Album shall be reduced by ten

(10%) percent of the otherwise applicable Recording Fund for each month (or portion thereof) until that Album is delivered; provided, however, Company shall not reduce the applicable Recording Fund below the actual Recording Costs for the Album concerned.

This fairly lengthy definition of the "Formula Amount" (and the calculations) is fine if the first recording sold well. If it didn't and the artist is really looking to get it together for the next shot, there may not be sufficient money in the account for these calculations.

(b) The Advance payable to you in connection with the First Album pursuant to paragraph 8.02(a)(i) shall be payable as follows: (i) _____ thousand Dollars ($_____) promptly following the complete execution hereof and (ii) the balance of the Advance (less all Recording Costs), if any, promptly following delivery to and acceptance by Company of the First Album.

(c) Each Advance payable to you pursuant to paragraph(s) 8.02(a)(ii)-(vi), if any, shall be made as follows:

(d) Upon Company's receipt of your notice that the recording of the Album concerned has actually commenced, Company shall pay you a portion of the applicable Advance equal to fifteen (15%) percent of the applicable minimum Recording Fund specified in subparagraph 8.02(a); and

If the advance is indeed used to finance the recording, then initial percent payment most likely need to be higher. Company shall pay you the balance of the Advance (less all Recording Costs), if any, promptly following delivery to and acceptance by Company of such Album.

What does "promptly" mean.........thirty days......six months??

8.03

(a) The aggregate amount of the compensation paid to (each of) you under this agreement shall not be less than the "Designated Dollar Amount" (as defined below) per Fiscal Year. "Fiscal Year", in this paragraph, means the annual period beginning on the date of commencement of the Term, and each subsequent annual period through the seventh such annual period, during the Term. [You hereby warrant and represent that all payments made to you under this agreement during each Fiscal Year shall be distributed equally among you.]

If (each of you has) (you have) not received compensation equal to the Designated Dollar Amount under this agreement for a Fiscal Year, the company shall pay (each of) you the amount of (any) (the) deficiency before the end of that Fiscal Year; at least forty (40) days before the end of each Fiscal Year you shall notify the company if (each of you has) (you have) not received compensation equal to the Designated Dollar Amount under this agreement for that Fiscal Year, and of the amount of the deficiency. Each such payment shall constitute an Advance and shall be applied in reduction of any and all monies due or becoming due to you under this agreement. The company may not withhold or require you to repay any payment made to you pursuant to or subject to this paragraph 8.03.

As used in this paragraph 8.03, the "Designated Dollar Amount" shall be:

Nine Thousand Dollars ($9,000) for the first Fiscal Year of this agreement;

Twelve Thousand Dollars ($12,000) for the second Fiscal Year of this agreement; and

Fifteen Thousand Dollars ($15,000) for each of the third through seventh Fiscal Years of this agreement.

If in any Fiscal Year the aggregate amount of the compensation paid to you under this agreement exceeds the Designated Dollar Amount, such excess compensation shall apply to reduce the Designated Dollar Amount for any subsequent Fiscal Years.

(d) You acknowledge that this paragraph is included to avoid compromise of the company's rights (including the company's entitlement to injunctive relief) by reason of a finding of applicability of California law, but does not constitute a concession by the company that California law is actually applicable.

These are the "play or pay" clauses. They state that if the company pays you these amounts, they have fulfilled their requirements of the agreement and they do not have to allow you to record, finance a recording, or do anything! In fact, in 8.03(b) the responsibility it put on you to notify them if you did not receive compensation. Unfortunately, this is standard language.

9. ROYALTIES.

9.01   Company will pay you an "all-in" royalty, during the term of copyright in the country concerned of Masters embodied in Phonograph Records delivered hereunder computed at the applicable percentage indicated in the Royalty Schedule below, of the applicable Royalty Base Price in respect of Net Sales of such Phonograph Records (other than Audiovisual Records) consisting entirely of Master Recordings recorded under this Agreement during the respective Contract Periods specified below and sold by Company or Company's licensees through Normal Retail Channels:

Be careful, normally "NRC Net Sales" in layman's terms is approximately the wholesale price.

ROYALTY SCHEDULE

UNITED STATES

Master Recordings made during the:	Albums	Singles	Long Play Singles
Initial Period			
First Option Period			
Second Option Period			
Third Option Period			
Fourth Option Period			
Fifth Option Period			

On albums, any figure starting around 24% would be standard. On singles 18%.

FOREIGN

Territory	All Records
Canada	% of the otherwise applicable rate set forth in the United States Royalty Schedule above in respect of Net Sales through Normal Retail Channels in the United States of the particular record concerned (i.e., Albums, Singles and Long Play Singles), without regard to any escalations.

Eighteen percent on albums and thirteen percent on singles.

All EU countries, Austraila, New Zealand and Japan	% of the otherwise applicable rate set forth in the United States Royalty Schedule above in respect of Net Sales through Normal Retail Channels in the United States of the particular record concerned (i.e., Albums, Singles and Long Play Singles), without regard to any escalations.

About the same in these countries as well.

Rest of World	% of the otherwise applicable rate set forth in the United States Royalty Schedule above in respect of Net Sales through Normal Retail Channels in the United States of the particular record concerned (i.e., Albums, Singles and Long Play Singles), without regard to any escalations.

Twelve percent for albums and nine percent for singles elsewhere.

The royalty rates set forth in this paragraph 9.01 are sometimes referred to herein as your "basic royalty rate(s)".

9.02   Notwithstanding anything to the contrary contained in the Royalty Schedule hereinabove, and with respect to each Album Delivered in fulfillment of your Recording Commitment hereunder, the royalty rate applicable to USNRC Net Sales of top-line Albums pursuant to the terms hereof shall be the royalty rate specified in the Royalty Escalation Schedule below.

ROYALTY ESCALATION SCHEDULE

Album recorded in fulfillment of the Recording Commitment for the:	USNRC Net Sales of top-line Albums (determined in accordance with Company's standard accounting procedures).
Initial Period	500,000 1,000,000
First Option Period	500,000 1,000,000
Second Option Period	500,000 1,000,000
Third Option Period	500,000 1,000,000
Fourth Option Period	500,000 1,000,000
Fifth Option Period	500,000 1,000,000

All negotiable!

9.03

(a) The royalty rate on Phonograph Records sold through direct mail or through mail order operations (including, without limitation so-called "record clubs") shall be one-half (?) of the otherwise applicable royalty rate if manufactured and sold by Company, and an amount equal to one-half (?) of the Net Royalty from the sale of those Phonograph Records if manufactured and sold by Company's licensees.

The 50% rate may be negotiated to a higher rate.

Secondly, a provision may be inserted that allows a percentage of "bonus" and "free" records to be accounted as records sold. There is the possibility that a hot album becomes one of the free introductory albums to hundreds of thousands of club members. The artist shouldn't be totally penalized for this.

(b) The royalty rate on Phonograph Records sold via telephone, satellite, cable, point of sale manufacturing or other means of direct transmission, now known or hereafter devised (herein collectively, "Electronic Transmission") shall be seventy-five percent (75%) of the otherwise applicable royalty rate if sold by Company and an amount equal to one-half (1/2) of the Net Royalty from sale of those Phonograph Records if sold by Company's licensees. Notwithstanding the foregoing, with respect to any Records sold via Electronic Transmission by Company or its licensees, Company shall have the option (which Company may exercise in its sole discretion) to pay to you in lieu of any royalty otherwise payable in connection with such Records, the same dollars-and-cents royalty payable hereunder for the equivalent Record (or, if no such equivalent Record exists, a comparable Record) in audio-only compact disc configuration at the time of transmission.

This is one of the few clauses that indirectly refers to the Internet. It is far too vague and needs negotiation.

From 2005 contract:

(iii)   The royalty rate for any Recordings hereunder licensed by Company or a Principal Licensee for On-Demand Usages shall be a percentage of Net Receipts equal to the [DRAFTING NOTE – USE 120% TO 130% - one hundred _____ percent (1_0%)] of the Basic U.S. Rate for the Record concerned; provided that, such credit to your royalty account shall not exceed the royalty amount that would otherwise be credited to your account hereunder for such use if Company or a Principal Licensee had distributed the Records concerned.

(e)   Notwithstanding anything to the contrary contained herein, for sales by Company or a Principal Licensee of: (i) Records in now widely distributed compact disc forms including Enhanced CD and CD Extra formats, the royalty rate shall be one hundred percent (100%) of the otherwise applicable royalty rate set forth in this agreement; and (ii) Phono Records in any form, format or technology not herein described, which is now known but not widely distributed or which hereafter becomes known, including Super Audio CD and DVD Audio ("**New Technology Formats**"), the royalty rate shall be seventy-five percent (75%) of the otherwise applicable royalty rate set forth in this agreement; provided that, if in any calendar year the revenues generated from the sale of Records in a particular New Technology Format exceed twenty percent (20%) of total United States recorded music revenues (as reported in a reputable published industry source such as IFPI's *The Recording Industry in Numbers*), then, with respect to sales of Records hereunder in any subsequent calendar years, such particular New Technology Format shall no longer constitute a New Technology Format and the royalty rate with respect to such particular New Technology Format shall be one hundred percent (100%) of the otherwise applicable royalty rate set forth in this agreement rather than seventy-five percent (75%).

(f)   With respect to Electronic Transmissions, the royalty rate shall be one hundred percent (100%) of the otherwise applicable royalty rate set forth in this agreement.

From "Definitions" Section:

"**Electronic Transmissions**" – Records sold by Company or through Company's distributors in the United States or by Company, Company's Principal Licensees or their distributors outside the United States other than as Phono Records including via telephone, satellite, cable, point-of-sale manufacturing, transmission over wire or through the air, downloading and any other methods now or hereafter known;

On-Demand Usages" – licensed usages of Records other than Phono Records as part of a service containing a functionality which permits a consumer to access a particular Recording or Recordings on a so-called "on-demand" basis including Subscription;

"Online Store Compilation" - a Compilation Record embodying Recordings that are individually selected and/or sequenced by an online retail store (such as amazon.com, listen.com, towerrecords.com, CDnow.com, pressplay.com and similar stores);]

"Subscription" – transmission of Records other than Phono Records to consumers, either by Company or through its distributors, its Principal Licensees or their distributors or another Person, in return for a subscription or other fee paid by the consumer to obtain access to such Recordings for a limited period of time and/or a limited number of uses or any other method of exploitation commonly recognized as a subscription service;

The record company's point of view changed considerably since 2001.

9.04   The royalty rate for the use of any Master as described in clause (a), (b), or (c) of this sentence will be one-half (?) of the basic royalty rate that would apply if the Record concerned were sold through Normal Retail Channels: (a) any catalog Phonograph Record sold by Company's special products operations or those of the distributor of the Records concerned (herein collectively "SPO's") to educational institutions or libraries, or to other SPO clients for their promotion or sales incentive purposes (but not for sale to the general public through Normal Retail Channels); (b) any Record sold by Company or Company's principal licensee in the country concerned in conjunction with a television and/or radio advertising campaign, during the calendar semi-annual period in which that campaign begins and the next two (2) such periods; and (c) any non-catalog Phonograph Record created on a custom basis for SPO clients. The royalty on any Record described in clause (c) will be computed on the basis of the SPO's actual sales price less all taxes and Container Charges. In respect of any Master Recording leased by Company to others for their distribution of Phonograph Records in the United States, Company will pay you fifty (50%) percent of Company's net receipts from Company's licensee. ("Net receipts", in the preceding sentence, means receipts as computed after deduction of all copyright, AFM and other applicable third party payments.) If another artist, a producer, or any other Person is entitled to royalties on sales of such Records, that payment will be divided among you in the same ratio as that among your respective basic royalty percentage rates.

This clause establishes the rate on special products to special customers.

9.05

(a) The royalty rate on any Budget Record or any "picture disc" (i.e., a disc Record with artwork reproduced on the surface of the Record itself) will be one-half (?) of the applicable basic royalty rate prescribed in paragraph 9.01. The royalty rate on any Mid-Priced Record will be seventy-five percent (75%) of the otherwise applicable basic royalty rate prescribed in paragraph 9.01. The royalty rate on any Record sold for distribution through military exchange channels shall be three-quarters (3/4) of the otherwise applicable basic royalty rate prescribed in paragraph 9.01. The royalty rate on any soundtrack Record will be seventy (70%) percent of the otherwise applicable basic royalty rate prescribed in paragraph 9.01 (provided, however, that on Masters licensed by Company for use on a soundtrack Record, the royalty rate shall be an amount equal to fifty (50%) percent of Company's net receipts received from such use). The royalty rate on any Record which is not an Album, Single or a Long-Play Single will be sixty (60%) percent of the applicable basic Album royalty rate prescribed in paragraph 9.01.

Negotiate separately!!

(b) The royalty rate on a Multiple Album will be one-half (?) of the applicable basic Album royalty rate prescribed in paragraph 9.01, if the Royalty Base Price of that Album is the same as the Royalty Base Price applicable to the top-line single-disc Conventional Albums marketed by Company or its Licensee in the territory where the Album is sold at the beginning of the royalty accounting period concerned. If a different Royalty Base Price applies to a Multiple Album, the royalty rate prescribed in the preceding sentence will be adjusted in proportion to the variance in the Royalty Base Price (but will not be more than the applicable Album royalty rate prescribed in paragraph 9.01). That adjustment of the royalty rate will be made by using the following formula:

(X divided by Y) multiplied by Z = adjusted royalty rate. (Subject to the parenthetical limit in the second sentence of this subparagraph.)

("X" represents the Royalty Base Price for the Multiple Album concerned; "Y" represents the Royalty Base Price for such top-line single-disc Records in the Multiple Album multiplied by the number of disc Records in the Multiple Album concerned; and "Z" equals the otherwise applicable basic royalty rate.)

(c) The royalty rate on any compact disc Record will be one hundred (100%) percent of the rate which would otherwise be applicable under this Agreement.

At least they are being fair by now including the standard configuration in the industry.

(d) The royalty rate on any New Media Record will be seventy (70%) percent of the rate which would otherwise be applicable hereunder; provided, in the event Company adopts a general policy applicable to the majority of artists signed exclusively to Company which provides for a royalty rate reduction with respect to Records in a particular New Media configuration more favorable to such artists than the royalty rate reduction provided herein, you shall receive the benefit of such general policy, on a prospective basis only.

In this clause the company is protecting itself from being omitted from an new "way" to receive product and digital downloading would be included here. The 70% can be negotiated.

9.06

(a) Except as otherwise specifically set forth herein, on Masters licensed by Company on a flat-fee or a royalty basis for the sale of Phonograph Records or for any other uses, the royalty rate shall be an amount equal to fifty (50%) percent of the Net Flat Fee or Net Royalty, as applicable, from such exploitation of the Masters.

(b) To the extent permissible at law, you hereby assign to Company all right, title and interest in and to any and all royalties or other payments to which you are or may become entitled to receive (herein "Your Share") under the Audio Home Recording Act of 1992, as it may be amended (the "Act"), or any implementing or similar legislation requiring the payment of copyright royalties in connection with the sale of recording devices or blank tapes or any other recordable device (e.g., digital audio tape, DCC). Upon receipt by Company of such royalties or payments, Company shall credit your royalty account with one hundred (100%) percent of Your Share of such royalties or payments received. In order to effectuate the foregoing, you shall execute and deliver to Company a letter of direction address to the Register of Copyrights of the U.S. Copyright Office and you agree to execute and deliver to Company any other document or documents as may be reasonably necessary to cause the payment to Company of Your Share of such royalties or payments. It is expressly understood and agreed that except as provided above in this paragraph 9.06(b), Company shall be entitled to retain for its own use and benefit any royalties or payments received by Company pursuant to the Act.

Another reservoir to recoup advances.

9.07   Notwithstanding anything to the contrary contained herein, on Audiovisual Recordings, the royalty rate shall be as follows:

(a) On Audiovisual Records manufactured and sold by Company's licensees, in the United States or elsewhere shall be an amount equal to fifty (50%) percent of the Net Receipts from the sale of those Audiovisual Records. On Audiovisual Records manufactured and sold by Company, the royalty rate shall be computed in accordance with the provisions of this Article 9 applicable to Conventional Albums, except: (i) on sales of Audiovisual Records in the United States the royalty rate pursuant to paragraph 9.01(a) above shall be deemed to be ten (10%) percent; (ii) on sales of Audiovisual Records outside of the United States the royalty rate shall be deemed to be five (5%) percent; and (iii) the Royalty Base Price of Audiovisual Records shall be as prescribed in paragraph 19.23 below.

(b) On Audiovisual Recordings licensed or otherwise furnished by Company for exploitation other than on Audiovisual Records, the royalty rate shall be an amount equal to fifty percent (50%) of the Net Receipts from that exploitation.

(c) The following amounts will be charged in reduction of all royalties payable or becoming payable to you under this paragraph 9.07:

(i) All royalties and other compensation which may become payable to any Person for the right to make any uses of copyrighted Musical Compositions in Audiovisual Records; and

(ii) All payments to record producers, directors or other Persons which are measured by uses of Audiovisual Records or proceeds from those uses, whether such payments are to be computed as royalties on sales, as participations in revenues, or in any other manner. (The amounts chargeable under the preceding sentence will not include non-contingent advances, but will include payments – including payments in fixed amounts - which accrue by reason that such sales, revenues, or other bases for computation attain particular levels.)

9.07 is the section that discusses the use of video in sync with recorded music. Major will pay a royalty based on "net sales" in the U.S., or by components of Major outside the U.S. All the percentages are negotiated by the attorneys.

9.08   Notwithstanding anything to the contrary contained in this Article 9:

(a) In respect of Joint Recordings, the royalty rate to be used in determining the royalties payable to you shall be computed by multiplying the royalty rate otherwise applicable by a fraction, the numerator of which shall be one (1) and the denominator of which shall be the total number of royalty artists whose performances are embodied on a Joint Recording. The term "Joint Recording" shall mean any Master Recording embodying the Artist's performances and any performances by another artist with respect to which Company is obligated to pay royalties.

This clause refers to coupling the artist with another artist. This clause needs to be negotiated and the artist needs to receive final veto power as to who s/he is coupled with. The formula must reflect the artist's status compared to other artists on the recording. If the artist is the biggest star on the recording the formula should reflect the receipt of the largest piece of the pie!

(b) The royalty rate on a Phonograph Record embodying Master Recordings made hereunder together with other Master Recordings will be computed by multiplying the royalty rate otherwise applicable by a fraction, the numerator of which is the number of Selections embodying Master Recordings made hereunder and contained on the particular record concerned and the denominator of which is the total number of Selections contained on such Record. The royalty rate on an Audiovisual Record containing a Audiovisual Recordings made hereunder and other audiovisual works will be determined by apportionment based upon actual playing time on the Record concerned.

(c) No royalties shall be payable to you in respect of Phonograph Records sold or distributed by Company or Company's licensees for promotional purposes, as cut-outs, at close-out prices, for scrap, at less than inventory cost or at fifty (50%) percent or less of the Record's highest posted wholesale price (whether or not intended for resale), as "free", "no charge" or "bonus" Records (whether or not intended for resale), to Company's employees or those of Company's licensees and their relatives, or to radio stations. In connection with the foregoing, you and Company hereby agree that (subject to additional short-term special programs) distributions of Phonograph Records on a "no-charge" basis shall be deemed to be as follows:

(i) With respect to Albums, fifteen (15%) percent of such Records are deemed distributed on a "no-charge" basis; and

(ii) With respect to Singles, twenty-three (23%) percent of such Records are deemed distributed on a "no-charge" basis.

(The calculation of Records deemed distributed on a "no-charge" basis pursuant to the foregoing clauses (i) and (ii) shall be deemed applicable, and such Records shall not be royalty-bearing, regardless of whether or not any such records are in fact invoiced to customers on a "no-charge" basis.)

(d) If records derived from the Masters are sold to distributors or others for less than Company's highest posted wholesale price, or at a discount therefrom, but for more than fifty (50%) percent of such wholesale price, then, for purposes of this paragraph, a percentage of such records shall be deemed non-royalty bearing records, which percentage shall be an amount equal to the percentage of such lesser amount or the applicable discount.

(e) Company may elect from time to time to compute and pay you royalties hereunder on a royalty base different than the Royalty Base Price provided herein, as long as such computation does not materially affect the net amount of royalties otherwise payable to you at that time hereunder.

All negotiable.

10.   ROYALTY PAYMENTS AND ACCOUNTINGS.

10.01   Company shall send to you statements for royalties payable hereunder on or before October 1st for the semi-annual period ending the preceding June 30th and on or before April 1st for the semi-annual period ending the preceding December 31st, together with payment of royalties, if any, earned by you hereunder during the semi-annual period for which the statement is rendered, less all Advances and other charges under this Agreement. Company shall have the right to retain, as a reserve against charges, credits, or returns, such portion of payable royalties as shall be reasonable in Company's best business judgment. With respect to Albums sold hereunder, Company's reserve shall not exceed thirty-five (35%) percent of the number of such records shipped, unless Company reasonably believes a particular release justifies a higher reserve. With respect to Singles sold hereunder, Company's reserve shall not exceed fifty (50%) percent of the number of such records shipped, unless Company reasonably believes a particular release justifies a higher reserve. Reserves shall be fully liquidated no later than the end of the fourth full accounting period following the period in which such reserve was initially established. Records returned will be apportioned between royalty-free records and records on which royalties are payable in the same proportion as such records were shipped to customers. You shall reimburse Company on demand for any overpayments, and Company may also deduct the amount thereof from any monies payable to you hereunder. Royalties paid by Company on Phonograph Records subsequently returned shall be deemed overpayments.

This clause sets out the accounting periods of the royalty statements, in this case they are semi-annual periods. The continuation is standard.

10.02   No royalties shall be payable to you on sales of Phonograph Records by any of Company's licensees or distributors until payment on those sales has been received by Company in the United States. Sales by a licensee or distributor shall be deemed to have occurred in the semi-annual accounting period during which that licensee or distributor shall have rendered to Company accounting statements and payments for those sales.

10.03

(a) Royalties on Phonograph Record sales outside of the United States shall be computed in the national currency in which Company's licensees pay to Company, shall be credited to your royalty account hereunder at the same rate of exchange at which Company's licensees pay to Company, and shall be proportionately subject to any withholding or comparable taxes which may be imposed upon Company's receipts.

Language should be inserted that asks that a foreign account be maintained in case payments are blocked by the government or for any reason.

(b) If Company shall not receive payment in United States dollars in the United States for any sales of Phonograph Records outside of the United States, royalties on those sales shall not be credited to your royalty account hereunder. Company shall, however, at your written request and if Company is reasonably able to do so, accept payment for those sales in foreign currency and shall deposit in a foreign bank or other depository, at your expense, in that foreign currency, that portion thereof, if any, as shall equal the royalties which would have been payable to you hereunder on those sales had payment for those sales been made to Company in United States dollars in the United States. Deposit as aforesaid shall fulfill Company's royalty obligations hereunder as to those sales. If any law, ruling or other governmental restriction limits the amount a licensee can remit to Company, Company may reduce your royalties hereunder by an amount proportionate to the reduction in Company's licensee's remittance to Company.

10.04

(a) Company will maintain books and records which report the sales of Phonograph Records, on which royalties are payable to you. You may, but not more than once a year, at your own expense, examine those books and records, as provided in this paragraph 10.04 only. You may make those examinations only for the purpose of verifying the accuracy of the statements sent to you under paragraph 10.01. All such examinations shall be in accordance with GAAP procedures and regulations. You may make such an examination for a particular statement only once, and only within two (2) years after the date such statement is rendered by Company under paragraph 10.01 (each such statement shall be deemed rendered when due unless you notify Company to the contrary in writing within 60 days after the applicable due date specified). You may make such an examination only during Company's usual business hours, and at the place where Company keeps the books and records to be examined. If you wish to make an examination you will be required to notify Company at least thirty (30) days before the date when you plan to begin it. Company may postpone the commencement of your examination by notice given to you not later than five (5) days before the commencement date specified in your notice; if Company does so, the running of the time within which the examination may be made will be suspended during the postponement. If your examination has not been completed within three (3) months from the time you begin it, Company may require you to terminate it on ten (10) business days' notice to you at any time; Company will not be required to permit you to continue the examination after the end of that ten

(10) business day period. You will not be entitled to examine any manufacturing records or any other records that do not specifically report sales or other distributions of Phonograph Records on which royalties are payable to you. You may appoint a certified public accountant to make such an examination for you, but not if (s)he or his/her firm has begun an examination of Company's books and records for any Person except you unless the examination has been concluded and any applicable audit issues have been resolved. Such certified public accountant will act only under a Letter of Confidentiality which provides that any information derived from such audit or examination will not be knowingly released, divulged or published to any person, firm or corporation, other than to you or to a judicial or administrative body in connection with any proceeding relating to this Agreement.

Several clauses may be inserted in 10.04(a). Language should be included that allows an accountant to postpone the examination of the artist's statements until he or she completes the present audit, should one be in progress.

The artist should negotiate for more time before the audit must begin, and less time to give notice.

(b) Notwithstanding the penultimate sentence of paragraph 10.04(a), if Company notifies you that the representative designated by you to conduct an examination of Company's books and records under paragraph 10.04(a) is engaged in an examination on behalf of another Person ("Other Examination"), you may nevertheless have your examination conducted by your designee, and the running of the time within which such examination may be made shall be suspended until your designee has completed the Other Examination, subject to the following conditions:

(i) You shall notify Company of your election to that effect within fifteen (15) days after the date of Company's said notice to you;

(ii) Your designee shall proceed in a reasonably continuous and expeditious manner to complete the Other Examination and render the final report thereon to the client and Company; and

(iii) Your examination shall not be commenced by your designee before the delivery to Company of the final report on the Other Examination, shall be commenced within thirty (30) days thereafter, and shall be conducted in a reasonably continuous manner.

(The preceding provisions of this paragraph 10.04(b) will not apply if Company elects to waive the provisions of the penultimate sentence of paragraph 10.04(a) which require that your representative shall not be engaged in any Other Examination.)

10.05   If you have any objections to a royalty statement, you will give Company specific notice of that objection and your reasons for it within two (2) years after the date such statement is rendered by Company under paragraph 10.01 (each such statement shall be deemed rendered when due unless you notify Company to the contrary in writing within 60 days after the applicable due date specified). Each royalty statement will become conclusively binding on you at the end of that two (2) year period, and you will no longer have any right to make any other objections to it. You will not have the right to sue

Company in connection with any royalty accounting, or to sue Company for royalties on Records sold during the period a royalty accounting covers, unless you commence the suit within that two (2) year period. If you commence suit on any controversy or claim concerning royalty accountings rendered to you under this agreement in a court of competent jurisdiction (as provided in paragraph 23.09 below), the scope of the proceeding will be limited to determination of the amount of the royalties due for the accounting periods concerned, and the court will have no authority to consider any other issues or award any relief except recovery of any royalties found owing. Your recovery of any such royalties will be the sole remedy available to you or the Artist by reason of any claim related to Company's royalty accountings. Without limiting the generality of the preceding sentence, neither you nor the Artist will have any right to seek termination of this Agreement or avoid the performance of your obligations under it by reason of any such claim.

Negotiate to extend the time to voice an objection and bring suit. Also it should be made clear that the terms of this clause are as stated unless there is fraud (which means there was intent to deceive), then a legal suit would be filed that introduce other remedies.

10.06   Company shall have the right to deduct from any amounts payable to you hereunder that portion thereof as may be required to be deducted under any statute, regulation, treaty or other law, or under any union or guild agreement, and you shall promptly execute and deliver to Company any forms or other documents as may be required in connection therewith.

10.07   Each payment made by Company to you or the Artist under this Agreement, other than union scale payments under Article 5 hereof, shall, at Company's election, be made by a single check payable to _____. All payments herein are contingent upon Company receiving properly completed W-9 and/or 1001 IRS tax forms, as applicable.

11.   MUSICAL COMPOSITION LICENSES.

11.01   You hereby grant to Company and Company's designees an irrevocable non-exclusive license, under copyright, to reproduce each Controlled Composition on Phonograph Records and to distribute those Phonograph Records in the United States and Canada.

11.02   Mechanical royalties shall be payable for each Controlled Composition on Net Sales of Phonograph Records and at the following rates:

(a)

(i) On Phonograph Records sold in the United States, the rate (the "United States Mechanical Rate") for each Controlled Composition embodied thereon shall be equal to seventy-five (75%) percent of the minimum statutory royalty rate (without regard to playing time) provided for in the United States Copyright Act which is applicable to the reproduction of Musical Compositions as of the date of the delivery of the first Master hereunder embodying the Controlled Composition in question.

[(ii) Notwithstanding anything to the contrary contained in the foregoing paragraph 11.02 (a)(i), with respect to USNRC Net Sales of all Phonograph Records in fulfillment of the Recording Commitment, the United States Mechanical Rate otherwise payable under paragraph 11.01(a)(i) above shall escalate to eighty-seven and one-half (87 ?%) of the United States Mechanical Rate on such sales in excess of five-hundred thousand (500,000) units and to one hundred (100%) of the U.S. Mechanical Rate percent on such sales in excess of one million (1,000,000) units.]

(b) On Phonograph Records sold in Canada, the rate (the "Canadian Mechanical Rate") for each Controlled Composition embodied thereon shall be equal to seventy-five (75%) percent of the prevailing rate agreed upon by the Canadian recording industry and the Canadian music publishing industry or its mechanical collection representative which is applicable to the reproduction of Musical Compositions as of the date of delivery to Company of the first Master hereunder embodying the Controlled Composition in question or, if earlier, as of the date that is sixty (60) days prior to the date upon which that first Master was required to be delivered hereunder; provided, however, in no event shall the Canadian Mechanical Rate be greater than the applicable United States Mechanical Rate.

11.03   Notwithstanding the foregoing:

(a)

(i) The mechanical royalty rate for a Controlled Composition contained on a Mid-Priced Record or a Budget Record shall be three-fourths (3/4) of the United States Mechanical Rate or the Canadian Mechanical Rate, as applicable. The mechanical royalty rate on a Controlled Composition, which is a copyrighted arrangement of a public domain work, shall be one-half (?) of the United States Mechanical Rate or the Canadian Mechanical Rate, as applicable. No mechanical royalties shall be payable on any Phonograph Records for which no royalties are payable pursuant to Article 9 above. No mechanical royalties shall be payable on any Controlled Composition having a playing time of less than ninety (90) seconds.

(ii) If ASCAP or BMI accords regular performance credit for any Controlled Composition which is an arranged version of a public domain work, the Mechanical Royalty rate on that Composition will be apportioned according to the same ratio used by ASCAP or BMI in determining the performance credit. Company will not be required to pay you at that rate unless you furnish Company with satisfactory evidence of that ratio.

(b) The maximum aggregate mechanical royalty rate for all Selections, including Controlled Compositions, contained on a Phonograph Record for sales in the United States or Canada shall be the product of (1): the United States Mechanical Rate (as set forth in paragraph 11.02(a)(i) above) or the Canadian Mechanical Rate, as applicable, for the first Master recorded in connection with the particular Album or EP project concerned and (2): eleven (11) for Albums (containing one (1) or more discs or the tape equivalent), five (5) for EPs, three (3) for Long-Play Singles and two (2) for

Singles, regardless of the number of Selections contained thereon. If the aggregate mechanical royalty rate applicable to all of the Selections embodied on any Phonograph Record hereunder shall exceed the applicable maximum aggregate royalty rate set forth above for that Phonograph Record, then the aggregate mechanical royalty rate for the Controlled Compositions, if any, contained thereon shall be reduced by an amount equal to such excess. If the aggregate mechanical royalty rate applicable to all of the Selections embodied on that Phonograph Record shall, even as reduced in accordance with the immediately preceding sentence, still exceed the applicable maximum aggregate mechanical royalty rate for that Phonograph Record, then you shall, upon Company's demand, pay Company an amount equal to the additional mechanical royalties payable as a result of that excess and Company may, in addition to all of Company's other rights or remedies, deduct that amount from any monies payable by Company hereunder or under any other agreement between you and Company or Company's affiliates.

11.04   Company will compute Mechanical Royalties on Controlled Compositions as of the end of each calendar quarter-annual period in which there are sales or returns of Records on which mechanical royalties are payable to you. On the next May 15th, August 15th, November 15th, or February 15th, Company will send a statement covering those royalties and will pay any net royalties which are due. Mechanical Royalty reserves maintained against anticipated returns and credits will not be held for an unreasonable period of time; retention of a reserve for two (2) years after it is established will not be considered unreasonable in any case. If any overpayment of mechanical royalties is made to any Person you will reimburse Company for it; Company may also recoup it from any payments due or becoming due to you. If Company pays any mechanical royalties on Records which are returned later, those royalties will be considered overpayments. If the total amount of the mechanical royalties which Company pays on any Record consisting of Master Recordings made under this agreement (including mechanical royalties for Compositions which are not Controlled Compositions) is higher than the limit fixed for that Record under subparagraph 11.03(b), that excess amount will be considered an overpayment also. Paragraphs 10.04 and 10.05 will apply to mechanical royalty accountings.

11.05   You shall, upon Company's request, cause the issuance to Company and Company's designees of mechanical licenses to reproduce on Phonograph Records Selections which are not Controlled Compositions and to distribute those Phonograph Records in the United States and Canada. Those mechanical licenses shall be at rates and on terms no less favorable to Company and Company's designees than those contained in the standard mechanical license issued by the Harry Fox Agency, Inc. or any successor with respect to Phonograph Records distributed in the United States and by CMRRA or any successor with respect to Phonograph Records distributed in Canada; provided, however, in no event shall those rates exceed one hundred (100%) percent of the applicable minimum statutory rates set forth in paragraph 11.02 above. You shall also, upon Company's request, cause the issuance to Company and Company's designees of mechanical licenses to reproduce Selections on Phonograph Records hereunder and to distribute those Phonograph Records outside the United States and Canada on terms no less favorable to Company and Company's designees than those generally applicable to

Phonograph Record manufacturers in each country in question. The obligation to account and pay mechanical royalties on sales of Phonograph Records outside of the United States shall be that of Company's licensees.

11.06   If the copyright in any Controlled Composition is owned or controlled by a person, firm or corporation other than you, you shall cause that person, firm or corporation to grant to Company and Company's designees the same rights as you are required to grant to Company and Company's designees pursuant to this paragraph.

11.07   You hereby grant to Company and Company's designees at no fee, royalty, or other cost to Company or Company's designees, the irrevocable, non-exclusive, worldwide right to reproduce and publicly perform each Controlled Composition on Audiovisual Recordings, to distribute Audiovisual Records embodying those Audiovisual Recordings, and to otherwise exploit in any manner and through any media those Audiovisual Recordings. You shall, upon Company's request, cause the issuance to Company and Company's designees, at no fee, royalty, or other cost to Company or Company's designees, the irrevocable, non-exclusive, worldwide right to reproduce and publicly perform each Selection which is not a Controlled Composition on Audiovisual Recordings and to distribute Audiovisual Records embodying those Audiovisual Recordings, and to otherwise exploit in any manner or media those Audiovisual Recordings. If Company or Company's designees shall pay any such fee, royalty, or other cost, you shall, upon Company's demand, pay Company the amount thereof, and Company may, in addition to all of Company's other rights and remedies, deduct that amount from any monies payable by Company hereunder or under any other agreement between you and Company or Company's affiliates. Without limiting the generality of the foregoing, it is understood and agreed that Company's rights under this paragraph 11.07 include the right to reproduce and publicly perform, at no fee, royalty or other cost to Company or Company's designees, Controlled Compositions and Non-Controlled Compositions in television and/or radio commercials advertising Phonograph Records made hereunder.

11.08   Any assignment, license or other agreement made with respect to Controlled Compositions shall be subject to the terms hereof.

12.   AUDIOVISUAL RECORDINGS.

12.01   Upon Company's request, you shall cause the Artist to appear for the making of Audiovisual Recordings embodying the Artist's performances on the following terms:

(a) Company shall designate the Musical Compositions which shall be embodied in the Audiovisual Recordings (Company shall consult in good faith with you with respect to such designation; provided, Company's inadvertent failure to so consult shall not be deemed a breach hereof). You and Company shall mutually designate the director, storyboard and script of each Audiovisual Recording. You and Company will mutually designate the producer of the Audiovisual Recordings, all other individuals rendering services in connection with the production of the Audiovisual Recordings, and the locations at and the dates on which the Audiovisual Recordings shall be produced. Provided you are in compliance with your material obligations hereunder, with respect to each Committed Album hereunder, Company agrees to produce one (1) Audiovisual Recording embodying a Master contained on the applicable Committed Album.

(b) Company shall pay the Audiovisual Production Costs in an amount not in excess of a written budget approved by Company in writing. The Audiovisual Production Costs shall mean and include all minimum union scale payments made by Company to the Artist in connection with the production of the Audiovisual Recordings, all payments which are made by Company to any other individuals rendering services in connection with the production of the Audiovisual Recordings, all other payments which are made by Company pursuant to any applicable law or regulation or the provisions of any collective bargaining agreement between Company and any union or guild (including, without limitation, payroll taxes and payments to union pension and welfare funds), all amounts paid or incurred by Company for studio, hall, location or set rentals, tape, film, other stock, engineering, editing, instrument rentals and cartage, transportation and accommodations, wardrobes, immigration clearances, any so-called "per diems" for any individuals (including the Artist) rendering services in connection with the production of the Audiovisual Recordings, together with all other amounts paid or incurred by Company in connection with the production of the Audiovisual Recordings. To the extent permissible under applicable union agreements, you and Artist hereby waive any right to be paid union scale payments in connection with the production of Audiovisual Recordings. The Audiovisual Production Costs shall constitute Advances hereunder and shall be recoupable as set forth in paragraph 12(f) hereof.

(c) The Audiovisual Recordings shall be produced in accordance with the rules and regulations of all labor unions and guilds having jurisdiction over the production thereof.

(d) You shall cause the Artist to fully cooperate with Company and Company's designees and to perform to the best of the Artist's ability in connection with the production of the Audiovisual Recordings.

(e) If the Audiovisual Production Costs exceed the budget approved by Company in writing as a result of any cause which is within your or the Artist's control, or if you or the Artist shall for any reason whatsoever delay the commencement of or not be available for any scheduled appearance by you or the Artist relating to the production of the Audiovisual Recordings, you shall, upon Company's demand, pay to Company an amount equal to the expenses or charges paid or incurred by Company by reason thereof. Company may, without limiting its other rights and remedies, deduct that amount from any monies payable by Company hereunder or under any other agreement between you and Company or Company's affiliates.

(f) One Hundred (100%) percent of the aggregate amount of Audiovisual Production Costs shall be recoupable from any and all monies payable to you from the exploitation of Audiovisual Recordings hereunder. Fifty (50%) percent of the Audiovisual Production Costs for each Audiovisual Recording may be recouped from your royalties on sales of Records which do not reproduce visual images or other exploitations of audio Master Recordings ("audio royalties").

12.02 Company shall be the sole owner of all worldwide rights in and to each Audiovisual Recording (including the worldwide copyrights therein and thereto). Without limiting the generality of the foregoing, it is understood and agreed that Company's rights to use your name and the name, likeness, and other identification of the Artist and biographical material concerning the Artist in the Audiovisual Recordings are set forth in Articles 6 and 7 hereof, wherein the terms "Master Recordings" and "Phonograph Records" shall include Audiovisual Recordings and Audiovisual Records, respectively.

Section Twelve should cover "covered videos" only. The company is requiring full ownership yet they are asking the artist to not only pay for the production costs, but also allow 50% of the cost of each video to be recouped from your audio royalty account! Tough negotiations are necessary and a new artist may have to accept this.

13. WARRANTIES, REPRESENTATIONS AND COVENANTS.

You hereby warrant, represent and covenant that:

13.01 You have the right and power and capacity to enter into this Agreement, to grant the rights granted by you to Company hereunder, and to perform all of the terms hereof, and you have not done and shall not do anything that will impair Company's rights hereunder. Without limiting the generality of the foregoing, no Musical Composition or any other material recorded by the Artist shall be subject to any re-recording or other restrictions.

Add the sentence "Except those listed below:" and then list all prior recordings made for other record companies, as the artist may have recorded for another label.

13.02 During the Term you and Artist shall become and remain members in good standing of any labor union or guilds with which Company may at any time have an agreement lawfully requiring your or the Artist's membership.

13.03

(a) All recording sessions for the Masters shall be conducted in all respects in accordance with the terms of the AF of M Phonograph Record Labor Agreement, of the AFTRACode for the Phonograph Industry, and of the agreements with all other labor unions and guilds having jurisdiction over the recording of the Masters.

(b) The information supplied by you pursuant to paragraph 4.03(b) above constitutes an accurate and complete listing of all individuals, vocalists, musicians and other performers whose performances are in fact embodied in such Masters and a corresponding description of the specified vocal, musical and/or other performances actually performed by each such person and embodied on such Masters.

13.04

(a) Your and Artist's names, masters, Selections embodied on masters and/or materials supplied to Company by you hereunder will not violate or infringe upon any common law or statutory right of any person, including, without limitation, any contractual rights, copyrights, rights of privacy, rights of publicity, trademark rights and rights to trade names. Neither you nor Artist shall "interpolate", "quote from," "sample", "borrow" or otherwise adapt any copyrighted music, copyrighted spoken words, copyrighted sounds, copyrighted words, copyrighted selections and/or copyrighted sound recordings (including, without limitation, any sounds accompanying copyrighted audiovisual works) owned or controlled by third parties in Masters ("Embodied Copyrighted Materials") without having first obtained the written consent of the applicable copyright proprietors of such Embodied Copyrighted Materials, and your failure to obtain such written consents shall be deemed a material breach of this Agreement; provided, always, that if Company, in the exercise of its reasonable business judgment, believes that Embodied Copyrighted Materials exist without such written consent from the applicable copyright proprietors, Company may withhold monies and/or royalties otherwise payable to you hereunder in amounts reasonably related to potential third party liability as a result thereof.

(b) You are the sole owner of the professional name(s) "_____" and no other Person has or will have the right to use such name in connection with Records during the Term other than Company. You shall not use a different name in connection with Records unless you and Company mutually agree in writing. You agree that Company may cause a search(es) to be instituted to determine whether there have been any third party uses for Record purposes of such name. Company may cause a federal application to USA federal registration of the name to be made in your favor for Record and/or entertainment purposes. You and Artist agree that, with respect to each such name, any and all amounts expended by Company pursuant to this paragraph will be deemed Advances. If the aforesaid search(es) indicate(s) that such name should not be used, Company and you shall mutually agree upon a substitute name for Artist. Nothing contained herein shall release you from your indemnification of Company in respect of Company's use of such name.

13.05

(a) There are no recordings embodying the Artist's performances which have not heretofore been commercially released in the Territory on Phonograph Records.

(b) Neither you nor Artist has heretofore granted any rights in and to any Controlled Composition to any music publisher or any other person.

Add the sentence "Except those listed below:" and then list all prior recordings made for other record companies, as the artist may have recorded for another label.

13.06   Neither you nor the Artist shall at any time, directly or indirectly, give or offer to give any consideration of any kind to any radio or television station or network, to any employee thereof, or to any person, firm, or corporation controlling or influencing that station or network's programming for the purpose of securing the broadcast or promotion of any Phonograph Records hereunder.

13.07   Except as otherwise specifically provided herein, Company shall have no obligation hereunder or otherwise to pay any person, firm, or corporation any amounts in connection with the exercise of any of Company's rights hereunder, including, without limitation, Company's rights with respect to the recording or exploitation of Master Recordings.

13.08   Artist has reached the age of majority prior to the date hereof.

13.09   You and Artist hereby waive any so-called "moral rights" you may have in the Masters and Records produced hereunder.

13.10   The Masters shall be free of any and all liens or and encumbrances.

13.11   Company's knowledge of facts which if true would constitute a breach of any warranty, representation or covenant made by you hereunder shall not impair or otherwise affect Company's entitlement to indemnification pursuant to paragraph 20 below or its other remedies hereunder.

[DRAFTING NOTE: IF NEITHER GRANTOR NOR ANY MEMBER OF ARTIST IS, AT THE TIME OF EXECUTION, A CALIFORNIA RESIDENT, ADD THE FOLLOWING, AND DELETE BRACKETS WHERE APPROPRIATE:

10.11   Grantor warrants and represents that, as of the date hereof, neither Grantor nor [any member of] Artist is a resident of the Sate of California. Grantor shall notify PRI immediately in the event that Grantor and/or [any member of] Artist becomes a resident of the State of California.]

14. RECORDING RESTRICTIONS.

14.01   During the Term neither you nor the Artist shall enter into any agreement or make any commitment which would interfere with your or the Artist's performance of any of the terms hereof nor shall the Artist perform for or render services in connection with the recording of any Master Recordings for any person, firm, or corporation other than Company. After the expiration or termination of the Term, the Artist shall not, prior to the later of the following dates, perform for any person, firm or corporation other than us, for the purpose of making Phonograph Records or Master Recordings, any Selection which shall have been recorded hereunder or under any other agreement between you and Company or Company's affiliates: (a) the date five (5) years subsequent to the date on which that Selection shall have been last delivered to Company in a Master Recording recorded hereunder, or (b) the date three (3) years subsequent to the expiration or termination of the Term (the later date in respect of any Selection being hereinafter sometimes referred to as the "Restriction Date"). Notwithstanding the foregoing, if any Selection recorded hereunder is not released on Records as of the date which is one (1) year after the expiration of the Term hereof, the Restriction Date for such selection shall be one (1) year after the expiration of the Term hereof.

If possible, negotiate fewer years.

14.02   Neither you nor the Artist shall at any time manufacture, distribute, sell or authorize the manufacture, distribution, or sale by any person, firm, or corporation other than Company of Phonograph Records embodying (a) any performance rendered by the Artist during the Term or (b) any performance rendered by the Artist after the expiration or termination of the Term of a Selection recorded hereunder if that performance shall have been rendered prior to the Restriction Date applicable to that Selection. Furthermore, neither you nor the Artist shall record or authorize or knowingly permit to be recorded for any purpose any such performance without in each case taking reasonable measures to prevent the manufacture, distribution, or sale at any time by any person, firm, or corporation other than Company of Phonograph Records embodying that performance. Specifically, but without limiting the generality of the foregoing, if during the Term the Artist performs any Selection or if after the Term the Artist performs any Selection prior to the Restriction Date applicable thereto, neither you nor the Artist will authorize or knowingly permit that Selection to be recorded unless pursuant to a written contract containing an express provision that neither that performance nor the recording thereof will be used directly or indirectly for the purpose of making Phonograph Records. Upon Company's request, you shall promptly deliver to Company a copy of the pertinent provisions of each such contract and you shall cooperate fully with Company in any controversy which may arise or litigation which may be instituted relating to Company's rights pursuant to this paragraph.

14.03

(a) During the Term, the Artist will not render any musical performances (audiovisual or otherwise) for the purposes of making any motion picture or other audiovisual work ("Picture", below) for any person, firm or corporation other than us, and no other person, firm or corporation other than Company will be authorized to produce, distribute, exhibit, or otherwise exploit any Picture which contains any musical performance (audiovisual or otherwise) by the Artist, without an express written agreement providing that:

(i) the Picture concerned will not contain performances by the Artist of more than two (2) Musical Compositions, in whole or in part; and

(ii) not more than one-half (?) of any version of the Picture may consist of featured musical performances (defined below) by the Artist or anyone else.

(b) "Featured musical performance", in this paragraph, means: any visual performance of a Musical Composition; and any background performance of a Musical Composition which is intended as a focus of audience attention, whether or not the visual matter is related dramatically to the lyrics or concept of the Musical Composition.

This clause not only deals with feature films, but also with commercials. The company is protecting itself from being excluded from revenue streams.

14.04 You may perform as a background musician ("sideman") accompanying a featured artist for the purpose of making Phonograph Records for others, provided:

(a) You have then fulfilled all of your material obligations under this Agreement, and the engagement does not interfere with the continuing prompt performance of your material obligations to Company.

(b)

(i) You will not render a solo or "step-out" performance; and

(ii) The musical style of the recording will not be so substantially similar to the characteristic musical style of Recordings made by you for Company so as to be likely to cause confusion with such Recordings.

(c) You will not record any material which you have then recorded for Company, and will not agree to be restricted from recording the same material for Company.

(d) You will not accept the sideman engagement unless the Person for whom the recordings are being made agrees in writing, for Company's benefit, that:

(i) Your name may be used in a courtesy credit to Company on the Album liners used for such Records, in the same position as the credits accorded to other side-men and in type identical in size, prominence and all other respects; and

(ii) Except as expressly provided in section 15.03(d)(i) above, neither your name (or any similar name), nor any picture, portrait or likeness of you will be used in connection with such Recordings, including, without limitation, on the front covers of Album containers, on sleeves or labels used for Singles, or in videos, advertising, publicity or any other for of promotion or exploitation, without Company's express written consent, which Company may withhold in its unrestricted discretion.

(e) Before you accept the sideman engagement you will notify Company of the name of the Person for whom the recordings are being made and the record Company which will have the right to distribute Records. Your notice will be addressed to Company's Executive Vice President, Business Affairs.

The purpose of this clause is to prevent the artist from being a featured artist on a record that is not his or her own. However, it also prevents the artist from acting as a sideman or a producer and should be negotiated out of the contract.

15. [THERE IS NO ARTICLE 15]

16. UNIQUE SERVICES.

16.01   You expressly acknowledge that your and the Artist's services hereunder are of a special, unique, intellectual, and extraordinary character which gives them peculiar value, and that in the event of a breach by you or the Artist of any term hereof, Company will be caused irreparable injury which cannot adequately be compensated by money damages. Accordingly, Company shall be entitled to injunctive relief, in addition to any other rights or remedies, which Company may have, to enforce the terms of this Agreement.

In this clause, insert the word "seek," before "injunctive relief..."

16.02 You acknowledge that your failure to timely complete your Delivery obligation will jeopardize Company's investment in the Artist in that it may adversely affect Artist's career and appearance in the public eye and will have an adverse impact upon Company's ability to properly market and promote records embodying Artist's performances and to build Artist's career. You further acknowledge that Company relies upon timely Delivery in order to establish its release schedule and marketing and promotional policies; that failure to timely Deliver adversely affects Company's ability to support its overhead costs, promotional costs and other expenditures necessary to properly record, promote and market phonograph records; and that such failure to timely Deliver will cause Company substantial damages in an amount not readily susceptible of computation.

Insert word "may" adversely affect the company's ability………

17. CERTAIN REMEDIES.

17.01 If you do not fulfill any portion of your Recording Commitment within thirty (30) days after the time prescribed in paragraph 3.02, Company will have the following options:

(a) to suspend Company's obligations to make payments to you under this Agreement until you have cured the default;

(b) to terminate the term of this Agreement at any time, whether or not you have commenced curing the default before such termination occurs; and

(c) to require you to repay to Company the amount, not then recouped, of any Advance previously paid to you by Company and not specifically attributable under Article 8 to an Album which has actually been fully Delivered. You will not be required to repay any such Advance to the extent to which you furnish Company with documentation satisfactory to Company establishing that you have actually used the Advance to make payments, to parties not affiliated with you or Artist and in which neither you nor the Artist has any interest, for recording costs incurred in connection with the Album concerned before Company's demand for payment. ("recording costs", in the preceding sentence, means items which would constitute Recording Costs if paid or incurred by Company.)

Company may exercise each of those options by sending you the appropriate notice. If Company terminates the term under clause 17.01(b) all parties will be deemed to have fulfilled all of their obligations under this agreement except those obligations which survive the end of the term (such as indemnification obligations, re-recording restrictions, and your obligations under clause 17.01(c)). No exercise of an option under this paragraph will limit Company's rights to recover damages by reason of your default, its rights to exercise any other option under this paragraph, or any of its other rights.

17.02 If because of: act of God; inevitable accident; fire; lockout, strike or other labor dispute; riot or civil commotion; act of public enemy; enactment, rule, order or act of any government or governmental instrumentality (whether federal, state, local or foreign);

failure of technical facilities; illness or incapacity of any performer or producer; or other cause of a similar or different nature not reasonably within Company's control; Company is materially hampered in the recording, manufacture, distribution or sale of records, then, without limiting Company's rights, Company shall have the option by giving you notice to suspend the running of the then-current Contract Period for the duration of any such contingency plus such additional time as is necessary so that Company shall have no less than thirty (30) days after the cessation of such contingency in which to exercise its option, if any, to extend the term of this agreement for the next following Option Period.

17.03 If Company refuses, without cause, to permit you to fulfill your minimum Recording Commitment for any Contract Period, (irrespective of whether or not you have commenced recording the particular Album for such Recording Commitment), other than as a result of an event or contingency referred to in paragraph 17.01 above, Company shall have no obligations or liabilities to you in connection therewith unless you shall notify Company of your desire to fulfill your minimum Recording Commitment for that Contract Period and within thirty (30) days after Company's receipt of that notice Company shall fail to advise you in writing that Company shall permit you to fulfill your minimum Recording Commitment for that Contract Period. If Company shall fail to so advise you in writing that Company shall permit you to fulfill your minimum Recording Commitment for that Contract Period, the Term shall expire as of the end of that thirty (30) day period and Company shall have no obligations or liabilities to you whatsoever in connection with Company's failure to permit you to fulfill your Recording Commitment for that Contract Period. Company shall, however, pay you promptly after the expiration of that thirty (30) day period, as an advance recoupable from royalties hereunder, with respect to your Recording Commitment for the Initial Period, the sum of Twenty Thousand ($20,000) Dollars, less any Advances or other monies already paid to you in connection with such Recording Commitment; and with respect to the First and any subsequent Option Period, an amount equal to the difference between the applicable Recording Fund minimum set forth in paragraph 8.02(a) for the Album then remaining unrecorded of your Recording Commitment for the Contract Period during which such termination occurs less one hundred (100%) percent of the Recording Costs for the last Committed Album recorded by you hereunder, less any Advances or other monies already paid to you in connection with such Recording Commitment; provided, however, in no event shall Company be obligated to so pay to you more than an amount equal to one-third (1/3) of the Recording Fund minimum for the Album then remaining unrecorded of your Recording Commitment for the Contract Period during which such termination occurs.

All negotiable if not struck entirely.

18. PRODUCER AND OTHER ROYALTIES.

18.01   You shall be solely responsible for and shall pay all royalties and other Compensation which may be payable to any producers of the Masters or to any others rendering services in connection with the recording of the Masters.

18.02   Notwithstanding the foregoing, Company may (but shall not be obligated to) enter into an agreement with any producer (or other royalty participant) of the Masters which provides for the payment by Company, rather than you, of royalties or other compensation payable to that producer. In that event (or in the event Company pays any such party pursuant to a letter of direction) Company may deduct any amounts payable by Company to that producer or director from any royalties or other sums payable by Company hereunder or under any other agreement between you and Company or Company's affiliates. Furthermore, for the purposes of the recoupment of any Advances or charges under this Agreement, the royalty rates contained in Article 9 with respect to those Masters shall be deemed reduced by the amount of the applicable royalty rates with respect to Masters which are contained in Company's agreement with any producer (or such party). Any Advances payable by Company to a producer (or such party) which are not recouped by Company from royalties payable to that producer may be recouped by Company from any royalties or other sums payable by Company hereunder or under any other agreement between you and Company or Company's affiliates.

This is an "all in deal."

19. DEFINITIONS.

19.01   The term "Advance" shall mean prepayment of royalties. Company may recoup Advances from royalties to be paid to you or on your behalf pursuant to this Agreement. Except as otherwise set forth herein, Advances shall be non-refundable.

19.02   The term "Album" shall mean an audio only long-playing Phonograph Record which is not an EP, Single, or Long-Play Single, and where the context requires, Master Recordings sufficient to constitute a long-playing audio only Phonograph Record.

19.03   The term "Audiovisual Record" shall mean a Record embodying an Audiovisual Recording. Without limiting the generality of the foregoing, any CD-ROM Record or other interactive audiovisual Record which is not intended primarily for audio playback shall be deemed to be an Audiovisual Record hereunder. For purposes of the preceding sentence, so-called "enhanced CDs" and CD-Plus Records are intended primarily for audio playback.

19.04   The term "Audiovisual Recording" shall mean every form of Master Recording embodying visual images.

19.05   The term "Container Charge" shall mean the applicable percentage, specified as follows, of the Gross Royalty Base applicable to the particular Record concerned: twelve and one-half (12 ?%) percent for Singles packaged in color or other special printed sleeves, and for Albums, EPs, and Long-Playing Singles in disc form packaged in Company's standard singlefold jackets without any special elements (such as, but not limited to, plastic, cardboard, or printed inner sleeves, inserts, or attachments); seventeen (17%) percent thereof for all other Albums, EPs or Long-Playing Singles in disc form, and for all other sound-only Phonograph Records in disc form; and twenty (20%) percent thereof for Audiovisual Records, all Phonograph Records in tape form, such as reel-toreel tapes, cartridges, cassettes (whether audio or video) and for all other recorded devices, but twenty-five (25%) percent for compact disc Records and all New Media Records.

The container charge for the standard configuration is 25% here and the artist should try to negotiate.

19.06   The term "Contract Period" shall mean the Initial Period or any Option Period of the Term (as they may be suspended or extended).

19.07   The term "Controlled Composition" shall mean a Musical Composition or other Selection, written or composed by you, the Artist, any producer of the Masters, or any other persons engaged by you in connection with the production of Masters, in whole or in part, alone or in collaboration with others, or which is owned or controlled, in whole or in part, directly or indirectly, by you, the Artist or any person firm or corporation in which you or the Artist have a direct or indirect interest.

19.08   The terms "Conventional Phonograph Record", "Conventional discs and tapes" and "Conventional Album" shall refer to discs or tapes of the quality used for the majority of units of a particular Phonograph Record released. If, at any particular time, Company has ceased to regularly manufacture plain, black "vinyl" disc records and only manufactures tapes, compact discs and/or "premium vinyl" (e.g., so-called "half-speed mastered") discs, then the terms "Conventional discs" or "Conventional Album in disc form", and the like, shall refer to conventional tapes.

19.09   The term "Delivery" or "delivery to Company" (or "Delivery to Company") or words of similar connotation used in connection with Master Recordings or Masters shall mean delivery to a person designated by Company at such location or locations designated by Company of fully-mixed, leadered, sequenced, equalized and unequalized master tapes in proper form for the production of the parts necessary to manufacture phonograph records therefrom, which Masters have been approved by Company as commercially and technically satisfactory for the manufacture and sale of Phonograph Records, and delivery to a person designated by Company at such location or locations designated by Company of all consents, approvals, copy information, credits, mechanical licenses and other material and documents (including those described in paragraph 4.03(b) above) required by Company to release Phonograph Records embodying those Master Recordings or Masters and to manufacture album covers or other packaging therefor. Company may (but shall not be obligated to) send you written notice of the date which Company deems to be the applicable date of Delivery to Company of any Master Recordings made hereunder. If you dispute the date of such notice, you shall give notice in writing to Company within ten (10) business days of Company's notice to you. Your failure to so notify Company shall be deemed your acceptance of the date contained in Company's notice. The sending of Company's notice shall be without prejudice to Company's rights and remedies hereunder if Company later discovers that such delivery has not been fully and completely made. Company's election to make a payment to you which was to have been made upon Delivery of Master Recordings or to release a Record derived from such Master Recording shall not be deemed to be its acknowledgement that such "Delivery" was properly made and Company shall not be deemed to have waived either its right to require such complete and proper performance thereafter or its remedies for your failure to perform in accordance therewith.

19.10   The term "EP" shall mean an audio only Phonograph Record embodying no fewer than five (5) different Musical Compositions and no more than seven (7) different Musical Compositions.

19.11   The term "Long-Play Single" shall mean an audio only Phonograph Record embodying no more than four (4) different Musical Compositions.

19.12   The term "Master Recording" shall mean every form of recording, whether now known or unknown, embodying sound, or sound accompanied by visual images.

19.13   The term "Masters" shall mean Master Recordings embodying the performances of the Artist recorded hereunder.

19.14

(a) The term "Mid-Priced Record" shall mean a Phonograph Record which bears a Gross Royalty Base at least twenty (20%) percent lower, but not more than thirty-five (35%) percent lower than the Gross Royalty Base applicable to Company's then-current highest prevailing "top-line" record of comparable repertoire and in the same configuration (e.g., Album, Multiple Record Set, Long Play Single, tape cassette, compact disc, etc.) released by Company or Company's licensees in the territory concerned.

(b) The term "Budget Record" shall mean a Phonograph Record which bears a Gross Royalty Base greater than thirty-five (35%) percent lower than the Gross Royalty Base applicable to Company's then-current highest prevailing "top line" record of comparable repertoire and in the same configuration (e.g., Album, Multiple Record Set, Long Play Single, tape cassette, compact disc, etc.) released by Company or Company's licensees in the territory concerned.

19.15   The term "Multiple Album" shall mean an Album which contains two (2) or more units of a particular configuration of Record, which is sold as a single unit.

19.16   The terms "Musical Composition" and "Composition" shall mean a single musical composition and, for the purposes of computing mechanical royalties hereunder, shall include medleys and spoken word pieces. Different versions of a Composition embodied on the same Phonograph Record will be considered one (1) Composition (and one(1) Selection) for all purposes hereunder.

19.17   The term "Net Receipts" shall mean an amount equal to the gross monies received by Company in the United States from a person, firm or corporation from the exploitation by that person, firm or corporation of rights in Audiovisual Recordings (including any monies received by Company for the use of Audiovisual Recordings in Audiovisual Records) less thirty (30%) percent of those gross monies as a distribution fee, and less all costs paid or incurred by Company in connection with the exploitation of those rights and the collection of those monies.

19.18   The term "Net Royalty" or "Net Flat Fee" shall mean the gross royalty or gross flat fee received by Company in the United States from a person, firm or corporation from the exploitation by that person, firm or corporation of rights in Masters (other than Audiovisual Recordings), less all costs paid or incurred by Company in connection with the exploitation of those rights and the collection of those monies, and less all royalties or other sums payable by Company to any person, firm or corporation in connection with the exploitation of those rights, except for royalties or other sums payable to producers of those Masters, which shall be borne solely by you.

19.19   The term "Net Sales" shall mean gross sales to wholesale and retail customers, less returns, credits and reserves against anticipated returns and credits.

19.20   The term "through Normal Retail Channels" shall refer to sales of Phonograph Records hereunder other than as described in paragraphs 9.03, 9.04, 9.05 (other than subsection (b) thereof), 9.06, 9.07 and 9.08 above;

19.21   The terms "Phonograph Record" and "Record" shall mean every form of reproduction, transmission or communication of Master Recordings, whether now known or unknown, embodying sound alone, or sound accompanied by visual images, distributed, transmitted or communicated primarily for home use, school use, jukebox use, and use in means of transportation, including, without limitation, discs of any speed or size, reel-to-reel tapes, cartridges, cassettes, or other pre-recorded tapes.

19.22   The term "New Media Records" shall mean Records in the following configurations: mini-discs, digital compact cassettes, digital audio tapes, laser discs, digital compact discs capable of bearing visual images (including, without limitation, CD-Plus and CD-ROM) and other Records embodying, employing or otherwise utilizing any non-analog technology, whether such Records are interactive (i.e. the user is able to access, select or manipulate the materials therein) or non-interactive, and whether now known or hereafter devised, but specifically excluding audio-only compact discs.

19.23   The term "Royalty Base Price" shall mean the amount specified below ("Gross Royalty Base") applicable to the Records concerned, less all excise, purchase, value added, or similar taxes (included in the Royalty Base Price) and less the applicable Container Charge:

(a) With respect to Records (other than Audiovisual Records) sold for distribution in the United States, the "Gross Royalty Base" shall be the suggested retail list price ("SRLP") for such Record; or if there is no SRLP, the lowest wholesale price payable by the largest category of Company's (or its distributor's) customers in the normal course of business with respect to such Records sold for distribution during the applicable semi-annual accounting period, multiplied by an "up-lift" of one hundred thirty (130%) percent.

(b) With respect to Records sold for distribution outside of the United States, the "Gross Royalty Base" shall be the same royalty base price on which Company is accounted to by its licensee in the country concerned provided that Company is accounted to based on the SRLP of such Records in the country concerned, or a substitute for an actual or hypothetical retail price ("Retail-Related Price"). If Company is accounted to based on a royalty base price other than a Retail-Related Price, the "Gross Royalty Base" for such Records shall be the published price to dealers ("ppd") in the country concerned for such Records, multiplied by an "up-lift" of one hundred twenty-six (126%) percent..

(c) With respect to Audiovisual Records, "Gross Royalty Base" shall mean Company's (or its distributor's) published wholesale price as of the commencement of the accounting period concerned.

19.24   The term "Selection" shall mean a Musical Composition, poem, dramatic work, comedy routine, or other verbal expression.

19.25   The term "Single" shall mean an audio-only seven (7") inch disc Phonograph Record or its tape or other equivalent, embodying no more than two (2) Compositions.

19.26   The term "Territory" shall mean the universe.

19.27   The term "other agreement between you and Company or Company's affiliates" and like words shall mean any other agreement between you, Artist or any entity furnishing Artist's services and Company or Company's affiliates which relates to recordings embodying Artist's performances.

19.28   The term "Person" "person" or "Party" shall mean any individual, corporation, partnership, association or other organized group of persons or the legal successors or representatives of the foregoing.

19.29   Notwithstanding paragraphs 19.02, 19.10, 19.11 and 19.25 above, if a particular record is marketed and priced by Company or its Licensees as a particular configuration of record (e.g., Single, Long-Play Single, EP, etc.), then, for royalty purposes only, such record shall be deemed to be such form of configuration.

20. INDEMNITY.

20.01   You hereby indemnify, save, and hold Company harmless from any and all damages, liabilities, costs, losses and expenses (including legal costs and reasonable attorneys' fees) arising out of or connected with any claim, demand or action which is inconsistent with any of the warranties, representations, covenants or agreements made by you in this Agreement, which has resulted in a final judgment or has been settled with your written consent (it being understood that your consent shall be deemed given to any settlement not in excess of Five Thousand ($5,000) Dollars). Notwithstanding the foregoing, if you withhold consent to any settlement which Company is willing to make, the foregoing indemnity shall apply and Company may settle such claim in its sole discretion unless you promptly assume all costs of defending against such claim, demand or action including, without limitation, court costs, reasonable attorneys' fees, and direct expenses theretofore incurred by Company in connection with said claim, demand or action; provided that in the event you assume said costs, Company shall nonetheless have the right to settle such claim, demand or action in its sole discretion without your consent, provided that, in such event, the foregoing indemnification shall not apply with respect thereto. You shall reimburse Company, on demand, for any payment made by Company at any time with respect to any damage, liability, cost, loss or expense to which the foregoing indemnity applies. Pending the determination of any claim, demand or action, Company may, at its election, withhold payment of any monies otherwise payable to you hereunder in an amount which does not exceed your potential liability to Company pursuant to this paragraph; provided, however, that if you shall deliver to Company an indemnity or surety bond, in a form and with a Company acceptable to Company, which in respect of such claim, demand or action shall cover the amount of such claim, demand or action and Company's estimated attorneys' fees and legal costs in connection therewith, then Company shall not withhold payment of monies otherwise payable to you hereunder in respect of such claim, demand or action; and provided further that Company shall liquidate any such withheld amounts if within twelve (12) months no lawsuit has been commenced and active settlement discussions are not then taking place. You may participate in the defense of any claim referred to in this paragraph 20 through counsel of your selection at your own expense, but Company will have the right at all times, in its sole discretion, to retain or resume control of the conduct of the defense of such claim.

21. ASSIGNMENT.

21.01

(a) Company shall have the right, at its election, to assign any of Company's rights hereunder, in whole or in part, to any subsidiary, affiliated, controlling or other related Company, and to any Person, firm or corporation owning or acquiring a substantial portion of Company's stock or assets, and any rights so assigned may also be assigned by the assignee. Company shall also have the right to assign any of its rights hereunder to any of its licensees in order to effectuate the purposes hereof. You shall not have the right to assign any of your rights hereunder.

It may be hard to take but non-negotiable.

(b) Notwithstanding the foregoing, you may assign your rights under this Agreement to a corporation, all of whose capital stock is owned solely by you, subject to the following conditions:

(i) The assignee will be subject to Company's approval in Company's sole discretion;

(ii) The assignment will not be effective until you have delivered to Company an instrument satisfactory to Company in Company's sole discretion effecting the assignment and the assignee's assumption of your obligations, and Company has executed that instrument to evidence Company's approval of it;

(iii) No such assignment will relieve you of your obligations under this Agreement; and

(iv) If such an assignment takes place, any further transfer of the rights assigned will be subject to the same conditions.

22. NOTICES.

22.01   All notices to be given to you hereunder and all statements and payments to be sent to you hereunder shall be addressed to you at the address set forth on page 1 hereof or at such other address as you shall designate in writing from time to time. All notices to be given to Company hereunder shall be addressed to Company to the attention of the Executive Vice President of Business Affairs at the address set forth on page 1 hereof or at such other address as Company shall designate in writing from time to time. All notices shall be in writing and shall either be served by personal delivery, mail, or telegraph, all charges prepaid. Except as otherwise provided herein, notices shall be deemed given when personally delivered, mailed, or delivered to a telegraph office, all charges prepaid, except that notices of change of address shall be effective only after actual receipt. A copy of all notices to Company shall be sent to {Name}, {Address}.

Insert in 22.01 that a courtesy copy of all notices by sent directly to the artist's attorney.

23. MISCELLANEOUS.

23.01

(a) This Agreement sets forth your and Company's entire understanding relating to its subject matter and all prior and contemporaneous understandings relating to the same have been merged herein. No modification, amendment, waiver, termination or discharge of this Agreement or any of its terms shall be binding upon Company unless confirmed by a document signed by a duly authorized officer of Company. No waiver by you or Company of any term of this Agreement or of any default hereunder shall affect your or Company's respective rights thereafter to enforce that term or to exercise any right or remedy in the event of any other default, whether or not similar.

(b) If any part of this Agreement is determined to be void, invalid, inoperative or unenforceable by a court of competent jurisdiction or by any other legally constituted body having jurisdiction to make such determination, such decision shall not affect any other provisions hereof, and the remainder of this Agreement shall be effective as though such void, invalid, inoperative or unenforceable provision had not been contained herein. If the payments provided by this Agreement shall exceed the amount permitted by any present or future law or governmental order or regulation, such stated payments shall be reduced while such limitation is in effect to the amount which is so permitted; and the payment of such amount shall be deemed to constitute full performance by Company of its obligations to you and Artist hereunder with respect to compensation during the term when such limitation is in effect.

23.02

(a) Company shall not be deemed to be in breach of any of Company's obligations hereunder unless and until you shall have given Company specific written notice by certified or registered mail, return receipt requested, describing in detail the breach and Company shall have failed to cure that breach within thirty (30) days after Company's receipt of that written notice or, if the breach cannot be cured within said thirty (30) day period, if Company does not commence to cure such breach within said thirty (30) day period and continue to so cure with reasonable diligence.

(b) Except with respect to: (i) your obligation to timely Deliver any Album hereunder, (ii) your warranties hereunder, (iii) where a specific cure provision is provided herein, (iv) breaches incapable of being cured, or (v) an application for injunctive relief, the failure by you to perform any of your obligations hereunder shall not be deemed a breach of this Agreement unless Company gives you written notice of such failure to perform and such failure is not corrected within thirty (30) days from the date you receive such notice.

23.03 Company's payment obligations under this Agreement are conditioned upon your full and faithful performance of the terms hereof.

23.04 Wherever your approval or consent is required hereunder, that approval or consent shall not be unreasonably withheld. Company may require you to formally give or withhold approval or consent by giving you notice of Company's request that you do so and by furnishing you with the information or material in respect of which the approval or consent is sought. You shall give Company written notice of your approval or disapproval or of your consent or non-consent within five (5) days after Company's notice is sent and, in the event of your disapproval or non-consent, your notice shall contain the specific reasons therefor. Your failure to give Company notice as aforesaid shall be deemed to be consent or approval, as the case may be, with respect to the matter submitted. In the event the word "you" includes members of a group, then, at Company's election, any member of the group shall have the right to give approval or consent on behalf of the entire group.

23.05 Nothing herein contained shall constitute a partnership, joint venture or other agency relationship between you and Company. Except as otherwise expressly provided herein, you and the Artist are performing your obligations hereunder as independent contractors. Neither party hereto shall hold itself out contrary to the terms of this paragraph, and neither you nor Company shall become liable for any representation, act or omission of the other contrary to the provisions hereof. You do not have the right to execute any agreement or incur any obligation for which Company may be liable or otherwise bound.

23.06 This Agreement shall not be deemed to give any right or remedy to any third party whatsoever unless that right or remedy is specifically granted by Company in writing to that third party.

23.07 The provisions of any applicable collective bargaining agreement between Company and any labor union or guild which are required by the terms of that agreement to be included in this Agreement shall be deemed incorporated herein as if those provisions were expressly set forth in this Agreement.

23.08 Except as otherwise expressly provided herein, all rights and remedies herein or otherwise shall be cumulative and none of them shall be in limitation of any other right or remedy.

23.09 **THIS AGREEMENT HAS BEEN ENTERED INTO IN THE STATE OF NEW YORK, AND ITS VALIDITY, CONSTRUCTION, INTERPRETATION AND LEGAL EFFECT SHALL BE GOVERNED BY THE LAWS OF THE STATE OF NEW YORK**

APPLICABLE TO CONTRACTS ENTERED INTO AND PERFORMED ENTIRELY WITHIN THE STATE OF NEW YORK. ALL CLAIMS, DISPUTES OR DISAGREEMENTS WHICH MAY ARISE OUT OF THE INTERPRETATION, PERFORMANCE OR BREACH OF THIS AGREEMENT SHALL BE SUBMITTED EXCLUSIVELY TO THE JURISDICTION OF THE STATE COURTS OF THE STATE OF NEW YORK OR THE FEDERAL DISTRICT COURTS LOCATED IN NEW YORK CITY; PROVIDED, HOWEVER, IF COMPANY IS SUED OR JOINED IN ANY OTHER COURT OR FORUM (INCLUDING AN ARBITRATION PROCEEDING) IN RESPECT OF ANY MATTER WHICH MAY GIVE RISE TO A CLAIM BY COMPANY HEREUNDER, YOU AND ARTIST CONSENT TO THE JURISDICTION OF SUCH COURT OR FORUM OVER ANY SUCH CLAIM WHICH MAY BE ASSERTED BY COMPANY. ANY PROCESS IN ANY ACTION OR PROCEEDING COMMENCED IN THE COURTS OF THE STATE OF NEW YORK ARISING OUT OF ANY SUCH CLAIM, DISPUTE OR DISAGREEMENT, MAY AMONG OTHER METHODS, BE SERVED UPON YOU BY DELIVERING OR MAILING THE SAME, VIA CERTIFIED MAIL, ADDRESSED TO YOU AT THE ADDRESS GIVEN IN THIS AGREEMENT OR SUCH OTHER ADDRESS AS YOU MAY FROM TIME TO TIME DESIGNATE BY NOTICE IN CONFORMITY WITH ARTICLE 22 HEREIN.

23.10   This Agreement shall not become effective until signed by you and countersigned by a duly authorized officer of Company.

23.11

(a) The paragraph headings herein are solely for the purpose of convenience and shall be disregarded completely in the interpretation of this Agreement or any of its terms.

(b) No deletion, addition, revision, change or other alteration in drafts of this Agreement prepared prior to the execution of this Agreement shall be used for the purpose of construction or interpretation of any term, provision or language of this Agreement.

23.12   Company may at any time during the Term obtain, at Company's cost, insurance on the lives of one (1) or more members of the Artist. Company or its designees shall be the sole beneficiary of that insurance and neither you, nor any member of the Artist, nor any person, firm or corporation claiming rights through or from you or the Artist shall have any rights in that insurance. You shall cause those members of the Artist as Company may designate to submit to such physical examinations and to complete and deliver such forms as Company may reasonably require and otherwise to cooperate with Company fully for the purpose of enabling Company to secure that insurance.

23.13   From time to time at Company's request, you shall cause Artist to appear for photography, artwork and similar sessions under the direction of Company or Company's duly authorized agent, appear for interviews with such representatives of newspapers, magazines and other publications, and of publicity and public relations firms as Company may arrange, and confer and consult with Company regarding Artist's performances hereunder and other matters which may concern the parties hereto. Artist shall also, if requested by Company, be available for personal appearances (including performances) on radio, television, record stores and elsewhere, and to record taped interviews, spot announcements, trailers and electrical transcriptions, all for the purpose of advertising, promoting, publicizing and exploiting records released or to be released hereunder and for other general public relations and promotional purposes related to the record business of Company or Company's subsidiary and related companies. Neither you nor Artist shall be entitled to any compensation from Company for such services, other than minimum union scale to Artist if such payment is required by applicable agreements.

23.14   Intentionally deleted.

23.15   You acknowledge that there exists no formal or informal fiduciary relationship between you and Company and that there exists no special relationship of trust and confidence between you and Company independent of the contractual rights, duties and obligations set forth in this Agreement, and that the future course of dealing between you and Company shall neither explicitly nor implicitly indicate such a relationship or the undertaking of any such extra-contractual duties or obligations by Company.

23.16   If Artist's voice should be or become materially and permanently impaired or if Artist should otherwise become physically or mentally disabled in performing, recording and/or personal appearances and/or if Artist should cease to pursue a career as an entertainer, Company may elect to terminate this agreement, by notice to you at any time during the period in which such contingency arose or continues and thereby be relieved of any liability for the executory provisions of this agreement.

24. GROUP ARTIST.

24.01.

(a) You warrant, represent and agree that, for so long as this agreement shall be in effect, Artist will perform together as a group for Company. If any individual comprising Artist refuses, neglects or fails to perform together with the other individuals comprising Artist in fulfillment of the obligations agreed to be performed under this agreement or leaves the group, you shall give Company prompt written notice thereof. (The term "leaving member" shall hereinafter be used to define each individual who leaves the group or no longer performs with the group, or each member of the group if the group disbands.) Company shall have the right, to be exercised by written notice to you within ninety (90) days following its receipt of your notice:

To continue with the services of any such leaving member pursuant to paragraph 24.04 below;

To terminate the Term of this agreement with respect to the remaining members of Artist whether or not Company has exercised its right to continue with the services of a leaving member;

To treat all the members of Artist as leaving members, and have the right to exercise its rights with respect to each in accordance with this Article 24.

(b) In the event that Company fails to send notice of its exercise of rights pursuant to paragraph 24.01(a) above, the Term of this agreement shall be deemed terminated with respect to such leaving member.

(c) If at any time Company believes or has knowledge that a member of Artist is or may be a leaving member, then Company shall have the right (but not the obligation) to exercise Company's rights in accordance with this Article 24. If Company sends a notice to you pursuant to this paragraph 24.01©, you shall have the right, within fifteen (15) days following the date of such notice, to furnish Company with affirmative documentation that the member of Artist shall continue to fulfill such member's obligations under this agreement and remain a member of Artist. Such documentation shall be satisfactory to Company in its sole discretion and shall include, without limitation, a signed notification from the member that such member shall continue as a member of Artist. Notwithstanding anything to the contrary expressed or implied in this paragraph 24.01©, Company's action or inaction with respect to Company's belief or knowledge that a member of Artist may be, or may become, a leaving member shall not act as a waiver of any of Company's duties, obligations, representations or warranties under this Agreement, including, but not limited to, those obligations under paragraph 24.01(a), or as a waiver of any of Company's rights or remedies under this Agreement.

Negotiate longer than fifteen days.

A leaving member, whether or not his engagement is terminated hereunder, may not perform for others for the purpose of recording any selection as to which the applicable restrictive period specified in paragraph 14.02 of this agreement has not expired.

A leaving member shall not, without Company's consent, use the professional name of the group in any commercial or artistic endeavor; the said professional name shall remain your property and the property of and those members of the group who continue to perform their obligations hereunder and whose engagements are not terminated; and, the person, if any, engaged to replace the individual whose engagement is terminated shall be mutually agreed upon by you and Company, and each such person added to Artist, as a replacement or otherwise, shall become bound by the terms and conditions of this agreement and shall execute a letter to Company in the form attached here as Exhibit A as a condition precedent to being so added. Changes in the individuals comprising Artist shall be made by mutual agreement between you and Company.

24.04   In addition to the rights provided in the preceding paragraphs, Company shall have, and you hereby grant to Company, an irrevocable option for the individual and exclusive services of each leaving member as follows: Said option, with respect to such individual, may be exercised by Company giving you notice in writing within ninety (90) days after Company receives your notice provided for in paragraph 24.01(a) above. In the event of Company's exercise of such option, you and such leaving member shall be deemed to have entered into an agreement with Company with respect to such individual's exclusive recording services upon all the terms and conditions of this agreement except that: (i) The Minimum Recording Obligation in the Initial Period shall be two (2) Sides, with a so-called "overcall" option, at Company's election, for sufficient additional Master Recordings to constitute up to one (1) Album, with an additional number (the "Number") of options granted to Company to extend the term of such agreement for consecutive option periods for one (1) Album each, each of which options shall be exercised within nine (9) months after delivery to Company of the Minimum

Recording Obligation for the immediately preceding contract period of such leaving member's agreement. The Number shall be equal to the remaining number of Albums embodying performances of Artist which you would be obligated to deliver hereunder if Company exercised each of its options, but in no event shall the Number be less than four (4); (ii) the provisions contained in paragraph 8.02 shall not be applicable, but Company shall pay all Recording Costs for Master Recordings to be recorded by such individual up to the amount of the budget approved by Company therefor; (iii) Company's royalty obligation to you in respect of Recordings by such individual shall be the payment to you of the royalties computed as set forth in this agreement but at only three quarters (3/4) the rates set forth herein; (iv) Company shall be entitled to combine such leaving member's account with Artist's account hereunder; and (v) Recordings by such individual shall not be applied in diminution of your Minimum Recording Obligation as set forth in this agreement.

Remember with all recording contracts an artist signs the contract as an individual and as a group member. The company will require the complete control over who is in the group, who leaves, and who will be allowed to continue to be a recording musician. Clause twenty-four requires the member to continue his/her career with the company. Some of this is negotiable.

From 2005 contract:

GROUP PROVISIONS

(a)   (i)   For the purposes of this agreement, the following definitions shall apply: (A) **"Leaving Member"** - (I) each individual member of Artist who refuses, neglects, fails or ceases for any reason (including dying or becoming disabled) to perform together with the other individuals comprising Artist in fulfillment of the obligations described in this agreement or who leaves the Group; (II) each individual member of Artist if Artist disbands or (III) each individual member of Artist with respect to whom Company exercises the option described in paragraph 20(a)(ii)(B)(I); (B) **"Leaving Member Event"** – the occurrence of any one (1) or more of the following events: (I) any one (1) or more individual members of Artist refusing, neglecting, failing or ceasing for any reason (including dying or becoming disabled) to perform together with the other individual members comprising Artist in fulfillment of the obligations under this agreement or leaving the Group [DRAFTING NOTE – ADJUST FOR KEY MEMBER SITUATION]; or (II) the disbanding of Artist; (C) **"Reunion Member"** - (I) each individual member of Artist who desires to recommence performing in a group of at least fifty percent (50%) of the members of Artist for the purpose of making Records; or (II) each member of Artist desiring to perform under any group name of Artist used by Company hereunder; and (D) **"Reunion Event"** - at least fifty percent (50%) of the individual members of Artist desiring to recommence performing together for the purpose of making Records or one (1) or more of such members desiring to perform under any group name of Artist used by Company hereunder.

(ii)   Notwithstanding paragraph 1, as used in this agreement, the term **"Artist"** refers jointly and severally to the individuals first mentioned herein as comprising Artist and to such other individuals who during the Term shall comprise Artist. You warrant, represent and agree that, throughout the Term, Artist shall perform together as a group (the **"Group"**) for Company. Artist's obligations under this agreement are joint and several and all references herein to [DIRECT DEAL - **"you"** or **"Artist"** and their possessive forms] [FURNISHING DEAL – **"Artist"**] shall include all members of the Group collectively and each member of the Group individually, unless otherwise specified. If any Leaving Member Event occurs during the Term, then: (A) you and each member of Artist shall give Company prompt notice thereof (the **"Leaving Member Notice"**) specifically referencing this paragraph 20(a); and (B) Company shall have, and each individual member of the Group hereby irrevocably grants to Company, the option, exercisable by notice (**"Company's Leaving Member Notice"**) to you within three (3) months after Company's receipt of the Leaving Member Notice: (I) to deem any or all members of Artist as Leaving Members in accordance with this paragraph 20 [DRAFTING NOTE – ADJUST FOR KEY MEMBER SITUATION]; (II) to obtain the individual and exclusive services of any or all Leaving Members; (III) to terminate the Term with respect to any or all Leaving Members; and/or (IV) to terminate the Term in its entirety without any obligation as to unrecorded or un-Delivered Masters. For the avoidance of doubt, each member of Artist who is not deemed to be a Leaving Member, as well as each Leaving Member with respect to whom Company does not terminate the Term, shall remain bound by this agreement. If Company deems any one (1) or more members of Artist as Leaving Members, then Company's Leaving Member Notice shall specify whether Company requires you to cause such Leaving Member(s) to record and Deliver Demos of at least four (4) completed, fully-mixed and previously-unreleased Masters (the "Leaving Member Demos"), to perform for a personal audition, or to record and Deliver Masters sufficient to comprise one (1) Album, all in accordance with paragraph 20(b); provided if Company's Leaving Member Notice does not so specify, then Company shall be deemed to have required you to cause such Leaving Member(s) to record and Deliver the Leaving Member Demos [DRAFTING NOTE – ADJUST FOR KEY MEMBER SITUATION]. Company shall have no liability or obligations to any Leaving Member unless Company elects to exercise its rights to the recording services of such Leaving Member in accordance with paragraph 20(b). [DIRECT DEAL - If Company terminates the Term with respect to a particular Leaving Member, then you shall be solely responsible for and shall pay all monies required to be paid to such Leaving Member in connection with any Recordings theretofore or thereafter Delivered for which royalties are payable to such Leaving Member and you shall indemnify and hold harmless Company against any claims relating thereto pursuant to the terms of paragraph 15(b).] No Leaving Member (whether or not his or her engagement is terminated by Company) shall, without Company's prior written consent: (I) perform for any Person other than Company for the purpose of recording any Composition as to which the applicable Re-recording Restriction has not yet expired; or (II) use the professional name of the Group in any commercial or artistic endeavor other than for Company. The person, if any, engaged to replace any Leaving Member shall be mutually agreed upon by Company and you. Each person added to Artist, as a replacement or otherwise, shall become bound by the terms and conditions of this agreement and shall execute this agreement and any other documents required by Company as a condition precedent to being so added. Neither Company nor you shall unreasonably withhold agreement with regard thereto; and, if agreement cannot be reached, Company may terminate this agreement by notice to you.

(b)   If Company exercises its option for the individual and exclusive services of any or all Leaving Members pursuant to paragraph 20(a)(ii)(B)(II), you and the Leaving Member(s) referred to in Company's Leaving Member Notice shall be deemed to have entered into a new and separate agreement (the **"Leaving Member Agreement"**) with Company with respect to each such Leaving Member(s)' exclusive recording services upon all the terms and conditions of this agreement except that:

(i)   If Company requires the applicable Leaving Member(s) to record the Leaving Member Demos, then you shall cause such Leaving Member(s) to record same in accordance with a budget approved by Company in writing and you shall Deliver the Leaving Member Demos. If Company requires that the applicable Leaving Member(s) perform for a personal audition, then you shall arrange for same at such place and time as Company may approve. Nothing in this paragraph 20 shall be deemed to require that Company request the Leaving Member Demos or a personal audition if pursuant to paragraph 20(a)(ii) Company elects to require such Leaving Member(s) to record and Deliver Masters sufficient to comprise one (1) Album [DRAFTING NOTE – ADJUST FOR KEY MEMBER SITUATION];

(ii)   By the later to occur of ninety (90) days after Company's receipt of the Leaving Member Notice or sixty (60) days after Company's receipt of the Leaving Member Demos or the date of the personal audition, as the case may be, Company shall have the option by notice to require you to cause the Leaving Member(s) concerned to record and Deliver Masters sufficient to comprise one (1) Album (the **"Leaving Member Recording Commitment"**). Without limiting the foregoing, if Company's Leaving Member Notice requires the applicable Leaving Member(s) to record and Deliver Masters sufficient to comprise one (1) Album, then Company's Leaving Member Notice shall be deemed to constitute the notice required by the preceding sentence. Company shall thereafter have the right to increase the Leaving Member Recording Commitment and the right to extend the term of the Leaving Member Agreement for option periods so that Company shall have the right under the Leaving Member Agreement to the same number of Albums (including optional Albums, i.e., Albums to be Delivered during optional Contract Periods) remaining un-Delivered under this agreement, provided that, notwithstanding anything to the contrary herein, Company shall have options for no fewer than [DRAFTING NOTE – LABEL CALL AS TO NUMBER - _____ (_) Albums] under the Leaving Member Agreement. (The first Album of the Leaving Member Recording Commitment pursuant to each Leaving Member Agreement is referred to in this paragraph 20 as the **"First Leaving Member Album"**, the second such Album is referred to as the **"Second Leaving Member Album,"** etc.);

(iii)   The terms of the following paragraphs shall not be applicable: [DRAFTING NOTE - INSERT APPLICABLE PARAGRAPHS];

(iv)   The Recording Fund for the First Leaving Member Album shall be seventy-five percent (75%) of the minimum Recording Fund set forth in paragraph 7 for the immediately preceding Committed Album Delivered under this agreement (**"Preceding Group Album"**), provided if you have not yet Delivered the First Album hereunder, then the First Album shall be deemed the **"Preceding Group Album"** for purposes of paragraphs 20(b)(iv) and 20(b)(v) only. With respect to each subsequent Album of the Leaving Member Recording Commitment, the Recording Fund shall be calculated in accordance with the provisions of paragraphs 7(c); provided that, "net royalties credited to your royalty account hereunder" as used in paragraph 7(c), shall mean net royalties credited to such Leaving Member's royalty account with respect to units of the particular Album of the Leaving Member Recording Commitment; the minimum Recording Fund applicable with respect to each subsequent Album of the Leaving Member Recording Commitment shall be the minimum Recording Fund for the immediately preceding Album of the Leaving Member Recording Commitment plus five percent (5%); and the maximum Recording Fund applicable to each such Album shall be two (2) times the minimum Recording Fund for such Album;

(v)   Company's royalty obligation in respect of Recordings constituting the First Leaving Member Album shall be seventy-five percent (75%) of the otherwise applicable rate set forth in paragraph 9 of this agreement for Recordings constituting the Preceding Group Album. The royalty rates with respect to all subsequent Albums of the Leaving Member Recording Commitment shall be seventy-five percent (75%) of the royalty rates applicable to the comparable Committed Album hereunder (e.g., for the Second Leaving Member Album, the Basic U.S. Rate shall be seventy-five percent (75%) of the Basic U.S. Rate applicable to the Committed Album immediately following the Preceding Group Album, provided if such comparable Album would be subsequent to the final Album of the Recording Commitment under this agreement, the royalty rates for each subsequent Album of the Leaving Member Recording Commitment shall be seventy-five percent (75%) of the royalty rates applicable to such final Album);

(vi)   Company shall only be entitled to recoup the Leaving Member Portion of the unrecouped balance of your royalty account hereunder as of the date of Company's Leaving Member Notice from royalties otherwise payable under the Leaving Member Agreement concerned and the unrecouped balance of the royalty account under the Leaving Member Agreement concerned from the Leaving Member Portion of the royalties otherwise payable hereunder in respect of Recordings made prior to the date of Company's Leaving Member Notice. [DRAFTING NOTE – ADJUST FOR KEY MEMBER SITUATION] As used in the preceding sentence, the term **"Leaving Member Portion"** shall be calculated by multiplying the unrecouped balance concerned by a fraction, the numerator of which shall be one (1) (or, if more than one (1) Leaving Member is performing together, such number of Leaving Members as are performing together) and the denominator of which shall be the total number of royalty-earning members constituting Artist as of the date of Company's exercise of its option with respect to such Leaving Member; provided that, if as of such date Artist has disbanded, the numerator and denominator shall both be deemed to be one (1);

(vii)   Recordings by a Leaving Member shall not be applied in diminution of the Recording Commitment or Delivery obligations described in paragraph 3; and

(viii) If there shall be more than one (1) Leaving Member for whom Company has exercised its option as provided in this paragraph 20(b) and two (2) or more of such Leaving Members shall, with Company's consent, elect to perform together as a duo or group, then (except as otherwise specifically set forth in paragraph 20(b)(vi)), Company shall have the right to treat such Leaving Members collectively as if they were one (1) Leaving Member for the purpose of this paragraph 20(b), including royalty rates, advances and other monies payable in respect of their joint Recordings pursuant to this paragraph 20(b).

(c)   Notwithstanding anything to the contrary contained in this paragraph 20, if any Reunion Event occurs within five (5) years after Company terminates the Term with respect to any or all member(s) of Artist based on Company's receipt of a notice claiming, or Company's good faith determination that, Artist has disbanded, then: (A) you and each of the Reunion Members shall give Company prompt notice that such Reunion Event has occurred (the **"Reunion Notice"**), specifically referencing this paragraph 20(c); and (B) Company shall have the option, exercisable by notice to you within thirty (30) days after Company's receipt of the Reunion Notice, to require you to produce and Deliver within thirty (30) days of Company's notice Demos comprised of at least four (4) completed, fully-mixed and previously-unreleased Masters featuring the performances of the Reunion Members, which Demos shall be recorded in accordance with a budget approved by Company in writing. Company shall thereafter have the right to reinstate this agreement with respect to the Reunion Members by notice to you on or before the later to occur of ninety (90) days after Company's receipt of the Reunion Notice or thirty (30) days after Delivery of the above-described Demos. If this agreement is so reinstated, Company hereby nevertheless acknowledges and agrees that its subsequent leaving member rights pursuant to paragraph 20(b) with respect to each Reunion Member whose services Company had previously terminated shall be subject to any agreement then-currently in force relating to such Reunion Member's solo recording services which was executed by such Reunion Member during the period in which his or her services hereunder had been terminated.

(d)   Company shall have the right, in its sole discretion, to rely on notice from you or any member of Artist that a Leaving Member Event or Reunion Event has occurred. In addition, your or any such member's failure or refusal to send any Leaving Member Notice or Reunion Notice shall not be deemed to limit Company's rights pursuant to this paragraph 20 if Company determines in its good faith judgment that a Leaving Member Event or Reunion Event, as applicable, has occurred. Company shall have no liability to you, Artist or any member thereof (including any Leaving Member or any Reunion Member) by reason of Company's acts or omissions based upon Company's receipt of any notice that a Leaving Member Event or Reunion Event has occurred or Company's good-faith determination that a Leaving Member Event or Reunion Event has occurred.

(e)   If you or any individual member of Artist wishes to record performances of any one (1) or more of the individual members comprising Artist, which such individual(s) remains a member of Artist and continues to perform his or her obligations hereunder, you and Artist shall give Company prompt notice thereof. Company shall thereafter have the irrevocable option to permit such member(s) of Artist to record such Recordings, and if exercised, such Recordings shall be acquired upon all of the terms and conditions set forth herein; provided that, if Company exercises such option, the financial terms set forth in paragraph 20(b) shall be applied with respect to such Recordings

The 2005 Group Section is far more comprehensive.

IN WITNESS WHEREOF, the parties hereto have this day signed in the spaces provided below.

{COMPANY}

By:_____
An Authorized Signatory

ACCEPTED AND AGREED:

_____
{ARTIST}

By:_____
An Authorized Signatory

EXHIBIT "A"

{COMPANY}

{ADDRESS}

As of {DATE}

Gentlemen:

Pursuant to an exclusive recording contract (the "Recording Contract") between _____ ("Grantor") and me, Grantor is entitled to my exclusive services as a recording artist and is the sole owner of the entire worldwide right, title and interest in and to the results and proceeds of my services as a recording artist under the Recording Contract, including, without limitation, master recordings embodying my performances and the phonograph records derived therefrom. I have been advised that Grantor is entering into a written agreement with you (the "Agreement"), pursuant to which Grantor is agreeing to furnish my services as a recording artist exclusively to you and pursuant to which you shall be the sole owner of the entire worldwide right, title and interest in and to the results and proceeds of my services as a recording artist. In consideration of your entering into the Agreement, and as a further inducement for you to do so, it being to my benefit as a recording artist that you enter into the Agreement, I hereby represent and agree as follows:

1.

    (a) I have read the Agreement in its entirety and fully understand the Agreement and all of the terms thereof were explained to me before signing this document.

    (b) Grantor has the right, insofar as I am concerned, to enter into the Agreement and to assume all of the obligations, warranties and undertakings to you on the part of Grantor contained therein, and Grantor shall continue to have those rights during the term of the Agreement and thereafter until all of those obligations, warranties and undertakings shall have been fully performed and discharged.

    (c) I shall fully and to the best of my abilities perform and discharge all of the obligations, warranties and undertakings contained in the Agreement insofar as the same are required of me and to the extent Grantor has undertaken to cause the performance and discharge by me of those obligations and undertakings.

2.   If during the term of the Agreement or any extensions or renewals thereof, Grantor shall, for any reason, cease to be entitled to my services as a recording artist or the results and proceeds thereof in accordance with the terms thereof or Grantor shall, for any reason, fail or refuse to furnish my services as a recording artist or the results and proceeds thereof exclusively to you as and when required under the Agreement or

Grantor shall commit any action or omission proscribed in the Agreement, I shall, at your written request, for the remaining balance of the term of the Agreement upon the terms contained therein, be deemed substituted for Grantor as a party to the Agreement as of the date of your notice to me. Without limitation of the foregoing, in the event I am substituted in place of Grantor as a party to the Agreement, I shall render all services and perform all acts as shall give to you the same rights, privileges and benefits to which you are entitled under the Agreement as if Grantor had continued to be entitled to my services as a recording artist and had continued to furnish my services as a recording artist and the results and proceeds thereof exclusively to you as and when required under the Agreement, and such rights, privileges and benefits shall be enforceable in your behalf against me.

3.   You and any person, firm or corporation designated by you shall have the perpetual, worldwide right to use and to permit others to use my name (both legal and professional, and whether presently or hereafter used by me), likeness, other identification and biographical material concerning me, for purposes of trade and advertising. You shall have the further right to refer to me during the term of the Agreement as your exclusive recording artist, and I shall in all my activities in the entertainment field use reasonable efforts to be billed and advertised during the term of the Agreement as your exclusive recording artist. The rights granted to you pursuant to this paragraph with respect to my name, likeness, other identification and biographical material concerning me shall be exclusive during the term of the Agreement and nonexclusive thereafter. Accordingly, but without limiting the generality of the foregoing, I shall not authorize or permit any person, firm or corporation other than you to use during the term of the Agreement my legal or professional name or my likeness in connection with the advertising or sale of phonograph records (including, without limitation, audiovisual records.)

4.   During the term of the Agreement, I shall not enter into any agreement or make any commitment which would interfere with my performance of my obligations under the Agreement, and I shall not perform or render services in connection with the recording of master recordings for any person, firm or corporation other than you. After the expiration or termination of the term of the Agreement, I shall not prior to the later of the following dates perform for any person, firm or corporation other than you, for the purpose of making recordings of phonograph records, any selection which had been recorded under the Agreement or under any other agreement between Grantor or me and you or your affiliates: (a) the date five (5) years subsequent to the date on which that selection shall have been last delivered to you in a master recording recorded under the Agreement; or (b) the date three (3) years subsequent to the expiration or termination of the term of the Agreement.

5.   No termination of the Agreement shall diminish my liability or obligation hereunder without your written consent.

6.   You may, in your name, institute any action or proceeding against me individually or collectively, at your election, to enforce your rights under the Agreement, under this guarantee or under the Recording Contract.

7.   I expressly acknowledge that my services hereunder and under the Agreement are of a special, unique, intellectual and extraordinary character which gives them peculiar value, and that if I breach any term hereof or of the Agreement, you will be caused irreparable injury which cannot adequately be compensated by money damages. Accordingly, you shall be entitled to injunctive relief, in addition to any other rights or remedies which you may have, to enforce the terms hereof or of the Agreement.

8.   Except as otherwise provided in Articles 15 and 24 of the Agreement and paragraph 9 below, I shall look solely to Grantor for any and all royalties, recording fees or other monies payable to me in respect of the recording of all recordings under the Recording Contract and under the Agreement and in respect of your manufacture, distribution, sale or other use or recordings recorded under the Agreement and all phonograph records and other reproductions derived therefrom, all throughout the world.

9.   I warrant and represent that, pursuant to the Recording Contract, each individual signatory hereto is guaranteed to receive from Grantor during each consecutive twelve (12) month period of the term of the Agreement ("Term Year") compensation of no less than the Designated Dollar Amount (as that term is defined in paragraph 24.03 of the Agreement) solely in respect of such signatory's services as a recording artist under the Recording Contract. If, for any reason, Grantor shall fail to pay to any signatory at least the Designated Dollar Amount during any Term Year, you shall pay to such signatory an amount which, when added to the amounts, if any, so paid by Grantor to such signatory during the Term Year, shall equal the Designated Dollar Amount. I agree that you shall have the right to demand that Grantor pay to you an amount equal to any amounts so paid by you pursuant to this paragraph, and you may, without limiting your other rights and remedies, deduct that amount from any monies payable by you under the Agreement or under any other agreement between Grantor or me and you or your affiliates. No later than thirty (30) days prior to the end of each Term Year, I shall advise you in writing of whether of not Grantor shall have paid to each signatory at least the Designated Dollar Amount during that Term Year. If in any Term Year the aggregate amount of the compensation paid by Grantor or you to any signatory exceeds the Designated Dollar Amount, such excess compensation shall apply to reduce the Designated Dollar Amount for any subsequent Term Years. I acknowledge that the provisions of this paragraph relating to the guaranteed payment to me of at least the Designated Dollared Amount during each Term Year and the corresponding provisions of the Agreement are intended to be construed and implemented is such a manner so as to comply with the provisions of Section 526 of the Code of Civil Procedure of the State of California and Section 3423 of The Civil Code of the State of California, concerning the availability of injunctive relief to prevent the breach of a contract in writing for the rendition or furnishing of personal services (although nothing contained in this paragraph 9 or elsewhere herein shall be deemed to make this agreement subject to the aforesaid statutory provisions).

10.   I, on behalf of myself and on behalf of any publisher or other person or entity which has or may have any interest in or to any Controlled Composition (as defined in the Agreement) hereby license to you mechanical reproduction rights with respect to each Controlled Composition upon the terms and at the mechanical royalty rates applicable to Controlled Compositions licensed to you by Grantor as set forth in Article 11 of the Agreement.

11.   If there is more than one (1) individual signatory to this agreement, our obligations hereunder and under the Agreement are joint and several, and your rights hereunder and under the Agreement apply with respect to each of us individually and collectively.

12.   **THIS AGREEMENT HAS BEEN ENTERED INTO THE STATE OF NEW YORK, AND ITS VALIDITY, CONSTRUCTION, INTERPRETATION AND LEGAL EFFECT SHALL BE GOVERNED BY THE LAWS OF THE STATE OF NEW YORK APPLICABLE TO CONTRACTS ENTERED INTO AND PERFORMED ENTIRELY WITHIN THE STATE OF NEW YORK. ALL CLAIMS, DISPUTES OR DISAGREEMENTS WHICH MAY ARISE OUT OF THE INTERPRETATION, PERFORMANCE OR BREACH OF THIS AGREEMENT SHALL BE SUBMITTED EXCLUSIVELY TO THE JURISDICTION OF THE STATE COURTS OF THE STATE OF NEW YORK OR THE FEDERAL DISTRICT COURTS LOCATED IN NEW YORK CITY; PROVIDED, HOWEVER, IF YOU ARE SUED OR JOINED IN ANY OTHER COURT OR FORUM (INCLUDING AN ARBITRATION PROCEEDING) IN RESPECT OF ANY MATTER WHICH MAY GIVE RISE TO A CLAIM BY YOU HEREUNDER, I CONSENT TO THE JURISDICTION OF SUCH COURT OR FORUM OVER ANY SUCH CLAIM WHICH MAY BE ASSERTED BY YOU. ANY PROCESS IN ANY ACTION OR PROCEEDING COMMENCED IN THE COURTS OF THE STATE OF NEW YORK ARISING OUT OF ANY SUCH CLAIM, DISPUTE OR DISAGREEMENT, MAY AMONG OTHER METHODS, BE SERVED UPON ME BY DELIVERING OR MAILING THE SAME, VIA CERTIFIED MAIL.**

Very truly yours,

SSN: _____   SSN:_____

Birth Date:_____   Birth Date:_____

SSN:_____   SSN:_____

Birth Date:_____   Birth Date:_____

SSN:_____   SSN:_____

Birth Date:_____   Birth Date:_____

INDEPENDENT LABEL:

If an independent label agreed to sign an artist, the contract would most likely be a per recording commitment which is also known as a "step deal." The step deal could encompass either a single-to-single contract based on sales, or a single-to -album commitment. However, it would probably not include much, if any, advance money.

BLANK RECORDS
EXCLUSIVE RECORDING AGREEMENT

This Agreement (the "Agreement") is entered into between Blank Records ("Company"), a sole proprietorship with its principle office located at ? North Pole, and

_____,

_____,

_____,

_____,

_____,

known collectively as **Group**, and performing under the name **Group** (referred to as "Artist.") All references to "Artist" include all members of the group collectively and individually unless otherwise specified.

The Parties agree as follows:

1. Exclusive Recording Services. During the Term or during and exercised options(as described below), Artist shall only render recording services for the Company and shall not, unless otherwise permitted under this Agreement, render recording services for any other party worldwide.

2. Term. The Artist's obligation to perform exclusive recordings services shall begin upon the latest signature date of this Agreement (the "Effective Date") and shall continue for 12 months after the delivery of the first Master Recording (the "Term").

3. Options. This Agreement includes an option structure which allows Artist to opt out or "Terminate" the Agreement upon which time the "Grant of Rights Upon Termination" section is triggered. The Terms of the option structure are as follows:

a) At the end of the initial 12 month Term the Artist may exercise an option to Terminate the Term. Intent to Terminate the Term must be made not less than 60 days prior to expiration of the initial Term or option in a writing signed by all members of Knife the Glitter. If this option to Terminate is not enacted in the above manner, the Term will continue for an additional 12 months beginning at the expiration of the previous Term.

b) At any point that material is recorded for release under this Agreement the option Term is automatically triggered for a period of 12 months following the delivery of the masters of the recorded material in question.

4. Termination of the Term. For whatever reason at the end of the initial Term, or at the end of any exercised option period, the Artist or the Company may Terminate this Agreement granted that 60 days prior written notice is given. Once this Agreement is Terminated, by these means, the Terms under the "Grant of Rights Upon Termination" section below are triggered. Please also see the "Termination of Agreement" section below.

5. Grant of Rights. Beginning on the date when a Master Recording is delivered to the Company, the Company shall be the exclusive owner of rights to all Master Recordings worldwide and in perpetuity. However, while the Company exclusively owns the rights to Records made within the Terms of this Agreement, Artist may unanimously veto specific uses of the album by the Company, solely with regards to advertising and promotion, which are inconsistent with Artist's artistic vision. Specific intent to veto must be embodied in writing, electronic or otherwise, and delivered to the Company within 1 week upon information regarding a specific use. Company will utilize its best efforts to inform Artist about specific uses of all Master Recordings.

a) Artist grants to Company all right, title and interest in the sound recording copyright (as provided under the U.S. Copyright Act of 1976 and international copyright treaties) to any Master Recordings delivered under this Agreement worldwide and in perpetuity. This grant of rights includes:

b) the exclusive right to manufacture copies of all or any portion of the Master Recordings;

c) the exclusive right to import, export, sell, transfer, release, license, publicly perform, rent, and otherwise exploit or dispose of the Master Recordings; and

d) the exclusive right to edit, adapt, or conform the Master Recordings to technological or commercial requirements in various formats now known or later developed. Rights granted under this subsection 5© must be approved first by the artist.

i) the exclusive right to reproduce or distribute in any medium, Artist's names, portraits, pictures and likeness for purposes of advertising, promotion or trade in connection with Artist or the exploitation of the Master Recordings. Artist shall be available from time to time to appear for photography, video performance, or the like, under the reasonable direction of Company. The Company shall give Artist at least 2 weeks notice prior to any such appearance. Artist shall not be entitled to any compensation for such services except for reimbursement of travel expenses.

ii) This subsection does not prevent the Artist or Artist's Management from utilizing personal funds for their own promotional efforts. However, the Company must be given reasonable and timely notice of any promotional efforts which the Artist or the Artist's Management funds themselves. Such reasonable notice shall not exceed 2 weeks prior to the execution of aforementioned promotional efforts set forth in this subsection 5(d)(ii).

6. Grant of Rights Upon Termination. Upon the expiration of the Term of this Agreement, or, if an option has been triggered, upon the expiration of that option the Company retains the following rights under this Agreement:

a) All exclusive rights under the subsections (a), (b), and (c) of Section 6 (the "Grant of Rights" section of this Agreement) continue in the Company worldwide and in perpetuity.

b) Company is entitled to 50% of all monies made from the continued sale of all Records released under this Agreement for a period of 24 months beginning on the date of Termination of the Term or option. This 24 month period is the "Termination Period"). After this 24 month period Company is entitled to 40% of all monies made from the continued sale of all Records released under the Agreement.

c) Company is entitled to 50% of all income streams that were created as a result of Company's efforts during the Term or any exercised option period including but not limited to sponsorships and publishing deals for a period of 24 months beginning on the date of expiration of the Term or option. This 24 month period is the "Termination Period"). Upon expiration of this 24 month period Company is entitled to 40% of aforementioned income streams.

d) This Section 8 does not include income streams created as a result of an Agreement between Artist and another recording Company during the Termination Period.

e) At any time subsequent to expiration of the Term, option, or Termination Term the rights granted to Company under this contract may be purchased outright by an Agreement reached between the Company and the purchasing party. Any material covered by this agreement may only she transferred with consent of the Artist.

7. Side-Artist Recording.
During the Term, Artist may perform as part of another Artist's recording project (a "side-Artist" performance) provided that:

a) the side-Artist recording does not interfere with obligations under this Agreement; and

b) the following credit is included on the side-Artist recording: "[Name of Group Member] appears courtesy of Blank Records."

8. Professional Name. With the exception of the Leaving Member sections of this Agreement, Artist will perform and record under the professional name Group. Artist will not use a different name in connection with the Master Recordings unless Artist and Company mutually agrees in writing.

9. Subsequent Recording of Compositions. Artist represents and warrants that Artist shall not record any composition contained on a Master Recording recorded under this Agreement at any period during the Term, the options, or during the Termination Period. Upon expiration of the Termination Period, Artist represents and warrants that no more than 3 songs from any 1 album released under this Agreement will be re-recorded and included on an album or set of albums or any other tangible medium released under Agreements subsequent to this Agreement without the express written consent of the Company.

10. Company Obligations.

a) *Replication*: The Company will cover all costs in connection with replication of technically satisfactory Master Recordings delivered by the Artist pursuant to this Agreement. This obligation also covers all re-pressing of any recordings made by the Artist pursuant to this Agreement.

b) *Merchandise:* Company shall supply Artist with various articles of merchandise, artistically approved by Artist. The amount, type, and time of delivery of specific items of merchandise are within the discretion of the Company.

c) *Promotional Services:* The Company will cover all costs in connection with promoting recordings released under this Agreement. A reasonable budgetary amount shall be allocated solely to promotional services for Artist. All means and methods of performing promotional services are within the discretion of the Company. This section does not prevent Artist or Artist's management from allocating funds to promotional efforts of Artists. However, Company must be given reasonable and timely notice of the nature of any such promotional efforts made by Artist or any entity other than the Company.

d) *Distribution:* Company will distribute all recordings delivered under this Agreement through traditional and non-traditional means worldwide. Company will make its best efforts to secure retail distribution for recordings released under this Agreement. Company will handle all the maintenance and accounting responsibilities associated with any distribution channels.

e) *General Clause:* Company is also obligated to develop and explore new promotional opportunities for the Artist both nationally and internationally. All new endeavors must be presented to the Artist within a timely manner and agreed upon by both parties before performance proceeds.

f) *Tour support:* In connection with any tours equal to or exceeding 18 dates in any 25 consecutive day period, and with sufficient prior noticed detailed below, the Company will use its best efforts to provide tour support in the following form: Promoting tour dates in the cities where street teams are available, using promotional tools artistically agreed upon by the Artist and the Company.

i) Company will utilize its best effort to contact local press in the cities where tourdates are being held.

ii) Company will set aside a reasonable initial capital outlay to support the Artist while on tour. These amounts are considered costs recoupable from Artists' record and merchandise sales. It is within the Company's discretion to allocate any amount of the tour support budget for promotion of the tour. Artist has the right to refuse any tour support from the Company.

iii) Artist is obligated to keep an accounting of all Records and merchandise sold while on tour and to return acquired funds from the sale of Records and applicable merchandise to the Company within 2 weeks upon completion of the tour. The Company reserves the right to contact Artist at any time during the tour and request an accounting from the Artist of the number of items sold and the monies received from record and merchandise sales while on tour. Artist will be given a reasonable amount of time not to exceed 48 hours to comply with said Company requests. Artist may only utilize merchandise funds upon timely notice and prior approval of the Company. Upon an emergency situation, Artist has the right to use merchandise funds for the necessities of life including food and gas expenses. Artist shall use their best efforts to contact the Company before merchandise funds are so used. However, all funds acquired from Record sales and merchandise provided by Company must be accounted subject to this section. No more than 25% of total proceeds from sales of merchandise provided by the Company, acquired while on tour, may be used for any expenses while Artist is on tour.

iv) The Company makes no claims to any monies paid by the venue to the Artist in connection with a performance, unless such monies as provided as payment for Records or merchandise.

v) Prior notice of scheduled tourdates sufficient to trigger the Company obligations above is at least 14 days prior to each scheduled tourdate.

vi) It must be noted that Artist is obligations to keep an accounting of and return all funds received from the sale of records and merchandise provided by the Company even for isolated shows. All Artist obligations under this subsection must be completed within 72 hours following each show.

vii) The Company reserves the right to alter the procedures for allocating merchandise for tours if the Company feels that these terms are not being complied with in a satisfactory manner.

11. Recoupable Costs. All monies spent by the Company in connection with Company obligations shall be considered a recoupable advance ("Advances"). All Advances shall be recoupable from monies made from the sale of Records released under this Agreement, merchandise supplied by the Company under this Agreement, and any other income streams created by the Company for the Artist pursuant to this Agreement.

a) Promotional recording and cutouts: Copies of any portion of the Master Recordings used for promotional purposes will be considered recoupable costs.

12. Routing Accountings and Payment of Monies to Artist. With this Agreement the Company enters into a payment structure with the Artist in which net profits from all

Artist's Records and merchandise sold are split 50%/50% between Artist and the Company after the Company is first reimbursed for all costs which are considered recoupable under this Agreement.

a) Routine Accountings

i) Recoupable costs accounted for: 30 days after the release date set for any record released under this Agreement Artist shall be provided with a full itemized list of all monies spent up to that date. After that date the following accounting procedures shall occur:

ii) From the date that the first accounting is made concerning monies spent in connection with any Records released under this Agreement, additional accountings will be made in which all monies made from the sale of Artist's Records and merchandise by means of distribution networks, tourdates, live performances, non-live performances, and all other purchase points, and monies brought in from all other income streams shall be calculated. All of this amount will be applied to the recoupable costs of the Company until recoupable costs are paid in full, unless otherwise mutually agreed upon by the Company and Artist. In addition, this accounting shall include all monies spent by Company in relation to Company obligations under this Agreement. This accounting shall be delivered to the Artist on the 28th of every other month following the first accounting.

1) Once the recoupable amount is paid off, the Artist will share in the net profits of the sales of Artist's Records and merchandise supplied by the Company on a 50%/50% basis. Where other payment percentages are specifically itemized for other particular income streams those amounts shall be followed (i.e. "Foreign Licenses" and "Flat Fee").

2) Once the first accounting is made after the release of a recording under this Agreement the Company may not exceed a budget of $300 per month without prior approval of the Artist. Artist has the right to halt any budgetary allocation made by the Company.

b) Payment of Monies to Artist: The monies which Artist is entitled to under this Agreement will be calculated as follows:

i) The first payment date for monies due to Artist under this Agreement will be made on the same date as the second accounting statement provided pursuant to Section 13(b). Subsequent payments will be made to the Artist on the 28th of every other month following the first payment. If late in any payment, Company shall pay a flat 2% rate of interest from the due date until paid.

ii) Artist has the discretion to elect to ear mark their % payment for either future costs related to Artist or for personal Artist use.

13. Foreign Licenses. Blank Records shall pay Group 40% of the net receipts paid to Blank Records under any foreign license during the Term of this Agreement after all Company costs are recouped.

14. Reserves. In computing Records sold, only Records for which Company has been paid or credited shall be considered sold. The Company reserves the right to withhold 20% of monies due to Artist under this Agreement as reserve payment against returns of Artist's Records to the Company.

15. Flat Fee. Blank Records shall pay Artist 40% of the net receipts paid to Blank Records under any flat fee license of the Master Recordings or any portion of the Master Recordings after all Company costs are recouped.

16. Statements; Audit. *Accounting request by Artist:* At any time the Artist may request an accounting of all monies expended for that Artist under this Agreement, and of all monies made, granted that Company is provided with not less than 14 days prior notice. Outside of an accounting request by Artist, Company shall present Artist with an accounting itemizing costs and sales revenues with regards to Artists Records and merchandise under the Terms set forth above in Section 13(a)(i) (the "Recoupable Costs Accounted For" section). The acceptance by Artist of any statement or payment does not prevent Artist later questioning its accuracy for a period not to exceed 1 year. Company shall keep accurate books of accountings covering all transactions relating to this Agreement. Artist or its representatives shall have the right upon reasonable written notice to audit the Company's books relating to sales of Artists Records and merchandise. These accountings do not include Records or merchandise sold while on tour. The method of accounting and organization of monies made from sales of Records and merchandise on tour will be determined subject to the Terms of this Agreement and will include and additional accounting procedures mutually agreed upon by Artist and the Company prior to the start of the tour.

17. Artist Promotional Records. The Company shall furnish to Group a total of 20 (4 per member) promotional Records at no charge. Artist may obtain further Records from Company at Company's then wholesale cost.

18. Artist Warranties.

    a) Artist warrants to Company that Artist has the power and authority to enter into this Agreement, that all recording made under this Agreement violate none of the applicable copyright laws, and that all necessary and appropriate rights and licenses have been or will be obtained within a reasonable amount of time with respect to the Master Recordings. Artist warrants that the Master Recordings are original to Artist except for material in the public domain and such excerpts from other works as may be included with the written permission of the copyright owners and that proper clearances or permission have been obtained from the Artists of any copyrighted material, including but not limited to any digitally reprocessed samples of material incorporated in the Master Recordings. Artist warrants that Artist's use of any name or moniker will not infringe on the rights of others and that Artist's use of any musical composition or arrangement will not infringe on the rights of others.

b) Artist further warrants that the Master Recordings do not:

i) contain any libelous material;

ii) infringe any trade name, trademark, trade secret or copyright;

iii) invade or violate any right of privacy, personal or proprietary right, or other common law or statutory right.

c) Artist hereby indemnifies the Company and undertakes to defend the Company against and hold the Company harmless (including but not limited to attorney fees and costs) from any claims and damage arising out of a breach of Artist's Warranties as provided above. Artist agrees to reimburse the Company for any payment made by the Company with respect to this Section, provided that the claim has been settled or has resulted in a final judgment against the Company or its licensees. Artist shall notify the Company in writing of any infringements or imitations by others of the Master Recording which may come to Artist's attention. The Company reserves the right to withhold the release of any Records embodying any Master Recordings if the Company feels that any part of this section has not been complied with.

19. Leaving Members.

a) If any member of Artist ceases to perform as a member of the group ("Leaving Member"), Artist shall promptly give Blank Records written notice of not less than 60 days.

b) If the group disbands, each member of the group shall be considered to be a Leaving Member and must give the Company written notice of leaving. More than two members leaving the band is considered to be disbandment unless otherwise determined by the Company.

c) In the event of disbandment Leaving Members shall be responsible for reimbursing Blank Records for the recording and manufacturing costs of any currently unsold Records manufactured or in the manufacturing process up to the date that notice of disbandment is made.

d) A Leaving Member shall not without the Company's consent, use the professional name of the group in any commercial artistic endeavor and said professional name shall remain the property of the group who continue to perform their obligations hereunder and whose engagements are not terminated.

20. Termination. Blank Records may Terminate this Agreement within thirty (30) days of the expiration of the Term or of any option. Artist can Terminate this Agreement if Company fails to pay monies due to Artist on time or if Company fails to accurately report accountings pursuant to Section 13 and the failure is not corrected within thirty (30) days after notice from Artist. Only upon Termination of this Agreement in this manner and subsequent to a judicial determination that Company did indeed fail to accurately report pursuant to Section 13 or pay monies due Artist pursuant to the Terms of this Agreement does the Company relinquish all rights granted under this Agreement.

If this Agreement is Terminated for a reason other than Company' failure to pay or accurately report monies due to Artist under this Agreement, the Termination shall not Terminate the underlying rights granted to Company by Artist or Company' obligations to continue to pay monies due to Artists under this Agreement.

21. Termination in the Event of Leaving Member. Within sixty (60) days of receipt of notice of any Leaving Member, as defined in the Leaving Member Section, Company shall have the right to Terminate the Agreement with respect to the remaining members of Artist. In the event of such Termination, all members of Artist shall be deemed to be Leaving Members. In this situation Company retains all right granted to the Company under this Agreement.

22. General. Nothing contained in this Agreement shall be meant to establish either Company or Artist a partner, joint venturer, or employee of the other party for any purpose. This Agreement may not be amended except in a writing signed by both parties. No waiver by either party of any right shall be construed as a waiver of any other right. If a court finds any provision of this Agreement invalid or unenforceable as applied to any circumstance, the remainder of this Agreement shall be interpreted so as best to effect the intent of the parties. This Agreement shall be governed by and interpreted in accordance with the laws of the State of North Pole. This Agreement expresses the complete understanding of the parties with respect to the subject matter and supersedes all prior proposals, Agreements, representations and understandings. Notices required under this Agreement can be sent to the parties at the addresses provided below. In the event of any dispute arising from or related to this Agreement, the prevailing party shall be entitled to attorney's fees.

23. Correspondence: All correspondence required by this Agreement shall be sent to the following addresses for each party:

- Company:

- Artist:

Artist Name: _____

Individual Band Member Signatures: _____

_____

_____

_____

_____

Artist Representative Name & Title:

_____

Artist Representative Signature:

_____

Artist Address:

_____

_____

Date: _____

Company Business Name:

_____

Company Representative Name & Title:

_____

Company Representative Signature:

_____

Company Address:

_____

_____

Date: _____

A simpler deal that needs little explanation.

MANAGEMENT/ENTERTAINMENT COMPANY

The simplest of the three contracts is the contract where the management/entertainment company want its artist on the company label and outsource the manufacturing and distribution.

DKE
44 ELM STREET
4TH FLOOR
NORTH POLE

Group members

d/b/a "Group Records"

_____

_____

_____

Dear Jim and Dave:

1.   (a) As you know, DKE is party to an agreement (the "RED Agreement") with RED Distribution, Inc. ("RED") with respect to the distribution of phonorecords and audiovisual records (in all formats) in the United States and Canada.. You have requested that your recently-recorded album entitled "Love Will" (the "Album") be distributed under the RED Agreement and that we provide other record label type services with respect to the Album. We agree to do so on the following terms.

(b) With respect to the period commencing on the initial commercial release of the Album and ending on the date which is seven (7) years thereafter (the "Term"), the Album will be exclusively distributed in the United States and Canada pursuant to the RED Agreement (or successor distribution agreement) and DKE will provide the services set forth below.

(c) In addition to the distribution services provided by RED at the applicable distribution fee set forth in the RED Agreement, DKE will provide, on your behalf and at your expense, sales, marketing, promotion, publicity and new media services with respect to the Album for an additional fee of ten (10%) percent of "Net Sales" (as such term is defined in the RED Agreement). The engagement of third parties to render any such services and the fees to be paid to such third parties shall be subject to your prior approval (it being understood that there shall be no additional charges if such services are provided "in-house" by DKE). Remaining proceeds from the sales of the Album shall be paid to you within 15 business days following our receipt of payment from RED. Reserves for returns and exchanges shall be maintained and liquidated in accordance with the applicable provisions of the RED Agreement.

(d) You will be responsible for all pre-approved costs of manufacturing copies of the Album and the Album's packaging, costs of artwork creation and all third-party costs incurred in connection with the marketing, publicizing, promotion and the like of the Album.

(e) You will also be responsible for all mechanical royalties in connection with sales of the Album and for any payments due to musicians, engineers, producers and all third parties rendering services in connection with the master recordings contained on the Album.

2.   (a) You also engage DKE, on an exclusive basis during the Term, to procure distribution agreements ("ROW Agreements") for the Album on your behalf in all countries of the world outside the United States and Canada. DKE will forward all offers it receives with respect thereto to you and will negotiate such offers in consultation with you. You will have absolute and final approval over the acceptance of any such offer and will review and execute any ROW Agreement. In addition to procuring such foreign distribution of the Album, DKE will act as marketing consultant with respect thereto and will act as liaison between you and any such distributor for the term of the relevant ROW Agreement.

(b) In consideration of such services, you shall pay or cause to be paid to DKE a fee equal to fifteen (15%) of all compensation (of whatever nature) earned by you or paid to you at any time in respect of all ROW Agreements.

3. You hereby make all customary warranties, including the warranties that you are fully empowered to enter into this agreement and that no master recordings contained on the Album (or the musical compositions embodied therein) or the materials constituting its packaging will infringe upon the rights of any party.

4. The parties agree that this agreement has been entered into in the State of North Pole and that the laws of the State of North Pole shall govern the validity, interpretation and effect of this agreement. Any dispute hereunder shall be subject to the exclusive jurisdiction of the federal or state courts located in city. If the foregoing accurately reflects our agreement, kindly sign below where indicated.

Sincerely,

DKE

By:_____

ACCEPTED & AGREED TO:

_____

Jim

_____

Dav

collectively d/b/a "

Group Records"

Some new artists believe the recording contract is an agreement "written in stone" and demand that every word be negotiated. Obviously both sides must feel comfortable with the language, not only for the financial aspects, but also more importantly, because the contract should be the basis for a long-term relationship. Although it provides the guidelines for this relationship, one cannot contractualize the strong company commitment that is necessary for the artist to succeed. Therefore, everything is negotiable.

SUMMARY

1. A successful artist-record company relationship is one of the most important business arrangements needed for success.

2. The record contract is one of the most important and usually complicated agreements in the industry.

3. An artist should not be expected to understand every clause in a major label contract.

4. A competent music attorney must negotiate the record contract for the artist.

5. Every item in a record contract should be considered negotiable, especially royalty rates.

6. Most new artists must settle for a contract less favorable to them than an established superstar.

7. In negotiations, a good rule-of-thumb to follow is, "if you don't ask for it, you won't get it."

PROJECTS

1. Team up and perform mock negotiations.

2. Find out if any bands you know have record contracts (even with small independent labels):

   a) ask the band if they understood the terms when they signed

   b) find out what they don't and do like about the contract

   c) ask them what they would like to renegotiate if they were given the chance

   d) ask to see the contract and compare the terms with the example in this chapter

   e) renegotiate the contract for them explaining what you would insert or strike

3. Research other agreements and compare their terms to the example in this chapter.

CHAPTER EIGHT
CARE AND FEEDING OF THE CREATIVE

BROWN'S "CONFUSIONAL MODEL OF CREATIVITY"

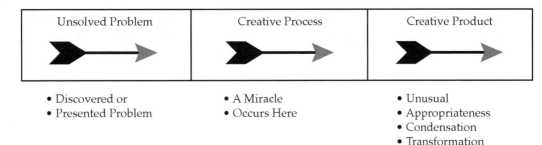

Unsolved Problem	Creative Process	Creative Product
• Discovered or • Presented Problem	• A Miracle • Occurs Here	• Unusual • Appropriateness • Condensation • Transformation

(Brown, Robert. "Confusional Model of Creativity". from *Handbook of Creativity*. Edited by Glover, Ronning, & Reynolds. Plenum Press, New York. 1989. pg. 30)

BY THE END OF THIS CHAPTER YOU SHOULD BE ABLE TO:

1. Discuss the characteristics of the creative process.

2. List the traits of the creative person and the creative product.

3. Discuss the factors that accompany age change that bring about a reduction in creativity.

4. Describe some methods to evaluate creativity.

5. Discuss the art and craft of songwriting.

6. List the characteristics of a potentially successful song.

7. Discuss how songwriters make money.

8. When given a songwriter/publisher agreement, discuss the important clauses.

9. Discuss the publisher's role in song exploitation.

10. List the six basic song uses that are revenue producing.

11. List the RIAA criteria for Gold and Platinum Video Awards.

12. Describe the first music videos and how they were presented.

13. Discuss the nonlinear concept of story evolution.

14. When given a recording contract, discuss the important issues of the video production clauses.

15. Discuss the differences among the live vs. audio vs. video media.

16. Discuss the role industry management should play in guiding creative talent.

THE CREATIVE PROCESS

Creativity itself is a quicksilver thing: an intangible, subjectively evaluated property,
often purchased in commercial circles by the slightest whim or fancy."
(*Buxton, Edward.* Creative People At Work. *Executive Communications, Inc. N.Y. 1975 pg ix.*)

How does it happen? Why do some people have it and others don't? What is the mystique about it? Can you learn to be creative? What's the big deal anyway?

The truth is that the people involved with the creative aspects of this industry are the highest paid. And one of the reasons they are the highest paid is because of the mystique that surrounds the creative process. Non-creative people find it magical that someone can be creative, a feat that is so superhuman that many will pay any price to be a part of the process.

Our creative thought is the function of the right hemisphere of the brain. The further to the "right" someone feels comfortable existing in, the more creative (but not necessarily useful), their output is. Accountants and scientists make daily use of the brain's left hemisphere. Because society has made laws and rules to govern its people, one must make use of the left side of the brain in order to survive. Supposedly, the more "centered" you are, the easier it is to cope with life's daily activities and the happier you are. Many creative people, (those referred to as "right sided"), are uncomfortable making business decisions. They find it tedious and boring to constantly use the left side of their brain. Besides, it's not as much fun. (This may be why so many entertainment attorneys are frustrated producers, songwriters, and musicians.)

This chapter explores the creativity as it pertains to this industry. It is divided into two sections, the creative process and the creative product. The areas investigated include: the creative personality; measuring creativity, guiding the creative talent, followed by a detailed description of the industry's creative products.

CREATIVE TRAITS

JACKSON AND MESSICK: FOUR CHARACTERISTICS OF CREATIVITY

Traits of the Person		Traits of the Product		
Intellectual Traits	Personal Traits	Product Properties	Standards	Reflective Reaction
1. Tolerance of Incongrutiy	Original	Unusualness	Norms	Surprise
2. Analysis and Intuition	Sensitive	Appropriateness	Context	Satisfaction
3. Open-mindedness	Flexible	Transformation	Constraint	Stimulation
4. Reflection & Spontaneity	Poetic	Condensation	Summary Power	Savoring

Source: Jackson and Messick. Copyright 1965 Duke University
Figure 8.1 John S. Dacey. Fundamentals of Creative Thinking. Lexington Books. Lexington, MA. 1989 pg. 7.

THE CREATIVE PERSONALITY

"The creative person is commonly regarded as being filled with new ideas and projects; he views life from surprising perspectives, formulates problems contrary to what he has been told by parents and teachers, turns traditional and seemingly self-evident conceptions topsy-turvy, and wants to retest the validity of accepted truths {{17 Smith,Gudmund J.W. 1990/f, p. 1}}."

When creative people are described in the music business, such phrases as self-centered and ego driven are used. "According to psychologists, the general view is that creative people have a stronger, more pronounced sense of self. Call it ego, pride of authorship, or a larger-than-normal need for praise and approval {{33 Buxton,Edward 1975/f, p. 1}}." One only needs to watch the annual telecast of the Grammy Awards presentation to agree.

Researchers have found the following characteristics (in one or more studies) differentiate highly creative persons from less creative ones. Obviously with a list so long, one or several of these traits can be found in every entertainment artist. So the characteristics noted in **Bold** are frequently attributed to creative people in the music business.

1. Accepts disorder	28. Full of curiosity	56. Resolute
2. Adventurous	29. Appears haughty and self-satisfied at times	57. Self-assertive
3. Strong affection		58. Self-aware
4. Altruistic	30. Likes solitude	59. Self-starter
5. Awareness of others	31. Independence in judgment	60. Self-confident
6. Always baffled by something	32. Independent in thinking	61. Self-sufficient
7. Attracted to disorder	33. Individualistic	62. Sense of destiny
8. Attracted to mysterious	34. Intuitive	63. Sense of humor
9. Attempts difficult jobs	35. Industrious	64. Sensitive to beauty
10. Bashful outwardly	36. Introversive	65. Shuns power
11. Constructive in criticism	37. Keeps unusual hours	66. Sincere
12. Courageous	38. Lack business ability	67. Not interested in small details
13. Deep and conscientious conventions	39. Makes mistakes	
	40. Never bored	68. Speculative
14. Defies conventions of courtesy	41. Nonconforming	69. Spirited in disagreement
	42. Not hostile or negativistic	70. Strives for distant goals
15. Defies conventions of health	43. Not popular	71. Stubborn
	44. Oddities of habit	72. Temperamental
16. Desires to excel	45. Persistent	73. Tenacious
17. Determination	46. Becomes preoccupied with problem	74. Tender emotions
18. Differentiated value-hierar-chy		75. Timid
	47. Preference for complex ideas	76. Thorough
19. Discontented		77. Unconcerned about power
20. Disturbs organization	48. Questioning	78. Somewhat uncultured, primitive
21. Dominant	49. Radical	
22. Emotional	50. Receptive to external stimuli	79. Unsophisticated, naive
23. Emotionally sensitive	51. Receptive to ideas of others	80. Unwilling to accept anything on mere say-so
24. Energetic	52. Regresses occasionally	
25. A fault-finder	53. Rejection of suppression as a mechanism of impulse control	81. Visionary
26. Doesn't fear being thought as different		82. Versatile
		83. Willing to take risks
27. Feels whole parade is out of step	54. Rejection of repression	84. Somewhat withdrawn
	55. Reserved	

Figure 8.3. Paul E. Torrance. Guiding Creative Talent. *Prentice-Hall Inc. Englewood Cliffs, NJ, 1962. Pg. 66-67.*

Also, creative people think of themselves as special. Therefore, when there is a lack of recognition outside of their own community of peers, it leads many to frustration. People often say that creative people are very difficult to work with, and some creative people feel they are prisoners of the whims of their audience. Emotions run on high in this business and managers must deal with each artist accordingly.

ONCE YOU HAVE IT, DO YOU HAVE IT FOREVER

"Creativity is a cognitive, attitudinal, personal trait that every person has to some degree (unless in a coma or of very low intelligence) {{33 Buxton,Edward 1975/f, p. x}}."

The peripherals of music industry are filled with people who were "one hit wonders". Why can't the successes be easily repeated? Obviously there is no one answer. However there have been studies concerning, among other things, age and creative productivity. Lehman (1953) found that the greatest contributions to their field were made by musicians between the ages of thirty and forty. Lehman (1956) also pointed out that not age itself, but the factors that accompany **age change** bring about reduction in creative production {{19 Torrance,E.Paul 1962/f, p. 100}}. Some of the general factors he found are listed in Figure 8.4.

1. A decline in physical vigor energy, and resistance to fatigue occur before the age of forty.

2. Sensory capacity and motor precision decline with age.

3. Serious illness and bodily infirmities have more negative effects on older than younger persons.

4. Creativity curves may be related to glandular changes.

5. Marital difficulties and sexual problems increase with age and may have a negative effect on creativity.

6. Indifference toward creativity may develop more frequently among older people because of the death of a loved one.

7. Older persons are more likely to be preoccupied with the practical demands of life.

8. Success, promotion, increased prestige, and responsibility may lead to less favorable conditions for concentrated work.

9. Having achieved these goals, those that desire prestige and recognition, rather than the creation of something new, strive less for achievement.

10. Easily won and early fame may lead to contentment with what has been done before accomplishing what could be the most creative work.

11. Non-recognition and destructive criticism may lead to apathy of older workers.

12. Negative transfer, resulting in inflexibility, may be more of a handicap among older workers.

13. Older workers may become less motivated because of these factors.

14. Younger people may be better educated and lived in more stimulating environments.

15. Psychoses, which occur more frequently in later life, may have clouded what was previously a brilliant mind.

16. Alcohol, narcotics, and such may have sapped an individual's productive power.

Figure 8.4. {{19 Torrance,E.Paul 1962/f, p. 101;}}.

So can you have it forever? Individuals are individuals and a general rule doesn't exist. However, as a word of caution, throughout history there have been few successful revolutionists over age forty.

CAN IT BE TAUGHT?

"I think that talented, creative people are going to be successful anyway. I don't think a training program has anything to do with It" {{33 Buxton,Edward 1975/f, p. 17}}.

Unfortunately in areas that do not require a great deal of technique or prerequisite skills, the above quote is usually true. The craft of any creative endeavor (such as songwriting) can be learned, but learning the craft does not necessarily make someone successful. What can be taught is how to recognize creative uses of a craft, and exercises can be designed to practice those uses. However, this is refining the craft not the art. Composers study the Mozart Symphonies to learn the mechanics of composing in the classical style and to acknowledge the genius in Mozart's artistic use of the tools. Students then imitate the Mozart classical style to explore his techniques. With practice they improve, and the techniques of the style are learned. The craft is refined. Although there are rules that govern the use of certain notes, the artistry lies in the choice of notes. The notes are chosen from what the composer hears, and what is heard is an individual's choice. And that is where the creativity lies!

EVALUATING CREATIVITY

Can creativity be measured without measuring the creative product? How is the evaluation criterion derived? Are there critical factors? Who is qualified to do the measuring?

The literature does not agree on a method for evaluating creativity. Although most would agree that a quantitative measure alone, such as record sales, would do an injustice to a large amount of quality work, but should a quantitative statistic play a role in the decision.

One method of measurement might be to identify creative people who are innovators by the number of representatives they spawn. For example, if someone decides to drive a car in reverse looking over his or her shoulder instead of in forward and no one chooses to pick up on the idea (the innovation) and drive like that (as a representative of the innovation), the original person who started driving in reverse would not be considered an innovator, but probably considered crazy! However, if several people liked the idea and started to drive in reverse, and then millions of people followed, the innovator would be considered a genius. If the driving fad lasted two weeks and then someone began driving sideways, driving backwards would be considered part of the evolution of modern driving and a creative step in reaching the current state of driving practices. Because millions became users or representatives of the innovation, the innovator would be recognized as highly creative. Therefore, using this logic, record sales as a quantitative measure, can be a valid part of the test for measuring creativity.

As a second example, if a composer composed a composition (an innovation) and no one performed it, it would not be considered a good work. However, if it received hundreds of performances (as representations) it would be.

A final definition of creativity, this one by Morris I. Stein reads, "Creativity is a process that results in a novel work that is accepted as useful, tenable, or satisfying by a significant group of people at some point in time {{34 Stein,Morris Isaac 1974-1975/f, p. vii}}." Stein is including a quantitative measure, by employing the acceptance by a significant group of people, ie: record buyers or listeners as the evidence of creativity.

THE CREATIVE PRODUCT
SONGWRITING

"At the dawn of the century Chas K. Harris published a little red book of rules and secrets called How To Write A Popular Song. To his readers he advised: Look at newspapers for your story line. Acquaint yourself with the style in vogue. Avoid slang. Know the copyright laws" {{20 Whitcomb,Ian 1972/f, p. 3}}.

Is it an art or a craft? Most debates settle with the compromise, "well it's both." This seems to be true as songwriting methods teach the mechanics of the craft but do not guarantee artistic or commercial acceptance. Some songs, such as Paul McCartney's "Yesterday" have great lyrics and a great melody, and others are successful because they fit the style that's in at the time (remember the big hit of the late 1970's "Shake Your Booty"). Concerning the craft, Harris gave very good advice. Most of what he said is still useful today.

In the Music Business Handbook, Baskerville suggests that if a song exhibits the following characteristics, it has very strong potential for making it in the marketplace:

1. is memorable; it sticks in the mind. This is accomplished particularly by use of a "hook"

2. has immediate appeal

3. uses some kind of special imagery

4. is well-crafted

5. everything lyrical and musical holds to a central theme

6. has an element of mystery {{21 Baskerville,David 1990/f, p. 29}}

Songwriting "how to" texts agree with Baskerville. There is a method to learning the craft, but creating hits cannot be guaranteed. Baskerville adds that the transformation of an artistic achievement into a commercial success may occur if the following takes place:

1. The song gets an appealing initial performance.

2. The record company promotes strong airplay.

3. The song and the record suit the taste of the current market.

4. The record is effectively distributed and is made readily available nationally.

These events fall beyond the scope of the creative process, and are the personal manager's responsibility to see that they occur.

MAKING MONEY AT IT

The key to receiving revenue from the efforts of songwriting is through the use of the song. In the business this is referred to as "exploiting the copyright" and is the main function of the song's publisher. Revenue producing uses include:

1. motion pictures
2. television
3. ringtones/ringbacks
4. sampling
5. homevideos/DVD
6. greeting cards
7. sheetmusic/folios
8. dolls, toys, music boxes, cereal boxes
9. interactive games
10. CD-ROM/multimedia audio visual configurations
11. record sales
12. trailers
13. limited edition collectibles
14. downloads
15. Broadway/OffBroadway/the road
16. video games
17. podcasting
18. subscription services
19. webcasting
20. new media
21. video on demand
22. dual disc
23. radio
24. satellite
25. mobile devices
26. remix
27. cell phone
28. compilation albums
29. special products albums
30. streaming
31. foreign countries
32. performances
33. advertising
34. lyric reprints
35. karaoke
36. theme parks {{115 Brebac, Jeff 2006;}}

Because revenue collection for the songwriter relies so heavily on the function of the song's publisher, the Songwriters Guild of America publishes a **Popular Songwriter Contract**. This songwriter/publisher agreement includes basic descriptions of all the revenue producing areas that are handled by the publisher for the songwriter. Although some major publishers feel that the contract is weighted in favor of the songwriter, and therefore insist on their own contracts, it is a good resource to use as a guide and an outline when beginning negotiations on one's own deal. Pay particular attention to all parts of clauses numbered **4, 6, 9,** and **18,** and the instructions included in parenthesis. Since the terms of the contract are based on the strength of the songwriter's track record, the percentages noted in each sub clause vary greatly. What follows is a reprint of those specific clauses with comments and advice. The information is somewhat dated but it is still useful. The complete contract can be accessed at: www.songwritersguild.com/guildcontract.html.

---

4.   In consideration of this contract, the Publisher agrees to pay the Writer as follows:

(a)) $.....as an advance against royalties, receipt of which is hereby acknowledged, which sum shall remain the property of the Writer and shall be deductible only form payments hereafter becoming due the Writer under their contract.

*In 4a, the advance money conditions are stated. The money is advanced free and clear, and will be paid back to the publisher **before** any royalties are distributed. This contract does not include a clause forbidding "cross-collateralization", which means that monies advanced against one song under the guise of this contract may be collected against the royalties on another song. As a songwriter, although you may not be in favor of this, it is a standard clause in the industry, and unproven songwriters must accept it.*

(b) In respect of regular piano copies sold and paid for in he United States and Canada, the following royalties per copy:...% (in no case, however, less than 10%) of the wholesale selling price of the first 200,00 copies or less; plus ...% (in no case less than 12%) of the wholesale selling price of copies in excess of 200,00 and not exceeding 500,00; plus ...% (in no case, however, less than 15%) of wholesale selling price of copies in excess of 500,000.

This is a sliding scale of percentages that should increase the songwriter's participation in revenues as the print sales increase. Here it is based on the wholesale selling price, and the percentages should be twice as large as if based on the selling price at retail.

(c) ...% (in no case, however, less than 50%) of all net sums received by the Publisher in respect of regular piano copies, orchestrations, band arrangements, octavos, quartets, arrangements for combination of voices and/or instruments, and/or copies of the composition sold in any country other than the United States and Canada, provided, however, that if the Publisher should sell such copies through, or cause them to be sold by, a subsidiary or affiliate which is actually doing business in a foreign country, then in respect of such sales, the Publisher shall pay to the Writer not less than 5% of the market retail selling price in respect of each such copy sold and paid for.

*This clause deals with the publishing of arrangements of the work outside of the U.S. and Canada. If the publisher signing the agreement publishes the work, the writer is entitled to at least 50% of the **net** sums received. However, if the publisher sells or licenses the copies through an affiliate or subsidiary in the foreign country, the writer will receive not less than 5% of the market retail selling price for each copy sold and **paid for**. Make note of the inclusion of the phrase "paid for". With foreign publications it is sometimes very difficult to receive payment, and furthermore there is a time lapse between the sale and delivery of funds. Also, this clause does not specify if the payment will be made in U.S. or foreign currency. Many foreign companies hold funds collected until the currency exchange rate favors them, and there could be a different rate on the day the check is written than on the day of the sale.*

(d) In respect of each copy sold and paid for in the United States and Canada, or for export from the United States, of orchestrations, band arrangements, octavos, quartets, arrangements for combinations of voices and/or instruments, and/or other copies of the composition (other than regular piano copies) the following royalties on the wholesale selling price (after trade discounts, if any): ...% (in no case however, less than 10%) on the first 200,000 copies or less; plus ...% (in no case, less than 12%) of all copies in excess of 200,00 and not exceeding 500,000; plus ...% (in no case, however, less than 15%) on all copies in excess of 500,000.

This clause pertains to orchestrations and other arrangements printed and sold in the U.S. and Canada, or printed and exported.

(e)

(i) If the composition, or any part thereof, is included in any song book, folio or similar publication issued by the Publisher containing at least four, but not more than twenty-five musical compositions, the royalty to be paid by the Publisher to the Writer shall be an amount determined by dividing 10% of the Wholesale selling price (after trade Discounts, if any) of the copies sold, among the total number of the Publisher's copyrighted musical compositions included in such publication. If such publication contains more than twenty-five musical compositions, the said 10% shall be increased by an additional ½% for each additional musical composition.

(ii) If, pursuant to a license granted by the Publisher to a licensee not controlled by or affiliated with it, the composition, or any part thereof, is included in any song book, folio or similar publication, containing at least four musical compositions, the royalty to be paid by the Publisher to the Writer shall be that proportion of 50% of the gross amount received by it from the licensee, as the number of uses of the composition under the license and during the license period, bears to the total number of uses of the Publisher's copyrighted musical compositions under the license and during the license period.

(iii) In computing the number of the Publisher's copyrighted musical compositions under subdivisions (i) and (ii) hereof, there shall be excluded musical compositions in the public domain and arrangements thereof and those with respect to which the Publisher does not currently publish and offer for sale regular piano copies.

(iv) Royalties on publications containing less than four musical compositions shall be payable at regular piano copy rates.

This clause deals with songbooks and folios that are published by the publisher and/or licensed by the publisher. It is a given, that the writer wants the printed editions of the song published, however, there is no mention as to if the songs are going to be coupled with other writer's works. The songwriter may insist that the material in all folios published is exclusively his/hers. Also make note that all percentages and numbers are negotiable.

(f) As to "professional material" not sold or resold, no royalty shall be payable. Free copies of the lyrics of the composition shall not be distributed except under the following conditions: (i) with the Writer's written consent; or (ii) when printed without music in limited numbers for charitable, religious or governmental purposes, or for similar public purposes, if no profit is derived, directly or indirectly; or (iii) when authorized for printing in a book, magazine or periodical, where provided that any such use shall bear the Writer's name and the proper copyright notice; or (iv) when distributed solely for the purpose of exploiting the composition, provided, that such exploitation is restricted to the distribution of limited numbers of such copies for the purpose of influencing the sale of the composition, that the distribution is independent of the sale of any other musical compositions, services, goods, wares or merchandise, and that no profit is made, directly or indirectly, in connection therewith.

In this clause free copies and other professional uses are explained. The writer has the power to limit such uses, especially regarding religious and governmental purposes.

(g) ...% (in no case, however, less than 50%) of: All gross receipts of the Publisher in respect of any licenses (including statutory royalties) authorizing the manufacture of parts of instruments serving to mechanically reproduce the composition, or to use the composition in synchronization with sound motion pictures, or to reproduce it upon electrical transcription for broadcasting purposes, and of any and all gross receipts of the Publisher from any other source or right now known or which may hereafter come into existence, except as provided in paragraph 2.

All other rights are discussed here. And although 50% is the standard split, the importance of all of these revenue-producing areas probably merits more detailed descriptions.

(h) If the Publisher administers licenses authorizing the manufacture of parts of instruments serving to mechanically reproduce said composition, or the use of said composition in synchronization or in timed relation with sound motion pictures or its reproduction upon electrical transcriptions, or any of them, through an agent, trustee or other administrator acting for a substantial part of the industry and not under the exclusive control of the Publisher (hereafter sometimes referred to as licensing agent), the Publisher, in determining his receipts, shall be entitled to deduct from gross license fees paid by the Licensees, a sum equal to the charges paid by the Publisher to said licensing agent, provided, however, that in respect to synchronization or timed relation with sound motion pictures, said deduction shall in no event exceed $150 or 10% of said gross license fee, whichever is less; in connection with the manufacture of parts of instruments serving to mechanically reproduce said composition, said deductions shall not exceed 5% of said gross license fee; and in connection with electrical transcriptions, said deduction shall not exceed 10% of said gross license fee.

Here the Publisher administers licenses for the material through a licensing agent, any and all fees for the services performed by the Publisher will be shared by the writer.

(i) The Publisher agrees that the use of the composition will not be included in any bulk or block license heretofore or hereafter granted, and that it will not grant any bulk or block license to include the same, without the written consent of the Writer in each instance, except (i) that the Publisher may grant such license with respect to electrical transcription for broadcasting purposes, A bulk or block license shall be deemed to mean any license or agreement, domestic or foreign, whereby rights are granted in respect of two or more musical compositions.

This is a particularly long clause (only partially reprinted here) that describes what a block license is. The Writer must give his/her consent before the Publisher is allowed to license two or more compositions together. It also includes exclusions, however, they are of standard practice.

(j) Except to the extent that the Publisher and Writer have heretofore of may hereafter assign to or vest in the small performing rights licensing organization with which Writer and Publisher are affiliated, the said rights or the right to grant licenses therefore, it is agreed that no licenses shall be granted without the written consent, in each instance, of the Writer for the use of the composition by means of television, or by any means, or for any purposes not commercially established, of for which licenses were not granted by the Publisher on musical compositions prior to June 1, 1937.

The Writer must give consent for any television or new delivery system use, such as internet streaming or downloading.

(k) The Publisher shall not, without the written consent of the Writer in each case, give or grant any right or license (i) to use the title of the composition, or (ii) for the exclusive use of the composition in any form or for any purpose, or for any period of time, or for any territory, other than its customary arrangements with foreign publishers, or (iii) to give a dramatic representation of the composition or to dramatize the plot or story thereof, or (iv) for a vocal rendition of the composition in synchronization with sound motion pictures, or (v) for any synchronization use thereof, of (vi) for the use of the composition or a quotation or excerpt therefrom in any article, book, periodical, advertisement or other similar publication. If, however, the Publisher shall give to the Writer written notice by certified mail, return receipt requested, or telegram, specifying the right or license to be given or granted, the name of the licensee and the terms and conditions thereof, including the price of other compensation to be received therefore, then, unless the Writer (or any one or more of them) shall, within five business days after the delivery of such notice to the address of the Writer herein designated, object thereto, the Publisher may grant such right or license accordance with the said notice without first obtaining the consent of the Writer. Such notice shall be deemed sufficient if sent to the writer at the address or addresses hereinafter designated or at the address or addresses last furnished to the Publisher in writing by the Writer.

This clause protects the writer against any unwanted licensing of his/her material.

(l) Any portion of the receipts which may become due to the Writer from license fees (in excess of offsets), whether received directly from the licensee or from any licensing agent of the Publisher, shall, if not paid immediately on the receipt thereof by the Publisher, belong to the Writer and shall be held in trust for the Writer until payment is made; the ownership of said trust fund by the Writer shall not be questioned whether the monies are physically segregated or not.

(m) The Publisher agrees that it will not issue any license as a result of which it will receive any financial benefit in which the Writer does not participate.

On all regular piano copies, orchestrations, band or other arrangements, octavos, quartets, commercial sound recordings and other reproductions of the composition or parts thereof, in whatever form and however produced, Publisher shall include or cause to be included, in addition to the copyright notice, the name of the Writer, and Publisher shall include a similar requirement in every license or authorization issued by it with respect to the composition.

6.   (a) The Publisher shall

(i) within ..... months from the date of this contract (the "initial period"), cause a commercial sound recording of the composition to be made and released in the customary form and through the customary commercial channels. If at the end of such initial period a sound recording has not been made and released, as above provided, then, subject to the provisions of the next subdivision, this contract shall terminate.

A new writer should negotiate for the shortest number of months that is agreeable, however, it is customary to give the publisher 12 to 18 months to secure a deal. The clause does not state which record labels would be acceptable, and there is a major difference between a release on Sony Records and one on "Pointless." A compromise might include "a commercial recording distributed by one of the five major record distributors, or a RIAA member label."

(ii) If, prior to the expiration of the initial period, Publisher pays the Writer the sum of $....(which shall not be charged against or recoupable out of any advances, royalties or other monies theretofore paid, then due, or which thereafter may become due the Writer from the Publisher pursuant to this contract or otherwise), Publisher shall have an additional .... months (the "additional period") commencing with the end of the initial period, within which to cause such commercial sound recording to be made and released as provided in subdivision (i) above. If at the end of the additional period a commercial sound recording has not been made and released, as above provided, then this contract shall terminate.

Here there are two figures to be negotiated. The sum allows the publisher to buy some additional time to secure a deal. This clause is included in case the publisher is working on a record deal and it's beyond his/her control to close when s/he would like. The writer should not give the publisher more than six additional months, and should receive a sum s/he feels comfortable with.

(iii) Upon termination pursuant to this Paragraph 6(a), all rights of any and every nature in and to the composition and in and to any and all copyrights secured thereon in the United States and throughout the world shall automatically re-vest in and become the property of the Writer and shall be reassigned to him by the Publisher. The Writer shall not be obligated to return or pay to the Publisher any advance or indebtedness as a condition of such reassignment; the said reassignment shall be in accordance with and subject to the provisions of Paragraph 8 hereof, and, in addition, the Publisher shall pay to the Writer all gross sums which it has theretofore or may thereafter receive in respect of the composition.

This is a clause that the Publisher will have difficulty signing as stated. S/he will want to participate in future revenues that may be generated due to agreements that s/he may have initiated but did not complete. Sometimes there is a compromise (a sunset clause) that suggests that if any revenue is generated during the first ...months immediately following the termination date, the Publisher will receive ...% of the sums.

(b) The Publisher shall furnish, or cause to be furnished, to the Writer six copies of the commercial sound recording referred to in Paragraph 6(a).

Remember that all numbers are negotiable.

(c) The Publisher shall

(i) within 30 days after the initial release of a commercial sound recording of the composition, make, publish and offer for sale regular piano copies of the composition in the form and through the channels customarily employed by it for that purpose;

(ii) within 30 days after execution of this contract make a piano arrangement or lead sheet for he composition and furnish six copies thereof to the Writer.

In the event neither subdivision (i) nor (ii) of this subparagraph © is selected, the provisions of subdivision (ii) shall be automatically deemed to have been selected by the parties.

Since sheets are no longer manufactured for every song recorded, (ii) would be sufficient.

9.   If the Publisher desires to exercise a right in and to the composition now known or which may hereafter become known, but for which no specific provision has been made herein, the Publisher shall give written notice to the Writer thereof. Negotiations respecting all the terms and conditions of any such disposition shall thereupon be entered into between the Publisher and the Writer and no such right shall be exercised until specific agreement has been made.

18.   Except to the extent herein otherwise expressly provided, the Publisher shall not sell, transfer, assign, convey, encumber or otherwise dispose of the compositions or the copyright or copyrights secured thereon without the prior written consent of the Writer. The Writer has been induces to enter into this contract in reliance upon the value to him of the personal service and ability of the Publisher in the exploitation of the composition, and by reason thereof it is the intention of the parties and the essence of the relationship between them that the rights herein granted to the Publisher shall remain with the Publisher and that the same shall not pass to any other person, including, without limitations, successors to or receivers or trustees of the property of the Publisher, either by act or deed of the Publisher or by operation of law, and in the event of the voluntary or involuntary bankruptcy of the Publisher, this contract shall terminate, provided, however, that the composition may be included by the Publisher in a bona fide voluntary sale of its music business or its entire catalog of musical compositions, or in a merger or consolidation of the Publisher with another corporation, in which event the Publisher shall immediately give written notice thereof to the Writer; and provided further that the composition and the copyright therein may be assigned by the Publisher to a subsidiary or affiliated company generally engaged in the music publishing business. If the Publisher is an individual, the composition may pass to a legatee or distributee as part of the inheritance of the Publisher's music business and entire catalog of musical compositions. Any such transfer or assignment shall, however, be conditioned upon the execution and delivery by the transferee or assignee to the Writer of an agreement to be bound by and to perform all of the terms and conditions of this contract to be performed on the part of the Publisher.

This clause does not allow the publisher to sell or trade any of the writer's songs without prior written consent of the writer. It protects the writer from being part of a package deal that the publisher may want to execute to obtain the rights to a song or catalog. However, if the publisher is sold to another music publisher in the business, then the writer cannot stop his/her material from being assigned, provided that the contract between the writer and the new publisher contains all of the terms included in this contract.

PUBLISHING

Record companies have taken over many of the responsibilities of the early music publishers, narrowing their role in exploiting the copyright. Today virtually all record companies own publishing firms. In fact, the top four publishing firms of 2009 are owned by the four majors and accounted for over sixty percent of the market share {{158 Christman, Ed 2009;}}. So the main function of the music publisher is to generate "covers" of their clients catalog. This may include the following:

1. covering the song for other markets by having a different artist record the song

2. completing several arrangements of the work ie: big band, piano arrangements, etc.

3. licensing the song for use in advertising, promotional commercials, or e commerce

4. licensing the song for print editions

5. permitting the song to be used with time-related visuals (synchronization)

6. sub-publishing the work for foreign income.

The consequence of these avenues of exploitation is the generation of income. The more ways a song is used, the better the chances that it will generate income. Recently, Billboard, wrote of five big ideas that publishers are employing today to boost income. They include: music in film; paring newcomers with legends; licensing lyrics for commercials; band-branded games; and signing songwriters {{161 Christman, Ed 2009;}}.

Traditionally, a publisher's strength is in the success of his/her catalog. Over the past decade, the size of the catalog has been of major concern. In the 1980's, bigger was better. Many catalogs were sold for what seemed like huge amounts of money. This was due to several reasons: Some companies were experiencing cash flow problems and needed revenue quickly; it was more cost effective to purchase an entire catalog than it was to purchase one or two hits; and lastly, with the development of new and different "delivery systems", it was advantageous to own the song rather than secure a license for one use. If you own the song, it is your option to license it or use it anyway you see fit. The strength is in the catalog!

There is a joke in the business; the idea of it is that Paul McCartney and the estate of Michael Jackson own all the songs that were ever written! It's true that they both own large catalogs (Yoko Ono and Paul joined together to purchase the remaining Beatle songs that Paul didn't already own, but were out bid by Michael), however, they own them not only for their respective egos, but because one of the surest safest investment in the music business is owning a song catalog.

SOURCES OF INCOME

Publishers (and songwriters) receive income from six basic song uses or licenses. They are:

1. mechanical licensing

2. performance licensing

3. synchronization licensing

4. jukeboxes

5. print licensing

6. foreign licensing

7. special use licensing

1. Mechanical Licensing   As a songwriter, if someone wants to manufacture (mechanically reproduce) a sound recording of your song, s/he must obtain a mechanical license from your publisher. In 1909, the statutory rate was $.02 per song and it cost $.03 to mail a letter. The current price for the license (the statutory rate) is $.091 per song or $.0175 per minute, whichever is greater, on every recording manufactured and sold, and it now costs over twelve times as great to mail a letter! (Obviously the rate has not kept up with inflation or the U.S. Postal Service rates, and has been quite a deal for the record companies.} The rate now in effect, was set and adjusted according to the Consumer Price Index by the now disbanded U.S. Copyright Tribunal, whose responsibilities have been taken over by the U.S. Copyright Office. If 500,000 copies of the recording are sold, the mechanical license generates $45,500 (500,000 X $.091), which is split between the songwriter and the publisher. Once the initial recording is released, if anyone is willing to pay the current statutory rate, the song's owner must issue the license. Since the rate is set by law, many feel that it discriminates against successful songwriters. For example, is a song written by Paul McCartney worth the same amount as one written by John Doe? Some feel that the licensing rate should be free to be negotiated on the open market. And in a way it is, through the use of the negotiated license. If the copyright holder agrees, the manufacturer (record company), may pay a rate lower than the statutory rate. If the record company is not the publisher of the song, the company will negotiate to pay 3⁄4 statutory rate (the standard in the industry) with the possibility of a graduated scale based on sales. This negotiated mechanical license is used throughout the industry, especially on initial recordings, where the statutory rate doe not apply, and when the artist is more famous than the songwriter. Also, if the artist is more famous than the songwriter, the record company may want to pay only $.02 on every recording manufactured and sold and may negotiate that rate with the song owner (publisher). Therefore on 500,000 copies sold, it would cost the company only $10,000 (500,000 X $.02) instead of $40,000.

In the U.S., most publishers issue mechanical licenses through one of the mechanical rights organizations. The largest is the Harry Fox Agency, who charges a fee (circa +5 %) for its services. The services include the issuing of licenses, collecting royalties, and auditing record companies as well.

2. Performance Licensing Another right the copyright owner is granted by law is the right to perform the copyrighted material in public. This includes the actual live performance of the work or the performance of a mechanical reproduction of the work. Consequently, the user of the work must obtain a license to broadcast a performance or have a live performance occur in his/her venue. Broadcast stations, internet broadcasts, phone services, satellite, webcasters, auditoriums, arenas, and clubs throughout the world, all obtain various types of performance licenses. Because the issuing of these licenses would be an enormous task for individual copyright owners, performing rights organizations act as clearinghouses for their respective clients.

In the U.S. there are three performing rights organizations (PRO's): ASCAP (American Society of Authors, Composers, and Publishers), BMI (Broadcast Music Incorporated), and SESAC (Society of European Stage Authors and Composers). ASCAP and BMI are the largest and not for profit. In order to receive payments, composer must exclusively belong to one of the three, however, a publisher may belong to all three. Their responsibilities include granting licenses, collecting royalties, and distributing the income to their clients.

The structures of the organizations include a broadcast licensing area, and a general licensing area. The broadcast license revenues are determined by a survey or logging procedure, where different broadcast performances are given a value (or a weight). A sophisticated formula determines how much revenue is produced by each performance.

The general licensing area issues licenses to venues. The fee for the license is determined by the capacity of the venue and various other factors. The revenue collected is distributed for the most part by the number of logged or surveyed **broadcast performances, rather than public performances**. Therefore, songs that are performed a great deal live but have ceased (or never were) to be played (performed) by broadcasters, lose out because they are disproportionately accounted for. The performing rights organizations are now surveying actual performances in the largest venues in the country, however, a system for accounting for every live performance in America has not been established.

The PRO's distribute the income (after expenses) individually to the writers and the publishers (usually on a 50/50% share basis). Performance license royalties are the only license royalties that are not funneled through the publisher to be split and distributed to the writer.

A performance right for digital transmission of a recorded performance has now been established. The right not only includes the songwriter and publisher but the performer as well. This is the only performance license granted in this country that includes the performer.

3. Synchronization Licensing Anytime music is combined with visual motion it becomes what is known as "time related" and requires a "synch license." These uses include music in motion pictures (theatrical releases or made for TV movies), and music videos. The producer of the work must obtain the license form the publisher. Obviously, revenue from synch licenses can be very substantial. The publisher collects these payments who in turn splits them (usually 50/50) with the writer.

4. Jukeboxes Prior to 1978, jukeboxes were exempt from copyright liability. A2001-2005 agreement with the PROs and the Amusement and Music Operators Association (AMOA), provided for a rate of $350 for the first box plus $59 per additional box with a consumer Price Index increase each year {{115 Brebac, Jeff 2006;}}.

5. Print Licensing Before the recording industry took over, music publishers printed sheet music of the songs that they owned. This is what it meant to publish! Today, only a few music publishers are in the print manufacturing business. Most license the rights to another company and receive a percentage of the revenue on the sheet music sold. They, in turn, pay the writer a small percent of what is received. Sheets or folios are not printed for every song recorded, and for new artists, they are not printed until it is determined that the record has "some legs." However, big hits can produce substantial folio revenue.

6. Foreign Licensing Foreign income is derive from licensing and subpublishing throughout the world. The percentage of revenues realized from each license is substantively lower than revenue from similar domestic uses. Exchange rates, tariffs, and distribution costs play a major role in how much income is generated. Some songwriters are counseled to retain their foreign rights and issue their own licenses. Although this sounds great, it may prove to be disastrous because the hardest aspect of foreign licensing is receiving the revenues (getting paid), and an individual songwriter may not have the resources a publisher may have to track down money due to them.

7. Special Use Licensing These licenses include using the music in advertising jingles, greeting cards, and other merchandise. Sponsors who want music in their commercial notify their advertising agency that may produce the music in-house, or rely on the services of a music supplier. The commercials may run in a national television campaign or a 15 second local radio spot. The use of the music may vary from using the original recording of the song followed by a voice over, as a background "bed" under a voice over, or the use of the music with lyrics selling the product sung to the original melody. Therefore the special use release of the song usually uses a form of a synch license as well.

Additional uses have developed including **ringtones**. The standard royalty structure has been the greater of a 10¢/10% formula. For example, if the consumer is charged $1.99 for the download, the royalty to the songwriter/publisher would be 19.9¢ (the higher of the 10¢/10% formula. Concerning **streaming**, the writer/publisher would currently split a quarter of a cent per stream, if the stream is longer than 30 seconds. The current rate for the use of a pre-existing song in a **video game** is 8¢ to 15¢ per game or a buy-out that would range from $2500 to $20,0000 + {{115 Brebac, Jeff 2006;}}. These rates are constantly being negotiated and can only be used as a guide.

The following chart sums up the normal income distribution between the publisher and the songwriter. These figures can be only be used as a guide.

INCOME

License	Split
Mechanical	Publisher collects 100% and pays affiliated composer 50%
Performance	PRO pays composer and publisher individual shares directly
Synchronization	Publisher collects and pays affiliated composer 50%
Jukeboxes	PRO pays publisher who pays affiliated composer his/her share
Print	Publisher collects 100% and pays composer small royalty at approximately $.10 per printed edition sold
Foreign	When received from foreign or subpublisher, 50% of income is paid to composer
Special Use	Publisher collects 100% and pays affiliated composer 50%

Figure 8.5

PERFORMING

LIVE

Only in the last 25 years has the technology been available to perform in the arenas and stadiums that are so common practice today. There is a great picture of the Beatles performing their now famous Shea Stadium Concert. The two baselines of the baseball diamond are lined with five foot sound columns, with six or seven speakers in each. That was the sound reinforcement system for the fifty thousand fans seated (and screaming) in the stands!

There was also less emphasis placed on the performance as another retailing opportunity for the artist. It was looked upon as another way of enhancing record sales, instead of a large revenue generating experience. Today a worldwide concert tour takes years to complete and produces millions for top artists in ticket and merchandising sales revenues. Today, artists are totally aware of the potential and power of the live performance, and approach the live show creatively, to bring the consumer the most unforgettable experience possible. CONCERTS DON'T SELL, EVENTS SELLOUT! (A more in-depth discussion of a show appears in Chapter Nine.)

VIDEO

How important is it? Should we spend the money? I don't know how to act anyway? Are we sure that they help sell recordings? Is everyone still releasing videos?

Videos had a strong impact on the business in the 1980s. The Recording Industry Association of America (RIAA) has established the quotas for Gold and Platinum video awards. Figure 8.4 lists the number of units needed to be sold for video singles, long forms, and matchbox sets to be certified as gold, platinum, and multiplatinum sellers. The upper levels are rarely met.

GOLD & PLATINUM AWARDS CERTIFICATION LEVELS

	Gold	Platinum	Multi-Platinum
Video Single	25,000 units: max. running time of 15 minutes: two songs per title	50,000 units: max. running time of 15 minutes: two songs per title	100,000 units: max. running time of 15 minutes: two songs per title
Video Long Form	50,000 units	100,000 units	200,000 units
Video Multi-Box	50,000 units	100,000 units	200,000 units

Figure 8.6 Gold and Platinum Awards Certification Levels (Audio and Video). Statistical Overview 1991. Inside the Record Industry. RIAA, Washington DC p. 16.

Although they represent only one-twentieth of the amounts needed for audio recording certifications, it should be noted that the configuration (or some form of video configuration) has never caught on with the consumer. Also, the sale of music videos has not come close to what had been expected. In the early 1980's, it was thought that consumers would no longer purchase audio recordings. Their sales would be replaced by long form videos of entire albums that would be watched as well as listened to. That never became a reality. Consumers seem to still want the freedom to do what they want when they want to, and use music in a variety of ways.

Promotional videos have become an industry staple. MTV recognized this in the mid 1980's and offered to pay major record companies for the exclusive right to exhibit new releases. The radio industry was astonished that MTV would be willing to pay for a service that radio stations have always received for free. However, MTV gambled that the way to stifle competition from other video presenters was to gain exclusivity to new releases and was willing to pay for that access. It proved to be a brilliant decision as MTV logo is synonymous with word video worldwide.

The forerunners to the modern videos were called "soundies". They surfaced in the 1940's, and "were an ambitious attempt to merge the jukebox concept with three minute filmclips" {{9 Denisoff,R.Serge 1986/f, p. 330}}. They were made by the Mills Novelty Company in Chicago who in 1941, also began manufacturing Panorams.

The Panorams were the hardware (viewing and listening machines) that were used to play the soundies. The screens were the size of two pieces of letterhead stationery, and selections were changed twice a month. Because racism prevailed, two separate catalogs were issued and distributed along color lines. Customers paid a dime to see a clip, almost entirely made of close-up shots with crude lip syncing. Because reels became outdated in a matter of days, the idea suffered from a built-in obsolescence.

The early modern videos were basically concert footage (either live or staged) of the group performing. During the early 1980's the concept video appeared. In some related loose form, the story told in the lyrics was acted out by members of the group. The concept was usually a nonlinear approach, where certain scenes and symbols would appear and reappear without any simple storytelling logic.

The nonlinear concept was new, exciting, and fresh to television. Up until that point, TV shows used a linear approach. For example, in a detective show, a crime would be committed and then solved. A situation comedy would set up a dilemma (situation), and then act out the solution. Soap operas would do the same thing, only they would add a few twists and turns to unravel the story over time.

The first network show to use the nonlinear approach over any length of time was NBC's Miami Vice. The fashion statements were perfect for the 1980's video viewing age group, and the quasi nonlinear concept with rock stars making guest appearances, gave the show a long run.

The concept music video is commonplace today. Video producers and directors must consciously develop concepts that compliment the artist's image. If it is so unbelievable that it's down right silly, it could, and has spelled trouble for the artist. Even video king, Michael Jackson was criticized for (and the video was quickly pulled) the smashing of the cars scenes from the Dangerous album's initial video.

Videos are not as essential today as there are few outlets showing them. Still record companies see the promotional importance of videos and the possibility that their sales or licensing may help revenue. Therefore, what was once a few paragraphs in a recording contract, still encompasses several pages. Below are key video clauses and commentary from a major recording contract. Use it as guide.

KEY VIDEO CLAUSES

1.

(a) In addition to ARTIST's recordings and PRODUCTIONS, production and delivery commitments as set forth in Paragraph # of this Agreement, PRODUCTIONS and ARTIST shall comply with requests, if any, made by COMPANY in connection with the production of Pictures. In this connection, PRODUCTIONS shall cause ARTIST to appear on dates and at places requested by COMPANY for the filming, taping or other fixation of audiovisual recordings. PRODUCTIONS and ARTIST shall perform services with respect thereto as COMPANY deems desirable in a timely and first-class manner. PRODUCTIONS and ARTIST acknowledge that the production of Pictures involves matters of judgment with respect to art and taste, which judgment shall mutually exercised by COMPANY and PRODUCTIONS in good faith, it being understood that if agreement cannot be reached, COMPANY's decisions with respect thereto shall be final.

In this contract, the artist's works are being produced by a company called PRODUCTIONS, and the COMPANY is requiring the artist to appear for "pictures" when asked. It also states that the record company will have the final word on the release of the audiovisual work, even though it plans on discussing the matter with the artist in good faith.

(b)

(i) Each picture produced during the Term of this Agreement shall be owned by **COMPANY** (including the worldwide copyrights therein and thereto and all extensions and renewals thereof) to the same extent as COMPANY's rights in master recordings made under this Agreement.

(ii) COMPANY will have the unlimited right to manufacture Videoshows of the Picture and to rent, sell, distribute, transfer, sublicense of otherwise deal in such Videoshows under any trademarks, tradenames and labels; to exploit the Picture by any means now or hereafter known or developed; or to refrain from any such exploitation, throughout the world.

(c)

(i) Following COMPANY's receipt of invoices therefor, COMPANY agrees to pay all costs actually incurred in the production of Pictures made at COMPANY's request hereunder, provided such costs have been previously approved by COMPANY in writing. In this connection, prior to commencing production of any Picture, PRODUCTIONS shall submit to COMPANY, in writing, a detailed budget for each Picture. Said budget shall include the following information: (i) the musical compositions and other material to be embodied thereon

(ii) the general concept therefor and (iii) the producer, director, and any other key personnel therefor. Following PRODUCTIONS' receipt of COMPANY's approval of said budget, PRODUCTIONS' shall commence production if the Picture. All costs incurred in excess of the applicable approved budget shall be PRODUCTIONS' sole responsibility and PRODUCTIONS agrees to pay any such excess costs on PRODUCTIONS' behalf, PRODUCTIONS shall, upon demand, reimburses COMPANY for such excess costs and/or COMPANY may deduct such excess costs from any and all monies due to PRODUCTIONS pursuant to this or any other agreement between the parties hereto. All sums paid by COMPANY in connection with each Picture shall be an advance against and recoupable by COMPANY out of all royalties becoming payable to PRODUCTIONS pursuant to this or any other agreement, provided that COMPANY shall not recoup more than fifty (50%) percent of such sums from royalties becoming payable to PRODUCTIONS pursuant to Paragraph # of this Agreement.

These clauses specify ownership and how production costs will be paid. It also addresses COMPANY'S right to cross-collateralize up to 50% of sum stated in an earlier paragraph. Remember that almost all percentages are negotiable.

(ii) Each of the following sums, if any, paid by COMPANY in connection with each Picture shall be an advance against and recoupable by COMPANY out of all royalties becoming payable to PRODUCTIONS pursuant to this or any other agreement, provided that COMPANY shall not recoup more than fifty (50%) percent of such sums from royalties becoming payable to PRODUCTIONS pursuant to Paragraph # of this Agreement:

Fifty percent is the standard sum.

(vi) With respect to records embodying Pictures made hereunder together with other material, royalties payable to PRODUCTIONS shall be computed by multiplying the royalties otherwise applicable by a fraction, the numerator of which is the amount of playing time in any such record of Pictures made hereunder and the denominator of which is the total playing time of all material in any such record.

(vii) As to Pictures embodying performances of ARTIST together with the performances of another artist or artists, the royalties otherwise payable hereunder shall be prorated by multiplying such royalties by a fraction, the numerator of which is one and the denominator of which is the total number of artists whose performances are embodies on such Pictures. COMPANY shall not require ARTIST to so perform with other artists without PRODUCTIONS' consent, however, if ARTIST does perform with other artists, such performance shall constitute consent.

The formula stated in vi and vii is okay for a short form video where the artist is the star of the picture. However, in a long form video, if the artist is the biggest star on the video and his/her performance does not constitute the majority of the playing time, then this formula would have to be negotiated.

(e)

COMPANY shall have the right to use and allow others to use each Picture for advertising and promotional purposes with no payment to PRODUCTIONS or ARTIST.

(f)

(i) During the Term of this Agreement, no person, firm or corporation other than COMPANY will be authorized to make, sell, broadcast or otherwise exploit audiovisual materials unless:

(A) PRODUCTIONS first notifies COMPANY of all of the material terms and conditions of the proposed agreement pursuant to which the audiovisual materials is to be made, sold, broadcast or otherwise exploited, including, but no limited to, the titles of the compositions covered by the proposed agreement, the format to be used, the manner of exploitation proposed and the identities of all proposed parties to the agreement, and

(B) PRODUCTIONS offers to enter into an agreement with COMPANY containing the same terms and conditions described in such notice and otherwise in the same form as this Agreement. If COMPANY does not accept PRODUCTIONS' offer within sixty (60) days after COMPANY's receipt of same, PRODUCTIONS may then enter into that proposed agreement with the same parties mentioned in such notice, subject to subparagraph

(f)

(ii) hereof and provided that such agreement is consummated with those parties within thirty (30) days after the end of that sixty (60) day period upon the same financial terms land condition set forth in PRODUCTIONS' notice and latter thirty (30) day period, no party except COMPANY will be authorized to make, sell, broadcast or otherwise exploit such audiovisual materials unless PRODUCTIONS first offers to enter into an agreement with COMPANY as provided in the first sentence of this subparagraph . . . .

(ii) If COMPANY does not accept an offer made to it pursuant to this subparagraph

(f), such nonacceptance shall not be considered a waiver of any of COMPANY's rights pursuant this Agreement. Such rights include, without limitation, the right to prevent PRODUCTIONS from exploiting audiovisual material featuring ARTIST in the form of Videoshows, and the right to prevent PRODUCTIONS from authorizing any use of masters owned by or exclusively licensed to COMPANY unless COMPANY so agree. PRODUCTIONS shall not act in contravention of such rights.

COMPANY is exercising a right to first refusal by asking for notice and a time period to respond. It also is stating that it is not given up any of its rights to masters.

MEDIA CHECK! LIVE VS. AUDIO VS. VIDEO

It is often said that artists that land a recording deal and don't make it fail because of one of two reasons: poor management (read this book) or a lack of understanding of the differences between the live performance and the recorded performance. So many artists have said "we don't know what happened man, we sounded so great on stage, but the excitement was not captured on our record." Demo recordings of many great young bands do not sound as good as the band does in a club. On the other hand, occasionally, bands that sell a whole bunch of records are disappointments when seen in concert. One of the reasons this happens is that young bands that play in clubs night after night become really proficient at playing in the live medium. And some bands with record deals make records that are produced by producers who understand the medium of recording and make great records.

Some things that work great on stage for a live performance can not be captured in the audio (recorded) medium. However, on the record, something different takes the place of the stage event to generate excitement. It many occur in the mix of the recording or something extra that is added to the arrangement. For example, listen to a Rolling Stone's record, the excitement that is generated by Mick Jagger prancing across the stage making faces at the audience, is somehow compensated for in the studio medium. Secondly, The Stones are not intimidated by the physical characteristics of the recording studio. They do not let the isolation of the studio hinder their performance. To capture their sound they layer tracks, double themselves, and use every studio trick ever invented (I'm certain that they invented quite a few themselves). The record is produced with the clear understanding that it must generate the excitement of the visual effects of their show without being seen. The producer understands the recording medium and its uniqueness.

Over the last twenty years, a third, yet different medium has become important. Artists must have an understanding of what is successful in the video medium. Television and computer screens (video) wash colors and make one appear to be heavier than s/he really is. Moving the camera or background scenery can create the illusion of movement. Lyrics and solos can be lip-synced to allow for exaggerated acting. Producers and directors make videos work. Again, it is the understanding of the uniqueness of the medium that is important.

As a manager, it is suggested that if an artist has not had studio experience, the making of an entire album master (rather than a demo) should be discouraged. More often than not, a great deal of expense is incurred, and the end result of the ego trip is a record that does not capture the live excitement of the band's club performances, nor reflect the artist's intent. The same must be said for the budget video. Leave it to the pros. In the end money will be saved.

GUIDING THE CREATIVE TALENT

What is the manager's role in guiding an artist? On page 63 in *Guiding Creative Talent*, Paul Torrance lists both general and specific goals in guiding creative talent. He lists the general goals as:

1. encouraging of a healthy kind of individuality

2. developing of conditions which will permit creativeness

3. regressing in the service of the ego and

4. counteracting pressures of regression to the average.

In order to achieve the general goals, he suggest obtaining the following specific goals as essential:

1. reward diverse contributions

2. help creative persons recognize the value of their own talents

3. avoid exploitation

4. accept limitations creatively

5. develop minimum skills

6. make use of opportunities

7. develop values and purposes

8. hold to purposes

9. avoid the equation of divergent with mental illness or delinquency

10. reduce overemphasis or misplace emphasis on sex roles

11. help them learn how to be less obnoxious

12. reduce isolation and

13. help them learn how to cope with anxieties, fears, hardships, and failures {{19 Torrance,E.Paul 1962/f, p. 63}}.

And who said management wasn't fun!

SUMMARY

1. The creative process is a function of the right hemisphere of the brain.

2. The creative process is different for different people and different for the same individual at different times.

3. Traits of the creative individual include being intuitive, open-minded, spontaneous, sensitive, flexible, and original.

4. Traits of the creative product include: unusualness, appropriateness, newness, and compactness.

5. Unless in a coma, everyone has some degree of creativity.

6. Research has found that the greatest contributions to their field were made by musicians between thirty and forty years old.

7. Factors that accompany age change bring about a reduction in creativity.

8. Creativity cannot be taught, but creative uses of a craft can.

9. Creativity can be evaluated by some quantitative measure.

10. Songwriting is both an art and a craft.

11. Songs that have a potential of being successful have certain characteristics.

12. Money is made from songwriting by exploiting the copyright.

13. The Songwriter's Guild of America publishes a Popular Songwriter's Contract that contains clauses describing all revenue producing areas.

14. The music publisher's role of exploiting the song's copyright includes many functions.

15. Publishers receive income form six basic song uses.

16. The publisher and songwriter usually split income on an equal basis.

17. The RIAA now lists criteria for Gold and Platinum Video Awards.

18. The first videos were called soundies and were viewed on panorams.

19. Many modern music videos use the nonlinear concept of story evolution.

20. Record company video clauses have grown larger and more complex.

21. Many artists with record contracts are not successful because they do not understand the differences between the live vs. audio and now video media.

22. Management must play a role in guiding creative talent.

PROJECTS

1. Think of someone you know who you feel is very creative. List his/her personality characteristics.

2. Analyze why a song is successful. List the characteristics that make it successful.

3. Discuss whether songwriting is an art or a craft.

4. Compile a songwriter/publisher agreement that is fair for both parties.

5. Discuss the nonlinear approach of story evolution in a current music video.

6. List the different characteristics of live vs. audio vs. video performance.

7. Discuss the role of management in the nurturing of creative talent.

CHAPTER NINE
TOURING

"I've made seven albums and two babies in the last five years, but it's not the same as touring.
There's something so positive about it . . . Not that you're adulated,
but that you feel euphorically encouraged and completely whole."
Tina Weymouth, formerly of Talking Heads . . . Rolling Stone Magazine: *RS 491*

"There are no bad shows. There are just bad deals." Alex Hodges, Executive VP, House of Blues
Concerts. N.Y. Times, *June 6, 2005*

BY THE END OF THIS CHAPTER YOU SHOULD BE ABLE TO:

1. Discuss the five basic tour objectives
2. Discuss the most productive routing for most tours
3. Discuss the procedure for securing a concert performance
4. Discuss the various concert performance fee structures
5. Discuss the basic budget lines for an artist's tour
6. Discuss the various categories of a concert contract rider
7. Discuss tour publicity
8. Discuss all aspects of staging and production
9. Discuss how to evaluate a tour's objectives
10. Discuss the manager's role before, during, and after the tour.

ITS HISTORY

Touring has always played a role in musicians' lives. From the eleventh to the end of the thirteenth centuries, many poet-musicians traveled the southern regions of France, singing lyric poetry. In America, during the nineteenth century, minstrel shows with singers, musicians and variety acts combed the south daily. Around 1900, vaudeville entertainers visited the newly developed industrial urban centers, playing one- nighters. In the early 1920's, jazz musicians traveled from New Orleans, up the Mississippi toward Chicago, performing in every city along the way.

The big bands of the 1930's and early 1940's really solidified the idea of musicians being "married" to the road. Stories about the effects of travel on a musician's physical and emotional well being from this era are numerous. Although the players have changed and our transportation systems have improved, the road is still an essential part of a musician's life.

Rock musicians and rock bands have taken on the role of the big bands of 1930's and 40's. Each metropolitan area and region of the country had its own favorite big bands in those days. They included the nationally famous bands of the era . . . The Benny Goodman Band, The Glen Miller Orchestra, The Duke Ellington Orchestra, and others. Today, local and regional rock bands hope to gather a following of fans who are as loyal and who will allow them to perform their own material. Eventually they hope this will lead to a recording contract with a nationally distributed record company.

The live performance has been and continues to be an important form of artist-to - consumer retailing. When someone purchases a ticket to see an artist perform, he or she is the consumer. The concert promoter is the retailer. The music is the product. And the live performance is a way of selling the artist's product. For this reason, performance, and touring remain very necessary aspects of an artist's career.

Fortunately, for successful musicians, "the road" no longer means an old bus, cheap hotels, junk food, and beer joints. Most artists tour to build a fanbase and experience the rewards that an immediate response from an audience provides. As a manager, you'll need to know why, when, and where to tour. Some guidelines follow. A timeline is included, showing, when certain aspects of tour preparation should be completed. Take note of the objectives you will want to accomplish during the tour. Finally, you will be given some pointers on how to evaluate the tour's success. In this example, the artist on tour holds a recording contract with a major label and performs in arena venues of approximately 10,000 seats or more.

TOUR OBJECTIVES

Why tour at all? It's very expensive, and it consumes a great deal of time and energy from the artist and the manager. However, in today's business, it's where the money is. A successful tour can meet useful objectives. Several of these are:

ONE: TO MAKE A CONNECTION WITH THE AUDIENCE AND CONVERT PASSIVE FANS INTO FANATIC FANS.

This is the central theme of this book's edition. Obviously, the artist's presence in a market increases the likelihood that the concertgoer will buy his or her recording and merchandise. In turn, the concertgoer will introduce the artist to prospective fans. A concert provides the opportunity for an audience to see the artist perform in person, and to identify with him or her. The tour should be announced and the tickets should go on sale as soon as the record is released.

TWO: TO PUBLICIZE THE EVENT AND MONETIZE ALL REVENUE STREAMS.

When an artist arrives in a city for a concert performance, he or she should spend the time wisely. The artist should make contact with the record company's local representatives (which generally include the promotion and sales representatives), radio stations and other media personnel, the local record retail community, and anyone else who might prove useful in furthering his or her career. These meetings, although sometimes tiresome and repetitious to the artist, pay off "down the road." These individuals appreciate the opportunity to meet the person behind the music, and the artist receives the opportunity to publicize all his or her website and products.

The New York Times reported the itinerary of the New York City visit of the band *Kings of Leon*.

Monday:	Video shoot in Rockaway, NJ.
Tuesday:	Letterman appearance; Irving Plaza show After party, sponsored by *Rolling Stone* Magazine. Nightcap
Wednesday:	Carson Daly's show Webster Hall show After party Nightcap
Thursday:	Interviews: MTV; Fuse; Q Magazine; Bass Player Magazine; Dinner photo shoot
Friday:	early bus to Philadelphia {{116 Carr, David 2005;}}

THREE: TO MAKE THE ARTIST'S PERFORMANCE "AN EVENT" ON A PERFORMANCE BY PERFORMANCE BASIS.

Unless an artist is well known enough to receive immediate national media exposure via "Entertainment Tonight," "The Today Show," or other news and information programs, a ground swell effect must be created on a market-by-market basis and on the internet. The objective is to develop a ripple effect that will extend to additional markets. Creating a media event pays off! They almost always sell out; most ordinary performances or concerts do not. Contests, give-aways, tie-ins with local sponsors, will help to distinguish your artist's concert as special. The same promotional "gimmicks" maybe used throughout the tour. But they must be tailored to every individual stop so they seem fresh and exciting.

FOUR: TO MAKE A PROFIT.

An artist may derive a tremendous amount of creative fulfillment from performing, and you may get personal satisfaction from managing. But the bottom line is the artist is in business. Tours earn a great deal of money for headliners. Recently however, there has developed the fear that high-ticket prices are turning off the consumer. Gross revenues are higher but attendance is down. As noted in Chapter Four, the highest grossing tour in 2008, was Bon Jovi performing ninety-nine sellout shows to 2,157,675 people and grossing $210,650,675, with an average ticket price (excluding fees) of $97.60.

Setting the ticket prices (scaling the house) is a complex issue. In a recent Billboard Magazine Commentary, Frank Luby and Jason Gelbort in discussing price sensitivity, assume that for every ten percent in the reduction of the average ticket price, fifteen percent more fans will buy tickets, a reasonable assumption they claim, with some variations. Also they state that from analyzing data, and learning the exact price sensitivity of your audience, you might be able to set a price that everyone makes money; however, it would not guarantee a sellout. And a price set too low would not necessarily be offset by additional ancillary income and thereby would not be the best solution {{154 Luby, Frank and Gelbort, Jason 2009;}}.

TOUR PREPARATION TIMELINE
Six Month Plan

PREPARING FOR THE TOUR
WHEN AND WHERE TO START

Deciding where to begin a tour depends upon a number of factors. If it's a baby band headling for the first time, the tour should begin far from media attention and industry visibility. This insulation gives the artist a chance to iron out unforeseen problems before moving into a major market. Problems may occur in the actual stage/performance, the technical production preparation, or the performance publicity. Major acts, rent a large warehouse, airplane hanger, or area, and setup, teardown, and run the performance before the tour's kickoff. These bands' anticipated tours begin with much media attention. One rule of thumb is to begin a tour a short time after the release of the record. By this time, the album's first single should be getting attention.

ROUTING

In which secondary market should the tour begin? In which secondary market will the artist draw a large enough audience to make a profit? Where is a good place to try out the material and warm up the show? Should the tour begin in the east or someplace in the Midwest? How many miles should the artist and the entourage travel between performances in each region?

The key to a successful tour is flexibility. As manager, you must be willing to add additional dates and reroute the artist at any time. The tentative routing of the tour should begin several months prior to its start (see Figure 9.1). It makes good business sense to begin somewhat close to the artist's home. People and equipment will only need to travel a short distance. If the artist lives in Atlanta, why cart the equipment across the country to begin in Boise, Idaho? Sketch out where (in which major market) you would like to be when you anticipate the record hitting its stride. If the artist is very popular, it doesn't matter if the concert is on a weekday or a weekend. If the artist has toured before, use the results of previous tours to rationalize why a certain routing should be successful.

Some variables may decrease the size of the anticipated audience. First, be aware of the other "traffic" in the market (traffic refers to concerts by competing artists). If your artist's audience has a limited disposable income, or the market's population cannot with stand a too heavy concert schedule, the concert attendance may be affected. Secondly, be aware of the economic conditions of the market. A depressed economy may seriously decrease the expected number of ticket sales in a geographic area; no matter how much publicity you have.

PROCEDURE

The process of securing a concert performance involves the artist's manager, the booking agent, and the concert promoter. The following is a typical sequence of events:

Step 1: The manager and agent arrive at a fee the artist is seeking for his or her performance.

This price is based on the tour's budget, and the artist's worth in the marketplace. If the artist is a "baby band," a tour budget is set and the attempt is made to average out the expectation over a number of dates. For example, if the artist needs to net $500/date to meet expenses, two dates may be booked to net $350, and two dates may be booked to net $650. For a major act, the artist basically has a performance price!

The price may be represented in four different forms:

1. A flat guarantee

2. A guarantee plus a percentage after verified expenses

3. A guarantee vs. a percentage

4. A percentage

1. A flat guarantee

Today, even though a headlining artist usually does not perform solely for a guaranteed price, it is still an option and is employed in state fair performances or where specific admission is not charged. However, a flat guarantee is most often the deal offered to an opening act. For example, **"The artist will perform one 45 minute set for $3500 flat guarantee."**

2. A guarantee plus a percentage after verified expenses

Many headlining artists require a concert promoter to guarantee them a sum of money to perform, and if the revenue is greater, they will also want to share in the profits from the number of tickets sold. This option assures them a sum of money in case ticket sales don't meet their expectations (see Figure 9.4). This example assures them a sum of money plus the 90% of the "overage". For example, **"The artist will perform for $160,000 guarantee plus 90% of the Gross Box Office Receipts after verified expenses, and 15% promoter's profit."** In this case, if the gross potential from the ticket receipts after taxes is $800,000 (20K seats at an average of $40 per), and the promoter has incurred expenses of $380,000 (the artist's guarantee is included in these calculations). The promoter would earn a 15% promoters fee of the $380,000 expenses or $57,000. Then the artist would receive 90% of the remainder or $363,000 (plus $160,000). The concert promoter would receive the fee of $57,000 plus 10% of the overage, $36,300.

```
$800,000  GP
-220,000  expenses
-160,000  artist guarantee
 -57,000  promoter's 15% profit  (of 380K expenses)
$363,000  (overage)
    x.90
$326,700  + $160,000 guarantee = $486,700 Artist receives


$363,000
    x.10
$36,300 + $57,000  15% fee = $93,300  Promoter receives
```

3. A guarantee vs. a percentage after verified expenses

This deal is generally for Superstar artists who demand a bigger share of the gross. The promoter will earn less money than in example two, because s/he takes on less risk. For example, **"The artist will perform for $160,000 guarantee vs. 90% of the Gross Box Office Receipts after verified expenses, whichever is greater."** In this case, if the gross potential from the ticket receipts after taxes is $800,000 and the promoter has incurred expenses of $220,000 (the artist's guarantee is not included in these calculations), the remainder would be $580,000. The artist would receive 90% of the remainder or $522,000. The concert promoter would receive the rest — $58,000.

```
$800,000  GP
-$220,000  Expenses
$580,000  Remaining
     x .90
$522,000  Artist receives


$ 58,000  Promoter receives
```

4. A percentage of Gross Box Office Receipts

On occasion, headlining artists may not require a concert promoter to guarantee a performance fee, but demand a higher percentage of the box office receipts. These are artists who are in demand at show time because of a long awaited release of an album or are just simply hot. The contract would read **"80% of the Gross Box Office Receipts."** In this case, if the gross potential from the ticket sales after taxes is $800,000, the split would be $640,000 for the artist and $160,000 for the concert promoter. Of course, the promoter must cover the expenses from his/her share.

```
$800,000 Gross Potential
     x.80
$640,000  Artist Received


$160,000  Promoter (and expenses)
```

This method gives the artist a greater percentage of the profit and may be demanded by management when a sellout is almost assured. All the previous examples were based on a sellout!

As stated in an article about Pace Concerts: "Pace Concerts expects to net 4 percent to 7 percent of a concert's gross after accounting for expenses and settling with the band" {{50 Mitchell, Rick/f, p. 8}}. Of course, in some instances the promoter might net closer to 10% or better.

Step 2: The agent solicits concert promoters in each region of the country, or calls venues in each region to put tentative holds on dates and then routes the tour.

The booking agent calls each concert promoter with the artist's price requirement and other details to determine if the promoter will buy or "pass" on the act's package. Even at this early stage, some negotiations occur concerning the selling price of tickets, and the scaling of the house (how many seats at what price). In fact, some managers insist that every item is thoroughly discussed. However, now the promoter must decide if he or she can deliver a sellout show.

In 1998, the concert business drastically changed. Robert Sillerman created SFX (for "S"illerman and his middle initials "F" and "X") Entertainment. One of the objectives of the company was to control the production of live concert performances throughout the world by owning the concert promotion business and the venues.

In 2000, Clear Channel Communications bought SFX in an all-stock deal. The company was founded in 1972 and owns over 1000 radio stations, domestic and foreign, in 47 or the 50 largest U.S. cities; 500,000 billboards; and 20 TV stations {{51 Mosemak, Jerry/f, p. 1B}}. The strategic plan and business model for the conglomerate is obvious. After all, why pay others when you can pay yourself!

In 2005 Live Nation was formed by a spin-off from Clear Channel. As of this writing, according to its webpage www.livenation.com, Live Nation has expanded and diversified its venue portfolio to include 26 of the top 30 U.S. DMA markets and, at present, owns and operates 45 amphitheaters and 35 clubs/theaters including the House of Blues and The Fillmore brands. A great many of concert promoters "signed on" to SFX and continue to work for Live Nation. Its business model allows promoters to continue to do business in each region.

Although quite a bit smaller than Live Nation, AEG is the second largest concert promoter. According to its webpage www.AEGLive.com, AEG Live is a subsidiary of Anschutz Entertainment Group, one of the leading providers of live entertainment and sports in the world. AEG Live has an international reach with regional and local presence in Los Angeles, New York, Las Vegas, London, Nashville, Houston, Dallas, St. Louis, Atlanta, Denver and Seattle. The webpage includes a complete list of their venues.

Tours

The consolidation of the concert business did not happen without controversy and several of the country's top concert promoters, including John Scher, did not take the deal. For example, Live Nation has agreed to very large artist guarantees and some agents feel that it has hurt the business. At Billboard Magazine's "Roadwork05" conference, Dixie Chicks' manager Simon Renshaw said: "A lot of the time I'm dealing with a guy I don't know in a large corporation ...... I know what they're going to do is marketing and promotion by rote: they're not going to be invested in the act, and you're like, you know what? I'll take the money and run ....."

In 2006, Live Nation inaugurated another approach to concert promotion. In return for investing millions of dollars in upfront money, Live Nation has completed 360Deals with some of the biggest artists on the scene. For example, in 2007, they made a deal with Madonna for a reportedly $120 million over ten years, and in 2008 they signed Jay-Z to a $150 million deal over ten years.

Professional and college sports, circuses, ice shows, auto shows, trade shows, etc. are held in arenas. At times, very few dates are available that allow sufficient time for concert setup and breakdow. Consequently, tentative holds on specific dates should be placed as early as possible.

It should be noted that venues are very much in competition with one another. A tour stop means thousand of dollars of revenue for just one performance. Therefore venues have taken on in-house marketing. As stated by Tim Ryan, President/CEO of the Arrowhead Pond of Anaheim, "I think the simple fact that a promoter knows that a particular arena promotes events, takes large risks and has invested in the necessary staff provides a comfort level. If a show has been on sale for a month and still needs a push, it is reassuring for them to know that they can pick up the phone and be connected to a department that is ready to help get it over the top" {{124 Waddell, Ray 2005;}}. In actuality, a booking agent told this author that in order to book the show, venues will actually be required to purchase a number of seats prior to the on-sale date.

Step 3: Dates are confirmed.

As the manager accepts the offers to perform, the dates are confirmed with each venue and the routing begins to take shape. Obviously, the number of miles between performances will differ in the west as compared to the northeast. After this decision has been made, the rest of the performance dates are accepted to complete the tour itinerary. According to Martin Atkins of TourSmart, the overwhelming majority of population centers are in the eastern part of the country where it is more cost effective to tour.

EAST V. WEST

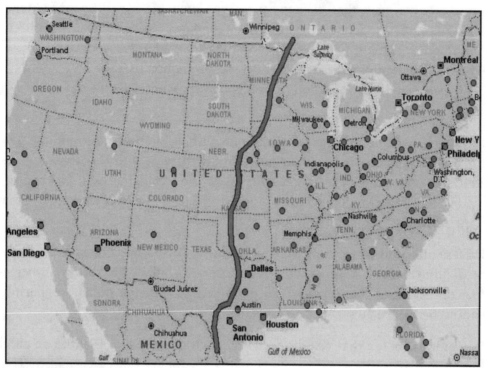

TOUR:SMART BY MARTIN ATKINS   **WWW.TSTOURING.COM**

The confirming of the dates indicates that a decision has been made as to the selling price of the admission tickets. According to Ray Waddell, "A rule of thumb for major festivals is that 60 – 70% of revenue comes from ticket sales, 10-20% from concessions, and 15–30% from sponsorships {{156 Waddell, Ray 2009;}}. Most ticket prices are set for an entire tour, however, there are times when the concert promoter in each region must negotiate an admission price that matches the economic conditions of his/her region that still meets all expenses, including a profit for him/herself. According to John Scher, a former heavy concert promoter and then head of Polygram Diversified Entertainment, the factors entering into the decision concerning how much to charge include: the artist guarantee and the cost of media advertising space and time {{52 Scher, John/f, p. 12}}. In the last several years, ticket prices have skyrocketed. Presently, top ticket prices for major tours have reached the $300+ mark.

In an article titled "Where The Money Goes" the breakdown of a $145 ticket to a Paul McCartney show was estimated as follows {{128 Knopper, Steve 2003;}}:

41.2% Artist Profit	59.74
21% Artist Expenses	30.45
18% Artist/Management Expenses	26.10
10% Ticketmaster	14.50
4.9% Venue rental and expenses	7.11
4.9% Promoter Profit	7.10
	$145.00

Concert ticket surcharges have caused ill feelings. Ticket surcharges include add-ons such as parking, ticket service charges, and facility fees. Generally, these fees are non-negotiable and the artist does not share in the revenue. "If they're putting $3-$5 on as a facility charge, what do we pay rent for?" asks Doc McGhee, manager of Kiss. "If you're talking 20,000 people in a shed, that's $100,000 the artist is not participating in. If you want to charge more rent, then do it. Don't call it something else" {{42 Waddell, Ray 2001/f, p. 1}}. Consequently, if a ticket is advertised at $50 and is really much higher, the artist looks insensitive and isn't participating in the extra revenue.

The author recently bought two tickets for a show online. See below.

Total Face Value	75.00
Facility Charge	4.00
Subtotal	79.00
Convenience Charge	18.10
Order Proc. Fee	3.55
TOTAL CHARGE	$100.65

BUDGET

The manager engages the business manager to compile a projected budget for the tour. A spreadsheet, illuminating a realistic picture of revenue and expenses is studied and a decision is made to determine the financial outcome of the tour. A manager can never be too conservative in estimating a tour budget! If an artist is "going out" for a guarantee against a percentage, the tour budget should be based roughly on the guarantee. Figure 9.3 is an example of a European tour budget with projected income and expenses estimated by the business manager.

30 Shows - 8 weeks / 56 days

PROJECTED TOUR INCOME $	PER WEEK	PER TOUR
INCOME – GUARANTEES - PER ITB	$16,570,168	
INCOME - OVERAGES	1,400,000	
17,970,168		
LESS: AGENCY COMMISSION @ 5%	(898,508)	
17,071,660		
SOUND & LIGHT REIMBURSEMENT	394,470	
17,466,130		
PROJECTED EXPENSES		
TOUR MANAGER	5,000	40,000
TOUR MANAGER - PRE TOUR TWO WEEKS/POST TOUR ONE WEEK	1,875	15,000
TOUR ACCOUNTANT	4,000	32,000
TOUR ACCOUNTANT - PRE AND POST TOUR	1,000	8,000
BAND SECURITY - @ 1500 GBP P/W	3,000	24,000
BAND TRAVEL - TO/FROM AIRPORT	350	2,800
BAND HOTELS	67,857	542,856
BAND – AIR FARES (INCLUDES AIRFARES IN EUROPE) @ $27,500 X 8	31,429	220,000
BAND – LOCAL TRANSPORTATION (EUROPE)	2,000	16,000
BAND - SUNDRY	3,500	28,000
BAND PHONES	625	5,000
BAND ENTOURAGE - PER DIEMS (TOUR MGR, TOUR ACCT, ASST & SEC. @ $75)	2,100	16,800
BUSSES - 4 @ 45K POUNDS PER TOUR	54,000	432,000
BUS DRIVER ALLOWANCE- $100 X 8 DRIVERS/ 7 DAYS + PERMITS	7,500	60,000
CONFETTI - 4 BLASTERS / 2,500 LBS CONFETTI	7,000	56,000
FLIGHTS - CREW - 35 COACH @ $1200	5,550	44,400
FLIGHTS - CREW - 10 BUSINESS @ $4,000	4,500	36,000
FLIGHTS - CREW - INTERNAL	3,500	28,000
CREW SHIRTS	1,850	14,800
ELECTRO DISTRO	10,000	80,000
FREIGHT CONTAINERS - 3 OUT 7 BACK @ $10,000 +$20K LOCATION	15,000	120,000
FREIGHT CARNETS	2,000	16,000
GENERATOR PACKAGE	18,000	144,000
HOTELS - CREW 4 NIGHTS P/W @ $200 x 44	35,200	281,600
LIGHTING FROM US	5,500	44,000
LIGHTS EUROPE - WEEKLY @ $65,000	65,000	520,000
MISC. VISA COSTS	1,000	8,000
MISC SUPPLIES	5,000	40,000
PAYROLL PRE TOUR-PREP/TECH/PROGRAMMER = $20000	2,500	20,000
PAYROLL PRE TOUR -	1,500	12,000
PAYROLL CREW	61,000	488,000
PAYROLL TAXES & W/C - 15%	11,231	89,850
PASSES/ITINERARIES	750	6,000
PER DIEM CREW - 44 X 7DAYS @ $50 = $15050	15,400	123,200
PHONES - REIMBURSE CELL PHONES	250	2,000
PRE TOUR COSTS-PW MEETINGS/FLIGHTS	500	4,000
PYRO-INCL PAYROLL/CRYO/ADMIN	95,000	760,000
REHEARSALS-LA & FIRST GIG REHEARSALS	19,565	156,521
RIGGIN PACKAGE - ALL EFFECT @ $17500 P/W	17,500	140,000
CABLE RIGGING - SYSTEM AND RIGGER	1,000	8,000
SOUND US - CONTROL PANEL FROM US	2,750	19,250
SOUND EUROPE	39,000	312,000
SET/STAGE-SET/SCISSOR LIFTS/STAGING ELEM.	13,000	104,000
TRUCKING US	3,750	30,000
TRUCKING EUROPE - 13 TRUCKS @ 50K POUNDS @$100K		1,300,000
TRUCK DRIVER ALLOW - 26 DRIVERS @ $100 P/D X 7 DAYS	18,200	145,600
VIDEO - FULL VIDEO SYSTEM & 6 TECHNICIANS	35,000	280,000
WALKIE TALKIES - SYSTEM FROM THE US	2,000	16,000
WARDROBE PREP	2,500	20,000
WAREHOUSE PREP-PREP/COORD./LOAD/UNLOAD	1,000	8,000
WIRELESS SYSTEMS- RENTAL PKG. IN EAR BUDS	1,000	8,000
AIR CHARTER	83,750	670,000
NON-APPEARANCE INSURANCE	38,750	310,000
PAYROLL SERVICE	250	2,000
FEDERAL EXPRESS/POSTAGE	1,000	8,000
ACCTG & LEGAL FEES	10,000	80,000
FOREIGN ACCOUNTANT	2,500	20,000
INSURANCE - GENERAL	6,406	51,246
FOOD	4,000	32,000
JYA OFFICE	3,000	24,000
	897,152	8,124,923
CONTINGENCY - 5 %	44,858	406,246
TOTAL COSTS BEFORE BAND MEMBERS AND MANAGER	942,010	8,531,169
PROJECTED PROFIT BEFORE MANAGER, BAND MEMBERS & FOREIGN TAXES	8,934,960	

TRAVEL AND ACCOMMODATIONS

Secure the services of a competent, reliable travel agent for booking hotel rooms, public transportation, and local car rentals. An agent's services are basically free, and an efficient one allows the manager to concentrate on the tour's other pressing issues. Trailer trucks and a band bus (provided the artist has agreed to this mode of travel) are usually leased separately from a leasing firm and are not the travel agent's responsibility.

CHOOSING AN OPENING ACT

All consumers respond to value for their money. When they purchase their tickets, many concertgoers are aware of who is the opening act. Therefore a hot opening act should increase ticket sales. If the agent, record company, or promoter hasn't forced an opening act on the show, a smart manager should look for an opening act that has had a level of success that will have name recognition with the audience. An opening act should have an image that complements the headliner. An act that has already toured should have a small base of ticket buyers already established. However, nothing guarantees that the opening act will help fill the seats. A manager must rely on his or her own intuition plus any hard data concerning the prospective opening act's performing ability.

Once the manager chooses the act, he or she must "buy" the act before some other act's manager does. The term "buying an act" means that the headliner's manager offers the act a series of performance dates for a flat guaranteed price per show. In return, most often, the opening act uses the headliner's sound system and lights. In special cases, the offer to the opening act is negotiated to include a guarantee and a bonus based on the number of tickets sold per concert. However, this occurs only when the opening act's career has such momentum that it is in a position to demand it, or the competition for the opening act's participation amongst several other headlining acts requires it.

THE CONTRACT

The agreement that is normally issued for a live engagement is a form of the American Federation of Musicians' live engagement contract. Because the AF of M licenses booking agents, the union logo appears on the booking agency's letterhead and/or contract form. The contract is a standard agreement that contains the name and place of the engagement, the name of the artist, the date and time of the performance, how much and how the artist will be compensated for the appearance, and other important information. The signatures that appear on the contract are the buyer of the show, usually the concert promoter, the artist (or representative of the artist), and the booking agent's; however the booking agent's role is only as a conduit or middleman.

The buyer or concert promoter is not recognized as an employer of the musicians, but rather a **purchaser**. As a purchaser, s/he is not libel for any damages or accidents that the musicians (and crew) might encounter, and has very little responsibility concerning the personal welfare of any of the performers. If the concert promoter was considered an employer, then the musicians performing would be subject to workman's compensation insurance and all other employee benefits bound by law. As the contract reads, the musician is considered an **independent contractor** and is responsible for declaring the net revenue of the proceeds on his/her income tax form.

(HEREIN CALLED "FEDERATION")

CONTRACT

(Form T-2)

FOR TRAVELING ENGAGEMENTS ONLY

Whenever The Term "The Local Union" is Used in This Contract, It Shall Mean The Local Union Of The Federation With Jurisdiction Over The Territory In Which The Engagement Covered By This Contract is To be Performed.

THIS CONTRACT for the personal services of musicians on the engagement described below is made this 24 day of February, 1999, between the undersigned purchaser of music (herein called 'Purchaser') and the undersigned musician or musicians.

1. Name and Address of Place of Engagement:

Flynn Theatre
153 Main St.
Burlington, VT 05401
Ph: Fax

Name of Artist:

2. Show Details:

Monday,   ...20___. Doors: 7:OOpm, ...:7:30pm, Capacity: 1,381, Ticket Scaling & Deductions: ,
Reserved:329 @ $32.00, Reserved 2:1,152 @ $23.50 Comp/Kill:-50 @ $32.00, Comp/Kill 2:-50 @ $23.50, Gross Potential:
$34,825.00.

3. Merchandising: 3a. On Sale:

80/20 Sells Artist

4. Compensation Agreed:

$12,500 GUARANTEE + 85% OF THE GROSS BOX OFFICE RECEIPTS AFTER VERIFIED EXPENSES AND 15% PROMOTER
PROFIT. PURCHASER TO PROVIDE AND PAY FOR SOUND AND LIGHTS PER ARTIST'S SPECIFICATIONS.
ARTIST TO RECEIVE 100% HEADLINE BILLING. SHOW TO BE AN EVENING WITH (NO SUPPORT).

5. Purchaser Will Make Payments As Follows:

50% ($6,250) DUE UPON ON SALE VIA CERTIFIED CHECK, MONEY ORDER OR BANK WIRE.

WIRE INFO:

6. No performance on the engagement shall be recorded, reproduced or transmitted from the place of performance, in any manner or by any means whatsoever, in the absence of a specific written agreement with the Federation relating to and permitting such recording, reproduction or transmission.

7. It is expressly understood by the Purchaser and the musicians who are parties to this contract that neither the Federation no the Local Union are parties to this contract in any capacity except as expressly provided in 6 above and, therefore, that neither the Federation nor the Local Union shall be liable for the performance or breach of any provision hereof.

8. A representative of the Local Union, or the Federation, shall have access to the place of engagement covered by this contract for purposes of communicating with the musician(s) performing the engagement and the Purchaser.

9. The agreement of the musicians to perform is subject to proven detention by sickness, accidents, riots, strikes, epidemics, acts of God, or any other legitimate conditions beyond their control.

10. Attached addenda and Artist's Rider are made part of this contract herein

IN WITNESS HEREOF, The parties hereto have hereunto set their names and seals on the day and year above written.

PURCHASER: ARTIST:

_____   _____

Figure 9.4

Figures 9.4 and 9.5 are actual engagement contracts issued by a booking agency to the headlining act. The name of the artist and the date of the event have been omitted, however, the other information is as it appeared on the original document. Figure 9.4's gross potential is considerably less than 9.5's.

Artist:		Show Dates:	Monday,	99
Deal Type:	Gross Split Point w/Promoter Profit			
Venue:	Flynn Theatre	**Promoter:**	–	
Address:	153 Main St.	**Address:**		
Burlington, VT 05401				

Ticket Scale	# Seats	Price	Gross
Reserved	329	$32.00	$10,528.00
Reserved	2115	$23.50	$27,072.00
Comp/Kill	-50	$32.00	($1,600.00)
Comp/Kill 2	-50	$23.50	($1,175.00)
TOTAL GROSS	1381		$34,825.00

Talent and Production Costs

	$12,500.00
Total Talent Costs	$12,500.00

Fixed Expenses

Advertising	$4,000.00	Rent	$2,450.00
ASCAP	$150.00	Runners	$100.00
Facility Services	$350.00	Security	$100.00
Hospitality	$1,500.00	Site Coordinator	$350.00
Local Production	$2,500.00	Spotlights	$262.50
Miscellaneous	$250.00	Stagehands	$2,500.00
Phones	$100.00	Towels	$50.00
Piano Tuner	$500.00	Ushers/Tix Takers	$200.00
Total Fixed Expenses			**$15,362.50**

Variable Expenses	Rate	Sellout	Guarantee	Ceiling	Total
BMI	0.30%	$104.48			$104.48
Insurance	1.78%	$619.89			$619.89
Total Variable Expenses					**$724.36**

Summary

Total Projected Show Costs	$15,362.50
Variable Cost at Sellout	$724.36
Talent and Production	$12,500.00
Breakeven Dollars & Tickets	$28,586.86
Concert Gross(less taxes)	$34,825.00
Less Promoter Profit	$4,288.03
Less Costs at Sellout	$28,586.86
Sharing Gross (Net Receipts)	$1,950.11

Earnings Potential

Artists Percentage	$1,657.59	85%	$14,157.59
Promoter Percentage	$292.52	15%	$4,580.55

Expenses must be documented on the night of the engagement and approved by the Artist's representative. Any expenses not documented shall be the Purchaser's sole responsibility. Producer requires notarized affidavits from all sources with whom commercials are placed including, but not limited to, radio stations, television stations, and print media, to be presented at settlement. If the Purchaser has other or greater expenses than those indicated above, the break figure shall not be affected. If however, the bonafide aggregate paid bills relating to any of the above listed costs shall total less than stated above, the break figure will be reduced accordingly.

_____	_____
Purchaser/Local Manager	**Artist**

Figure 9.4

Line 2 expresses the show details, including, date of the performance, and also includes the time the doors will open, the time the headliner will go on, and the capacity of the house. It also states the prices of the tickets, excluding any service charge, the scaling of the house, the types of tickets (general admission or reserve), the number of complimentary tickets at each price level, and the gross potential for a sellout.

Line 3 is the merchandising arrangement; in this case the artist will sell the merchandise and receive 80% of sales. 3a list the date the tickets will go on sale.

Line 4 contains the terms of how the compensation will occur. For this performance, the headliner is receiving **a guarantee of $12,500 plus 85% of the gross box office receipts after verified expenses and 15% promoter profit.** The percentage is based on the amount of tickets the promoter sells. A sellout will reap the artist and the promoter considerably more money than less than a sellout, as discussed earlier in this chapter. The list of verifiable fixed expenses and variable expenses appears towards the end of the contract and has been agreed upon by the buyer and the artists' representatives. This deal is called a "gross split point w/promoter profit." If the concert is a sellout, the revenue moves the deal into the "splits" and at a sellout, the earning's potential are calculated as presented at the end of the contract. The artist gross potential is $12500. + $1657.59 (85% of override) = $14,157.59

Line 5 states how the payment will be made. Artists usually demand about 50% of guarantee upon the signing of the contract. Should the promoter really screw up, this amount is non-refundable. It also locks in the performance date. Without a considerable amount of money upfront, the artist might be asked to perform somewhere else and have to decline the offer believing that s/he is already booked for a performance that may never happen.

Line 6 states that the performance may not be recorded or transmitted with a specific agreement allowing such to occur. The A F of M has insisted on this language since commercial recordings began.

The second page of the contract itemizes the deal. This should be studied. It reinforces the fact that the artist spends his/her own money on (85% of) the show's expenses.

AMERICAN FEDERATION OF MUSICIANS OF THE UNITED STATES AND CANADA
(THERIN CALLED FEDERATION)

CONTRACT

(FORM T-2)

FOR TRAVELING ENGAGEMENTS ONLY

Whenever The Term "The Local Union" Is Used For This Contract It Shall Mean The Local Union Of The Federation With Jurisdiction Over The Territory In Which The Engagement Covered By This Contract Is To Be Performed.

THIS CONTRACT for the personal services of musicians on the engagement described below is made this 20 day of October 1997 between the undersigned purchaser of music (herein called Purchaser) and the undersigned musician or musicians.

1. **Name and Address of Engagement:** _____
   Name of Artist:_____

   Number of Musicians: 4   Number of Vocalists: 1

2. **Date(s) of Engagement, Daily or weekly schedule and daily clock hours:**
   Wednesday_____ 1997 Doors: 6:30 PM Opening Act: 7:30PM Opening Act: 8:00PM
   Headliner: 9:15 PM   Capacity: 14,612 Ticket Scaling: 8,087 @ $65.00 6,525 @ $35.00
   Gross Potential: $754,030 00 . There is an additional $2 00 Facility Fee to patrons at the box office TicketMaster patrons are subject to Ticket Master service fees. On Sale Date: _

3. **Type of Engagement**: Concert   3a. Merchandising Deal: 60/40 Venue Sells

4. **Compensation Agreed:** $300,000   All Inclusive Guarantee vs. 85% of the gross box office receipts after verified expense whichever is greater. (Headliner to receive $187,500 Guarantee plus a $15,000 Production Fee. Opening Act to receive $97 500 Guarantee. Headliner to pay any overages due Opening Act.)

5. **Purchaser Will Make Payments As Follows:** 50% ($93,750)   Due upon on sale via certified check money order or bank wire. Balance Due immediately prior to performance via, cash certified check or money order.

6. No performance on the engagement shall be recorded, reproduced, or transmitted from the place of performance in any manner or by any means whatsoever in the absence of a specific written agreement with the Federation relating to and permitting such recording reproduction or transmission.

7. It is expressly understood by the Purchaser and the musicians who are parties to this contract that neither the Federation no the Local Union are parties to this contract in any capacity except as expressly provided in & above and, therefore, that neither the Federation nor the Local Union shall be liable for the performance or breach of any provision hereof.

8. A representative of the Local Union, or the Federation, shall have access to the place of engagement covered by the contract for purposes of communicating with the musicians performing the engagement and the Purchaser.

9. The agreement of the musicians to perform is subject to proven detention by sickness, accidents, riots, strikes, epidemics, acts of God, or any other legitimate conditions beyond their control.

10. Attached addenda and Artist's Rider are made part of this contract herein.

IN WITNESS WHEREOF, The parties hereto have hereunto set their names and seals on the day and year above written.

PURCHASER: _____   ARTIST: _____

Figure 9.5

FIXED EXPENSES

/97 WEDNESDAY

CAPACITY: < 14,612>
POTENTIAL: $754,030.0

TOTAL: $615,275.00
New York, NY 10001

Expense Categories	Ind.	Budget Amount	Notes
FLAT RENT/ BLDG EXP.	F	16,000.00	INCL. SPOTLIGHTS, PHONE/LINES
ADVERTISING	F	70,000.00	CLEANING, MEDICAL, POLICE, FIRE
ASCAP/BMI	F	925.00	SECURITY, STAGEHANDS, USHERS,
CATERING	F	7,000.00	TIX TAKERS & BOX OFFICE
ADDT'L PHONE LINES	F	600.00	$300 PER LINE
INSURANCE	F	9,000.00	$321 + $0.57 PER HEAD
PRODUCTION MANAGER	F	750.00	
RUNNERS (3)	F	450.00	
SECURITY	F	1,200.00	
TOWELS	F	200.00	
FURNITURE RENTAL	F	1,200.00	
CREDIT CARD CHARGES	F	1,200.00	
MISCELLANEOUS	F	750.00	
TRANSPORTATION	F	2,500.00	
* INTENTIONALLY OMITTED	F	2,500.00	
ARTISTS GUARANTEE	F	300,000.00	
		$615,275.00	

Expenses must be documented on the night of the engagement and approved by Artist's representative. Any expenses not documented shall be the Purchasers sole responsibility. Producer requires notarized affidavits from all sources with whom commercials are placed including, but not limited to, radio stations, television stations, and print media, to be presented at settlement. If the Purchaser has other or greater expenses than those indicated above, the break figure shall not be affected. However the bona fide aggregate paid bills relating to any of the above listed costs shall total less than breakeven stated above, the break Figure will be reduced accordingly.

ACCEPTED and AGREED TO:

PURCHASER:_____ ARTIST:_____

Figure 9.5

Line 2 expresses the date of the performance, and also includes the time the doors will open, the time any support act will begin, the time the headliner will go on, and the capacity of the house. It also states the price of the ticket, excluding any service charge, the type of ticket (general admission or reserve), the gross potential for a sellout (including taxes), and the date tickets will go on sale.

Line 3 includes the type of engagement and 3a the merchandising arrangement. 3a may list the company that will handle the merchandising, or the percentage arrangement, ie. 60/40 if the venue concessionaires are to be involved with the physically selling the merchandise.

Line 4 contains the terms of how the compensation will occur. For this performance, the headliner is receiving **a guarantee vs. 85% of the gross box office receipts after verified expenses whichever is greater.** The percentage is based on the amount of tickets the promoter sells. A sellout will reap the artist and the promoter considerably more money than less than a sellout, as discussed earlier in this chapter. The list of verifiable or fixed expenses appears at the end of the contract as an addendum and has been agreed upon by the buyer and the artists' representatives. If the concert revenue moves the deal into the splits, the artists' guarantee of $300,000 does not enter the calculation of expenses, because they stand to earn a considerably larger amount of money. This example is rare, as the opening act is performing for a very high guarantee and will take part in the splits.

Line 5 states how the payment will be made. Artists usually demand about 50% upon the signing of the contract. Should the promoter really screw up, this amount is non-refundable. It also locks in the performance date. Without a considerable amount of money upfront, the artist might be asked to perform somewhere else and have to decline the offer believing that s/he is already booked for a performance that may never happen.

Line 6 states that the performance may not be recorded or transmitted with a specific agreement allowing such to occur. The A F of M has insisted on this language since commercial recordings began.

THE CONCERT CONTRACT RIDER

The most important reason for the existence of a contract rider is to inform the promoter of the artist's expectations and requirements, and to protect the artist against any unforeseen difficulties. Is there a way to react to a problem legally? Is there some language in the written agreement that will allow the artist to cancel the performance? Do we really need twelve cases of French wine in the dressing room after every show?

Of course, there are other reasons for attaching a rider to a contract. Some artists want to feel as at home on the road as they possibly can, and they expect the concert promoter to see that they do. Others carry a spectacular visual production and massive sound systems that have extraordinary technical needs. Specific requirements for this sophisticated equipment should be listed in the rider.

Most concert riders include the following categories. Some artists require more details on some categories than others. For the concert promoter, the technical requirements are most important since they will insure the promoter's preparedness concerning everything from electrical power to the number of stagehands needed.

RIDER CATEGORIES

Riders usually carry a statement indicating that no other document will super cede its power. For example:

NO INDIVIDUAL BAND RIDER ON THIS TOUR WILL SUPER CEDE THIS RIDER. THIS IS THE ONLY RIDER BEING USED AND THE OFFICIAL RIDER FOR THE HEADLINER'S 2009 TOUR. IF YOU HAVE RECEIVED ANY INDIVIDUAL RIDERS FROM ANY OF THE BANDS ON THIS TOUR FOR YOUR DATE, PLEASE PUT THEM IN THE SHOW FILE AND REFER ONLY TO THIS ONE. IF ANY BANDS CALL ABOUT ADVANCING THE SHOW, PLEASE REFER THEM TO THE TOUR MANAGER. ALL ADVANCING FOR THE SHOWS ON THIS TOUR WILL BE THROUGH THE TOUR MANAGER, AND THE PRODUCTION MANAGER, AT THE CONTACT INFORMATION ABOVE…

The following are the usual categories found in a concert rider.

1. Billing and Advertising

Headlining artists require "100% sole star billing" in all advertising and publicity for the show. This means that nothing else connected with the performance will be larger than the artist's name.

2. Cameras/VCRs/Recorders

Cameras or recorders of any type are not permitted by the artist (with the exception of the press) unless specific arrangements have been made.

3. Financial Considerations (including ticket sales, merchandising requirements and insurance)

Specifics concerning the guest list and other box office requirements are listed. Concert expenses not detailed in the actual contract are also listed. The purchaser's obligations as to the sale of concert merchandise, and the artist's rights are also specified. On some tours, the official concert merchandise is sold by the venue's concessionaires, and on others, the artist employs personal vendors as well.

The purchaser (concert promoter) must provide for full public liability insurance coverage to protect against any accidents during the load in, operation, and load out of the equipment. The purchaser must also carry insurance that excludes any of the artist's entourage from any claims that may arise due to the personal injury of an audience member.

4. Backstage Accommodations, Catering, and Security

Although this section of the rider makes for the most humorous reading, the essential aspects of these three areas cannot be ignored.

Specifics concerning backstage accommodations are not only important to the artist, but also the crew and management. Some "legs" of tours last six to eight months. The road becomes home! Hassle free comfort is important in maintaining one's health, sanity and concentration.

The same is true for the catering requirements. Everyone in the crew must eat a nourishing, balance diet. Energy levels must be maintained and fatigue must be kept at a minimum. Dietary requirements such as beefless meals or special diets due to medical needs must be honored.

Backstage access, security, and safety are the responsibility of the purchaser. It is here that details are specified.

5. Crew Arrangements

Accommodations and catering requirements must be specified for the crew as well. Meals must be served at the times specified and other essentials, such as showers and restrooms must be available. Space for truck and bus parking must be reserved, as well as information concerning medical emergency facilities.

6. Productions and Technical Requirements

As previously stated, this is the most important aspect of the concert rider. It usually appears as the very last category of the rider as it is torn out and given to the production manager. Specific electrical requirements and the purchaser's responsibility for hiring the carpenters, electricians, spotlight operators, stagehands, riggers (climbing and ground), truck loaders, forklift operators, etc. are listed. Remember, the actual success of the artist's presentation relies heavily on the total compliance with this section of the rider. Riders also make it clear that the headliner is in charge of the production. Here is an example:

> *Artist's Company shall have the sole and exclusive control, creative and otherwise, over the means and methods utilized in the production, presentation, and performance of the Engagement. Purchaser shall fully and promptly comply with all of Artist's Company's directions in connection with the Engagement. Without limiting the foregoing, Purchaser agrees that Artist's Company (and Company's designees) shall have sole and exclusive control over the following and Purchaser represents and warrants that any and all equipment and the venue itself and its contents are in good working order throughout the performance from load-in through the end of the engagement:*

(a) All aspects of the Performance;

(b) All lights, sound, doors, mix, and equalization levels and security in the stage, console, and backstage areas, as well as the choice of camera shots to be used in the live video feed for television production or airing the performance on the video screens in the Venue;

(c) ©All ventilation, air conditioning, and heating systems in the Venue;

(d) All power and electricity

(e) Showtime(s) and running orders of the artists performing nightly including the sound checks.

All sound and light technicians shall be fully competent and aware of the importance of consistent production in the Artist's performances. These technicians shall report to Artist's production manager (or other designee) at least thirty (30) minutes prior to sound check and again thirty (30) minutes prior to Showtime for a pre-show briefing, if needed. Any overtime resulting from any technicians' tardiness shall be paid for by Purchaser and shall not become a show expense.

Entertainment business magazines and websites include articles on the elaborate production requirements of tours. Convoys of tractor-trailer trucks and banks of computers are normal parts of the shows of all headline acts today. Visit http://360.u2.com for a look at the 2010 tour staging. For an interview with Paul McGuiness, visit Ray Waddell's interview, U2 Manager Paul McGuiness: Billboard Q&A in Billboard Magazine, September 26, 2009.

7. Cancellation and Force Majeure

Usually the artist states that if any member of the act or production staff becomes ill (or incapacitated), the artist maintains the right to cancel (and not be obligated to reschedule) the show. The force majeure clause also includes other events beyond the control of the artist, such as civil unrest or other Acts of God.

8. Legal Remedies

In case of any breech of the contract by the purchaser or any damages, this section specifies the legal remedies available.

Originally (way back when), concert riders were initiated because promoters agreed to supply certain production requirements and then didn't. For example, the artist would request a stage with dimensions of 64'x 48'x 8' high. The promoter would say "no problem" and then deliver a stage that was only 4' high! However, today this is only nostalgia. Delinquent or unprofessional concert promoters do not stay in business. Cutting extraneous expenses can be critical to the profitability of a tour. As mentioned earlier, most headlining artists perform for a percentage of the profits. While the artist receives a percentage of every $50 ticket sold, it is also true that the artist looses a percentage for every $50 spent on expenses!

RECORD COMPANY SUPPORT

In some instances, record companies contribute tour support money to new artists lucky enough to be an opening act. This is sometimes negotiated into the artist's contract and then administered by the artist development department. Today a brand usually sponsors an established artist.

Record companies determine the fan support for the artist in each market by subscribing to the various industry tabulators such as Nielsen Soundscan and Broadcast Data System. They want to keep track of how the recording is selling in the performance market and they'll want to do whatever is needed to increase sales.

Record companies may also want the act to perform in markets where the record isn't selling. Since the artist's agent would like to sell as many concert tickets as possible, s/he wants the artist to perform where the record is doing well. If this occurs, it is up to the manager to solve this dilemma.

CHOOSING MATERIAL FOR THE PERFORMANCE

Another question facing the artist and the manager is what to perform on the tour. The audience wants to hear songs that are familiar. The artist may be tired of performing hits that are often years old and wants to perform new material. How many songs should be included from the new album? How many songs should be repeated from the last tour? When should the hits be performed? Should any cover material, such as rock classics, be included? For his last appearance dates in Giants Stadium, Springsteen performed several of his hit albums in their entirety on separate nights.

When deciding what to perform, one rule of thumb is to choose material that works well in the live setting. Simpler tunes may work best. A good rule is to give the audience as much familiar material as possible and save the biggest hit for the encore. The old show business adage still holds true: "Leave them wanting more!"

TOUR REHEARSAL

Each artist sets his or her own rehearsal schedule for the tour. The schedule is based on how long it's been since the band has played together or how many new players will be added for this tour. Most bands rehearse for only a few weeks as a group before the tour begins. The material to be performed should be chosen before rehearsals begin.

Before the start of the tour, if possible, it's useful to hold the final tour dress rehearsals in the opening arena. An artist's manager will book the arena for a few days to a week before the beginning of the tour, and rehearse the music and production. These dress rehearsals benefit the production crew. However, they also give the artist an opportunity to rehearse different stage moves and choreography. When this is not possible, a large space should be used that can accommodate the show. The Rolling Stones have used an airplane hanger.

PRODUCTION PREPARATION

As a tour headliner, the artist is responsible for the concert staging. To allow for competitive bidding for the actual construction of the stage and rigging, the stage production design should be completed as far in advance of opening night as possible. The manager and the tour production manager should receive estimates for the production budget and then meet with a designer for the actual design. A computer drawing to scale or an actual scale model should be completed at least two months before the beginning of the tour. Considered the most elaborate concert staging ever assembled is the present U2 360 tour. See the production at: http://www.u2ticketnews.com/u2-news/1-latest-news/164-u2-360-tour-production.html.

Depending on the design, the production development budget for a headlining act can run into the millions. Artists generally own the stage production rather than lease it and, most often use it for only one tour.

TRANSPORTATION

The vehicles used to transport tour equipment are usually leased. If a highway breakdown occurs, the leasing company is responsible for transporting the equipment to the arena. It is important to work with reputable tour leasing companies that offer commercial leasing agreements.

TOUR PUBLICITY

The tour should be announced to the media in conjunction with the release of a product. There are mixed opinions as to the importance of any announcement that doesn't publicize a specific date. However, most managers do release a press announcement with details about the entire tour. The release is then disseminated on the artist's webpage and to various publications throughout the country. If the artist retains the services of a publicist, then the publicist uses his or her influence to get the information published. Posters and other tour paraphernalia that uses the artist's name and likeness are usually licensed to a merchandising company. This will be covered in the next chapter.

ENTOURAGE

The number of people that travel with the artist varies. They include: musicians, support crew, and guests. The concert rider contains the list of entourage members that travel with the band and the crew–members that are hired locally for each specific site.

ROAD CREW

A road crew consists of sound people, lighting people, stage construction people, drivers, etc. The production manager usually hires the crew for the entire tour. A simple policy is "Don't pay people until you need them!"

TOUR MANAGER

The tour manager (road manager) is responsible for the logistics of transporting the artist during the tour and for the daily activities of the entire tour entourage. S/he must be organized, articulate, and able to make decisions under stress. The tour manager sometimes acts as the tour "accountant." His or her responsibilities include "settling" the show with the promoter by receiving payment for each performance, as well as handling the weekly petty cash needs. The tour manager usually begins receiving a salary weeks before the tour begins. At this time s/he begins advancing the initial concert dates with the promoters, reviewing the transportation and hotel arrangements, and compiles a tour-book that lists the specifics for every date on the tour. S/he also meets with the manager and accountant to determine what bookkeeping and other duties will be expected.

SECURITY

Artists either contract their own security personnel for the entire tour and/or rely on the security personnel contracted by each concert promoter for each performance.

INSURANCE

The entire tour must be covered by the various forms liability insurance (refer back to the budget section). Sometimes artists also purchase performance cancellation insurance. This means that if a performance is cancelled for any reason, the artist receives a percentage of his or her fee. Performance cancellation insurance premiums are very expensive. The manager usually budgets the fee into the artist's performance price. Promoters carry weather insurance for outdoor events.

DURING THE TOUR

MANAGER'S RESPONSIBILITIES

As a manager, you must carry on the daily activities of the management office, and handle the maintenance and execution of all unforeseen emergencies! Since every tour date is a major financial transaction involving thousands, if not millions of dollars, it's your responsibility to see that every date is successful.

Typically, there are ten to twenty performances on sale simultaneously. You should telephone every responsible promoter daily. You should also arrange for and monitor 90% of all details for each show. You must keep track of the artist on the road, as well as promotional materials, ticket sales, radio spots, and the media coverage for each performance. This requires good organizational skills. Forms are designed to help keep track of all the promotional materials, press interviews, and concert production details.

ARTIST FATIGUE

Fatigue can lead to sloppy performances. That's why it's important to schedule periodic days off for the artist and make certain they remain days "off" rather than just days without a performance. The artist should not give interviews or attend rehearsals on these days (unless it is absolutely necessary). And, it's also important to keep all tour problems away from the artist. The tour manager should solve the problems. Lastly, a proper diet and rest are essential to the artist's health. An artist who is in good shape will be in a better frame of mind with a positive attitude.

SETTLING WITH THE PROMOTER

The artist representative (usually the tour accountant) and the concert promoter make the financial settlement for the date on the night of the performance. When the box office has tallied the evening's receipts, the financial transaction takes place. Most often it occurs after the first few songs of the headliner's set. The promoter submits his or her expenses incurred in producing the performance, and the figures are totaled per the written contract. If the expenses appear to be in excess if what was anticipated, they are negotiated. However, artists work with the same concert promoters for many dates and a mutual respect is reached. Figure 9.6 is a show settlement form. This is an actual form from a 2003 show in Virginia. The following is an explanation.

Settlement

City:	Manassas	Show Date:		Weather:	Cloudy/ Mild
State:	Virginia	Venue	Nissan Pavilion	Total Gross	$353,168.50

BOX OFFICE

	Manifest Capacity	Available	Kills	Comps	Sold	Price	Gross
Ticket Price #1	3,833	481	132	323	2,897	$75.00	$ 217,275.00
OOS	140				140	$77.00	$ 10,780.00
Ticket Price #2	1,867	1263		96	486	$55.00	$ 26,730.00
OOS	15				15	$57.00	$ 855.00
Ticket Price #3	3,183	2070	76	176	851	$35.00	$ 30,135.00
OOS	79				79	$57.00	$ 6,923.00
Ticket Price #4	9,005	2688	8	4699	1,591	$25.00	$ 42,275.00
OOS	211				211	$27.00	$ 5,697.00
L-Type	2,569				2,569	$6.50	$ 16,698.50
Voucher	980				980	$10.00	$ 9,800.00
W-Voucher	784				784	$0.00	$ -
Ticket Price #12					0	$0.00	$ -
Ticket Price #13					0	$0.00	$ -
Ticket Price #14					0	$0.00	$ -
Ticket Price #15					0	$0.00	$ -
Ticket Price #16					0	$0.00	$ -
Totals	22,667	8,442	216	5,296	10,713		$353,168.50

COMPLIMENTARY TICKET RECONCILIATION

	PL1	PL2	PL3	TOTAL
Building/Suites				0
Tour/Artist				0
Promoter				0
Promotion				0
Relotech				0
House Dress				0
Total	0	0	0	0

Gross Receipts	$ 353,168.50
Facility Fees $4.50	$ (48,208.50)
Tax #1 1.00%	$ (3,116.42)
Tax #2 0.00%	$ -
Net Gross Receipts	$ 311,841.58
Show Expenses	$ (168,100.00)
Net Show Receipts	**$ 143,741.58**
% of Gross	39.6%

COMP CHECK 5296

SHOW EXPENSES

Description	Budget	Venue	Promoter	Tour/Artist	TOTAL
Advertising	-				
Print	-	-	-	-	-
Radio	-	-	-	-	-
Television	-	-	-	-	-
Production	-	-	-	-	-
Fees	-	-	-	-	-
Total Advertising	-	-	-	-	-
Artist	-	-	-	-	
ASCAP/BMI	-	-	-	-	-
Barricade	-	-	-	-	-
Box Office/Ticketing	-	-	-	-	-
Catering	7,500.00	7,500.00	-	-	7,500.00
Cleaning	-	-	-	-	-
Conversion	-	-	-	-	-
Dressing Room/Furniture	-	-	-	-	-
Electrical	-	-	-	-	-
Electricians	-	-	-	-	-
Equipment Rental	-	-	-	-	-
Fire	-	-	-	-	-
FOH Staffing	-	-	-	-	-
Generator	1,100.00	-	-	1,100.00	1,100.00
Loaders	-	-	-	-	-
Medical	-	-	-	-	-
Miscellaneous	-	-	-	-	-
Parking	-	-	-	-	-
Payroll Tax	-	-	-	-	-
Police	-	-	-	-	-
Production	-	-	-	-	-
Production Staffing	-	-	-	-	-
Rent (House nut)	112,500.00	########	-	-	112,500.00
Runners	-	-	-	-	-
Security	-	-	-	-	-
Spotlights	-	-	-	-	-
Staffing - Other	-	-	-	-	-
Stagehands	-	-	-	-	-
Staging	-	-	-	-	-
Support	47,000.00	46,500.00	500.00	-	47,000.00
Telephones	-	-	-	-	-
Towels	-	-	-	-	-
Transportation	-	-	-	-	-
Ushers & Takers	-	-	-	-	-
TOTAL EXPENSES	168,100.00	########	500.00	1,100.00	168,100.00
Variable Costs:					
Rent (if Variable)		-	-	0.0%	-
Credit Cards		-	-	0.0%	-
Box Office		-	-	0.0%	-
Insurance	-	-	-	$0.00	-
Other		-	-	0.0%	-
Total Costs	168,100.00	########	500.00	1,100.00	168,100.00

BUILDING SETTLEMENT

Net Gross Receipts	$ 311,841.58
Less:	
Expenses Paid by Building	$ (166,500.00)
Cash Draw Tour/Artist	$ -
Cash Draw Promoter	$ -
Other	$ -
Add:	
Building Deposit	$ -
Net Due Promoter From Building	$ 145,341.58

TOUR SETTLEMENT

Net After Expenses	$ 143,741.58
(not including chargebacks)	
Guarantee	
vs. % Deal 90%	$ 300,000.00
%	
Witholding at source	$ -
Cash Advance	$ -
Chargebacks	$ (2,029.22)
TOTAL DEDUCTIONS	$ (2,029.22)
DUE TOUR BEFORE DEPOSIT	$ 297,970.78

COMBINED NOS PAYMENT DUE

Artist Guarantee	$ 300,000.00
Artist Overage	$ -
Production Reimbursement	$ 1,100.00
DUE TOUR BEFORE Deductions	$ 301,100.00
Less:	
Deposits to Agency	$ (31,250.00)
Total Deductions	$ (2,029.22)
NOS DUE ARTIST	$ 267,820.78

PROMOTER LOSS	$ (156,258.42)
NOS PAYMENT DUE	
Guarantee	$ 300,000.00
Overage	$ -
Production Reimbursment	$ 1,100.00
DUE TOUR BEFORE Deductions	$ 301,100.00
Total Deductions	$ (2,029.22)
Deposit to MTLtd	$ (31,250.00)
Cash Advance	$ -
Witholding at source	$ -
tickets	$ (314.00)
Comp excess	$ -
NOS DUE ARTIST	$ 267,506.78

Figure 9.6

1. The Total Gross for the concert was $363,168.50. The upper section shows how the house was scaled and the resulting gross dollar amount.

2. Section #5 shows the gross receipts ($363,168.50); facility fees ($48,208.50); and taxes ($3118.42) coming to the Net Gross Receipts (NGR) ($311,841.58).

3. Show expenses were $168,100, as noted on the left side under Show Expenses. The Net Show Receipts (NSR) were $143,741.58 or 39.6% of gross. (Note that promoters usually hope that the breakeven point is about 70% or keeping expenses at about 30%.)

4. The Building Settlement is the calculation to arrive at what the venue owes the promoter. NGR less building expenses ($166,500) or $145,341.58.

5. The Tour Settlement calculation takes the NSR and compares it to the guarantee. If the NSR is greater than the guarantee then the artist receives an "overage" (split point) that has been negotiated for the show. In this case, without a profit being earned from the show, the artist had to settle for the guarantee of $300,000.

6. Combined NOS Payment Due lists who gets what. The artist paid for the generator hence the extra $1100. After all is said and done, there was no overage to split, the promoter lost a chunk of money, and the artist received their guarantee.

The show was dismal for the promoter and the artist agreed to return for less of a deal.

From time to time, a mathematical error may occur. To avoid this, it is important for the tour manager/accountant to check and recheck all figures. A 2% error on a $240,000 performance fee is $4800. The same error could cost the artist $96,000 if it was multiplied over 20 shows!

AFTER THE TOUR

After the tour ends and everyone has rested, the entire experience should be evaluated to see which of the objectives have been met. The obvious question is: Did the tour make money and how much? However, the other tour objectives are important as well. Did the artist increase his or her visibility in a given market? Has the artist increased his/her fanbase? Have any left? Why? On a market-by-market basis, did any or all concert(s) reach the status of being recognized as an event? Does the artist consider the tour successful? Do you? What was learned from the total experience?

SUMMARY

1. The main objectives for any tour are: to increase the artist's visibility in a given market; to increase the number of industry players on an artist's team and win their loyalty; to make the artist's performance an "event" on a performance-by-performance basis; to provide an opportunity to perform in a major market when the record is reaching its stride; and to make a profit.

2. A tour should begin in a secondary market close to the artist's home.

3. The booking agent and manager should work closely to arrive at all the specifications for the tour.

4. The procedure for booking a tour entails: the manager and agent arrive at a price the artist is seeking for the performance; the agent solicits concert promoters in each region to inquire about bookings; the promoter or agent puts a tentative hold on a venue for a specific date; and dates are confirmed.

5. Tour budgets should be based on conservative estimates.

6. An opening act should be chosen on its ability to generate ticket sales.

7. A concert rider should protect the artist against any unforeseen difficulties. The categories should include: billing and artist approval; recording; financial considerations; backstage accommodations and catering; crew arrangements; cancellation; and legal considerations.

8. Material for concert performance should be familiar to the audience and should work well in a live setting.

9. Production preparation should include the actual staging specifications.

10. The entire tour should be announced to the press no earlier than two months in advance.

11. During the tour, the manager must monitor 90% of all details for each show on a daily basis.

12. After the tour, the experience should be evaluated.

PROJECTS

1. Cost out a three-day regional tour, including a budget (with real cost figures) for expenses.

2. Draw up a production budget, including a sound system, lights, and staging, musicians, hotels, buses, trucks, etc.

3. Formulate a fair and meaningful concert rider, including the categories listed in this chapter.

4. Write a press release announcing an artist's tour.

5. Role play the job of a concert promoter; negotiate a contract for a performance, and submit a realistic list of expenses using the Gross Split Point Deal method.....do the math!

CHAPTER TEN
MERCHANDISING, ENDORSEMENTS, SPONSORSHIPS, & BRANDING

"Perhaps more than ever before, corporate America recognizes the power of music marketing."
William Chipps, senior editor of IEG Sponsorship Report

BY THE END OF THIS CHAPTER YOU SHOULD BE ABLE TO:

1. Discuss the differences between merchandising, endorsements, and sponsorship and branding.
2. Discuss the five basic ingredients in a merchandising deal.
3. Discuss how the revenues are shared.
4. Compute the average revenue splits in a merchandising deal.
5. List the factors that contribute to the size of the artist's advance money.
6. Discuss the procedures for prosecuting offenders.
7. Discus four important issues concerning product endorsements.
8. Discuss the important areas of an endorsement deal.
9. Discuss sponsorships that exist in the business.
10. Discuss all aspects of branding.

The areas of merchandising, endorsements, and sponsorship have been very lucrative for many artists. But none of them compare to the amount of revenue that branding can produce. Compared to endorsements, merchandising and sponsorship were relatively new to the entertainment business. Now, more than ever before, the exploitation of the artist's name and/or likeness as a property right, represents important promotional and revenue vehicles. When an artist becomes a brand in him/herself and ties in to new media, the income potential seems to be virtually endless.

THE DIFFERENCE

MERCHANDISING

In general terms, merchandising is the buying and selling of goods for profit. In the entertainment industry, these goods feature the name or likeness of the artist (and usually the artist's recordings) on every good produced. The owner of the artist's name or likeness has the legal right (property or "personality" right) to exploit it for either promotional reasons or as a means of generating income.

ENDORSEMENTS

When an artist endorses a product he or she gives support or approval to the product for a set fee for a limited time. Usually, this represents a relationship between the artist and the product. Caution must be used when choosing a product to endorse. No endorsement deal is worth the possibility of deteriorating the artist's image. Today, more than ever, image is "everything".

SPONSORSHIP

A business (or corporation) that pays an artist a fee for the right to associate its name or logo with the artist's appearance is a sponsor. The name may blatantly appear on a banner hung behind the stage in a concert hall or on merchandise sold, or it may be tastefully incorporated into posters advertising the event. Today, many sponsorship deals also include product and brand endorsements.

BRANDING

As stated in Chapter Four, the fifth definition of "brand" by *Webster's New World Dictionary* states: a. an identifying mark or label on the products of a particular company b. the kind of make of a commodity. In concert with the second definition, the entertainment business has embraced "branding" as a vehicle for the artist to reach a broader audience and add revenue to his/her income. Artists design their own line of a commodity or become a brand in themselves. By becoming a brand in themselves, they can be associated with any number of products that will take on their identity.

MERCHANDISING

ITS HISTORY

Artist merchandising seriously began in the rock business in the early 1970's. Winterland Productions, which is one of the biggest merchandising companies in the business, began in the early 1970s by selling Grateful Dead T-shirts at one of their concerts at the Winterland Ballroom in San Francisco {{13 Rohter, Larry/f, p. D9}}. However, not many people recall any substantial exploitation of an act's name prior to the Peter Frampton "Live" tour in the mid-1970's. In any case, merchandising was more or less a dirty word to the Woodstock generation, and was not a factor in the exploitation of the counterculture of the 1960's. A former employee of the Filmores East and West could not recall any act selling T-shirts or other paraphernalia in either hall.

Now it's big business. Worldwide revenues are now in the billions of dollars, and on some tours, a staggering average of $10+ a ticket is generated from the sale of tour merchandise.

HOW DOES IT WORK?

Tour merchandising is the primary source of merchandising revenue. Fan Club, e commerce, retail, and direct mail merchandising are growing, but revenue still depends on the loyalty of the group's fan base. Thanks to the internet, the industry has discovered direct to consumer marketing.

One of the most successful companies is *MusicToday* that started as the online merchandising arm for the Dave Mathews Band. Their mission is "to help both emerging and established artist harness the power of the Internet to deliver their music, merchandise, and message to the growing global community of music fans on the Internet." What is unique about *MusicToday* is that they build stores on the internet which are client-branded in that they match the look and feel of the artist's site. So if a customer clicks on SHOP at one of their 500 client's web sites, it brings them to a *MusicToday* built and hosted store that looks just like the artist's site {{121 Grossweiner, Bob and Cohen, Jane 2006;}}.

Although the number of merch companies has grown considerably, when dealing with any of the big companies for tour merchandising, the basic procedure is as follows:

1. Several months prior to the start of a tour, the manager will contact one or several merchandising companies and ask them to bid for on merchandising the tour. If the artist does not have any product value in the marketplace (even though he or she may have a recording contract), the merchandiser may pass on the tour, or may offer to merchandise the tour without offering any advance money. If the artist has a proven merchandising track record, the merchandiser will examine the tour dates and determine the past and projected **"per-head gross."**

2. The manager and merchandiser agree on the terms of the contract.

3. The merchandiser designs the graphics for the products and brings the designs to the manager for approval. If the tour coincides with the release of a recording (and it should), then the recording should be incorporated into the merchandising graphics.

4. The merchandiser and the manager decide which products are to be manufactured. T-shirts are mandatory. Some groups estimate that they sell shirts to a quarter of their fans. The other products should be priced to cover the

spending power of the audience. In other words, there should be something for every pocketbook. Common items include: T-shirts, baseball shirts, sweatshirts, visors, caps, posters, and buttons. However, towels, undergarments, sheets & pillowcases, and soccer balls have also been offered!

5. The manager approves all of the items to be merchandised accepting only high quality pieces.

THE DEAL

There isn't a standard merchandising deal in the music business. The power of the artist in the marketplace plays a major role in determining who receives the biggest piece of the pie. Some merchandisers will take a smaller share of the revenue to have the prestige of merchandising a superstar's tour. The number of dates on the tour and the number of countries covered are also factors.

Usually, a manager will give the merchandiser the right to exploit the name and likeness of the artist for the purpose of selling merchandise for a negotiated royalty . . . with a minimum guarantee or an advance against the royalty. The royalty for the license is negotiated and computed on either the wholesale or retail prices of the products, based on the number sold.

For an established act, the length of the deal usually coincides with the length of the tour. If the deal is with a new artist, the merchandiser will specify that the length of the deal run at least until the monies are recouped, for fear of not making any profit. In either case, the artist must guarantee to perform a set number of dates.

Lately, venues have been demanding as much as 40% of the sales which has been passed on to the consumer.

The revenue splits are roughly as follows:

Cost of the goods (including freight, security, etc.) 25-35%.

Venue (arena) receives 20-40% commission. This arrangement may vary depending on whether the merchandiser works the concessions or the venue's concessionaires are used and the venue's notoriety.

Merchandiser receives 5-10%.

Artist royalty is 15-30% or higher, depending upon his or her status.

For example:

$30.00 shirt
-10.50 cost (35%)
$19.50
-$9.00 venue (30%)
$10.50
-$2.70 merc (9%)
$ 7.80 artist (26%)

Advance money: A number of factors come into play when negotiating the artist's advance. Obviously, the size of the advance is based on the volume of business expected. This is calculated on the number of tour dates and the volume of business transacted on previous tours. Advances may range from $10,000 to $1,000,000+. The manager may negotiate a higher royalty rate in lieu of an advance if cash is not needed.

Normally, the agreement will contain a personal guarantee by the performer that minimum tour obligations will be met. If they are not met, unrecouped advances (unlike record company advances) will be repayable, with interest, by the performer.

Because the concert business has been so risky, advances have been given in increments throughout the tours {{62 Ungar, Paul B. 1992/f, p. 51}}.

Selloff. The merchandiser will want to sell-off unsold goods. The manager should negotiate a time limit that extends beyond the tour for the sell-off to occur. The merchandiser should not be permitted to manufacture any additional merchandise. This prevents merchandise to be sold for an unlimited time under the old contract.

Ownership. There are usually three ways to handle the merchandising rights. The artist can grant the rights to the record company, grant the rights to a merchandiser, or handle merchandising independently. Since the mid-1980's, record companies have not permitted new artists sole ownership of the recording jacket's artwork or graphics. They have made it clear that they intend to take part in all merchandising that bears the name or likeness of the artist. It may be stated in the contract as follows: **"If Records receives any payments for any use of your name or picture in connection with merchandise other than Phonograph Records, your royalty account will be credited 50% of the net amount of those receipts, after deduction of the following expenses."** The manager may negotiate the ownership (or a bigger share) from the record company to the artist for a price.

Bootlegs And Counterfeits. During a major artist's tour, products featuring the tour logo are in such demand and sell so well that bootleg and counterfeit products are big business. Since official tour merchandise is marketed outside the arena as well as inside, a concert-goer may not know if the product he or she buys in the parking lot is "official" or not. Nor may he or she really care! Therefore, the bootlegger doesn't care if the products he or she sells are exact replicas of official products. If a bootlegger incorporates the artist's name, and the tour specifics, the product has the potential to sell as well as the "official" product. In fact, some claim that at times the bootleg products are better designed!

Stopping Them. Obviously, it's disturbing to the artist and manager to see bootleg and counterfeit products sold at a concert. However, it's usually the merchandiser's responsibility to police the tour.

There are several ways to curtail the sale of bootleg and counterfeit products. According to Graff, suits may be filed based on trademark infringement under the Federal Lanham Act; copyright infringement under the Federal Copyright Act; and unfair competition and misappropriation of the right of publicity under common law. An enforcement procedure is important, although many merchandisers do not always find it cost effective.

Until the 1980's, the best procedure was to obtain a court order prohibiting the sale of unauthorized merchandise. However, the merchandiser had to bring the bootlegger into court before a judge would grant the injunction. However, with the result of the **Matter of Vuitton et Fils, S.A.606F.2d.1 (2d Cir. 1979)** case, an ex parte temporary restraining order (TRO) can be obtained from a court without notice to the defendant. This allows the plaintiff to obtain an injunction, without first notifying a bootlegger, and restrains the unauthorized activities for a limited time period, usually ten days, after which the court will consider granting a preliminary injunction which will remain in effect during the pendency of the case {{63 Sloctnick, Barry I. 1992/f, p. 53}}. Because some bootleggers don't really have legal addresses, the courts have allowed "John Doe" TROs to be served by marshals. These TROs are enforceable during specified times and areas, usually within a three-mile radius of the concert hall, during several hours before and after the concert. This has been very helpful in curtailing the business of bootlegging.

Following is a merchandising agreement with comments in italics.

TYPES OF DEALS

Andy Allen outlines the following at: http://www.cityshowcase.co.uk/index.php?section=FeatureDetail&FeatureID=0S1zQcC0zS

SUPPLY-ONLY DEAL

This deal requires you to accept the merchandise and then take responsibility for the sales. You can either appoint someone to sell for you or can strike up a deal which involves the venue supplying personnel. You may encounter concession-hall fees or site-rental fees, but these are usually only charged at larger venues. At the end of the show the staff will return whatever stock is left over along with the cash they have taken, minus their percentage, which is generally 25% of cash taken, although at some larger venues they can charge more. This figure is calculated on the retail price. This means that the artist will actually be charged 29.38% of the net, or 25% of the gross.

ROYALTY-RATE DEAL

In a Royalty-Rate deal, the rate is calculated on gross sales. It's important to note, however, that gross sales are considered to be the retail price less taxes, and on some occasions the concession fee from a venue is also deducted before the royalty rate is calculated. On average the Royalty Rate is usually in the region of 25% to 35%, but – depending on how large an artist you manage – you may be able to negotiate a better rate, should the tour generate a higher income, or even to have an increase written into the deal, depending on performance of the tour. A merchandiser will generally offer a lower rate in foreign territories, which usually tends to be 75%-80% of the domestic rate.

SPLIT-PROFIT DEAL

This deal is organized by the merchandiser responsible for the supply and sale of products on tour and for then analyzing the figures at the tour's conclusion. Once calculated, an agreed split of the profits can be anywhere between 65/35 and, in extreme cases, 90/10. Generally, however, the average split is calculated between 70/30 and 80/20, in favor of the artist. It should be noted, however, that the merchandiser may take an administration fee, based on gross sales.

RETAIL

A merchandiser will generally sell your T-shirts, sweatshirts, caps and other merchandise to a specialist music merchandise wholesaler. (The Royalty Rates for merchandising span anywhere from 10% to 25% of wholesale.) Furthermore, they will attempt to procure licensing deals with other non-clothing merchandisers to merchandise other goods – for example, posters and badges. In consideration, they will take a percentage of roughly 20% of the Royalty Rate agreed with the sub-licensee. The agreed royalty rate will be generally 10% to 15% of wholesale.

E-commerce or mail-order will result in the receipt of approximately 20%-30% of gross sales {{143 Allen, Andy 2005;}}.

RE: RETAIL MERCHANDISING AGREEMENT

Ladies and Gentlemen:

This will confirm our agreement by which we shall have the exclusive retail merchandising rights regarding you, the artist and collectively professionally known as the artist.

1.   Territory: World.

Rights:

Exclusive right throughout the term to use your name(s), group name(s), approve likenesses and other approved identification ("Licensed Property") in connection with the manufacture, distribution, advertising, and sale of merchandise to the public, to be offered for sale and sold through retail distribution channels and on the site of your live concerts. The rights granted to us hereunder with respect to retail sales include the execution of licenses for the implementation of our retail rights, and specifically exclude fan club sales, mail order sales and phone order sales. All rights not expressly granted hereunder are expressly reserved by you.

2.   We agree that we shall not, without your prior written consent, (i) utilize the Licensed Property in connection with so-called commercial "tie-up" arrangements or (ii) enter into any endorsement arrangement pursuant to which you agree to endorse goods or services of any kind.

3.   Term:

The term of this agreement shall be for a period of one (1) year commencing on January 1, it being understood that should you be on tour on January 1, the tour rights only hereunder will continue until that particular tour leg is completed. Upon the expiration of earlier termination of the term as provided hereunder all rights granted to us shall cease and revert to you automatically subject to the provisions of paragraph 7, below, and as may be otherwise specified hereunder.

4.   Royalties.

(a) Tour; Ninety percent (90%) of our "tour net profits". The term "tour net profits" shall be defined as our "tour net sales" less hall and vendor commissions (not to exceed thirty percent [30%] of gross receipts), cost of goods sold (including artwork), road expenses (which shall be deemed to be no greater than five percent [5%] of net sales), freight and mutually agreed upon miscellaneous expenses. The term "tour net sales" shall be defined as gross proceeds actually received by us from the sale of tour merchandise less sales taxes actually included in the sales price, value added taxes, import and customs dues and reasonable and customary costs of on-site bootleg security pertaining solely to the rights granted hereunder.

Included in this clause are important definitions as well as the basics of the entire deal. Ninety percen appears to be a big piece of the pie, however, upon closer reading, the ninety percent is ninety percent of 65%, and not including freight and miscellaneous expenses. A limit of thirty percent has been placed on hall and vendor commissions......in reality many halls are receiving forty percent! This is addressed in "d" below.

(b) Retail: Fifteen percent (15%) of our Wholesale Receipts up to Two Hundred Fifty Thousand Dollars ($250,000.00) of gross receipts; sixteen percent (16%) of our Wholesale Receipts between Two Hundred Fifty Thousand One Dollars ($250,001.00) through Five Hundred Thousand Dollars ($500,000.00) of gross receipts' and seventeen percent (17%) of our Wholesale Receipts in excess of Five Hundred Thousand Dollars ($500,000.00) of gross receipts. "Wholesale Receipts" are all monies actually received by us or our agents or credited to our or their account from the retail sale of products less sales taxes, returns or credits on returns.

The retail deal is worded so that as sales increase the artist's percentage increases. Again these percentages do not include taxes, returns, etc.

(c) Licensing: Seventy five percent (75%) of our License Receipts. "License Receipts" are the total of all monies or other compensation payable or credited to our account by the licensees under licenses entered into under this agreement.

(d) We agree that upon your request we will sell T-shirts hereunder for Fifteen Dollars ($15.00), Notwithstanding the foregoing, in the event that hall fees exceed thirty five percent (35%) of the gross receipts, the parties agree that the selling price of T-shirts will be adjusted accordingly, upon the mutual agreement of the parties.

5. <u>Products.</u>

(a) You will provide us with a reasonable number of color transparencies or equivalent full color artwork sufficient to enable us to produce T-shirts, sweatshirts, and other specialty wearable items. All costs of creating or originating photographs, color transparencies or equivalent artwork shall be advances, which are recoupable from monies payable to you hereunder,

(b) We shall not manufacture products hereunder (except for samples) without your prior approval of the design and quality of such product, which approval may be withheld in your sole discretion. Your failure to reject any product within ten (10) days after submission of same to you shall constitute your disapproval of same.

*(c)*You shall have the right to approve In writing each license agreement, which we propose to enter hereunder.

6. <u>Warranties.</u>

(a) You warrant, represent and agree that (i) you exclusively own and control all rights in and to the names, group names and other identification of every kind, and all rights covered herein, (ii) you have not taken and shall not, during the term, take any action which would limit in any manner our full enjoyment of such rights in the Territory, (iii) you have the right to grant and do hereby grant the right to use on products hereunder the album artwork and all photographs, artwork or other materials furnished by you to us, and (iv) our use of such materials will not infringe the rights of any person and the rights granted to us hereunder shall not conflict with the rights of any person. You agree to indemnify and hold us harmless from any loss, cost, damage, liability or expense arising out of any claim, demand or action by a third party which, If proven, would constitute a breach of this agreement and which claim, demand or action is reduced to final, non-appealable judgement.

(b) We warrant, represent and agree that (1) we have the right to enter into this agreement and perform all of our obligations hereunder, (ii) all wearable products shall be made of one hundred percent (100%) cotton unless otherwise requested by you, and (iii) all Products hereunder shall be of the same style, fabric and quality as the samples which are approved by you pursuant to paragraph 5, above. We agree to indemnify and hold you harmless from any loss, cost, damage, or expense arising out of any claim, demand or action by a third party which, it proven, would constitute a breach of this agreement and which claim, demand or action is reduced to final, non-appealable judgement.

7. **Unsold Merchandise.** We will have the non-exclusive right, for a period of ninety (90) days after the expiration of the term (the 'Sell-Off Period"), to dispose of any unsold merchandise remaining after the term (provided that we shall not have the right to manufacture merchandise during the Sell-Off Period or to sell those unsold products which are in excess of a reasonable inventory of same in light of anticipated demand as of the expiration of the term and provided, further, that we shall not manufacture products prior to the expiration of the term in excess of anticipated demand during the term) through retail distribution channels only and will pay to you a royalty equal to fifty percent (50%) of our Wholesale Receipts. In connection with the foregoing, we shall not sell any merchandise during the Sell-Off Period at a discount price without your prior written consent. During the Sell-Off Period, you shall have the right to purchase any unsold products from us at our cost in respect of same less only the royalty which would otherwise be payable to you pursuant to paragraph 4, above. At the expiration of the Sell-Off Period, we shall destroy all unsold products and furnish you with an affidavit certifying same.

This is a very important clause in the agreement because it defines the sell-off period (which is ninety days after the expiration of the one year term) and what rights are granted to deplete the inventory, should any remain. This clause blocks excess manufacturing of goods and bargain pricing.

8. <u>Force Majeure.</u>

(a) If, by reason of any cause or causes beyond our control or that of any affiliate or subsidiary, (i) the enjoyment by us, or our subsidiaries or affiliates of any rights or benefits hereunder is interfered with or otherwise becomes impossible or impracticable, or (ii) the performance of our obligations hereunder Is interfered with or otherwise becomes impossible or impracticable, then we shall be relieved of such obligations (other than the obligation to account and make payments to you hereunder), and the periods of time in which we shall be obligated to take any actions shall be suspended, for the period during which we are so affected. If any suspension imposed under this paragraph by reason of an event affecting no merchandise manufacturer or distributor except us continues for a period in excess of sixty (60) days after the commencement of the applicable event, you may request us, by notice, to terminate the suspension within fifteen (15) days after our receipt of your notice. If we do not do so, the term hereof will terminate at the end of that fifteen (15) day period or at such earlier time, which we may designate by notice to you, and all parties will be deemed to have fulfilled all of their obligations under this agreement except those obligations which survive the end of the term.

(b) If, by reason of any cause or causes beyond your control the performance of any of your obligations hereunder or our ability to tour is interfered with or otherwise becomes impossible or impractical, then you shall not be responsible for any loss, cost or damage to us occasioned as result thereof.

The force majeure clause appears in all contracts relating to live performance. The clause protects against any "acts of God" such as tornados, hurricanes, civil violence, or causes "beyond your control".

9.   Accounting. Accountings and payments will be on a monthly basis within thirty (30) days following the end of each month during the term. Not later than forty five (45) days following the expiration of the term, we will render a final accounting and will pay to you the balance of royalties, if any, shown to be due pursuant to such statement.

10.   Books and Records

(a) We shall keep, maintain and preserve for three (3) years following expiration or earlier termination of the term, complete and accurate records and accounts of all transactions relating to this agreement. Such records and accounts shall be available for inspection, copying and audit at any time or times during or within three (3) years after the term (but not more frequently than once a year) during reasonable business hours, upon reasonable notice by you, specifying the statements with respect to which you seek examination, at your sole cost and expense.

(b)   (i) Such examination shall be limited to those books and records which relate to you and which are necessary to verify the accuracy of the statement or statements specified in your notice to us. All information furnished by us to auditors or sent to us by auditors including; without limitation, any reports prepared by auditors, shall be held confidential by all parties and used solely for the purpose of identifying and settling claims and disputes that arise under this agreement. Unless documents or information to any person or entity not a party hereto other than attorneys and business representatives.

(ii) In the event that any audit conducted by a certified public accountant reveals an under-reporting of royalties to you of more than ten percent (10%) less than the royalties to which you were entitled under this agreement, we shall reimburse you for the reasonable and customary coat of such audit.

(c)   Each royalty statement rendered to you shall be final, conclusive, and binding on you and shall constitute an account stated unless objected to within three (3) years after the same is delivered to you. You shall be foreclosed from maintaining any action, claim or proceeding against us in any forum or tribunal with respect to any statement or accounting due hereunder unless such action, claim or proceeding is commenced against us in a court of competent jurisdiction within four (4) years from rendition of such statement or accounting.

11.   Gratis Products. We shall provide you with fifty (50) gratis units of each product produced by us hereunder.

12.   Ownership of Logo(s) and Designs: Uses By Third Parties.

(a) It is acknowledged that the copyrights in and to any and all artwork and designs created by you and/or furnished to us by you hereunder shelf be owned exclusively by you or your designee and we shall have no rights therein except the right to use the some on products In accordance with the terms of this agreement. We agree to place an appropriate legend, in the form supplied by you, on all products in order to provide public notice of your copyright and trademark rights, No inadvertent failure by us to place such legend on any product hereunder shall be a breach of this agreement, but we shall use best efforts to cure such failure prospectively, on the next manufacturing run after our receipt of notice of such failure.

You acknowledge and agree that, with respect to any artwork created or originated by us, we shall own such artwork; provided, however, that you may repurchase such artwork at our cost after the term.

13.   Cure of Default.

As a condition precedent to any assertion by either party that the other is in default in performing any obligation contained herein, the party alleging the default must advise the other In writing of the specific facts upon which it is claimed that the other is in default and of the specific obligation which it is claimed has been breached, and the other party shall be allowed a period of thirty (30) days (or, solely with respect to payments by us to you, ten [10] days) after receipt of such note within which to cure such default.

14.   Resolution of Disputes.

All disputes arising out of or in any way associated with this agreement, including its execution, performance or breach, shall be governed exclusively by the laws of California, whose courts shall have exclusive jurisdiction.

15.   General.

This agreement cannot be assigned by you without our specific written consent We shall have the right to assign this agreement or any rights hereunder to any third party owning or acquiring a substantial interest in our company or our assets or to any-affiliated company.

This agreement sets forth the entire understanding between the parties with respect to the subject matter and suspends all prior agreements and understandings.

Any notices required or desired to be sent hereunder shall be in writing and shall be sent by registered or certified mail, return receipt requested, to the other party at the address herein above provided, unless either party notifies the other in writing of a change of address. This shall be deemed effective when received. In the event you notify us of a change in your address, we shall thereafter furnish a courtesy copy of notices sent hereunder to our attorney.

(a) If either party hereto brings any action, suit or proceeding arising from or based upon this agreement against the other party hereto, then the prevailing party shall be entitled to recover from the other its reasonable attorneys' fees in connection therewith in addition to the costs of such action suit or proceeding.

Please sign below to indicate your agreement with the terms of this letter.

Very truly yours,

By_____

An Authorized Signature

Accepted and Agreed to:

By: _____

An Authorized Signature

HOW TO MAKE A T-SHIRT THAT REALLY SELLS

Dell Furano, CEO of Live Nation Merchandise offers this advise:

1. Tie the T to the Tour

2. Limit the options- More is not More

3. Be Style-Inclusive

4. Weigh the cost of each print

5. Stand out from the crowd-literally {{149 Nagy,Evie 2009;}}

ENDORSEMENTS

Product endorsement has long been a part of the entertainment industry. Celebrities have endorsed products through TV and radio advertisements and print ads for years. In 1998, the Wall Street Journal reported that Elton John received $5 million from Citibank to appear in its global ad campaign.

Others have allowed (licensed) their names or likenesses to be used in conjunction with product promotion. The royalties may be high, but caution should be taken before consenting to an endorsement deal.

As stated earlier, an endorsement represents a relationship between the product and the artist. Potentially, it can represent income or damage the artist's image, and no endorsement is worth that risk. The manager should exercise caution and investigate the following before signing an agreement.

1. Is the product valid? How effective is it?

2. Is it harmful? Will certain interest groups be against its use?

3. Will the artist's fans believe the artist uses the product?

4. How accurate are the products claims? Does it do what it claims to do?

5. Has it been tested by an independent laboratory and given its seal of approval?

6. Does the artist use the product? If not, he or she should live with it to see if he or she feels comfortable with it.

As well as the income potential, the endorsemen should also be evaluated in terms of its effect on the long-range career goals.

THE DEAL

An ad agency will usually approach a manager inquiring about the possibility of an endorsement. As a manager, if you are seeking an endorsement deal, a big fan in an account services department can be helpful in working a deal.

The important areas of the contract are:

1. The length of time a commercial will appear or a print ad will run.

2. The region or number of regions of the country where the commercial or print ad will appear.

3. The media for which it is intended.

4. Advances against a royalty deal.

5. Residuals from the airing of a commercial

6. Creative control…. Does the artist have any input?

7. Rights. Who will own what?

The cola war has been going on for over a decade. Whitney Houston, Paula Abdul, Ray Charles, Christina, and Britney have been spokespersons for either Coke or Pepsi. Market researchers believe that the consumer associates (and hopefully remembers) who is endorsing what so much so that brand endorsements are popular today. (This author feels that overexposure degrades the very definition of the word "artist.")

SPONSORSHIP

Non-record company tour sponsorship is extremely active in the industry. Usually the sponsor pays the artist outright for the right to associate its name or logo with an artist's appearance. This usually involves some sort of bidding opportunity for the right, and in many instances is connected to an endorsement deal. The artist may be required to guarantee that s/he will complete a certain number of appearances. Sometimes the sponsor will want to pay for the advertising of the brand and the tour; with cash as tour support included.

For the 1981 tour, it's reported that the Rolling Stones received over $500,000 plus advertising from Jovan (a subsidiary of Beecham Group LTD.). Also in the 1980s, Rod Stewart received $4 million from Canada Dry, the Jacksons received over $5 million from Pepsi, Julio Iglesias received over $30 million from CocaCola in a multitier deal. In the early 2000s, Shania Twain received an estimated $2 million for her first national concert tour, including local tour ads. Celine is hooked up with Ericsson mobile phones, and Blink 182 dresses in Billablong clothing {{32 Waddell, Ray 2000;}}. Forbes Magazine reported that Britney Spears' deal with Pepsi accounted for at least 25% of the $38 million she earned in 2001. Recent deals have included Rascal Flatts with J. C. Penny; Keith Urban and the Clorox Co. (KC Masterpiece sauces); and U2 for Blackberry {{159 Waddell, Ray 2009;}}.

Another form of sponsorship that has a history in the industry involves media companies and non-record companies teaming up. For example, MTV or another broadcaster contributes a certain amount of tour support for the right to an exclusive broadcast performance of an artist. The broadcaster, with the non-record company support, sells the show to radio station affiliates who sell air-time to local advertisers.

One of the more interesting hookups was the Ameriquest Mortgage-sponsored Rolling Stones On Stage tour. Since 1989, such companies as Volkswagen, Tommy Hilfiger, Budweiser, Sprint, E-Trade, AT&T Wireless and T-Mobile have sponsored The Stones' tours. Ameriquest broke in to rock sponsorship with the Paul McCartney halftime show in Super Bowl 2005. According to Jay Coleman, CEO of Entertainment Marketing & Communications International, "Ameriquest will be supporting it with millions of dollars in television advertising. Spots will tie into this tour and their sponsorship of this tour across the country and will keep the band and the brand front and center. If one judges a brand by the company they keep, standing next to the Rolling Stones is a great place to be {{123 Waddell, Ray 2005;}}. In fact, according to the IEG Sponsorship Report, North American companies will have spent an estimated $1.1 billion to sponsor venues, festivals, and tours in 2009, up almost 4% from 2008 {{152 Peoples, Glenn 2009;}}

Sponsorship can mean millions to an artist. If appearances in commercials are included in the deal, several million dollars can be guaranteed. Jive Records believes that commercial/sponsorship exposure for the artist, can and does give the artist additional exposure to a different audience that translates into record sales. Obviously, sponsorship deals can represent a great deal of money and be very lucrative for an artist. Therefore, companies, such as Entertainment Marketing International, usually take about a 15% commission from the party seeking a deal {{54 Heider, Adam/f, p. 30}}.

BRANDING

Branding has been covered extensively in Chapter Four, however product tie-ins seem endless and the following is a list of some of the most successful.

50 Cent	G-Unit video game; clothing line; shoe deal; collaboration with Jacob the Jeweler
The Black Eyed Peas	Partnerships with NBA, Dr Pepper, Verizon, Best Buy; Apple iPod; Honda Civic Hybrid
Sean "Diddy" Combs	Bad Boy WW Ent. Empire has restaurants and fashion; Sean John Fragrances;
Destiny's Child	McDonalds; WalMart; Pepsi;
Beyonce	Tommy Hilfiger; Loreal; House of Dereon clothing; {{125 Mitchell, Gail 2006;}}.

The concept is to develop the artist as a brand and then tie in to specific consumer brands that fits the image.

Another interesting trend is the attempt to attract the interest of the tween-age kids. Some creative tie-ins have included: Ashanti and Mattel for her "Diary" Juice Box personal video player (LL Cool J, Ashlee Simpson, and the Cure also have Juiceware deals); Mattel's *Famous Friends of Barbie* dolls, featuring Destiny's Child, Raven, LeAnn Rimes. Lindsay Lohan is an addition to the My Scene Barbie line. To quote guitarist Slash, "It's extremely flattering and humbling to be immortalized in plastic" {{126 Traiman, Steve 2005;}}. The Pussycat Dolls signed a deal with Hasbro Toys to create a line of fashion dolls modeled on the six members. The dolls will be $15 at retail and sell to the 6 to 9 year olds (Interscope label will receive a royalty) {{127 Leeds, Jeff 2006;}}.

There isn't a set standard deal for endorsement/branding, and as usual, the bigger the star the bigger the deal. Where and when it will reach oversaturation is anyone's guess.

SUMMARY

1. Merchandising is the buying and selling of goods with the artist's name or likeness on them for profit. An artist endorses a product by giving support or approval of it for a set fee. A business that pays an artist a fee for the right to associate with him or her is called a sponsor.

2. Merchandiser's largest expansion in the rock music field occurred in the mid 1970's.

3. Revenue from tour merchandising averages billions of dollars a year.

4. The procedure for acquiring a merchandising deal is as follows: The manager calls merchandisers and asks them to bid on merchandising the tour. The terms of the contract are agreed upon and the merchandiser designs the products. The manager approves all of the items to be merchandised.

5. The revenue from the merchandising is split between the maker of the goods, the venue, the merchandiser, and the artist.

6. Advance money is based on the volume of business expected.

7. The record company shares in the merchandising revenue unless the artist buys the ownership of the graphics and artwork from the record company.

8. Bootleggers and counterfeits are difficult and time consuming to prosecute.

9. Several issues should be investigated before endorsing a product. Namely, is the product effective? How accurate are its claims? Does the artist use the product?

10. Poor endorsement choices can have a negative effect on the artist's image.

11. Several areas of importance in an endorsement contract include: The length of the advertising run, audience reach, media, advances, residuals, creative control, and rights.

12. Most tour sponsorship is reserved only for major acts.

13. Branding of an artist provides extensive revenue streams.

PROJECTS

1. Design a logo for a group that incorporates the group's image.

2. Locate a local silkscreen company that will create a silkscreen for the artist's merchandise.

3. Locate a local company that would like your artist to endorse a product and negotiate a deal.

4. Do the same for a sponsorship deal

5. Locate local sponsors and connect a local artist with a company.

CHAPTER ELEVEN
BUSINESS MANANGEMENT

"The business manager's primary function is to maximize client's earnings while safeguarding their capital."
Marshall M. Gelfand and Wayne C. Coleman in *The Musician's Business & Legal Guide.*
Mark Halloran (ed.) Prentice Hall, 1991. *Pg. 153.*

BY THE END OF THIS CHAPTER YOU SHOULD BE ABLE TO:

1. Describe the role of the business manager.
2. Describe the various functions s/he performs.
3. Discuss the various fee structures.
4. Discuss how to choose a business manager.
5. Using your knowledge of project management, discuss in detail how to prepare a funding proposal.
6. Prepare a budget for a project.

There are a million stories in the rock business about artists and their money. And there are two million stories in the business about artists without their money! When money comes quickly it sometimes gets "lost in the shuffle." Take Kiss for example, as reported in the New York Times: a former employee said that "she was told by an accounting firm that about $700,000 in cash had somehow fallen through the cracks" {{64 Fabrikant,Geraldine 1997/f, p. 7}}. The financial woes of Mick Fleetwood from Fleetwood Mac are also well documented (see "There's No Stopping Tomorrow" by Geraldine Fabrikant, New York Times, November 30, 1997 Bus. Sec. Pg. 1), as are Marvin Gaye's, Jerry Lee Lewis', and Wayne Newton's.

One of the saddest tales is that of Stanley Kirk Burrell, a.k.a. "Hammer." Hammer's "Please Don't Hurt Me" sold 18 million copies. He won three Grammys, had a private jet, movie offers, his own record production company, and a cartoon show. According to Forbes, he earned $33 million in 1990 and 91. By 1996 his income totaled over $50 million. It has been estimated that if Hammer had invested conservatively, he could have enjoyed an annual income of $3 to $5 million for the rest of his life.

Instead, he spent over $11 million to build a house and bought 17 cars. While on tour, he stayed at the best hotels, traveled by private jet. Consequently, his debts total $13.7 million with only $9.6 million in assets. One business associate who is owed money by Hammer summed it up by saying, "In this business you have overnight-success stories, but they tend to go down very quickly. They think it will always be as good as it is now" {{66 Cassidy, John 1996/f, p. 62}}.

BUSINESS MANAGER

THE ROLE:

Income generated in a single year has skyrocketed recently. Billboard reported that twenty artists made at least $38 million in 2005 with U2 and The Rolling Stones generating $255+ million and $152+ million respectively. To combat the horrors of the "Hammer" story, business managers are playing a greater role in the management of the artist's finances. Their relationship, as with the personal manager, is a fiduciary one, and the artist must have total confidence in their judgment. Many business management firms also act as accountants, and play a role in the daily fiscal activities. Therefore, the breath and depth of their role varies.

CONTRACT

Business management contracts are fairly straight forward. Figure 11.1 below is a standard contract for study.

ABC BUSINESS MANAGEMENT SERVICES LLC

Dear   :

This letter is to outline an agreement for the terms and objectives of our engagement and the nature and limitations of our services.

We propose to provide these services during the Term (as defined below):

1) **TERM** - Either party shall have the right to terminate this agreement at any time by written notice to the other party. Thereafter, the Term shall automatically be renewed for additional one (1) year period(s), each commencing on the date following the expiration of the immediately proceeding period unless you or we send a notice to the contrary to the other party prior to the expiration of the Initial Period or any subsequent, then current period.

2) **COMPILE** - from our/your information the annual and interim balance sheets and related statements of income, retained earnings/accumulated deficit.

3) **CASH DISBURSEMENTS** - Our office reviews all your bills and invoices rendered to you and if proper, generate checks drawn on the various checking accounts and after approval by you or a member of your management company, sign and deliver such checks to the appropriate parties. We will retain a payroll service to issue payroll checks for your various entities and will make all payroll tax deposits with the relevant government agencies. You hereby authorize and direct us to pay (INSERT ARTIST MANAGEMENT FIRM). its management commission in accordance with your management agreement and to provide same with copies of all relevant statements.

4) **CASH RECEIPTS** – We will establish bank accounts for your various entities. We will receive monies for you to be deposited into your various bank accounts. We will collect monies payable directly to you from various sources. These monies are deposited immediately, and at the time of deposit, a bank stamped copy of the deposit is attached to the cash receipt.

5) We will provide bookkeeping and accounting services with respect to all of your bills, expenditures, tours, engagements, contracts, and other activities in the Entertainment Industry (as that term is commonly understood).

6) At the end of the month, we will reconcile bank accounts and prepare a detailed listing of each check drawn on your accounts, the opening and closing balance in the detailed general ledgers and a detailed statement of all transactions in such month.

7) In our relationship, we are often advisors, not advocates, regarding investment advice. We will advise you on tax implications if any, or specific matters you bring to our attention.

8) We are not investment counselors, brokers, or stock agents. We can only advise you on the implications of the investment in light of today's tax laws and economy.

9) **TAX COMPLIANCE, TAX PLANNING** - We will prepare all Federal, State and Local income tax returns for all of the business entities related to and in addition, all payroll and related tax returns for such business entities will be prepared and filed as needed. We will not audit or verify the data you submit, although we may ask you to clarify it, or furnish us with additional data. Further, on an ongoing basis, we will meet with you to discuss tax-planning matters.

10) **INSURANCE** - We will advise you on proper and appropriate insurance reasonably desirable for your professional career. We will pay premiums for insurance bills that are either sent to us directly from your insurance company or forwarded to us by you. If you do not forward insurance premium billings to us, we cannot be responsible for a lapse or cancellation in your coverage.

For insurance premium billings mailed directly to us by the insurance company, where payment must be authorized by you, you must be made aware that a delay in your authorization can result in a lapse or cancellation of coverage.

No insurance will be binding until:

Figure 11.1

FUNCTIONS

Below are lecture notes from Mr. Van Duyne who performs business management duties for Kiss, Dave Mathews Band, Three Doors Down, The Rascals, and others. He outlines the functions of a business manager for "baby bands" as well as established artists, and then discusses the sources and uses of income.

"KEEPING TRACK OF IT ALL"
Aaron Van Duyne III, CPA

Fall, 2008

Business management is the handling of one's financial affairs directly through the receipt of funds and the payments of expenses and the overseeing of others such as investment managers. The business manager becomes a family office for most artists – meaning that the management work usually goes well beyond the entertainment industry into other areas of the artist's life. These areas have included for me, real estate sales and purchases, investments in businesses outside of music, farms, wineries and vineyards, movie production, theatre production, motor vehicle development, art world sales, etc. In addition the business manager may handle the financial affairs of other members of the artist's family such as parents, children, spouses and others ensuring all the while the taxes are prepared and paid.

I. **Meeting with the new client**

    a. **Baby artist/band**

        Need to create entity structure – LLC, C or S-Corp

           a. Obtain desired names and alternate names for entities

           b. Obtain name, address, SS# and DOB for each owner (member/shareholder) plus phone numbers and email addresses

           c. Obtain Federal and State ID#s

           d. Open bank accounts for each entity and possibly for artists such as tax reserves

                i. Set-up with a payroll service; start registration process in States that touring will occur

                ii. Register with performance rights societies – ASCAP, BMI, SESAC

                iii. Register songs with Library of Congress if not already done

                iv. Work with group to develop songwriter's agreements among writers and related song splits

                v. Set up 401K or other pension type plan

                vi. Prepare applications for AFTRA membership and AFM to obtain health insurance and pension benefits

                vii. Obtain insurance (baby band coverage)

                      1. General liability

                      2. Auto – this is where the driver licenses come in handy

                      3. Equipment – need list of all equipment to be insured by actual description, serial number and initial cost

                      4. Workers compensation (by state statute in most states)

                      5. Foreign touring insurance, if required

                      6. Health, disability and life insurance

viii. Obtain copies of prior year's tax returns for each member/shareholder

ix. Obtain artist manager information plus copy of agreement with artist/band

x. Obtain attorney information and any related agreement with attorney

xi. Set-up Federal Express and UPS accounts

xii. Set-up American Express account - frequent flier miles

xiii. Work with the artist's manager and attorney for recording, publishing and merchandise agreements

xiv. Prepare letters of direction to be signed by artist directing all future artist earnings be sent directly to business manager

xv. Establish wireless phone account

b. Established artists

i. Letters of direction to performance societies, publisher, booking agent, record label and any other source of business

ii. Obtain copy of recording agreement

iii. Obtain copy of publishing agreement

iv. Obtain copy of merchandise agreement

v. Obtain copy of all licensing and sponsorship agreements

vi. Obtain all other agreements, i.e. producer, mixer, etc.

(Now the management works begins):

II. Sources and Uses of Artist's Funds:

Sources:

1. Advances for touring

   a. Merchandise advance

   b. Tour support from record label

   c. Sponsorships

   d. Promoter advance

2. Touring income
   a. Guarantees paid to booking agent
   b. Overages from performance
   c. Pre-ticket sales and band ticketing
   d. Meet & Greet events
   e. Private engagements
   f. Merchandise royalties
   g. Merchandise sales

3. Recording
   a. Advances for recording and living expenses
   b. Royalties from record sales
   c. Royalties from video sales
   d. Public performance royalties (foreign only)
   e. Royalties from use of masters in commercials, film, etc.

4. Publishing
   a. Advances for writing and living expenses
   b. Mechanical licensing - publishing and writer
   c. Performance - publishing and writer – foreign and domestic
   d. Synchronization – publishing and writer
   e. Sheet music – publishing and writer
   f. Sales of publishing or co-publishing arrangement
   g. Ringtones – music on cell phones, etc.

5. Merchandise
   a. Retail royalties from merchandise company
   b. Books/biographies written by artist
   c. Books/biographies written by others
   d. Auction of artist equipment, costumes, memorabilia
   e. Retail royalties from major department and specialty stores
   f. Musical equipment royalties and sales
   g. Sale of custom merchandise – autos, motorcycles, condoms, autographed items (gold records, lithographs, etc.), coffins, etc.
   h. Sales of merchandise via band website

6. Licensing

    a. Partnerships with organizations such as NASCAR, GM, Nokia, Nintendo, Pepsi, NHL, NFL, Playboy, Showtime, HBO, etc.

    b. Royalties from die cast custom cars

    c. Royalties from comic books/trade magazines

    d. Royalties from commercials

    e. Royalties from use of trademark and name & likeness of artist (Coffee houses, amusement rides, etc.)

    f. Royalties from artist credit card

    g. Royalties from telephone and other debit cards

7. Live appearance (other than touring)

    a. Television appearances

    b. Movie appearances

    c. Broadway Vegas theatrical stage performances

    d. Appearances at collector shows

    e. University & other private speaking engagements

8. Other

    a. Fan Club memberships

    b. Broadway/Las Vegas show of artist likeness

    c. Cartoon show of artist

III. USES

1. Tour related expenses

    a. Rehearsals including renting stadiums, airport hangers, studios, pre-tour crew payroll, airfares and lodging, etc.

    b. Deposits for sound & lights, trucking, busses, pyros, laser, video production, etc.

    c. Booking agency fees

    d. Insurances – health, general liability, workers compensation, life, disability, non-appearance, auto, aircraft, etc.

    e. Salaries – for band members and crew includes tax withholding in all States and Cities that require same

    f. State and City withholding taxes for corporation

    g. Support bands

    h. Pension plans

    i. Hotels, catering and per diems

    j. Telephone, fax, cells, and internet connections

    k. Leased equipment invoices such as sound and lights, trucking, busses, pyros, laser, video production, barricades, communication equipment, etc.

    l. Limousines and vans for to and from hotel and venue

    m. FedEx, UPS and postage

    n. Airfares band and crew including jet charter rentals

    o. Artist and business manger fees

    p. Freight carriers

    q. Itineraries and laminates

    r. Costume/wardrobe purchases and maintenance

    s. Hairstyling and make-up

    t. Office expenses and supplies

    u. Legal and accounting fees

    v. Crew shirts

    w. Generators

    x. Stage and show production designs

    y. AFofM memberships dues

    z. Storage facilities

    aa. Pre-tour tax filings with foreign authorities & post-tour foreign tax filings

    bb. Medical expenses, personal trainers and masseuses

    cc. Litigation arising from incidents while touring

2. Recording royalties

    a. Legal fees for contract negotiations and attorney's finder fees

    b. Artist and business management fees and attorney commissions

    c. Producer's fees

    d. Audit fees

    e. Royalty payments to artists

    f. AFTRA/SAG membership dues

3. Publishing royalties

    a. Legal fees for contract negotiations

    b. Artist and business management fees and attorney commissions

    c. Royalty payments to writers and co-publishing

    d. Audit fees

4. Merchandise
   a. Legal fees for contract negotiations
   b. Artist and business management fees and attorney commissions
   c. Purchase of merchandise to be sold directly by artist
   d. Distributions to artist
   e. Audit fees
   f. Artist's storage facilities and fulfillment houses

5. Licensing
   a. Legal fees for contract negotiations
   b. Artist and business management fees and attorney commissions
   c. Distributions to artist
   d. Audit fees
   e. Name and likeness fees to artist
   f. Trademark fees paid to artist company

6. Live appearance
   a. Legal fees for contract negotiations
   b. Artist and business management fees and attorney commissions
   c. Audit fees
   d. Distribution to artist

7. Other
   a. Website design
   b. Maintenance of fan club
   c. Public relations and publicity

BUSINESS MANAGENT CLASS FALL 2008
MEIEA PRESENTATION APRIL 2, 2004

Figure 11.2

CHOOSING A BUSINESS MANAGER

Reputations are usually built on word of mouth recommendations. As stated in Chapter One, a good personal manager will suggest to his/her client the names of several reputable business managers, and then allow the artist to make the choice. A good personal manager will also emphasize to his/her client, that this is an important decision, which could affect many short and long term goals of the career.

FINANCING A PROJECT

It would be a wonderful world if everyone had enough capital to fund any creative idea. But it isn't. Some say, it would be a wonderful world if we still worked on the barter system of trading. But we don't. Although some people outside the entertainment industry think performers make "money for doing nothing," at the beginning of a career, there just doesn't seem to be enough available. Since robbery is against the law, attempts at raising capital for a project must be completed in an organized, convincing, businesslike manner.

Assuming that the artist is signed with a record label, the most often vehicle for borrowing money is a draw against the artist's royalty account. Assuming the artist is successful, another source of funds is a bank. However, assuming that both these resources are not available to the artist, a capital funding proposal needs to be developed.

THE DEAL

There are many ways to structure a capital investment deal. Below are four such possibilities. Before any deal is structured a business manager should be consulted.

1. **A loan:** The simplest and easiest way to get money is for someone to loan it you and you pay s/he back. You can compose a loan agreement describing the amount of money that is being borrowed and how and when it is will be paid back (a promissory note).

2. **A limited partnership:** As described in Chapter Two, a limited partnership is sometimes setup so that the   person loaning money becomes a partner that will share in income resulting from the project. S/he risks only   the sum being borrowed, and takes on no additional liability.

3. **A corporation:** Someone may loan money in return for a number of shares in a corporation. The amount of shares received in exchange is based on the amount of money loaned in relation to the number of shares outstanding. Similar to a limited partner, the only risk is the amount invested (loaned), and no additional liability is assumed.

4. **A securitization:** A music-royalty securitization is a method where an artist or songwriter issues bonds that give the artist immediate access to cash and the bond-holder/s receive/s an attractive, stable investment. David Bowie's bankers floated the first $55 million worth of bonds in 1997, issuing them against future royalties. Publishing assets clearly have the best value for application to the securitization transaction, basing the deal on future earnings {{65 Benz,Matthew 2002/f, p. 21}}.

THE PLAN

Adapting the tools of project management discussed in Chapter One to a capital seeking proposal is one method of organizing the plan. Figure 11.2 lists the categories that should be included. A discussion follows.

FUNDING PROPOSAL
(BASED ON PROJECT MANAGEMENT)

I.   Problem Statement

II.   Background Statement

III.   Goals & Objectives

IV.   Procedures

V.   Plan

VI.   Schedule

VII.   Budget

VIII.   Financing Structure

IX.   Success Indicator

X.   Executive Summary

I.   **Problem Statement** An explanation of what is perceived to be needed, what this project entails, and why it has been determined to be a solution.

II.   **Background Statement** This section usually begins with a description of the artist and his/her organization, his/her financial condition, the current status of his/her career, successes and any special attributes or awards that may persuade someone to believe that the artist is someone special. A description of similar situations and how the successful completion of the project solved a similar problem, must be included. This section should also include a thorough description (including statistical information) of the music business.

III.   **Goals and Objectives** The goals and objectives, (both long an short term) of the project must be clearly stated.

IV.   Procedures It is sometimes helpful to list what has to be completed before the actual plan is presented. This is especially true when the plan is very complicated and contains steps that are unique to the music business. For example, if one is seeking funds to support a tour, production, security, and catering requirements might seem elaborate to someone outside the industry.

V.   The Plan It is here that how the steps of the plan are to completed is clearly described. Who is responsible for doing what is clearly listed. If a marketing plan is needed, it should be included here. All aspects of the plan must be able to be explained easily, and no aspect of the project should be left to chance.

VI.   The Schedule Describing when the steps are to be completed is the main function of this section. Critical path analysis, a method to determine what aspect of the project will take the longest, should be performed first, so that unrealistic deadlines are not proposed. The schedule should remain flexible.

VII. The Budget The budget should also include the financial statement showing the present financial condition of the artist's company requesting funding. If the artist has been in business for three years or more, the financial condition of the past three years should also be included.

VIII.   Financing Structure The financing requirements are included in this section. The structure and responsibilities of the company loaning the funds, such as the formation of a limited partnership are described here. How and when the funds will be paid back are included. The projected time it will take to payback the loan is also described. The business manager must known the current "going rate" for such a project so that the artist does not pay too much for the deal.

IX.   Success Indicators Projected sales should be described in intervals to act as progress report. Inherent risks and possible problems should be indicated.

X.   Executive Summary This should be a one page description of the deal including all the basic requirements and financial conditions. It is intended for executives that do not have time to read the proposal. It should be concise and businesslike with an eye-catching appeal.

The old saying "you can't make money without spending money" is more true or truer than ever. What seems also to be true today, is the saying "to make a lot you need to risk a lot."

SUMMARY

1. The role of the business manager varies from artist to artist.

2. The basic functions are: accounting, collecting funds, budgeting, tax advising, and investment advising.

3. Any funds collected should be deposited in the artist's account in full and then drawn against when needed.

4. One should make certain how the fee for services is to be collected and what it is based on.

5. Business managers work on hourly fees, percentage of income, and retainers.

6. The artist's business manager has a fiduciary relationship with the artist, and should be chosen by the artist and not the manager.

7. The financing of a project will come forth easier if the funding proposal is organized, convincing, and businesslike.

8. The procedures used in project management can be adapted to be used in a proposal seeking capital.

PROJECTS

1. Develop a funding proposal for a project using actual cost estimates and a realistic time-line.

2. Ask the class to develop a funding proposal and have individuals role play as investors by examining each other's proposals.

3. Prepare a budget for a local artist.

CHAPTER TWELVE
LEGAL BATTLES

"The first thing we do, let's kill all the lawyers."
Shakespeare, Henry VI, Part 2 Act IV, Scene II

[The author thanks students from his personal management classes for their research in updating information concerning the cases listed in this chapter. Further updates may be required.]

The following are selected cases of artist manager disagreements that resulted in very publicized lawsuits. In the entertainment industry, when a substantial amount of income is achieved over a relatively short period of time, it is not unusual for allegations of the misappropriating of funds to arise. Although the law suits may result in large attorney fees, this is an "ego driven" business based on relationships, where emotions play a major role, and when someone is suspected of a misappropriation, the usual response is "I don't care what it costs, I'm going to get that sucker!" The truth of many settlements is that the attorneys are the real winners.

In reality, many artists young or old, fail to read or fully comprehend the artist-manager agreement, and consequently set themselves up for misunderstandings. Secondly, most contracts use terms like "reasonable effort" or "best effort" to describe the behavior expected by the parties, which are obviously open to a broad range of interpretation. What follows are lawsuits that were filed for a variety of reasons. They were chosen as a representation of the various misunderstanding that occurs. Because the entertainment industry can be a very private business, these legal battles come with different degrees of available information. They are meant to be used as learning tools for students, and not intended to be partial to the artist or manager involved. Much of the new background information was retrieved from Wikipedia.org.

TABLE OF CHAPTER CONTENT

BEE GEES VS. ROBERT STIGWOOD

THE BACKGROUND

The Bee Gees, Barry, Robin, and Maurice Gibb are pop singers from Australia who became one of the most successful recording groups in the world in the late 1970's. As a result of the overwhelmingly successful movie "Saturday Nite Fever," their soundtrack album, recorded for RSO Records, sold over twenty million records worldwide, and is considered by most as one of the crowning achievements of the disco era. Barry's falsetto vocals became a familiar sound on radio, television, and in elevators, supermarkets, and health clubs All accounts support that the Bee Gees were on top of the industry.

Robert Stigwood, an entertainment mogul also from Australia is the principal owner the Robert Stigwood Group. Under the umbrella of the RSO Group are a number of companies that encompass many aspects of the business. In addition to RSO Records, there is a personal management firm, and a number of music publishing companies. Stigwood is considered a giant in the worldwide entertainment industry.

THE DILEMMA

In October 1980, the Bee Gees filed suit in a New York State Supreme Court that Stigwood had cheated the act out of more that $16 million through a pattern of fraud, breach of trust, and conflict of interest. Filed on behalf of the three, the suit asked for upwards of $75 million in damages and other costs from a host of Stigwood related companies. They sued for release from all their ties with Stigwood, and charged that he deliberately mismanaged them to his own advantage and withheld millions of dollars in royalties

Details of the claim asked for $75 million from Stigwood; $75 million from Polygram, which owned half of the Stigwood Group companies; $50 million in punitive damages; and additional millions in interest and back royalties. They also asked for the return of all the Bee Gees' master recording and copyrights, and a release from all their many contracts with Stigwood {{87 Kirkeby, Marc 1980/f, p. 22}} The suit alleged that Stigwood diverted millions of dollars from them by creating self-servicing corporate entities that hid money and delayed royalty payments. The three brothers hired Paul McCartney's brother-in-law, John Eastman, to represent them, who negotiated Paul's release from the Beatles and from Allen Klein.

On the emotional level, the Bee Gees became insecure about the monopoly Stigwood had in every aspect of their career. He was their personal manager since 1968, and head of their record company. They were also signed to his publishing firm. In 1980 they questioned, as their manager, why Stigwood didn't solicit them deals from any other record companies or publishing firms. After all, as a manager, he took twenty-five percent of their gross earnings for twelve years. Weren't they entitled to negotiate deals through competitive bidding?

The suit continued to allege that Stigwood fraudulently failed and refused to account properly for royalties and other income and hid the fact that he owed them large sums of money {{87 Kirkeby, Marc 1980;}}. In fact they conducted their own audit and found that they were owed millions in unpaid royalties dating back to 1968.

The Stigwood group called the suit "revolting" and countered by claiming the whole suit was just a way for the three to renegotiate a better contract. Stigwood appealed in London England for an injunction against anyone who tried to usurp his interests in the group. Stigwood denied all charges and executives at RSO Records claimed that the group was being paid "excessively high royalties" and owed their careers to Stigwood.

THE RESOLUTION

Although it was widely speculated that the case would be very difficult and last for quite a number of years, the suit was settled out of court and all charges dropped. Details of the settlement were not revealed, however, an industry representative claims that Stigwood gave up his rights to the group and released them from their RSO Records deal but retained their catalogue.

BILLY JOEL VS. FRANK WEBER

Index No. 20702/89
Supreme Court of New York, New York County

THE BACKGROUND

Billy Joel is one of the biggest record-selling artists in the world. Starting out as a songwriter/piano player, his first shot at the big time, came as the singer/songwriter/ keyboards player in a keyboard and drum duo called "Attila". Recording solo albums for Columbia since the 1970's, Joel has gained the attention of the college age. In fact, at one time he was tied with the Beatles as having the largest number of platinum albums. Several worldwide tours have grossed him hundreds of millions of dollars as well.

Joel's rise to stardom did not come overnight nor without setbacks. His history as a singer in piano lounges in Los Angeles is public knowledge. His loss of ownership to many of his songs to various "parasites" in the industry is also a common hazard of this industry.

His career is bigger than ever. His marriage and subsequent divorce to supermodel Christie Brinkley has added to the aura of his public persona. He gained superstar status in the 1980's and continues to enjoy the status in the 2000's.

Frank Weber is Joel's ex-brother-in-law who began managing him in 1979. Also named in the suit were his wife Lucille, his brother-in-law Richard London, and two other in-laws. Weber's prior experience in the industry is not known.

THE DILEMMA

On September 25, 1989, Billy Joel filed a $90 million lawsuit against Frank Weber, accusing him of misappropriating recording royalties and tour funds over a period of ten years {{83 Flick, Larry 1989/f, p. 96}}. According to the papers filed in New York State Supreme Court, Weber "maliciously defrauded" Joel while being paid millions of dollars annually in management commissions, and funds from Joel's tours and record royalties.

Details of the allegations include:

1. misappropriation of $2.5 million in unauthorized, interest-free loans,

2. $10 million loss from risky investments,

3. double-billed Joel for production costs for music videos shot by a Weber controlled company,

4. and obtained loans from CBS Records for Joel, using his copyrights as collateral.

Joel also asked to void his 1980 agreement with Weber and block him from any further compensation. Weber moved to have the claims dismissed at the start of the hearings. He claimed he was innocent. Rumors in the industry suggested that Joel's new wife at that time, Christie Brinkley, convinced Joel that his former wife's family was unfaithful to his career, and the suit was filed with a great deal of ill feeling and mixed emotions.

THE RESOLUTION

The court ruled against Weber on counts of fraud and embezzlement, and awarded Joel $2 million as compensation for funds that were allegedly drawn from Joel's bank account {{79 Flick, Larry 1990/f, p. 94}}.

Although Joel was awarded $2 million in the spring of 1990, as of May 1991, Joel collected only $250,000 from Weber. Weber has filed for bankruptcy. Consequently, Joel pursued Weber's accountants and attorney claiming they had a role in the improper transfer of $1.5 million of Joel's assets {{84 Lichtman, Irv 1991;}}!

On February 25, 1993, Judge Lehner of the New York Supreme Court awarded Joel $675,670.68 in a summary judgement concerning two real estate partnership distributions. The remaining claims have yet to have hearings scheduled.

Weber filed an $11 million suit against Brinkley alleging that she induced Joel to terminate the management agreement. A New York judge has moved a dismissal of the complaint as a spouse is unnamed against a claim of interference and cannot be forced to testify against his or her spouse or reveal details about private conversations.

In April 1995, Joel's attorney, Leonard Marks, filed a motion in the Supreme Court of the State of New York to discontinue action without prejudice from the case so that the plaintiff is free to file a new suit on the same claim. However, at this time further action would be a waste of time and money.

LISA MARIE PRESLEY VS. TOM PARKER & RCA RECORDS

Probate Court, Memphis TN.

THE BACKGROUND

(This suit was filed on behalf of Elvis' daughter, Lisa Marie in 1980.)

Elvis was (and might still be) **THE KING**. He was one of the biggest stars in the entire entertainment business, attracting audiences whose ages ranged from "eight to eighty." For years, his records represented one-half of RCA Records' sales. He has over 700 hundred charted songs recorded on dozens of hit albums to his credit.

Colonel Tom Parker had been Elvis' personal manager since 1956. Legend has it that the colonel and Elvis didn't have a written agreement. A handshake and trust held their relationship together on a 50%-50% basis for those many years. Many consider Parker the brains behind Elvis' enormous success. After all, it was Parker's idea to convince RCA Records to buy his contract from Sam Phillips at Sun Records in Memphis for the total sum of $40,000.

Parker was once a carnival barker. He was known to have no problem with saying anything to anyone. In fact, he was known as one of the industry's biggest practical jokers.

RCA Records is one of the oldest continuously operating record labels in the USA. RCA is a subsidiary of BMG a major international entertainment company with facilities throughout the world. Historically, their emphasis has been in the recording and releasing of country and classical music.

THE DILEMMA

A court-appointed guardian of Lisa Marie Presley, then twelve years old, filed a report on July 31, 1981 accusing Col. Tom Parker and RCA Records of "collusion, conspiracy, fraud, misrepresentation, bad faith, and overreaching" in their business dealings with Elvis {{88 Kozak, Roman 1981;}}. Central to the charges was the 1973 sale of royalty rights to Presley's entire catalog to RCA for $5 million, to be split equally between Elvis and the colonel. With Elvis in the 50% tax bracket, his net would only be $1.35 million, and he would forfeiture of all future rights! This was certainly not a sound business decision on Parker's part for Elvis, however, it did provide a nice income for the 63 year old Parker.

The report also cited a number of side deals that the Colonel made with RCA, the Hilton International Hotel in Las Vegas, and Management III. Blanchard E. Tual, the court appointed attorney filing the suit, also claimed that Elvis lost considerable revenue by never playing outside the U.S.

Tual claimed that he never performed outside the country because Parker was never naturalized as an American citizen, and was really Andreas Cornelus van Kuijk, born in Holland on June 26, 1909.

Elvis tended to ignore any attorney's advice and put his entire fate in Parker's hands. Elvis went along with the buyout by RCA that was suggested by Parker, even though the contract was not due to expire until 1975. Furthermore, RCA Records had not purchased any of its other artists' master catalogs. The new 1973 seven year contract called for a royalty rate of 10c per single and 50c per album for U.S. sales, half of which was to paid to "All Star Shows," the Colonel's company. At the time, other stars such as the Rolling Stones and Elton John were getting twice the royalty and paying half the commission rates to their management.

Some of the side deals cited were the agreement that RCA Records would pay All Star Shows $675,000 over seven years, and RCA Records Tours would additionally pay the same for "planning, promotion, and merchandising." Parker would also receive 10% of RCA Tours profit. RCA agreed to pay Parker a $50,000 consulting fee and another $350,000 of All Star Tours for planning, promotion, and merchandising. Tual reported that with these deals, Elvis would gross $4.65 million, while Parker would make $6.2 million, plus 10% of all tour profits.

The contract contained a "no audit clause" which did not allow an Elvis representative to examine the books! By 1972, Elvis physical and emotional condition did not allow him to evaluate any agreements, and it seems obvious that Parker was interested in cashing in before the King's inevitable early expiration.

Another side deal was with the Hilton. Parker was provided with a year-round suite of offices and hotel rooms, all the food and beverages for his home in Palm Springs, and free transportation to Las Vegas anytime that he requested it. Parker was also a notorious gambler, good for $1,000,000 per year at the hotel tables. Included in this deal were the services of Elvis at $100,000 to $130,000 per week. A fee that was surpassed by acts of far less value.

THE RESOLUTION

A settlement was made on behalf of Lisa Marie. However, the Colonel never was convicted of enough crimes to spend any time in jail. He died a free man.

LAURA BRANIGAN VS. SUSAN JOSEPH

THE BACKGROUND

Laura Branigan is a pop singer that enjoyed a number of hit records on the Atlantic label in the 1980s. Her personal manager at the time was Susan Joseph, a partner of Henry Marx in Grand Trine Management. Marx is also a partner in Ram Promotions, an independent record promotion company. Branigan is married to Laurence Kruteck who is also her business manager.

THE DILEMMA

In 1985, Branigan sued Joseph for failing to fulfill her obligations of the personal management agreement. Branigan then terminated her agreement with Joseph. Specifically mentioned in the suit was the use of $125,000 of Branigan's money for independent promotion of her records. Also at issue was the claim that Joseph misrepresented the role offered to Branigan in an Australian film {{85 Terry, Ken 1987;}}.

Branigan claimed that the $125,000 spent on independent promotion was improperly spent by Ram Promotions, which was the company hired by Joseph to do the job. Branigan also claimed that Joseph was a partner in the company. Over $1 million was spent on independent promotion of Branigan's records over a two year period.

The testimony revealed that Branigan had reservations about the role in the Australian film. However, she already committed herself to the project when she filed suit in 1985.

According to Joseph's attorney, Branigan's husband, Kruteck, induced her to breach the contract with Joseph.

THE RESOLUTION

Branigan lost her suit against Joseph. A jury granted Joseph's counterclaim filed in federal court on November 30, 1987. They found that Joseph had not breached the contract or her fiduciary duty to the singer. Also she was not a partner in Ram Promotions. They awarded $509,238.74 to Joseph, and levied $100,000 punitive damages against Kruteck, as they believed he induced Branigan to breach the agreement. This settlement was very unusual because juries do not normally award punitive damages against a third party.

MICHAEL LANG VS. JOE COCKER

THE BACKGROUND

Joe Cocker is a blues oriented singer with an unusual stage presence. When he performs in his raspy voice, he contorts his body and releases spasms with his hands and arms that make him appear to be suffering from a crippling disease. Cocker hit the international scene in the early 1970's with a cover version of the Beatles' "A Little Help From My Friends." His career has had its ups and downs, however, he does sell records and makes concert hall appearances.

Michael Lang and Better Music Inc. began managing Cocker in 1977. The agreement expired in 1980 but the parties agreed to continue under its terms and conditions. In 1984 they entered into a new agreement.

THE DILEMMA

On March 26, 1992 Michael Lang and Better Music Inc. filed suit in federal court in New York City against Joe Cocker and Adaven Productions, which sometimes acts as Cocker's agent, claiming that Cocker agreed to pay Better Music 15% of his gross earnings from recordings, concerts, merchandising rights, song royalties, and TV appearances during the term of the 1977 agreement. The suit names several albums made under the original agreement as well as singles from the soundtracks of "An Officer And A Gentleman" and "An Innocent Man" {{86 Miller, Trudi 1992;}}

The suit claims damages of $1 million for breach of contract and $1 million for the plaintiffs' services, 15% of the net from Cocker's recordings and concert appearances, as well as court costs.

Better Music continued to manage Cocker until August 19, 1991 when they were notified by the singer that he no longer required Lang's services and would no longer pay him.

THE RESOLUTION

Cocker's attorney denies Lang's claims and said Cocker will counter sue.

PRINCE VS. CAVALLO, RUFFALO, & FARGNOLI

Los Angeles Superior Court

THE BACKGROUND

Prince is considered one of the most innovative performers in the business. His creative endeavors in addition to performing include producer, songwriter, screenwriter, movie star, and multi-instrumentalist. His mixture of raw sexual appeal with rhythm and blues has made him a huge success with crossover appeal.

THE DILEMMA

His former managers Robert Cavallo, Joseph Ruffalo, and Steve Fargnoli reportedly filed suit against him in Los Angeles Superior Court February 1, 1991 claiming that he owes them $600,000 that he agreed to pay when he released them from their responsibilities. The three assert that they were able to collect potential earnings when he ignored their career advice. They further claim that the disagreement occurred when Prince decided to release his records "in competition with one another."

In October 1991, Prince released the Diamonds and Pearls Cd, which contained a track entitled, "Jughead," which was Prince's artistic expression of the stereotypical music manager. Fargnoli was convinced that the song was specifically written to mock him. He filed a $5 million suit against Prince's Paisley Park Studios claiming "defamation of character." The suit was eventually thrown out of court {{78 Lichtman, Irv 1991;}}.

THE RESOLUTION

A settlement has not been reached.

ANITA BAKER VS. SHERWIN BASH, DAVID BRAUN, RANDY BASH

Los Angeles Superior Court

THE BACKGROUND

Grammy-winning artist Anita Baker is one of the greatest r & b singers of the 1990's. As an Elektra artist, her records have sold consistently well and she is recognized as one of today's most enduring female stars. Ms. Baker possesses great crossover appeal, as she is popular with the pop and jazz audiences as well.

THE DILEMMA

Ms. Baker has filed a breach-of-contract cross-complaint against former manager Sherwin Bash, former attorney David Braun, and Randy Bash, who administered her catalog through Big Heart Music. The filing occurred on May 14, 1996, claiming "fraud and deceit, breach of fiduciary duty, breach of contract, defamation and slander, intentional infliction of emotional distress, civil conspiracy, and attorney malpractice"{{ 68 Reynolds, J R. 1996; 1996;}}.

Her action stems from a default judgment filed by Sherwin Bash in February, 1996, for "damages, back royalties, unpaid commissions, other revenue sources and court costs." Baker stated: "Management firms and large labels don't pay you. [Bash] thinks that he should live off me the rest of my life."

The suit follows another action against Bash that was filed before the labor commission of California that alleges that Bash's BNB Associates acted as a talent agent without being licensed in that state. Baker entered into a 5 year personal management contract with BNB at a commission rate of 15% in 1983 and again in 1988, with an option to terminate in 1991. Baker terminated the agreement but retained BNB on a as needed basis for 10%. On December 13, 1994, Baker advised Bash that the management contract was terminated. Therefore, her agreements with BNB are unenforceable because BNB was unlicensed and that claims on existing and future commissions, royalties, or other sums arising from previous contracts be voided. Baker's suit claims that the defendants "knowingly and willfully conspired and agreed among themselves to further their own self-interest at Baker's expense."

THE RESOLUTION

A settlement has not been reached.

STEPHEN HUTTON VS. KID ROCK AND TOP DOG RECORDS

U.S. District Court, New York

THE BACKGROUND

Kid Rock has enjoyed a successful career mixing metal with rap. He has sold millions of records reciting nasty lyrics, and has performed his stage antics to sold out audiences throughout the world.

THE DILEMMA

Hutton sued Rock and his company, Top Dog Records for at least $4 million in July of 2000 alleging breach of contract and unjust enrichment (a person unfairly gets a benefit by chance, mistake or another's misfortune for which the one enriched has not paid).

THE RESOLUTION

Reportedly, the suit was settled out of court and in a joint statement, Hutton and Rock said that there were glad the case has been settled fairly and that the litigation has been brought to an end {{81 Newman, Melinda 2001;}}.

DAVID LEE ROTH VS. EDMUND ANDERSON

Los Angeles Superior Court

THE BACKGROUND

Just a gigolo………….

THE DILEMMA

Roth filed a lawsuit against his former manager for selling unauthorized Roth Tshirts and other memorabilia on his Web site. Roth authorized Anderson to sell "certain limited surplus merchandise" in exchange for previous management and consulting services. Anderson was not authorized to make copies of the merchandise or create new Roth products. Roth authorized him to set up a website to sell the stuff on condition that Roth approve its design and that Anderson would terminate the site when Roth asked. Roth told him to take down the site. Anderson did but then allegedly put it back up at another location and is continuing to sell merchandise without permission {{80 Skanse, Richard 1999;}}.

THE RESOLUTION

?

HENRY NEWMAN VS. HOOTIE & THE BLOWFISH

THE BACKGROUND

Hootie & the Blowfish enjoyed one of the biggest debut albums in industry history by selling over fourteen million copies of Cracked Rear View. In 1996, the Atlantic Records recording artists also won a Grammy for the Best New Artist.

THE DILEMMA

Henry Neuman, the group's former manager slapped the group with a $150 million lawsuit claiming that he was wrongfully excluded from the band's recording contract. The group called the suit "meritless."

Neuman says that he discovered the band while he was hosting a talent showcase in Rock Hill, North Carolina, and signed a managerial contract with a term of three years.

He claims that the group blew him off when the record went big by pressuring him into signing a release from his contract.

THE RESOLUTION

Terms of the settlement were not disclosed, but lawyers for the band happily reported that it was cheaper to settle than to go to court!

INGA VAINSHTEIN VS. JEWEL (KILCHER) AND HER MOTHER, LENEDRA CARROLL

California Superior Court, Los Angeles

THE BACKGROUND

Jewel is one of today's most successful artists. With several platinum albums charted, she is one of the industry's top performers. Born in Utah, she spent her early years living in Alaska performing in Eskimo villages with her singer/songwriter father. After graduation from the Interlochen Fine Arts Academy she moved to San Diego to live with her mother. Performing her own material, she played coffeehouses in the area and met Vainshtein who signed on as her manager in 1993. Later that year, she was picked up by Atlantic Records.

THE DILEMMA

In November of 1998, Vainshtein filed a $10 million lawsuit charging Jewel and her mother with wrongful termination of her 'three album cycle' managerial contract. Vainshtein is seeking compensatory and punitive damages claiming that she is owed millions in commissions. She maintains that Carroll shadowed her as a comanager to learn how to handle her daughter's business, and then fired her. The suit goes on to claim that Carroll convinced the singer that advice from Vainshtein had to be approved by a "channeler" (named Jack Snyder) who evaluated the advice by communicating with some entity referred to as "Z!" Furthermore, Carroll pressured her into sharing a portion of her commissions and directed that commission payment be calculated based on net, rather than gross earnings.

THE RESOLUTION

The California Labor Commission ruled that the management contract between Jewel and Inga is void because Inga used illegal tactics in booking Jewel's appearances while she was manager, voiding the contract (supposedly without a booking license). Vainshtein has filed an appeal to the ruling and is requesting that she be paid $1,843,450 in commissions {{82 Morris, Chris 1998;}}.

LOU PEARLMAN VS. 'N SYNC

Federal Court, Orlando, FLA

THE BACKGROUND

'N Sync, the boy band that followed in the footsteps of another Pearlman group, The Backstreet Boys, sold more than 7 million copies of their debut album in 1998. Presently, they are in the mist of a worldwide tour which, when completed, should be one of the largest grossing tours in history.

THE DILEMMA

On October 12, 1999, Pearlman, the group's creator and manager filed a $150 million law suit against them and Zomba Recording. The suit cited breach of contract and an injunction was also filed barring them from using the name 'N Sync, claiming that Pearlman had exclusive ownership.

Pearlman created, developed, and financed the boys and was instrumental in landing their exclusive distribution deal with BMG. The deal was for five albums, and they were signed to a subsidiary of BMG and then licensed to RCA.

The dispute began in July of 1999 "when the group claimed that Pearlman and his firm, Trans Continental, failed to fulfill its contractual obligations." The group then left RCA for Jive (of which Zomba is the parent company).

Pearlman's attorney, Michael Friedman, said that it is absurd to think that now that the group has been made rich and famous, they can just turn their backs on Pearlman and go someplace else. Pearlman is seeking $100 million in compensatory damages and $50 million in punitive damages.

On November 2, 1999, "N Sync filed a $25 million counter suit. The group claimed that Pearlman's financial arrangements made them virtually "indentured servants" of Trans Continental. They claimed that Pearlman et. al received 55% of all gross touring revenue plus 37.5% of the net; 75% of all record royalties and 100% of any advances; 80% of the merchandising; 100% of the music publishing; and 55% of gross celebrity endorsement monies, plus 37.5% of the net from such deals. (Pearlman filed an affidavit stating that $13 million was given to the band over the past two years.)

The court documents said that the band members "have been victims of a con man who has become wealthy at their expense. They have been cheated at every turn by Pearlman's fraud, manipulation and breach of fiduciary duty. As a final affront, Pearlman now seeks the aid of a federal court to ratify his theft and leave 'N Sync unable to pursue its career."

Group member J.C. stated that Pearlman was an "unscrupulous businessman who while hugging us and calling us family was picking our pockets, robbing us of our future and endangering our health." He also said that "Pearlman dissuaded the group from consulting lawyers, never showed them contracts for the label deals, and pressured them to hire Johnny Wright as manager and pay him more than the Backstreet Boys did in order to shift Wright's focus to "N Sync."

THE RESOLUTION

On November 24, 1999 Judge Ann Conway denied Pearlman's request for an injunction. On December 27, 1999 an agreement was reached that was not disclosed to the public. Some sources say that 'N Sync will pay royalties to BMG as part of the settlement {{71 Newman, Melinda 1999;}}.

LEANN RIMES VS. WILBUR RIMES AND LYLE WALKER

U.S. District Court Dallas Texas

THE BACKGROUND

As a teenage novice, Leann Rimes shot straight to the top of the country and pop charts with a voice reminiscent of Patsy Cline's. Today, as a holder of several Grammy awards, she is considered one of country music's top stars as she transforms her image from the teenage sensation to a sex symbol.

THE DILEMMA

In a suit filed May 2, 2000, Leann is suing her father, Wilbur, and former manager, attorney Walker claiming they took $7 million from her over a five year period. She claims that they paid themselves excessively as co-managers, keeping 30% of her income. The suit says that an artist of her stature "should pay 10% or less for competent management services."

She alleges breaches of fiduciary duty, constructive fraud, conspiracy, and breach of contract. Leann seeks an accounting of all transactions involving the defendants and actual damages to be determined but including at least $7 million in "excessive and unreasonable management fees" {{89 Horwitz, Carolyn 2000;}}.

THE RESOLUTION

All resolutions came after LeAnn's stepmother released recordings that allegedly showed LeAnn to be a manipulative and a very demanding spoiled person. In March, 2001 Rimes settled with Walker with financial terms not disclosed. In February 2002, she settled with Wilbur with financial terms not disclosed.

CHRISTINA AGUILERA VS. STEVEN KURTZ

California Superior Court Los Angeles

THE BACKGROUND

The former Mousecateer won a Grammy as best new artist in 2000, and has sold more than 7 million copies of her debut album for RCA. As a current player in the "cola wars" she has rocketed to the top of the music business in about two years.

THE DILEMMA

Aguilera, who filed suit on Oct. 13, 2000, is seeking to break the management agreement and alleges that Kurtz, Marquee Management and co-manager Katrina Sirdofsky committed fraud and breached their fiduciary duties. "Kurtz exercised improper, undue, and inappropriate influence over her professional activities, as well as her personal affairs." The action also claims that the contract allowed Kurtz to collect 20% of any and all Aguilera's "Commissionable income" earned for an indefinite period of time. "The true facts are that Kurtz did not place Aguilera's interests above his own; did not act fairly and honestly in protecting her rights and interests; did not advise her independently of his own interests; took actions which inured to his own benefit; and took actions adverse to her interests" {{74 Morris, Chris 2000;}}

THE RESOLUTION

?

TRENT REZNOR VS. JOHN MALM JR.

U.S. District Court, New York

THE BACKGROUND

Trent Reznor is the lead singer of Nine Inch Nails and the only "real" member of the platinum recording group. NIN were the most popular industrial group ever and was largely responsible for bringing the music to a mass audience. NIN built up a large alternative rock fan base right around the time of Nirvana's mainstream breakthrough. Reznor wrote melodic, traditionally structured songs where lyrics were a focal point. His pop instincts not only made the harsh electronic beats of industrial music easier to digest, but also put a human face on a style that usually tried to sound as mechanical as possible.

THE DILEMMA

On May 19, 2004 Reznor filed in court for breach of contract, fiduciary duty and conspiracy. The complaint says that Malm and J. Artist Management took improper control of his finances and legal documents and the defendants withheld money he earned and refused to turn over books and records of financial transactions. After TVT Records signed Reznor in 1989, he and Malm entered a management agreement and the two formed Nothing Records and J. Artist Management Merchandise splitting the profits equally. In 1993, Malm had Reznor sign NIN trademark registrations, and Reznor claims that he was not aware that they made Malm part owner. In 1994, the management agreement expired but the two orally agreed to continue working under the same terms. Zia Modagger, Reznor attorney claims that Malm never had a lawyer represent Reznor in any of the deals. Prior to trial, Judge Jed Rakoff held that Malm knew the earlier deal was not longer fair to Reznor because it required commissions paid without the standard deductions.

THE RESOLUTION

On May 27, 2005, Reznor was awarded $2.9 million (actually in a countersuit, as Malm had initiated a legal battle against Reznor) as the court found Malm liable for fraud. The jury awarded $1 million for overpayment of commissions and additional $1 million was awarded for unpaid loans. Reznor could be awarded an additional $1.5 million to the verdict {{130 Butler, Susan 2005;}}.

MATISYAHU VS. JDUB MANAGEMENT

THE BACKGROUND

Matisyahu is a member of the Chabad-Lubavitch Hasidic community in the Crown Heights section of Brooklyn, New York, which was led by its Rebbe, Rabbi Menachem Mendel Schneerson. Matisyahu was born Mathew Miller, on June 30, 1979 in West Chester, Pennsylvania and his family eventually settled in White Plain, New York. He was brought up a Reconstructionist Jew, and for some time during those years he played by the alias "MC Truth" for MC Mystic's Soulfari band. He eventually turned to Orthodox Judaism, and today performs in the reggae style. Matisyahu means gift of God. His 2005 release Live at Stubb's and his current release Youth have both gone gold.

THE DILEMMA

Via a phone call on March 1, 2006 Matisyahu informed his management, "JDub" that their services were no longer needed. In fact, he has been represented by new Management: former Capitol Records President, Gary Gersh. Aaron Bisman and Jacob Harris are partners running "JDub" which is a not-for-profit label, events and management team that promotes Jewish music. Bisman and Harris claim that Matisyahu has three years remaining on a four year contract. They also claim that they have promoted him as a pop star, convincing him to play clubs and not synagogues. The two argue that they have acted in good faith and have always had a strategic vision to make his a long-term career and not a novelty act {{131 Werde, Bill 2006;}}.

LEONARD COHEN VS. KELLY LYNCH

Los Angeles Superior Court, CA

THE BACKGROUND

Leonard Cohen, is a Canadian poet, novelist, and singer-songwriter. He is considered one of the most distinguished and influential songwriters of the twentieth century. His musical career has largely overshadowed his prior work as a poet and novelist, although he has continued to publish poetry sporadically after his breakthrough in the music industry. Musically, Cohen's early songs are based in folk music, however, beginning in the 1970s, his work shows the influence of various types of popular music and cabaret music. Cohen's music has become very influential on other singer-songwriters, and more than a thousand cover versions of his work have been recorded.

THE DILEMMA

On August 15, 2005 Cohen sued former manager of 17 years, Kelly Lunch, claiming that in 1997, she fraudulently sold his publishing and artist royalties after he entered a retreat for $12 million, leaving him with only $150,000. In 1993, after his successful album and tour he entered a Zen retreat for nearly five years. His income proceeded to decline in those years and the complaint alleges that Lynch did not accept a corresponding decline in her income. He also alleges that Lynch set up a corporate structure that allowed her to steal over $5 million and have complete control over his retirement savings. Cohen is seeking more that $5 million in punitive damages and other remedies.

CHRIS CORNELL VS. SUSAN J. SILVER

California Superior Court, Los Angeles, CA

THE BACKGROUND

Chris Cornell, born July 20, 1964 in Seattle is an American guitarist/singer-songwriter most well-known for being the lead singer of Soundgarden and Audioslave. He began his musical career as a drummer, before moving on to become a singer and guitarist. Due to his singing abilities and vocal range, Cornell gained nearly as much fame as Soundgarden. His ability to soar into falsetto and through heard voice effortlessly often defies many a normal singer's natural timbre, giving him a high harmonic overtone or timbre to his voice. In late 1994, after touring in support of the album Superunknown, doctors discovered that he had severely strained his vocal chords. Under medical directive, Soundgarden had to cancel several shows to avoid permanent damage to Cornell's vocal chords. Cornell is currently the vocalist in the critically and commercially successful alternative rock quartet Audioslave, backed up by the former members of Rage against The Machine.

THE DILEMMA

On November 28, 2005 Cornell sued his ex-wife and one-time manager, Susan J. silver for more than $1 million in damages. Cornell alleges that Silver conspired with other representatives of Soundgarden to direct funds owed to Cornell to other members of his former band. Silver called the allegations absurd and states no wrongdoings {{137 Walsh, Chris M. 2005;}}.

BRADEN MERRICK VS. THE KILLERS

U.S. District Court, Las Vegas, NV

THE BACKGROUND

The Killers is a synth rock band from Las Vegas, Nevada, who formed in 2002. The band is comprised of Brandon Flowers (vocals, synthesizer), Dave Keuning (guitar), Mark Stoermer (bass), and Ronnie Vannucci Jr. (drums and vocals). In 2004 they had a multi-platinum hit with Hot Fuss. Much of The Killers' music is based on British influences and on the music of the 1980s, particularly New Wave music. Since going platinum, the band (and principally Flowers) has managed to incite a few rivalries - most notably with The Bravery and Fall Out Boy, which, ironically, are both labelmates (Island Records). Flowers has said that these bands, especially The Bravery, are riding on the coattails of the success of The Killers.

THE DILEMMA

On February 21, 2006 Braden Merrick and his company, From the Future, sued band members for $16 million for breach of contract and interference with that contract. Merrick claims that band did not have grounds to terminate his 2003 contract. The band claims that Merrick was in independent A&R rep who first wanted to shop a deal, then manage the band; however, then went to work for the band's label. Merrick contends that he was a regional consultant for a major label when he found the band on the Internet; that label passed on the band. Merrick's company then entered a management agreement with the band. Island Def Jam picked up the band and released Hot Fuss. Then Merrick began working for IDJ without disclosing the fact to the band. A source close to the band says that Merrick was often unreachable, failed to attend meetings and mishandled opportunities{{132 Butler, Susan 2006;}}.

JENNIFER LOPEZ VS. BENNY MEDINA

Los Angeles Superior Court, CA

THE BACKGROUND

J-Lo!

THE DILEMMA

In June 2003, after five years of management, J-Lo is suing Benny Medina alleging that he diverted and misappropriated monies belonging to her. Medina who is credited with molding the Bronx-born beauty into a superstar said that the accusation is both untrue and offensive. J-Lo claims that Medina went behind her back and took an inappropriate consulting fee of over $100,000 on a project of hers. She also claims that Medina prevented other agents and managers from speaking with her. According to the court papers Lopez alleges that Medina acted in a manner detrimental to the best interest of her and in a manner which adversely affected her business, personal and financial interests {{134 Holson, Laura M. 2003;}}.

RICKY MARTIN VS. ANGELO MEDINA

New York Supreme Court

THE BACKGROUND

"Living la vida loca"!

THE DILEMMA

Ricky Martin Enterprises filed suit against Medina on February 17, 2004 for unearned management commissions through the assertion of claims for unjust enrichment, breach of agreement and breach of fiduciary duty. Martin seeks $2.5 million. The suit refers to several advances that Martin received from Sony Music. Legal experts have described the suit as unusual, given that managers are entitled to commissions when artist received their money. After more than twelve years, Martin and Medina parted ways amicably in September 2003, however, Medina filed a $63.5 million countersuit alleging breach of contract, unjust enrichment and pain and suffering {{133 Cobo, Leila 2004;}}.

THE FRAY VS. GREGG LATTERMAN

U. S. District Court, CO

THE BACKGROUND

The Fray is one of the important new artists on the scene today. Thanks to the popularity of their music on television, their tour is considered one of hottest tickets. The songwriting of the duo is thought of as pop with an indie twist.

THE DILEMMA

Joseph King and Issac Slade (The Fray) filed suit against their manager, Gregg Latterman in U.S. District Court on September 14, 2009 over copyright ownership of their songs. King and Slade wrote the 2005 hits "Over My Head (Cable Car)" and "How to Save a Life." The suit claims that Latterman obtained partial ownership when the band signed a publishing agreement in July 2005. The band claims that Latterman said that his company, Gregg Alan Corp., was "getting only a finder's fee." Instead the band alleges that he obtained ownership "to a portion of the composers' music through the agreement." {{148 Anonymous ;}}

THE RESOLUTION

?

TONI BRAXTON VS. BARRY HANKERSON

THE BACKGROUND

Toni Braxton's debut album was a No. 1 hit and sold ten million copies worldwide. She received Grammys in 1993 for Best New Artist and Female R&B Vocal Performance, and repeated the R&B FVP award the next year.

THE DILEMMA

The lawsuit accused Hankerson of putting his financial interests ahead of hers and inducing the singer to leave Arista Records for Blackground Records, the manager's label. Her lawsuit claimed that Hankerson owed her at least $10 million for dirty dealing that caused to leave the lucrative Arista deal through fraud, deception and double-dealing.

THE RESOLUTION

Under the settlement, she is free to pursue new projects following the return of $375,000 advance to Hankerson.

Braxton will be responsible for paying royalties from next album to Hankerson {{162 Anonymous 2009;}} {{163 Anonymous 2009;}}.

EVE VS. WIHELMINA ARTIST MANAGEMENT

New York Supreme Court

THE BACKGROUND

Eve was one of a new breed of commercially viable female MCs to hit the rap scene during the late '90s. Eve had hits with the R&B Top Ten "Gotta Man" and "Love Is Blind," and was a guest on Missy "Misdemeanor" Elliott's hit "Hot Boyz."

THE DILEMMA

Rapper **Eve**, her company, Blondie Rockwell, Inc, her manager **Troy Carter**, and Innovo Group executive, Anthony Ottimo were hit with a breach of contract lawsuit in New York Supreme Court on June 27, 2003. Eve entered into an exclusive two year deal with Wilhelmina in May of 2001 that allowed the company to represent her in the field of commercial marketing activities which include modeling, runway, fashion, commercials, spokesperson deals, tour sponsorships, celebrity endorsement, licensing and product placement. The lawsuit alleges that Eve negotiated a side deal with Ottimo to launch her Fetish clothing line after Wilhelmina introduced the parties. In addition, the lawsuit alleges that Wilhelmina was never paid for negotiating contracts with Reebok and Candies Shoes, and that Eve attempted to sever ties with the company without paying the company its commissions. The lawsuit did not include a specific dollar amount requested for damages {{164 Anonymous 2003;}}.

THE RESOLUTION

?

PROJECTS

1. Lawsuits involving some of the biggest stars in the music business were purposely omitted from this chapter so that students would have the opportunity to investigate the cases as a project. Two of those cases involved the following people and should be researched: Bruce Springsteen vs. Mike Apel, and Bob Dylan vs. Albert Grossman.

2. Pick any suit from the chapter and role-play the two sides of the argument. Draw logical solutions.

3. Further investigate any of the above cases.

4. Examine the trade papers for current artist-manager suits and investigate.

CHAPTER THIRTEEN
"RAP" UP

"...to see WMG become a music-based company rather than a songs and record company"
Edgar Bronfman, Chairman/CEO Warner Music Group

THE FUTURE

The shift in power has occurred. The savvy entrepreneurial artist manager has the potential to be in control of every aspect of the artist's career. Established superstars are creating new revenue streams, and demanding lucrative deals. Below is the Billboard Magazine, 2009 top five moneymakers. All were over fifty years old and toured {{157 Waddell, Ray 2009;}}:

Artist	Gross Revenue
1. Madonna	$242,176,446
2. Bon Jovi	$157,177,766
3. Bruce Springsteen	$156,327,964
4. The Police	$109,976,894
5. Celine Dion	$ 99,171,237

The more successful artists are branding themselves and/or hooking up with all sorts of products outside the entertainment industry. The internet has somewhat leveled the playing field, however, the old models are still surer bets for many. Because of technological advances, devices once used only for communication, are now used for entertainment, and e-commerce. Record labels, once the most important component of an artist's career, are revising old business plans, inventing new ones, creating new revenue streams, building partnerships, and taking cues from the millions of entrepreneurs on the internet.

As Warner Music Group (WMG) chairman/CEO, Edgar Bronfman stated: his vision is to see WMG become a music-based company rather than a songs and record company. In referencing the album King by southern rapper T.I., Bronfman said that the product was not just released as an album. It encompassed more than 200 retail SKU's including individually sold album tracks, more than a half dozen bonus cuts, mastertones, ringback tones, video ringer, wallpaper, music videos and original videoclips {{139 Garrity, Brian 2006;}}. The future could look bright for a full service entertainment company. Recently commenting in Billboard, artist manager, Al Branch (Kanye West, Lil Wayne) suggested that the 360 deals need to be expanded and " the full-service entertainment company of the future will not only bankroll superstars, it will hire qualified executives to maximize the resulting profits {{165 Branch, Al 2009;}} In other words, experts in each aspect of the revenue streams will control that aspect of the artist's career.

And with a plug for the indies, Bruce Iglauer, President of Alligator Records commented: "In this tough new music business, many smart artists continue to realize that their best opportunities won't come from working on their own or from the ever shrinking world of majors. Instead, they are increasingly turning to enterprising and innovative indie labels as partners {{160 Iglauer, Bruce 2009;}}. Recently, a Billboard Magazine poll asked "have internet and digital distribution (components of the Long Tail) closed the gap between "the hits" and the less established artists during the past five years?" Forty-three percent answered yes; forty percent said no; and seventeen percent said maybe, the Long Tail has given little or no sales boost to emerging artists {{166 Anonymous 2009;}}. Consequently, for many, a savvy label can be a great asset. (Recently reported, the Long Tail has not done very much for the end of the tail, as even though sales of hit albums are down, the effect has spread out down the tail and not just at the end {{167 Peoples, Glenn 2009;}}.)

Lastly, if labels, publishers, artists, digital music services, etc. decide to all work together, we might see:

- Contracts that no longer restrict record companies on how they may license and market recordings

- Major labels and representatives of indie labels and unsigned artists become the only companies that directly license the recordings to online services

- Every song on the recordings properly licensed with only a few organizations administering licenses

- One publisher handling the rights for each song, regardless of the number of writers and/or publishers in the cut in

- Every company that identifies and tracks recordings and compositions uses the same data standards {{139 Garrity, Brian 2006;}}.

It look like the future is yet to come!

APPENDIX

APPENDIX

The following list of websites was compiled by Dr. E. Michael Harrington, Professor of Intellectual Property & Entertainment & Music Business at Belmont University, Nashville, TN. Michael is also a Copyright/Intellectual Property Consultant and Music Copyright Expert Witness and can be reached at emichaelharrington.com

BIBLIOGRAPHY: WEBSITES: JOURNALS/MAGAZINES/NEWSPAPERS/TV/RADIO

Ars Technica	http://arstechnica.com/index.ars
BBC News	http://news.bbc.co.uk/
Billboard	(http://www.billboard.com)
Boston Globe	(http://www.boston.com/globe/)
Boston Phoenix	http://www.bostonphoenix.com/
Bureau of National Affairs	http://www.bna.com/ilaw/
Business 2.0	http://www.business2.com/
Business Week	http://www.businessweek.com/
CNET News.com	(http://www.news.com)
CNN	(http://www.cnn.com)
CNNfn	(http://www.cnnfn.com)
Google News	http://news.google.com/
National Public Radio	(http://www.npr.org)
New York Times	(http://www.times.com/)
Office.com	(http://www.office.com/)
PR Newswire.com	(http://www.prnewswire.com)
Public Broadcasting System	(http://www.pbs.org)
RollingStone.com	(http://www.rollingstone.com/ sections/home/text/default.asp)
Salon	(http://www.salon.com/)
Silicon Valley.com	(http://www.siliconvalley.com/)
SlashDot.org News for Nerds	http://Slashdot.org/
Sonicnet.com	(http://www.sonicnet.com)
Tech Law Journal	(http://www.techlawjournal.com/)
The Village Voice	(http://www.villagevoice.com/)
WGBH	(http://www.wgbh.org)
Wired News	(http://www.wired.com)
Yahoo.com	(http://www.yahoo.com)
ZDNet.com	(http://www.zdnet.com/)

BIBLIOGRAPHY: WEBSITES: ORGANIZATIONS/INDIVIDUALS

Archive.org	http://www.archive.org
Belmont Univ. Copyright Society	http://www.belmontcopyright.org
Berkman Center for Internet & Society (of the Harvard Law School)	(http://cyber.law.harvard.edu)
Big Champagne	http://www.bigchampagne.com/
Boing Boing Net	http://www.boingboing.net/
Boucher Fair Use address	http://www.techlawjournal.com/ intelpro/20010306boucher.asp
Boycott The RIAA	http://www.boycott-riaa.com
Business Software Alliance	http://www.bsa.org/
Cornell University Law School	http://www.law.cornell.edu
Cornell IP	http://www.law.cornell.edu/topics/copyright.html
Creative Commons	http://www.creativecommons.org/
Cyberspace Law Institute	http://www.cli.org
Digital Consumer	http://www.digitalconsumer.org/
Digital Consumer News	http://www.digitalconsumer.org/news.html
Digital Law Online	http://www.digital-law-online.com/
Electronic Frontier Foundation	http://www.eff.org
EFF Deep Links	http://www.eff.org/deeplinks/
Ed Felten	http://www.freedomtotinker.com/
Findlaw.com	(http://www.findlaw.com/)
Franklin Pierce Law Center	http://www.ipmall.fplc.edu/
Future of Music Coalition	(http://www.futureofmusic.org/)
Gnutella	(http://www.Gnutella.wego.com)
GrepLaw	http://grep.law.harvard.edu/
E. Michael Harrington	www.emichaelharrington.com
Harvard Law School	(http://www.law.harvard.edu)
Home Recording Rights Coalition	http://hrrc.org/
Intellectual Property & Tech...	http://infoeagle.bc.edu/bc_org/avp/law/st_org/iptf/
Intelproplaw.com	(http://www.intelproplaw.com/)
International IP Institute	http://www.iipi.org/
Internet Patent News Service	http://www.bustpatents.com
IP Justice	http://www.ipjustice.org/
KaZaA	http://www.kazaa.com
Legal Information Institute	(http://www.law.cornell.edu/topics/copyright.html)
Lawrence Lessig	http://www.lessig.org/
Lessig at the USSC 02-1009	http://www.aaronsw.com/2002/eldredTranscript
Lessig at 2003 SXSW (3/03)	http://www.onlisareinsradar.com/ archives/001012.php#001012
Lessig v. RIAA	http://www.pbs.org/newshour/forum/ june03/copyright.html
Lessig (Free Culture)	http://cyberlaw-temp.stanford.edu/freeculture.pdf
Declan McCullagh's Politech	http://www.politechbot.com/
Megalaw.com Copyright Law	http://www.megalaw.com/top/copyright.php
Movie Archive	http://www.archive.org/movies/movies.php
Napster	(http://www.napster.com/)
National Public Radio	(http://www.npr.org/)

Negativland	(http://www.negativland.com)
New York University Law School	http://www.law.nyu.edu/library/intprop.html
Nolo.com	(http://www.nolo.com)
Ocean State Lawyers for the Arts	http://www.artslaw.org/
Open P2P	http://www.openp2p.com/
Opposing Copyright Extension	(http://www.public.asu.edu/~dkarjala/)
Oyez (USSC Multimedia)	http://www.oyez.org/oyez/frontpage
Patentcafe.com	http://www.patentcafe.com/
Peer-To-Peer Guardian	http://xs.tech.nu/
Poisoned Project	http://poisonedproject.com/poisoned.php
Public Broadcasting System	(http://www.pbs.org)
Public Domain Music	http://www.pdinfo.com/
Public Knowledge	http://www.publicknowledge.org/
Purdue Online Writing Lab	http://owl.english.purdue.edu/
Puretunes.com	http://www.puretunes.com/
Razorpop	http://www.razorpop.com/
Michael Roberston	http://www.michaelrobertson.com/
Mike Rowe	http://www.mikerowesoft.com/ (now defunct)
Pamela Samuelson	(http://ei.cs.vt.edu/~cs6604/f97/Samuelson.htm)
Samuelson Law, Technology…	http://www.law.berkeley.edu/cenpro/ samuelson/index.html
Signal or Noise? Future of Music on the Net (2/25/2000 conference)	(http://cyber.law.harvard.edu/ events/netmusic_agenda.html)
Signal or Noise? Briefing Book	(http://cyber.law.harvard.edu/events/ netmusic_brbook.html)
Signal/Noise 2K5 Briefing Book	http://cyber.law.harvard.edu/events/ SignalNoiseBBFINAL.pdf
John & Ben Snyder	http://www.salon.com/tech/feature/ 2003/02/01/file_trading_manifesto/index.html
Nick Taylor	http://www.nicktaylor.us/
Brad Templeton	(http://www.templetons.com/brad/copyright.html)
Tollbooths on the Digital Highway	http://www.pbs.org/now/transcript/ transcript_copyright.html
Top Secret Recipes (trade secrets?)	http://www.topsecretrecipes.com
Trustyfiles	http://www.trustyfiles.c1om/
http://www.emediawire.com/releases/ 2004/3/emw109750.htm	
WGBH	(http://www.wgbh.org/wgbh/
When Works Pass Into P. D.	http://www.unc.edu/~unclng/public-d.htm
Wiki-Law	http://wiki-law.org/mwiki/index.php?title=Main_Page
WIPO	http://wipo.org
Yahoo Intellectual Property Directory	(http://www.yahoo.com/Government/ Law/Intellectual_Property/)
Peter K. Yu	http://www.gigalaw.com/articles/ 2002-all/yu-2002-08-all.html

BIBLIOGRAPHY: WEBSITES: MUSIC/WORLD MUSIC

ArtistsDirect.com (formerly UBL)	(http://ubl.artistdirect.com/)
Beatles	http://www.beatles.com/
CD Baby	http://www.cdbaby.com/
Chuck D, Public Enemy	(http://www.slamjamz.com/)
Cuba	http://www.cuba.com
Miles Davis	(http://www.milesdavis.com/)
The Dead (Grateful Dead)	http://www.dead.net/
Descarga.com	(http://www.descarga.com/)
The Doors	(http://www.thedoors.com/)
Ellipsis Arts	(http://www.ellipsisarts.com/)
Experience Music Project	http://emplive.com/index.asp
First Vienna Vegetable Orchestra	http://www.gemueseorchester.org/anfang_e.htm
Folk Alliance	http://www.folk.org/
FreeBurma.org	(http://www.freeburma.org/)
GEMM	http://www.gemm.com/
Global Music Network	(www.gmn.com)
Hindu Server	(http://www.hinduonline.com/)
Jimi Hendrix	(http://www.jimihendrix.com/)
Insurgent Country	http://www.insurgentcountry.com/
Int'l Library African Music	(http://archive.ilam.ru.ac.za/home.asp)
Johnny D's Restaurant & Music	(http://www.johnnyds.com/)
Just Plain Folks	http://www.justplainfolks.org/
Leo's Lyrics	http://www.leoslyrics.com/
Luaka Bop Records	(http://www.luakabop.com/cmp/index.html)
Listen.com (Rhapsody)	http://www.listen.com/
Lyric Find	http://www.lyricfind.com/
Madagascar Cdography	(http://www.froots.demon.co.uk/madagcd.html)
Magnatunes.com	www.magnatunes.com
Bob Marley's Bibliography	(http://www.nlj.org.jm/docs/bobbibo.html)
The Marley Store	(http://www.bobmarley.com/)
Roger McGuinn	http://www.ibiblio.org/jimmy/mcguinn/index.html
Pat Metheny	(http://www.patmethenygroup.com/)
Motown	(http://www.motown.com/)
MP3.com	http://www.mp3.com/
National Library of Jamaica	(http://www.nlj.org.jm/)
NetBeat.com	(http://world.netbeat.com/)
Notaviva.com	http://www.notaviva.com/
Okayplayer.com	http://www.okayplayer.com/
Online Classics Network	(www.onlineclassics.net)
La Plaza	(http://www.wgbh.org/wgbh/pages/laplaza/)
Pearl Jam	http://www.pearljam.com/
Pollstar.com	(http://www.pollstar.com/)
Public Domain Music	http://www.pdinfo.com/
Public Enemy	(http://www.publicenemy.com/)
Puerto Rico Governor's Site	(http://fortaleza.govpr.org/)
Puerto Rico Official Site	(http://www.puertorico.com/macie.html)
Putumayo World Music	(http://www.putumayo.com/)
Rapstation.com	(http://www.rapstation.com/)
Rhino Records	(http://www.rhino.com/)
Rhythm Music Magazine	(http://www.gorhythm.com/)
Rock & Roll Hall Of Fame	http://www.rockhall.com/

Rough Guides Music	(http://www.roughguides.com/music/index.html)
Rounder Records	(http://www.rounder.com/)
Rykodisc Records	(http://www.rykodisc.com/)
Ravi Shankar Foundation	(http://www.ravishankar.org/)
Ravi Shankar Links	(http://home.columbus.rr.com/woodstock1969/artist/ravi_shankar.html)
Scooter Scudieri	http://www.firstrockstar.com/
SESAC	(http://www.sesac.com/sesac.html
Sing365.com	http://www.sing365.com/
Sirius Satellite Radio	http://www.siriusradio.com/main.htm
Smithsonian Folkways Recordings	(http://web2.si.edu/folkways/)
TAXI (A & R, record deals, etc.)	http://www.taxi.com/
They Might Be Giants	http://www.theymightbegiants.com/
Tin Pan South	http://www.tinpansouth.com/index.cfm
Ultimate Band List	(http://www.ubl.com)
Caetano Veloso	(http://www.caetanoveloso.com.br/site.htm)
World Music	(http://www.worldmusic.org/)
World Music Network	(http://www.worldmusic.net/home/index.html)
Frank Zappa fansite	(http://www.science.uva.nl/~robbert/zappa/)
Frank Zappa Official Homepage	(http://www.zappa.com/)

BIBLIOGRAPHY: WEBSITES: U. S. GOVERNMENT

Bill Summary and Status (108th)	http://thomas.loc.gov/bss/d108query.html
Bill Summary and Status (109th)	http://thomas.loc.gov/bss/d109query.html
Rep. Rick Boucher (D-VA)	http://www.house.gov/boucher/internet.htm
Broadcast and Audio Flag Hearings	http://commerce.senate.gov/hearings/witnesslist.cfm?id=1704
CIA World Factbook	http://www.cia.gov/cia/publications/factbook/index.html
Copyright Legislation 109th Congress	http://www.copyright.gov/legislation/
Digital Media Consumers' Rights Act	http://www.house.gov/boucher/docs/dmcra108th.pdf
Federal Courts Finder	http://www.law.emory.edu/caselaw/
Library of Congress Homepage	(http://www.loc.gov/)
Library of Congress	(http://www.loc.gov/library/)
Rep. Zoe Lofgren	(D-CA) http://www.house.gov/lofgren
Smithsonian Institution	(http://www.si.edu/)
State Trademark Agencies and Databases	http://statetm.tripod.com/
U. S. Census Bureau	http://www.census.gov/
United States Code	http://www4.law.cornell.edu/uscode/
U. S. Congress on the Internet	http://thomas.loc.gov/
U. S. Copyright Office	(http://www.copyright.gov)
U. S. Federal Trade Commission	http://www.ftc.gov/
U. S. Patent & Trademark Office (Home)	(http://www.uspto.gov/)
U. S. Patent & Trademark Office (Trademark Information)	(http://www.uspto.gov/web/menu/tm.html)
U. S. Supreme Court Copyright Decisions	http://www.law.cornell.edu/supct/cases/copyrt.htm
U. S. Trademark Electronic Search System	http://tess2.uspto.gov/bin/gate.exe?f=tess&state=9l9rsl.1.1

BIBLIOGRAPHY: WEBSITES: INTERNATIONAL & INTERNATIONAL GOVERNMENT SITES:

African Regional Intellectual
  Property Org.   http://www.aripo.org/
Australia IP Australia   http://www.ipaustralia.gov.au/
Australasian Performing
  Arts Association   http://www.apra.com.au/
Australian Copyright Council   http://www.copyright.org.au/
Australian Record Industry
  Association   http://www.aria.com.au/
Australia EFA   http://www.efa.org.au
BBC News   http://news.bbc.co.uk/
Berne Convention
  (September 9, 1886)   http://www.wipo.int/treaties/
                                      en/ip/berne/trtdocs_wo001.html
British Music Rights   http://www.bmr.org/menu.html
British Music Rights
  Issues and…   http://www.bmr.org/html/issues.html
Canada Copyright Act   http://laws.justice.gc.ca/en/C-42/index.html
Canada Bill C-32   http://www.parl.gc.ca/bills/government/
                                      C-32/C-32_3/C-32TOCE.html
Canada, Neighbouring
  Rights Collective of   http://www.nrdv.ca/english/aboutFAQ.htm
Canadian Coalition For
  Fair Digital Access   http://www.ccfda.ca/
Canadian Intellectual
  Property Office   http://strategis.ic.gc.ca/sc_mrksv/cipo/
                                      welcome/welcom-e.html
Canadian Musical
  Reproduction Rights   http://www.cmrra.ca/default.htm
Canadian Private
  Copying Collective   http://www.cpcc.ca/english/index.htm
Canadian Trademark Office   http://strategis.ic.gc.ca/cipo/
                                      trademarks/search/tmSearch.do
China, Constitution of
  the Republic of   http://www.usconstitution.net/china.html
    http://www.taiwandocuments.org/constitution01.htm#C009_
      http://english.people.com.cn/constitution/constitution.html
China Copyright Law   http://www.chinaiprlaw.com/english/laws/laws10.htm
Chinese Law Resources
  on the Internet   http://www.law.wustl.edu/Chinalaw/intersou.html
China IP Law Explained   http://www.qis.net/chinalaw/lawtran1.htm
Collection of Laws for
  Electronic Access   http://clea.wipo.int
Copyright Board of Canada   http://www.cb-cda.gc.ca/new-e.html
Cultural Traffic   http://www.carleton.ca/ces/conference_fr.html
Denmark Consolidated Act
  on Copyright   http://www.kum.dk/sw4550.asp
Europa – European
  Union Online   http://europa.eu.int/index_en.htm
Fair Copyright Canada   http://www.faircopyright.ca/
Foreign Law Online
  (Univ. of Chicago)   http://www.lib.uchicago.edu/~llou/global.html
Germany Copyright Law   http://www.iuscomp.org/gla/statutes/UrhG.htm
Guardian   http://www.guardian.co.uk/
Guardian – Internet News   http://www.guardian.co.uk/internetnews/

India Copyright Act 1957   http://www.naukri.com/lls/copyright/cpwrt.htm

International Federation
  of Phonographic…   http://www.ifpi.org

International IP Institute   http://www.iipi.org/

International Institute of IT
  (India)   http://www.isquareit.com/

Internet Law (The Register)   http://www.theregister.co.uk/internet/

Japan Copyright Law   http://www.cric.or.jp/cric_e/clj/clj.html

Korea Herald   http://www.koreaherald.co.kr/index.asp

Korea Law   http://www.moleg.go.kr/mlawinfo/
       english/htms/list01.html

Korea Patent Act   http://www.moleg.go.kr/mlawinfo/
       english/htms/html/law26.html

Korea Trademark Act   http://www.moleg.go.kr/mlawinfo/
       english/htms/html/law27.html

Law Gazette (UK)   http://www.lawgazette.co.uk/homeframe.asp

Law Society of Ireland   http://www.lawsociety.ie/

Mechanical-Copyright
  Protection Society   http://www.mcps.co.uk/

Michael Geist (Canada)   http://michaelgeist.ca/

Norway Copyright Act   http://www.unesco.org/culture/copy/
       copyright/norway/fr_sommaire.html

Online Rights Canada   http://www.onlinerights.ca/

Phonographic
  Performance Limited   http://www.ppluk.com/ppl/ppl_fd.nsf/home?openform

Rome Convention
  (October 29, 1961)   http://www.wipo.int/treaties/en/ip/
       phonograms/trtdocs_wo023.html

Statute of Anne
  (1710 copyright law)   http://edge.net/~flowers/Statute%20of%20Anne.htm

Teosto Finnish Composers'
  Copyright Society   http://www.teosto.fi/teosto/webpages.nsf/
       Frames?ReadForm&English

UK Patent Office (Copyright)   http://www.patent.gov.uk/copy/index.htm

UK Patent Office (Design)   http://www.patent.gov.uk/design/index.htm

UK Patent Office (Patent)   http://www.patent.gov.uk/patent/index.htm

UK Patent Office (Trademark)   http://www.patent.gov.uk/tm/index.htm

World Intellectual
  Property Organization   http://wipo.org

BIBLIOGRAPHY: WEBSITES:
MUSIC & ENTERTAINMENT INDUSTRY

American Federation
  of Musicians   http://www.afm.org/
       http://www.afm.org/public/join/mpjgame.gif

AFM Local 802   http://www.local802afm.org/

American Federation of
  Television & Radio Artists   http://www.aftra.org/

American Guild of Music Artists   http://www.musicalartists.org/HomePage.htm

American Guild of Variety Artists   http://americanguildofvarietyartists.visualnet.es/

Arbitron   http://www.arbitron.com/home/content.stm

ASCAP   (http://www.ascap.com/)

Association of Talent Agents   http://www.agentassociation.com/frontdoor/newsstand.cfm

Azoz.com   http://www.azoz.com/

Belmont University Copyright Society (BUCS)	http://www.belmontcopyright.org
Berklee Music Shares	http://www.berkleeshares.com/
BMI	(http://www.bmi.com/)
Eric Boehlert on Clear Channel	http://www.salon.com/ent/clear_channel/
Jeff Brabec & Todd Brabec	http://www.musicandmoney.com/index.html
Buddy Lee Attractions, Inc.	http://www.buddyleeattractions.com
Joy Butler (music publishing)	http://www.goodnightkiss.com/joybutler.html
Canadian Musical Reproduction Rights	http://www.cmrra.ca/default.html
Capitol Records	http://hollywoodandvine.com/
CD Baby	http://www.cdbaby.com/
Celebrity Justice	http://celebrityjustice.com
Christian Music Managers	http://christianmusic.about.com/od/managers/
Clear Channel Communications	http://www.clearchannel.com/main.html
Clear Channel Sucks	http://www.clearchannelsucks.org/
CMJ (College Music Journal)	http://www.cmj.com/
Columbia Artists Management, Inc. (CAMI)	http://www.cami.com/
Community Broadcasters Association	http://www.communitybroadcasters.com/
Concerts West	http://www.aeglive.com/flash.php
Consumer Electronics Association	http://www.ce.org/
Country Music Television	http://www.cmt.com/
Country Music Television Canada	http://www.cmtcanada.com/
Country Review	http://www.countryreview.com/news/
Coverville	http://www.coverville.com/
Digg	http://digg.com/
Digital Media Association	http://www.digmedia.org/
Digital Music (Dmusic)	http://boycott.dmusic.com/
DJ Times	http://www.djtimes.com/original/index.htm
Dotmusic.com (BT legal music service)	http://www.dotmusic.com/
Dramatists Guild of America	http://www.dramaguild.com/
DVD Backup Buddy	http://www.dvdbackupbuddy.com/
DVD Squeeze	http://www.dvdsqueeze.com/
Echomusic	http://echomusic.com/main.php?content=about
EMI	http://www.emigroup.com/
Encore	http://www.celebrityaccess.com/news/
eTree.org	http://etree.org/
Fullaudio	http://www.fullaudio.com/index.jsp
Future of Music Coalition	http://futureofmusic.org/
Garage Band.com	http://www.garageband.com/
Gavin	http://www.gavin.com/
Gillett Entertainment Group	http://www.geg.ca/eng/mainPage.cfm
Grammy.com	http://www.grammy.com/
Harry Fox Agency	http://www.nmpa.org/hfa.html
Hit Song Science	http://www.hitsongscience.com/
House Of Blues	http://www.hob.com/
House of Blues Concerts Canada	http://www.hob.com/venues/concerts/canada/
How To Copy DVD's	http://www.howtocopydvds.com/
Impala (Independent Music Companies Assoc.)	http://www.impalasite.org/

Information Technology Association of America	http://www.itaa.org
International Alliance of Theatrical…(IATSE)	http://www.iatse.lm.com/
International Association of Assembly Managers	http://www.iaam.org/
International Music Managers Forum	http://www.immf.net/
International Recording Media Association	http://www.recordingmedia.org/
Internet Movies	http://www.internetmovies.com/
IPodder.org	http://ipodder.org/
Janis Ian	http://www.janisian.com/
Just Plain Folks	http://www.justplainfolks.org/
Kathode Ray Music	http://www.kathoderaymusic.com/tipsheet/
Dina LaPolt	http://www.lapoltlaw.com/main.html
Lefsetz (Bob Lefsetz newsletter)	http://lefsetz.com/
Listen.com (Rhapsody)	http://www.listen.com/
Media Consolidation (PBS "Now" 6/13/2003)	http://www.pbs.org/now/politics/fccchanges.html
Magnatune.com	http://magnatune.com/
Media Bistro	http://www.mediabistro.com/
MIDEM The International Music Market	http://www.midem.com/
Motion Picture Association of America	http://www.mpaa.org
Music Business Journal at Berklee	http://www.thembj.com/
Music Contracts	http://www.musiccontracts.com/
Music Industry Association of Canada	http://www.miac.net/pages/frame.html
Music Managers Forum (US)	http://www.mmfus.com/
MusicNet	http://www.musicnet.com/
Music Performance Trust Funds	http://www.mptf.org/home/index.html
Musictoday.com	http://www.musictoday.com/
Nashville Songwriters Association International	http://www.nashvillesongwriters.com/
National Association of Broadcast Employees…	http://union.nabetcwa.org/nabet/front.html
National Association of Broadcasters	http://www.nab.org/
National Association of Music Merchants	http://www.namm.com/
National Association of Recording Merchandisers	http://www.narm.com/
National Conference of Personal Managers	http://ncopm.com/
National Music Publishers Association	http://www.nmpa.org/
New Radio & Performing Arts, Inc.	http://www.turbulence.org/
Pass Along Networks	www.passalongnetworks.com
Pollstar.com	http://www.pollstar.com/
Pressplay	http://www.pressplay.com/
Pro-Music.org (IFPI about online music)	http://www.pro-music.org/
Public Domain Music	http://www.pdinfo.com/

Pump Audio	http://www.pumpaudio.com/
Puretunes.com	http://www.puretunes.com/
Record Company Addresses	http://www.dirtynelson.com/linen/special/label.html
Recording Industry Association of America	http://www.riaa.org/index.cfm
Rhythm Music Magazine	http://www.gorhythm.com/)
Rock On TV	http://www.rockontv.com/
Screen Actors Guild	http://www.sag.org/
Secure Digital Music Initiative (SDMI)	http://www.sdmi.org/
SESAC	http://www.sesac.com/sesac.html
SFX Sports Group	http://www.sfx.com/
Sirius Radio	http://www.siriusradio.com
Songwriters Guild of America	http://www.songwriters.org/
Sonicblue	http://www.sonicblue.com/
Sony	http://www.sonymusic.com/
Sony BMG	http://www.sonybmg.com/
Sound Exchange	http://www.soundexchange.com/
South By Southwest	http://www.sxsw.com/
Star Polish (Advice)	http://www.starpolish.com/advice/
Talent Agencies Act, California Civil Code 1700	http://www.modelingscams.org/1700.html
Time Warner	http://www.timewarner.com/corp/
TiVo	http://www.tivo.com/home.asp
TV Shows on DVD	http://www.tvshowsondvd.com/
Vans Warped Tour	http://warpedtour.launch.com/
Vivendi Universal	http://www.vivendi.com/vu2/en/_home/home.cfm
Warner Brothers	http://www2.warnerbros.com
Weblisten.com	http://www.weblisten.com/
William Morris Agency	http://www.wma.com/
XM Satellite Radio	http://www.xmradio.com/
Yahoo! Music Industry Websites	http://dir.yahoo.com/Entertainment/ Music/Music_Industry_Resources/

REFERENCES

Allen, A. (2005). *Merchandising advise from the experts.* Retrieved August/22, 2005, from http://www.cityshowcase.co.uk/index.php?section=FeatureDetail&FeatureID=0S1zQcC0zS

Amicone, M. (2002, September 21). Management 2002: Today's career-caretakers wear many hats, and their on-the-job training never stops. *Billboard*, , 31-32, 34, 42.

Anderson, C. (2009a). Free music. *Free* (pp. 153-154). New York, New York: Hyperion Books.

Anderson, C. (2009b). Free music. *Free* (pp. 154-155). New York, New York: Hyperion Books.

Baskerville, D. (1990). *Music business handbook & career guide* (5th ed.). Los Angeles: Sherwood Pub. Co.

Baskerville, D. (2006). Part V: The recording industry. *Music business handbook and career guide* (8th edition ed., pp. 354). Thousand Oaks, CA: Sage Publications.

Becker, H. S. (1963). *Outsiders: Studies in the sociology of deviance.* London: Free Press of Glencoe.

Benz, M. (2002). Music & money: Securitization: Who it's right for, and when. *Billboard - the International Newsweekly of Music, Video and Home Entertainment, 114*(17), 21-22, 28.

Bigger, S. (1996). Entertainment group name: Selection and protection. In M. E. Halloran (Ed.), *The musician's business and legal guide* (Rev. 2nd ed., pp. 12-22). Upper Saddle River, NJ: Prentice-Hall.

Billboard.biz poll. (2009). *Billboard Magazine,* (November/14), 6.

Brabec, J., & Brabec, T. (2006). *Sources of income* (Fifth ed.). New York: Schirmer Trade Books.

Branch, A. (2009). The deals of the future. *Billboard Magazine,* (November/21), 4.

Braxton released by blackground, sues ex-manager. (2009). Retrieved November/23, 2009, from http://www.billboard.com/bbcom/news/article_display.jsp?vnu_content_id=1003532374

Braxton settles suit against ex-manager. (2009). Retrieved November/23, 2009, from http://new.music.yahoo.com/toni-braxton/news/braxton-settles-suit-against-ex-manager

Bruno, A. (2006, April 22). Rum and coke with digital tunes. *Billboard*, , 5.

Butler, S. (2005a, September 3). (Un)licensed to book. *Billboard*, , 22.

Butler, S. (2005b, June 11). Reznor wins suit. *Billboard*, , 10.

Butler, S. (2006, March 11). Old story, new twists: Manager sues killers. *Billboard*, , 13.

Buxton, E. (1975). *Creative people at work.* New York: Executive Communications.

Cassidy, J. (1996, August 26). Under the hammer. *The New Yorker Magazine*, , 62.

Christman, E. (2005, March 12). This means warcon! *Billboard*, , 1-64.

Christman, E. (2009). Universal still tops. *Billboard Magazine,* (February/21), 11.

Christman, E., & Garrity, B. (2005, March 26). Edgar's digital play: Web, mobil initiatives are keys to warner IPO. *Billboard*, , 54-55.

Christman, E., Mitchell, G., Donohue, A., & Prince, E. (2009). Big idea. *Billboard Magazine*, May/16, 24-26, 28.

Cobo, L. (2004, March 13). Medina countersues martin. *Billboard*, , 6-83.

Crosley, H. (2006, April 15). T.I.MELINE of a hit. *Billboard*, , 12.

Denisoff, R. S., & Schurk, W. L. (1986). *Tarnished gold: The record industry revisited.* New Brunswick, N.J: Transaction Books.

Elliott, S. (2005, May 2). CBS and its many partners hope you can't help falling in love with elvis presley this month. *New York Times*, pp. C6.

Eve hit with lawsuit by wilhelmina artist management. (2003). Retrieved November/24, 2009, from http://new.music.yahoo.com/eve/news/eve-hit-with-lawsuit-by-wilhelmina-artist-management--12048355

Fabrikant, G. (1997, February 23). The bad boys start watching their pockets. *New York Times*, pp. 3.1.

Fact sheet public enemy. Retrieved November/13, 2009, from http://www.sellaband.com/projects/publicenemy/plan

Flick, L. (1989, October 7). Billy joel sues former manager for $90 mil. *Billboard*, , 96.

Flick, L. (1990, April 7). Billy joel gets $2 mil in suit. *Billboard*, , 94.

The fray sues manager over copyrights to songs. Retrieved september/15, 2009, from http://encore.celebrityaccess.com/print.php?encoreId=212&articleId=32380

Freedman, J. (2003, June). Sacre blew. *Money*, , 24.

Garrity, B. (2006a, April 15). New revenue on tap. *Billboard*, , 28-29, 30.

Garrity, B. (2006b, June 17). The new sku review. *Billboard*, , 27-31.

Gleason, R. J. (1969). *The jefferson airplane and the san francisco sound*. New York: Ballantine Books.

Grossweiner, Bob and Cohen, Jane. (2006). *Industry profile: Andrew snowhite*. Retrieved June 16, 2006, from http://www.celebrityaccess.com/news/profile.html?id=28

Hansen, B. (1992). Doo-wop. In A. DeCurtis, J. Henke & H. George-Warren (Eds.), *The rolling stone illustrated history of rock & roll: The definitive history of the most important artists and their music* (3rd ed., pp. 92-101). New York: Random House.

Harding, C. (2008). Promo spots provide coveted showcase for music. *Billboard Magazine*, (September/27), 11-12, 13, 14,15, 16, 17, 18, 19, 20, 21, 22.

Hearn, E. R. (1996). Forms of business entities to use in starting your own business. In M. E. Halloran (Ed.), *The musician's business and legal guide* (Rev. 2nd ed., pp. 23-34). Upper Saddle River, NJ: Prentice-Hall.

Hefflinger, M. (2009). *Public enemy to produce fan-financed album viz SellaBand*. Retrieved October/6 http://www.dmwmedia.com/news/2009/10/06/public-enemy-produce-fan-financed-album-sellaband

Heider, A. (1998, August 6). The company they keep. *Rolling Stone*, , 30.

Holson, L. M. (2003, July 14). When jenny dumped benny. *New York Times*, pp. D1-8.

Horwitz, C. (2000, May 20). Leann rimes. *Billboard*, , 36.

Iglauer, B. (2009). Labels are here to stay. *Billboard Magazine*, (July/4), 6.

Kirkeby, M. (1980, Novembeer 13). Bee gees sue stigwood, charge missmanagement. *Rolling Stone*, , 22.

Knopper, S. (2003, April 3). Where the money goes. *Rolling Stone*, , 57-61.

Kozak, R. (1981, August 15). Parker, RCA accused of fraud in elvis dealings. *Billboard*, , 1.

Kraski, M. (2005). Record labels and artist as partners. *The 2005 International Conference of the Music and Entertainment Educators Association*, University of Miami, Miami, Fl. 7.

Laing, D. (1998). The world record industry in 1997. *Popular Music*, 17(3), 328-329.

LeBlanc, L. (2006, April 15). Nettwerk making each act A label. *Billboard*, , 7-8.

Leeds, J. (2006, April 17). As pop music seeks new sales, the pussycat dolls head to toyland. *New York Times*, pp. C1-3.

Lewis, G. (1980, Fall). Positive deviance: A labeling approach to the star syndrome in popular music. *Popular Music and Society*, , 73-79.

Lichtman, I. (1991a, March 2). Inside track. *Billboard*, , 79.

Lichtman, I. (1991b, May 25). Inside track. *Billboard*, , 80.

Luby, Frank and Gelbort, Jason. (2009). Ticketonomics part II. *Billboard Magazine*, (May/2), 4.

Marcone, S. (2006). *Current sales data and what the "long tail" might do*. Unpublished manuscript.

Miller, T. (1992, April 18). Ex-manager sues joe cocker. *Billboard*, , 34.

Milom, M., Esq. (2006). *The impact of new business models on artists*. Retrieved May 30, 2006, from http://www.musicrow.com/

Mitchell, R. (1995, March 19). The music mogul. *Houston Chronicle*, pp. 8.

Morris, C. (1998, December 12). Former manager sues jewel and her mother. *Billboard*, , 6.

Morris, C. (2000, October 28). Aguilera sues her manager: Claims breach of duties; kurtz is 'disappointed'. *Billboard*, 112, 12, 24.

Mosemak, J. (2000, March 1). Entertainment clout builds. *USA Today*, pp. B1.

Nagy, E. (2009). How to: Make a T-shirt that really sells. *Billboard Magazine*, (October/24), 16.

Newman, M. (2001, March 24). Kid rock settles suit with ex-mgr. *Billboard*, , 3.

Newman, M. (1999, November 13). 'N sync responds to trans Con/BMG suits. *Billboard*, 111, 8.

Paoletta, M. (2005, October 1). What's in A name. *Billboard*, , 30-31.

Paoletta, M. (2006a, May 6). Inside pitch. *Billboard*, , 20-22.

Paoletta, M. (2006b, February 18). The name game. *Billboard*, , 26-27.

Peoples, G. (2009a). Finding the perfect fit. *Billboard Magazine*, (June/6), 12.

Peoples, G. (2009b). The long tale? *Billboard Magazine*, (November/14), 24-25, 26, 27, 28.

Rapaport, D. S. (2003). *A music business primer*. Upper Saddle River, N.J: Prentice Hall.

Recording Industry Association of America. (1900s). Annual report of the recording industry association of america. [Ar.]

Reynolds, J. R. (1996, June 8). Anita baker suing her former manager, lawyer, and publisher. *Billboard*, 108, 12, 15.

Rohter, L. (1991, January 8). Pop-music fashion becomes a sales hit. *New York Times*, pp. D1.

Sanneh, K. (2006, May 11). Do you remember the good old days of CD's? this band does. *New York Times*, pp. E1-E8.

Scher, J. (1994, January). Why are ticket prices so high? *Musician Magazine*, , 12.

Shemel, S., & Krasilovsky, M. W. (1985). *This business of music* (Rev. & enl. 5th ed.). New York: Billboard Publications.

Skanse, R. (1999, December 9). In the news. *Rolling Stone*, , 27.

Sloctnick, B. I. (1992, April). Are bootleggers walking away with the performance profit center? *Agent & Manager*, , 53.

Smith, G. J. W., & Carlsson, I. M. (1990). *The creative process: A functional model based on empirical studies from early childhood up to middle age*. Madison, Conn: International Universities Press.

Soocher, S. (1987, September). Protecting band names: A legal survival kit. *Musician Magazine*, , 45.

Stein, M. I. (1974-1975). *Stimulating creativity*. New York: Academic Press.

Stim, R. (2004). *Music law: How to run your band's business* (4th ed.). Berkeley, CA: Nolo.

Terry, K. (1987, December 12). Branigan loses lawsuit. *Billboard*, , 69.

Torrance, E. P. (1962). *Guiding creative talent*. Englewood Cliffs, N.J: Prentice-Hall.

Traiman, S. (2005, March 5). Licensers toy with artists' images. *Billboard*, , 43-44.

Ungar, P. B. (1992, March). Negotiationg concert agreements during a recessionary period. *Agent & Manager*, , 51.

Waddell, R. (2005a, July 9). Ameriquest lends stones tour support. *Billboard*, , 23.

Waddell, R. (2005b, June 18). In-house marketers get the gig. *Billboard*, , 25-27.

Waddell, R. (2006, April 29). Touring pulls out of slump. *Billboard*, , 7-8.

Waddell, R. (2008). Ten years after consolidation swept concert promoters, the dominance of live nation and AEG defines the industry. *Billboard Magazine*, (4, october), 27-28,29.

Waddell, R. (2009a). 2009 money makers. *Billboard Magazine*, (February/21), 24-25, 26, 27.

Waddell, R. (2009b). Brands in concert. *Billboard Magazine*, (May/23), 16.

Waddell, R. (2009c). *Study: Music sponsorships to reach new high in 2009*. Retrieved April/29, 2009, from http://www.billboard.biz/bbbiz/content_display/e3i9c779034c7476d10e9a2ed3a2

Waddell, R. (2000, December 16). Country: Fan fair: Change of venue, attitude in 2001. *Billboard*, 112, 39.

Waddell, R. (2001, May 26). Mounting concert ticket surcharges provoke dissent. *Billboard*, 113, 1, 36.

Walsh, C. M. (2005, December 10). Rocker cornell sues former manager. Billboard, , 5.

Werde, B. (2006, March 25). Matisyahu's misstep? *Billboard*, , 10.

Whitcomb, I. (1972). *After the ball*. London: Allen Lane the Penguin Press.

White, E. (1999, October 5). `Chatting' a singer up the pop charts - how music marketers used the web to generate buzz before an album debuted. *Wall Street Journal*, pp. B.1.

INDEX